Producing Instructional
Systems

Instructional Development 1

Producing Instructional Systems

Lesson Planning for Individualized and Group Learning Activities

A J Romiszowski

Kogan Page, London/Nichols Publishing, New York

To Helena Romiszowska and Lina Pastor, without
whose encouragement, patience and gentle pressure,
the book would not even have reached manuscript
stage.

First published in Great Britain in 1984 and reprinted in 1986 by
Kogan Page Ltd, 120 Pentonville Road, London N1 9JN

British Library Cataloguing in Publication Data
Romiszowski, A. J.
   Producing instructional systems.
   1. Educational technology
   I. Title
   371.3'07'8   LB1028.3
   ISBN 0-85038-224-6
   ISBN 1-85091-012-X (Pbk)

Published in the United States of America by
Nichols Publishing Company, Post Office Box 96, New York, NY 10024

Library of Congress Cataloging in Publication Data
Romiszowski, A. J.
   Producing instructional systems.
   Companion vol. to: Designing instructional systems.
   1. Instructional systems — Planning.   I. Title.
   LB1028.35.R653 1984   371.3   83-2287
   ISBN 0-89397-085-9
   ISBN 0-89397-244-4 (Pbk)

Printed and bound in Great Britain by
Anchor Brendon Ltd, Tiptree, Essex

Contents

Acknowledgements

No book of this nature can be produced without the assistance and inspiration, both direct and indirect, of many people and organizations. I would like to take this opportunity to thank all of them and single out some who were particularly helpful.

First, I am indebted to Anne Howe and Nick Rushby for reading some sections of the manuscript and making many valuable comments. I would also like to thank the many students on various courses who struggled through some of the chapters and contributed ideas that were later incorporated. In particular, I should mention the postgraduate students of educational technology at the State University of Rio de Janeiro and at Concordia University in Montreal.

Second, I acknowledge and thank those who gave permission to reproduce their work or contributed directly with original ideas: Madeleine Morin for the scuba diving instructional plan; Henry Ellington, Fred Percival and Eric Addinall for their ideas on simulation-gaming and for permission to use some of their examples; John Sloane for the FORMULON card game; Anthony Hodgson for the COMMUNI-KIT; Sivasailam Thiagarajan for the IDIOTS game. I must also thank Anne Valery, to whom I am indebted for so much and who introduced me to I'M NOT NEBUCHADNEZZAR.

Third, I mention the organizations and projects that furnished the opportunities to work with other instructional designers and to develop many of the ideas and examples presented here. I should single out: the staff of the Learning Systems Unit at Middlesex Polytechnic for collaboration in the early years when the systems approach was formed; the training department of the Pressed Steel Company and the Cranfield Institute of Technology for ideas and opportunities to develop industrial training simulators; projects of the United Nations Development Programme, based at CENAFOR and TELEBRAS in Brazil, as well as many client-organizations in four continents, which provided opportunities to implement many varied technical training and vocational education projects and to develop many of the practical examples presented in this book; the Organization of American States and the Brazilian Ministry of Education and Culture, through its Educational Technology Foundation (FUNTEVE) for opportunities to develop projects on the 'other side of the education/training fence', at both school and university levels; the Brazilian Association for Educational Technology (ABT) and the Foundation for the Development of Public Servants (FUNCEP) for implementing distance education courses for the training of officers and educational technologists, the design and development of which contributed yet another facet of experience, and many practical examples used in the book; finally, Professor Avi Bajpai, Director of the Centre for the Advancement of Mathematics Education in Technology (CAMET), the University of Technology, Loughborough, for supervising my Doctoral thesis many years ago, thus directing me towards research into the individualization of the instructional process which forms the theoretical backbone of this book.

Fourth, I thank all the staff of Kogan Page and, in particular, Loulou Brown for succeeding, against all odds and despite all manner of transatlantic communication problems, to transform the book from manuscript to finished product.

Preface to the Instructional Development Series

This two-volume work on the development of instruction is planned as a companion to an earlier book — *Designing Instructional Systems.*

This earlier book dealt with the decision-making process involved in overall course planning and curriculum design — the initial macro-design stages of a project. The present work continues on to the micro-design stages of lesson and instructional materials development. The work is divided into two volumes. Volume 1, *Producing Instructional Systems*, deals with lesson planning for individualized instruction in the conventional classroom environment, as well as the planning of small group learning situations, simulations and games. Volume 2, *Developing Auto-Instructional Materials*, deals with the development of many different types of materials, including programmed instruction, structural communication, various styles of structured writing, audio and audiovisual instruction and the many types of computer-based materials now being introduced in both education and training.

Taken together, these two volumes give extensive coverage of practical techniques for the development of instruction.

It is quite useful to draw a distinction between instructional *design* and instructional *development*, although some authors seem to use the two terms synonymously. It is true that in some cases it is difficult to separate 'design' (what happens on the drawing board) and 'development' (what happens in the workshop). The two processes are interrelated, forming an iterative cycle of design, development, re-design, etc. However, development requires the existence of a practical try-out situation and prototype products or services ready to be tried out. This is not a requirement of the initial design stages of a project, which may be a largely theoretical exercise, based on the experiences gained in other projects or on principles gleaned from a study of the literature. We differentiate between design and development in the context of instruction and it is this that distinguishes the present work.

Designing Instructional Systems laid the foundations for a systematic approach to the planning of instruction in both educational and training contexts, leading the reader through two levels of decision-making:

1. Is an instructional system really necessary?
2. What should be its overall structure?

These are the political and strategic levels.

Instructional Development takes the reader on to practical application of the plans prepared at these earlier levels. Naturally, this involves further, more detailed, design, as well as the actual production of prototype lessons and materials. These prototypes, when tested, may lead to further detailed re-design or even to changes in the initial overall plans. However, the emphasis is on production and testing and the further design decisions are very detailed, topic-specific or 'tactical'. These decisions may also be conveniently classified into two levels:

3. The decisions involved in the detailed planning of lessons and exercises.
4. The decisions involved in the preparation of instructional materials.

Very often, these two levels of decision-making are performed by one and the same person, as in the case of a teacher who prepares his own materials to be used as part of the lessons that he gives. It is also very common, however, for the materials production tasks to be the responsibility of specialists, the lesson planner merely selecting appropriate existing materials or orienting the specialist materials producer.

One reason, therefore, for dividing this work into two volumes is to aim more precisely at these two groups of readers.

Another reason for the division is the sheer size of the task. To deal thoroughly with these two levels of instructional development in one book either would have produced an unwieldy tome, or size and space restrictions would have prevented the inclusion of many examples (an essential feature of a practical treatment of the techniques discussed).

However, bearing in mind the possibility of two distinct groups of readers lesson planners and material producers — every effort has been made to make the two volumes self-contained. Essential basic concepts are defined in both volumes, so the reader may accompany the theoretical argument without necessarily having to refer to both volumes.

The same independence is achieved, in relation to the earlier *Designing Instructional Systems*, by the summary, in early chapters, of the principal conceptual schemata developed and used as the basis for practical decision-making.

However, there is a continuity and coherence within the books, best illustrated by the two 'world maps' of instructional design and development presented on the following two pages. The first map summarizes the principal content of the earlier book, *Designing Instructional Systems*.

The second map summarizes the principal aspects of instructional development covered in the present work. Volume 1 is mainly concerned with Level 3, and Volume 2 deals with Level 4. This map shows clearly how these more detailed levels of decision-making are dependent on earlier decisions taken at the initial design levels. The reader who has read *Designing Instructional Systems* will discover a strong thread of continuity running throughout the book. Some of the chapters in the present book, which summarize the basic theoretical approach adopted, may be found to be redundant in this case. Readers may prefer, however, to refresh their memories of the concepts and schemata developed earlier and which now come to play an important part in the instructional development process. This may be particularly important if some time has elapsed since the earlier book was read.

It is hoped that the structure of the content in the present work will enable the two volumes to be used conveniently as both initial reading or later reference material.

Alexander Romiszowski, April 19

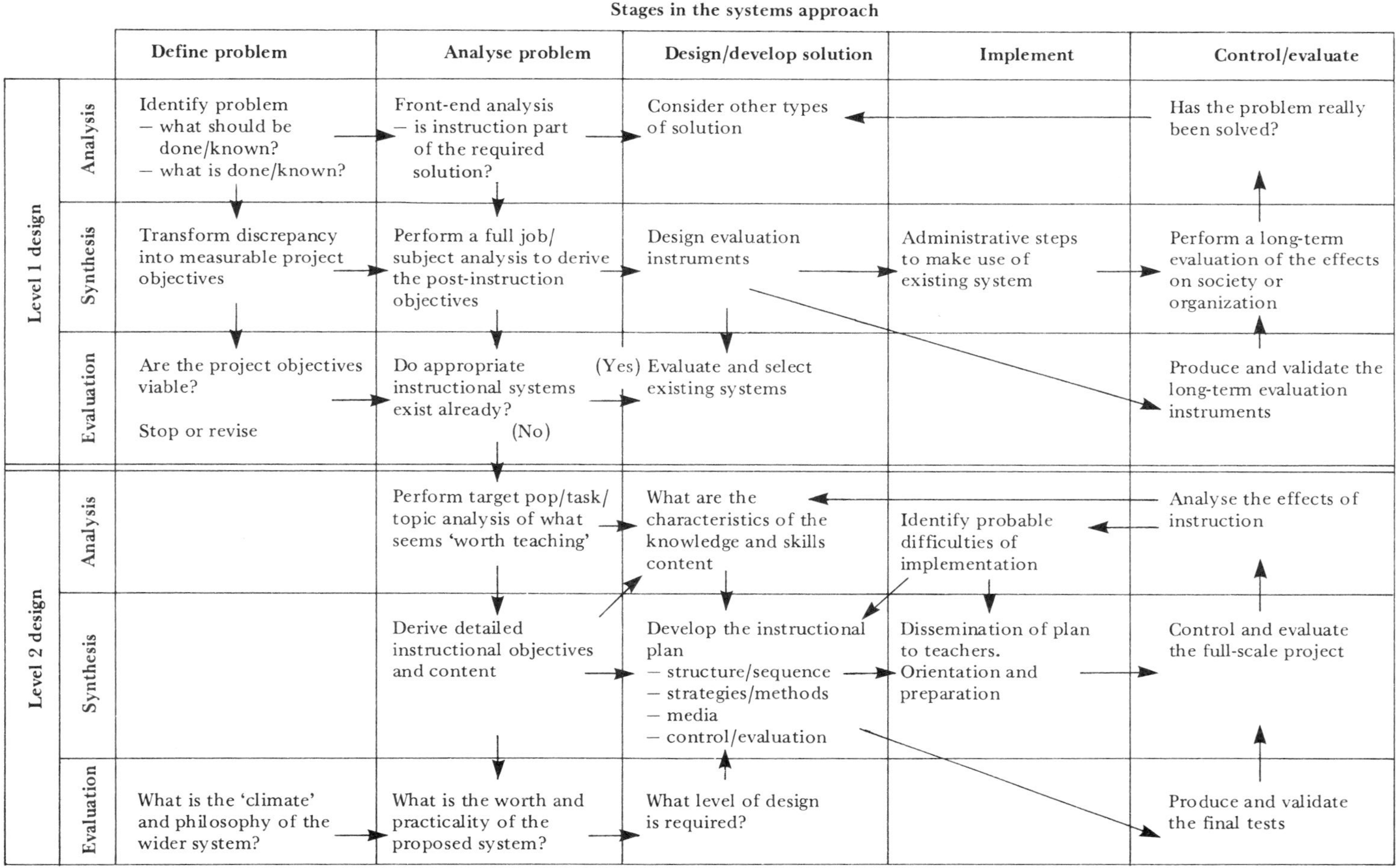

Stages in the systems approach

		Define problem	Analyse problem	Design/develop solution	Implement	Control/evaluate
Level 1 design	Analysis	Identify problem — what should be done/known? — what is done/known?	Front-end analysis — is instruction part of the required solution?	Consider other types of solution		Has the problem really been solved?
	Synthesis	Transform discrepancy into measurable project objectives	Perform a full job/subject analysis to derive the post-instruction objectives	Design evaluation instruments	Administrative steps to make use of existing system	Perform a long-term evaluation of the effects on society or organization
	Evaluation	Are the project objectives viable? Stop or revise	Do appropriate instructional systems exist already? (Yes) (No)	(Yes) Evaluate and select existing systems		Produce and validate the long-term evaluation instruments
Level 2 design	Analysis		Perform target pop/task/topic analysis of what seems 'worth teaching'	What are the characteristics of the knowledge and skills content	Identify probable difficulties of implementation	Analyse the effects of instruction
	Synthesis		Derive detailed instructional objectives and content	Develop the instructional plan — structure/sequence — strategies/methods — media — control/evaluation	Dissemination of plan to teachers. Orientation and preparation	Control and evaluate the full-scale project
	Evaluation	What is the 'climate' and philosophy of the wider system?	What is the worth and practicality of the proposed system?	What level of design is required?		Produce and validate the final tests

Map 1 *World map of the 'initial design' stage of an instructional design project*

Stages in the systems approach

Level	Phase	Define problem	Analyse problem	Develop solution	Implement	Control/evaluate
Level 3 design	Analysis	Inputs defined at earlier stages: — Objective — Content — Instructional plan — Project resources — Existing materials — Target population	Analyse the detailed instructional objectives and content	Identify appropriate teaching tactics	Identify difficulties of implementation	Analyse the effects of each lesson/unit
Level 3 design	Synthesis		Analyse the instructional plan to define a lesson sequence	Develop detailed plans for each lesson, including material specifications	Develop an implementation plan; Train teachers	Pilot project field-test the system in real conditions
Level 3 design	Evaluation		Analyse the existing instructional materials	Do existing materials meet specifications? (Yes) (No)	Do all teachers have the necessary skills/experience?	Produce and validate lesson tests
Level 4 design	Analysis		Analyse the target population characteristics in detail	Perform a behavioural analysis in fine detail	Identify suitable samples of the target population	Analyse the effects of each sequence or exercise
Level 4 design	Synthesis		Select the format for each exercise	Develop the materials — programmed texts — infomaps — structural — audiovisual, etc	Develop a production and validation schedule	Developmentally test the materials on small groups
Level 4 design	Evaluation			Evaluate for accuracy and consistency (expert evaluation)	Implement on a one-to-one basis and revise as necessary	Produce and validate criterion test items

The 'problem' has been fully defined at Levels 1 and 2, as has the overall form of the solution. Level 3 is concerned with the detailed tactics of each lesson — what learners and teachers should do at each stage of the instructional process. Level 4 is concerned with the development of special instructional materials.

Introduction to *Producing Instructional Systems*

Producing Instructional Systems deals with the micro level of decision-making which takes place when an overall plan of a new instructional system is transformed into a working reality. The intended readership is therefore composed of teachers, instructors, training analysts and others who plan the detailed tactics of instruction. The bulk of the book is devoted to systematic lesson planning, in the context of a general philosophy of individualized instruction. Individualization is not to be taken here in the sense of self-study, but rather as the creation of a self-correcting, adaptive system of instruction, sensitive to the individual needs and learning difficulties of the target students.

The first part of the book analyses this concept of individualization as the 'frequency of adaptive, student-centred, on-line decisions, taken during the process of instruction' and shows how this concept may be applied in real, practical teaching-learning situations. We see that although the majority of individualized systems of instruction make heavy use of specially prepared, often self-instructional, materials, their really important characteristic is adaptability to student characteristics at the tactical level.

This adaptability may be obtained in both individual and group instruction situations. Indeed, very often, it is necessary to use the dynamics of a group situation in order to create the variety of experience necessary for adaptation to individual student characteristics.

However, target population characteristics are but one element to be taken into account at the tactical level of lesson planning and execution. Other important factors are the content of the lesson and its specific instructional objectives. These factors are closely interlinked and quite complex, there being so many different types of content and objectives, each influencing the choice of instructional strategies and tactics. In order to assist the lesson planner in making his choice, several conceptual schemata have been developed. These are presented in Part 2 of the book, together with a summary of their use as tools for the overall, or *strategic*, planning of instructional systems, a topic that was more fully treated in the earlier book *Designing Instructional Systems*. This part of the present book is, however, more than a concise summary of the earlier work, as it also shows the practical application of the theoretical schemata to the design of several instructional systems.

The practical examples introduced in Part 2 act as a springboard for the development of Part 3. This is the main part of the book, devoted to the development and practical application of a lesson planning model that allows one to take into consideration the content and objectives of the proposed lesson, together with the characteristics of the target population, when selecting and implementing specific instructional tactics. This model is applied to the development of expositive classroom instruction, experiential group-learning exercises and a variety of both expositive and experiential simulations and games.

A further important aspect of this model is that it focuses the lesson planner's attention on the 'learner learning', rather than the 'teacher teaching' aspects of the instructional process, thus ensuring that the lesson promotes an interactive, two-way communication process. This interaction is, furthermore,

	Part 1 *Theory base:* Individualization of instruction	**Part 2** *Strategy:* Macro instructional design	**Part 3** *Tactics:* Micro instructional design – lesson planning
Analysis Techniques for understanding the problem	1 The individualization of instruction: analysis of the concept	4 The analysis of knowledge and skills: a new model for instructional design	7 The third level of analysis: selecting and planning the tactics of instruction 8 The structure of knowledge and its analysis 9 The structure of skilled behaviour
Synthesis Designing a solution	2 The structure of individualized instructional systems	5 A review of instructional design: the first two levels	10 A model for the preparation of lesson plans 11 The planning of group learning activities 12 Producing instructional simulations and games
Evaluation Looking at the proposed solution – and re-thinking	3 Some individualized systems: an evaluative review	6 Some typical instructional plans: an evaluation	13 The evaluation of an instructional system 14 Evaluating the evaluation system: why lessons fail 15 Establishing perspectives: where do we go now?

used as the basis for the planning of a continuous, on-line, formative evaluation and control system as an integral part of the lesson plan. It is this aspect of the model that promotes the adaptive individualization of the instructional process, whatever the strategy, tactics, group structure or media employed. The last chapters are devoted to this important aspect of planning for individualization.

The chapters in each of the three parts of the book are sequenced to move from the *analysis* of basic concepts and principles, to the *synthesis* of schemata, strategies, techniques and special instruments that may assist the lesson planner in his task. Finally, these planning tools are themselves subjected to *evaluation*, through the study of specific examples of their application to the development of lesson plans. In order to assist the reader to be selective in reading the chapters that are of most immediate relevance, the overall grid structure of the book is presented in the preceding table. Given a reasonable level of prior knowledge of instructional design and development, the reader should be able to use the book selectively, by reading either a specific row or column of the matrix. Those interested in analysis and basic concepts may read across the top-row chapters of all three parts. Those primarily interested in tools and techniques may opt for the second row. Those primarily concerned with evaluation may choose the third row, although it is not all that independent of the previous two rows. The three parts may also be read independently if the reader is already familiar with the earlier book *Designing Instructional Systems*.

PART 1.
Theory Base: The Individualization of Instruction

Overview

The first part of this book is designed to act as a theory base for the other three parts. The principal aim of the book is to develop approaches to, and specific techniques for, the production of instructional systems that are capable of being adapted to the individual needs, difficulties, interests and capabilities of students. There are so many different approaches to the individualization of instruction that perhaps the very meaning of the term is no longer clear. Our aims in the first three chapters are, therefore, first, to clarify the concept of 'individualization of instruction', second, to identify some of the principal factors in the design of systems of individualized instruction, and third, to analyse and evaluate some well-known systems.

Chapter 1 examines the concept of individualization of instruction. It opts for a definition that places emphasis on the frequency with which the instructional system is adapted to the needs and abilities of the learner. An historical review of early attempts at individualization leads to the identification of some of the facets of this complex concept. We note that individualization may occur at various levels, with varying frequency, in both individual and group learning, on the basis of pre-planned, prescribed decisions taken by the instructional designer, or on the basis of exploratory decision-making by the learner. This leads us to consider the need for a system of classification of approaches to individualization.

Various classifications are analysed, and a new, more complete, system is developed. This is based on four questions: What aspects of the instructional system are individualized?, When (ie at what level of design and with what frequency) are the decisions to individualize taken?, Who takes the decisions (teacher, learner, a pre-planned system or some combination of the three)?, and How is the individualization effected? These questions are used as the basis for the design of an analysis instrument which may be used for the planning or evaluation of individualized instruction systems.

Chapter 2 investigates the four levels of instructional design at which individualization decisions may be taken. We analyse the decisions which are characteristic of Levels 1 and 2 and the lesson planning and materials development decisions which are characteristic of Levels 3 and 4. The latter decision levels — the 'micro design' levels — are identified as the main area of interest in this book.

The chapter also emphasizes the importance of instructional media and materials in most systems of individualized instruction. These may be instructional media, which, by taking over a sizeable part of the teacher's routine instructional tasks, release him or her to perform the new tasks of managing the system, diagnosing individual difficulties and acting as a personal tutor. Alternatively, they may be support materials, designed to create opportunities for exploration, manipulation and discovery, in individual or small group learning.

Three basic approaches to the control of individualized systems of instruction are identified: prescriptive control, pre-planned by the teacher or an instructional designer; democratic control, in which decisions are taken by the learners, with the assistance of the teacher or some pre-prepared guidance system; and cybernetic control, in which the instructional system is capable of learning something about the special characteristics of each learner from an analysis of his or her response pattern, and can take decisions tailor-made to the learner's current needs.

This leads to a discussion of the various philosophical views on individualization, and their implications for the choice of system characteristics. The chapter ends with a consideration of the role of the computer in realizing the, as yet unachieved, ideals of the proponents of individualized instruction.

Chapter 3 analyses a series of well-known systems of individualized instruction, applying the concepts developed in Chapter 1 and the considerations regarding design discussed in Chapter 2. The examples are classified in a two-dimensional matrix, according to the principal media used for instruction and the principal control strategy employed. This schema and the preceding analyses are then used to identify and evaluate some of the main trends apparent in the current use of mediated, individualized instruction systems on both sides of the Atlantic.

1. The Individualization of Instruction: Analysis of the Concept

1.1 Introduction

'To many educators, the one tutor — one student relationship — the Socratic
dialogue — represents the ideal for higher education. They bemoan that the tutorial
system, as practised in Oxford or Cambridge, cannot be economically applied in the
less well-endowed universities. But as a product of the Oxbridge system, I do not
bemoan this.

   If the tutor is indeed Socrates, and if the students are highly motivated, articulate
and informed, then there may be no better system. But if (as was the case in my
time) the students are less than perfect, or the tutors untrained in the skills of tuition
(and generally much more interested in their research than in the students), then
I can think of no more disastrous system.'

This passage is taken from a speech Sir Walter Perry, former Vice-Chancellor of
the Open University, delivered at the International Conference on New Methods
of Post-Secondary Education, Caracas, Venezuela in September 1976. That
conference focused on two main themes — education at a distance (eg the
Open University) and individualization (eg the Keller Plan).

   The quote is from the opening speech of a panel discussion entitled
Individualization and education at a distance — two strange bedfellows one
may think. Yet members of the panel suggested that in *some respects, some*
Open University-type courses are more individualized than many traditional
school- or college-based courses. Other speakers disagreed, and it soon became
obvious that there were as many different concepts of individualization as
there were members of the discussion panel.

   This chapter identifies the main characteristics of individualization,
investigates attempts to construct a taxonomy for classifying and comparing
the many practical schemes or plans for the individualization of instruction,
and suggests a method for describing in a standardized way exactly how a
particular system is individualized.

1.2 Individualized learning or instruction?

It has often been said that all learning is individualized. After all, the learner
learns — and nobody can do it for him. Teachers can *help* learners to learn,
and they can do this in a variety of ways. Some methods give more
consideration to the individual learner than other methods, and in this sense
they are more individualized.

   Teachers may help learners to learn in ways other than by instruction. They
may exercise guidance or offer counselling, or remove obstacles to efficient
learning (such as cramped or noisy study conditions), or provide extra resources
(by lending books), and so on. However, our concern here will be restricted to
the processes of communicating information to the learner, stimulating
relevant learning activities, evaluating the result of those activities and taking
remedial action if necessary. This we have termed *instruction*. We are therefore
concerned with the individualization of instruction.

1.3 Approaches to the individualization of instruction

Historical background

Instruction, or at least some of it, has always been individualized. Only in the more recent past has the major part of instruction ceased to be individualized (or small group-based) and become large group-centred. This has perhaps been one of the penalties of rampant civilization, or at any rate it appears to be perceived as such, as attempts to find new ways of individualizing instruction recur in every generation. Rousseau's *Emile* is still sometimes held up quite seriously as a model for modern education,* and MacPherson (1972) quotes the following gem.

The Studebaker Exercises

'To accompany the Studebaker Economy Practice Exercises in Arithmetic (a set of programmed materials, complete with cardboard frames, immediate reinforcement and the like) published in 1916, the publishers stated:

"With the increasing scientific studies in education, the traditional "average"child has passed out of existence, and the complexity of the teaching problem has become much more apparent.

Consequently, educators have ceased their attempts to apply "average" methods of instruction. It is now fully realized that, if the processes of education are to yield adequate return for the effort, time and money spent, the extreme and numerous individual differences always present in every class must be recognized and treated.

Since one grows educationally only when his particular needs are met, and since the customary mass instruction cannot possibly furnish the variety of methods and materials necessary to meet the varying abilities represented in any group of individuals, it is imperative that a form of instruction be used that will, to the largest degree, permit each child to work according to his needs."

It could have been written in 1972. In fact, it probably will be.'

And so it was. The last time I came across virtually the same discovery, voiced in almost the same words, was in 1982, in the sales literature of an interactive video system manufactured by Sony.

The search for tutor substitutes

The hankering after a return to the economically unfeasible one learner/one tutor relationship has for a long time led to speculations and designs for tutor substitutes. Indeed, long before the self-instruction boom, attempts of various types had been made to organize education in ways which would optimize the amount of consideration given to the individual learner.

The development of individualized instructional programmes began in the latter part of the nineteenth century (Harris, 1960). Although the main current of educational practice has continued fixed in its course, increasing numbers of programmes that allow for differences among students have been proposed and developed (De Haan and Doll, 1964; Shane, 1962).

Arguments for breaking down uniformity of instruction gained support with the appearance of instruments for measuring human abilities shortly after the turn of the century. It became clear that students differ not only in intelligence, but also in creativity (Wallach and Kogan, 1965) and in various elements of intellect (Guilford, 1967). It also became clear that great differences between competence and performance are possible, and that inequalities in intellect, physical ability, and social behaviour, marked in childhood, 'increase as students move through the grades' (Thomas and Thomas, 1965).

Diversity of approaches

Some of the early proposals for changing the traditional system were referred to as individualized programmes; others exhibit the hallmarks of individualization even though they do not bear the title; and to these may be added still others, not necessarily associated with the school but obviously individualized — tutorials, correspondence courses, and informal programmes of independent study.

* Proponents of this approach might also be inclined to agree with Quintilian's reputed dictum that 'if only books could be so written that one page would only reveal itself to the reader once the previous page was quite understood, our educational problems would be over.'

Together, such programmes constitute a diverse family. They are based on different interpretations of individualization. They are inspired by different philosophies and theories and influenced by different technologies. In fact, the term 'individualized instruction' is used to describe such a varied assortment of curricula that it is no longer a useful, descriptive category of instructional methods.

It has become necessary to qualify the term by defining exactly *what* about a course is individualized and *how* it is individualized. This we shall attempt to do in a moment. But to illustrate the diversity, let us consider some of the well-known plans which have appeared during the past 100 years or so, both in the USA and in the UK.

In the USA Preston Search had, by 1888, initiated the Pueblo Plan, a laboratory scheme permitting a student to pace his own coverage of the course (Search, 1894). Parkhurst's Dalton Laboratory Plan (1922) and Carleton Washburne's Winnetka Plan (1963) presented self-instructional units that each student worked through as fast as he could.

In the UK, elements of individualization were introduced with the monitorial system. The free choice approach at Summerhill (Neill, 1960) is a completely different aspect of the concept. And in the Leicestershire Plan (Featherstone, 1967) the 'integrated day' concept presented yet another approach, aiming to adapt the school to the individual.

The self-instruction trend With the boom of programmed instruction in the early 1960s we were treated to yet another interpretation: individualization as self-paced individual study of prescribed material (usually common to all the students in a group). The self-pacing element briefly caught the imagination of educators, and linear programmes were seen as the new road to individualization.

However, people soon remembered that learning involved more than just reading. Branching programmes appeared (Crowder, 1963), and were soon followed by even more complex adaptive teaching machines, such as the SAKI keyboard instructor (Pask, 1960) and the Edison Responsive Environment or talking typewriter — a multi-media reading machine which adapts to the individual student's learning pattern in complex ways (Moore, 1962).

This trend has continued with the development of computer-based learning systems, beginning as rather sophisticated branching teaching machines (eg PLATO I), moving to programmes of drill and practice in routine skills (Suppes, 1968) and, finally, to computer-based instructional systems which simulate real-life business and social problems. We are now on the verge of developing viable systems of conversational programming which would enable the simulation of the one-to-one tutorial situation in all its essential aspects — the general-purpose adaptive teaching machine.

The group dynamics trend Yet another approach to individualization has been the growth of independent study: project-based work, Quest programmes, student-directed learning, etc. Such independent study may be carried out by the individual alone, or may be designed for small-group work, but it is still termed individualization, as it breaks down the larger group and ensures that each member of the small group has a task to perform.

Other types of group situations have been developed with the individual in mind. In sensitivity training, T-groups are used to enable individuals to learn to react appropriately to other individuals. In more specific training situations, role-playing and other simulation techniques are employed. Games are now commonly employed as instructional techniques, not only in elementary schools, but right up through the school system, into university, business and the professions. A well-structured instructional game ensures that each individual engages in learning-directed activities, while involved in a group situation.

Finally, the simple expedient of grouping (according to ability, interest or other criteria), although currently passing through a phase of unpopularity, is seen by some as a powerful and, indeed, necessary way of individualizing instruction.

1.4 Sorting out the approaches

With so many approaches to the individualization of instruction, it is necessary
to develop some way of classifying and describing them.

Gibbons'   One may adopt a variety of parameters. Maurice Gibbons, in his book
classification *Individualized Instruction: A Descriptive Analysis* (1971), divides strategies
for individualization into strategies which are employed in the group situation
and strategies which impinge on the individual. He then subdivides each into
active, responsive or permissive, depending on who directs the activity (that is,
who makes the decisions).

His final subdivision is concerned with the teacher-student interaction. In
group situations, the main determinant is whether the teacher works with the
whole group or with sub-groups, and, in individual learning situations, whether
the teaching is direct or indirect, (ie mediated).

This 'family tree' classification is rather rigid. Many instructional systems
are partly individual study-, partly group study-based. Indeed, MacPherson
(1972) suggests that any well-designed system would probably be a mixture.
Some decisions regarding options in the course will be taken by the learner;
others must be taken by the teacher, or are determined by the system itself.
Some activities will involve teacher-student contact; others will be mediated
by packaged presentations (both self-instructional and group).

Edling's   It is important to focus on *who* makes *what* decisions, and *when*. A simple
model   classification, suggested by Edling (1970), is summarized in Figure 1.1.

Methods and media	Objectives	
	School determined	Learner selected
System determined	Individually diagnosed and prescribed (IPI, PLAN, some CAI)	Personalized (many CAI systems)
Learner selected	Self-directed (learning resource centres, some multi-media kits)	Independent study (Project, Quest)

Figure 1.1 *Edling's model for the classification of individualized*
systems (adapted from Edling, 1970)

This classification, though useful, makes no direct mention of learner groupings
or learning pace (often considered key factors in individualization), although all
the examples quoted by Edling happen to involve self-instruction or small
groups under self-paced learning conditions, as if this was an essential ingredient

However, it is by no means clear whether a CAI course which allows the
learner to select his objectives is any more or less individualized than the
system at Summerhill (Neill, 1960), which also allowed the student to select
the lessons he attends. If there is a difference then surely it lies in what happens
within the lesson. How does the lesson adapt to the learner? Which experience
is more individualized: a linear programme in which all students read the same
material (albeit at their own pace) or a traditional lesson where all the students
have been selected by some diagnostic procedure so that the teacher has an
inventory of their learning problems?

A third   We might add a third dimension to Edling's model by constructing a
dimension   hierarchy of potential individualization, based on the degree to which a system

can adapt a presentation automatically to the needs of the individual learner. This is the degree to which a given instructional system is a self-regulating system. We may measure this by the frequency of adaptive decisions taken by the system.

A fourth dimension to consider is the level within a course at which individualization takes place. At which of the following levels does it occur?

1. At the course level: do students simply exercise their option to take or not to take a given course? Do they do this on the basis of a systematic consideration of the course objectives or simply because of individual whims? (Level 1 of individualization.)
2. At the course unit level: course options are planned in the light of the overall objectives of the course, the interdependencies of the units and the resources available. Neglecting the constraint of resources, reasonable course options are few in most courses with tightly defined, specific objectives, and many when objectives are ill-defined. (Level 2 of individualization.)
3. At the lesson level: lessons usually form a sequence, one building on the other. If this is so, is it reasonable at this level to talk of learner-selected objectives? Do we mean simply that learning rate, sequence and perhaps to some extent the methods and media, are individualized? Or do we mean that the learner can select some objectives over and above the common core of essential objectives? (Level 3 of individualization.)
4. At the individual, detailed objective level: the options would appear much the same as at the lesson level (ie learning rate, sequence, methods/media), but on a more micro scale, and therefore individual choice is exercised more often. (Level 4 of individualization.)

One may consider these levels of individualization as another way of expressing the frequency with which decisions are made — in terms of four broad frequency bands.

1.5 Key factors in describing individualization schemes

We have identified four relevant questions that one may ask of any instructional scheme that purports to be individualized:

1. What is to be individualized?
2. When (with what frequency) will the course adapt to the individual?
3. Who decides?
4. How does the system adapt to the individual?

1.5.1 What may be individualized?

The majority, though not all, of individualization schemes allow the learner to work on his own, at his own pace, for at least part of his study time. However, many other characteristics of a course can be, and in some schemes are, individualized. Some of the more obvious and more important characteristics which may be individualized include:

1. *Pace of study.* Students may be constrained to learn at a predetermined pace (as when listening to a lecture or viewing a TV programme), or they may be allowed to work at varying paces (as in programmed instruction, independent study, or small group discussions).
2. *Materials or media.* Students may be allowed to choose (or be assigned to on the basis of past performance) alternative versions of a lesson in different media, or alternative lessons leading towards the same objectives.
3. *Methods of study.* Students may receive alternative lessons differing in the instructional strategy adopted (eg expository or discovery) and/or

in the detailed tactics of instruction (eg choice of examples, number of problems to be worked, amount of hints given to the learner, sequenc of topics, etc).

4. *Content of study.* Students may receive alternative lesson content, eithe as a means of tailoring a course to the individual's own objectives (the liberal view of education) or as a means of selecting material familiar or interesting to the individual to be the vehicle for the attainment of broader educational objectives (the 'process' view of education).

5. *Objectives of study.* Course objectives may be varied, either for liberal reasons or in order to adapt courses to the different aptitudes of individuals or the different needs of the organization (the product view of education).

1.5.2 When does individualization take place?

As Gibbons (1971) points out, the term ' "individualized instruction" suggests a distinction to "non-individualized instruction", but it is impossible to un-individualize instruction. Every programme is unavoidably individual to some degree by the perception each person has of it and the response he makes to it.' Thus individualization is relative — a matter of degree.

A four-level model

I have elsewhere suggested (Romiszowski, 1976) a scale of frequency bands, depending on whether individualization decisions are taken:

1. For a course
2. For each unit within a course
3. For each objective within a unit
4. For each learning step taken to achieve the objective.

This scale is elaborated later in this chapter into an analysis schema for individualized instruction which combines the What?, When? and Who decide factors.

1.5.3 Who decides?

The decisions to individualize may be taken by:

1. *The student himself*, when he chooses a particular course option or a particular textbook.
2. *The teacher*, who may prescribe individual objectives or media or extra content.
3. *The system itself*, which may have built into it a diagnostic device whicl automatically adapts the presentation to the individual student. This is the case with the branching style of programmed learning (Crowder, 1963) and with many computer-based learning systems.
4. *Any combination of student, teacher and system.* This is the most common situation, involving a joint decision between student and teacher, taken in the context of the overall system.

1.5.4 How does the system adapt to the individual?

Two important factors

Two factors are identified as of importance:

1. The style and type of instructional materials employed in the system, and the way in which the learners select and have access to the materials
2. The role of the tutor or instructor (if there is one) in the system, both as a medium of instruction and as a medium for management and contro

It is apparent that there are innumerable different ways of trying to answer the How? question. In practice, a reply to this question generally requires a detailed description of the system in question. The What?, When? and Who? questions may, however, be used to compare the general structure and philosophy of different schemes.

		What course parameters individualized?				
Who makes the decisions?		Time and rate of learning	Materials and media	Sequence and methods	Content and examples	Objectives
Frequency of decision to individualize (When)	1. Total course	Student	✕	✕	←	System→ (diagnostic tests)
	2. Every unit	← Tutor and student →				✕
	3. Every lesson	Student and (System)	✕	System	✕	✕
	4. Every learning step	Student	✕	System	(System)	✕

(a) Example of use of analysis form to describe an individualized remedial mathematics course used at Middlesex Polytechnic (lower half completed for a 'branching PI' unit)

3. Every lesson	Student	✕	✕	✕	✕
4. Every learning step	Student	✕	✕	✕	✕

(b) Example of lower half, completed for a 'linear PI' unit

3. Every lesson	Student and tutor	(Tutor)	Tutor	(Tutor)	✕
4. Every learning step	Student and tutor	(Tutor)	Tutor	(Tutor)	(Tutor)

(c) Example of lower half completed for an individual tutorial

(Note: Brackets are used to indicate occasional rather than systematic and regular decisions.)

Figure 1.2 *Use of analysis form to describe an individualized system*

1.6 A proposed form for the description of individualized systems

The form shown in Figure 1.2 (see p 9) is a useful method of analysing and comparing existing systems of individualized instruction. It has also proved to be a useful planning tool when deciding which aspects of a course ought to be individualized and which ought not to be.

The example shown in Figure 1.2 is an analysis of the individualized remedial mathematics course offered at the Middlesex Polytechnic, which is described elsewhere (Hamer and Romiszowski, 1969; Romiszowski, Bajpai and Lewis, 1976).

Explanation of the analysis form   A few words of explanation — the answers to the How? question — will help to explain the chart.

Level 1. At the course level, course objectives are adapted by the system to the individual's needs — a diagnostic test (marked automatically) prescribes the *units* (there are 22 in all) which need to be studied. Theoretically, there is no overall time limit for the student to complete the prescribed units. He may plan his own timetable.

Level 2. At the unit level there is no choice of objectives; the objectives are the same for any student studying the unit. However, generally, there is a choice of methods and media available to achieve the objectives. The choice is made by the tutor and student jointly (typically, the choice would be between a branching PI unit on a teaching machine, a printed assignment to take home or an individual tutorial). However, mastery of the unit's objectives is always monitored by the tutor, who will require the student to repeat a unit, use an alternative presentation, etc if required in order to achieve mastery. Thus the time spent on a unit is effectively adjusted to the individual student's needs by the tutor.

Levels 3 and 4. At the lesson and step levels, the analysis would be different for alternative sets of materials. The bulk of the materials used are branching programmes in teaching machines. The analysis (as shown for these materials) indicates standard lesson objectives and media, but the content (example: type and number of problems), and the methods (alternative explanations) are varied automatically by the system to suit the individual learner's error pattern. The student, of course, controls his learning rate, but is occasionally forced by the system to repeat sections or to attempt extra problems, with a consequent time penalty.

In the case of a different medium of instruction, the analysis at the learning step level may be quite different. For example, a linear (Skinnerian) learning programme individualizes only the learning rate. Methods and content stay the same for all students. On the other hand, when the tutor gives an individual tutorial all the factors (except the overall objectives in this case) may be adapted to the individual student. The extent to which this happens in practice depends on the skill and creative adaptability of the tutor. At the least creative extreme, he is no more (perhaps less) adaptive than a simple branching programme.

These examples illustrate the sensitivity of the chart suggested as a form for describing a given individualized scheme. Other classifications (eg Edling) deal only in gross generalization, and do not define the frequency of decision. The suggested chart is simple to understand and use, both for analysis of existing systems and for the design of new ones.

2. The Structure of Individualized Instructional Systems

In Chapter 1 we analysed the concept of individualization, in order to show its complexity, in terms of *what* aspects of the instruction are individualized, *who* takes the decisions and at *what level* (or with what frequency) the decisions are taken. We shall now proceed to the question of how to perform the design of individualized systems of instruction. We shall use four basic characteristics of instructional systems as dimensions which we should specify during the design process.

These dimensions are:

1. The levels at which individualization takes place and the aspects to be individualized.
2. The principal media or agents of instruction.
3. The systems of control used.
4. The overall educational/philosophical viewpoints which lead us to wish to individualize the instructional process.

2.1 Levels of individualization

Virtually any course may be individualized as a whole; the student may choose to take it or leave it. It is only at the course unit level that individualization really begins to have meaning. However, at this level, individualization decisions are restricted to a choice of units that will make up the course. These units may vary in objectives, content, instructional methods or delivery media, or any combination of these. The student may select these himself, may be guided by a teacher, or may have his selection options restricted by some master plan, be it compulsory common core curriculum or a decision algorithm built into a computer-managed instructional system, such as project PLAN (Flanagan, 1968).

A comprehensive list of possible approaches to individualization is given in an article by Stephen Willoughby (1976):

1. Some students have simply been eliminated from the schools or the classes by the school authorities.
2. Various forms of homogeneous grouping or tracking have been tried.
3. Grouping within classes has been tried by many teachers.
4. Students (and their parents) have been allowed to choose which courses they would study, especially in the upper grades.
5. Some students have been used as teachers' helpers to try to improve the learning of other students.
6. Differentiated assignments have been tried, usually consisting of special remedial work or enrichment.
7. Occasionally, parents have been asked to provide special help for certain students, either directly or through a paid tutor.
8. Teachers often provide special help or inspiration to specific students outside the regular class period, as well as within the class.
9. Various forms of team teaching have been tried to help meet the needs of individual pupils.
10. Flexible scheduling on a school-wide basis has also been tried in an

attempt to meet the needs of individuals more efficiently.

11. Non-graded schools have been created to allow for progress through ability, achievement, and so on, rather than simply through the process of ageing.
12. Continuous progress plans (similar to Item 11) have also been used.
13. 'Free schools', based on the Summerhill School plan have been tried.

The items in this list are all organizational solutions which affect grouping, scheduling or grading systems and may have little influence on the instruction methods employed. Indeed, all these strategies could be applied at the course or unit levels without any attempt at individualization at the lesson or learning step levels.

However, we are more interested in systems which permit individualization at these lower levels. We are particularly interested in studying systems which modify the *way* that students learn (not just what they learn or when they learn), and systems that supplement or extend or even partly replace the human teacher. (We come back to this aspect later in Chapter 2.)

Of the 13 techniques listed above, perhaps the only one which of necessity modifies the way that teachers teach, and therefore the way that learners learn, is the team teaching approach. This approach generally forms part of a more complex system of individualization. The teachers released from large-group lecturing perform small-group or individual tutorial functions or manage resource-based learning systems. This technique will be discussed in the context of other systems which make use of it, rather than in its own right. The other techniques will not be discussed in detail.

Let us now turn to the remainder of Willoughby's list of techniques:

14. Computer-assisted instruction in one form or another has been installed in many places in the recent past.
15. Programmed instruction, with and without machines, has been employed.
16. All sorts of other methods based on advances in technology have been explored. These have included individual and small-group use of films, videotapes and audiotapes (often combined with filmstrips or slides).
17. Partial or complete independent study, in which children read appropriate material to learn certain topics, has been fairly popular recently.
18. A system of contracts in which children agree to complete a certain amount of work in a certain time has been tried in some schools.
19. Performance-based curricula, in which the goal is for students to perform certain activities at a certain level of competence.
20. Laboratories and resource or materials centres have been set up as a means to help individualize instruction.

This list includes techniques which imply that individualization proceeds to the lower lesson and possibly learning step levels. Most of the items also imply the use of media to take over a substantial part of the instructional task from the teacher.

2.2 Media of instruction

In his excellent book *Resources for Learning* L C Taylor (1971) says:

We can conceive of a number of different systems of learning being used in schools. Foremost among them is the teacher-based system familiar to us all in the classroom. Other systems already tried here or abroad are: book-based, book-and-boy-based, assignment-based, radio-and-television-based, computer-based. At first sight, it seems a daunting complexity, but we may find the appearance of conflict between these systems misleading . . .

We can start by noting that whatever system is used in a school, the teacher is assumed to be present. The most extreme exponents of programmed learning threatened to reduce the teacher to a cipher, but with regard to schools this was 1984 stuff and scarcely conceivable. Teachers are plainly of critical importance in caring for and about children; the inspiration, encouragement, control and guidance they provide matters profoundly. Further, no one but the teacher on the spot can perceive and supply the particular needs of a particular child at a particular moment. Neither the teacher's pastoral nor his tutorial functions can be replaced. When we talk about alternative systems of learning, then, we are asking only where, principally, the *burden of instruction* should rest.

Taylor then goes on to make the point that the essential difference between teacher-based and media-based instruction is that the accent moves from the teacher teaching to the learner learning. The teacher in the 'traditional' teaching situation (whatever that is) supplements his presentation with visual aids, refers the learners to textbooks and sets reading assignments, etc. However, he remains the principal medium of instruction and the principal learning resource at the learners' disposal — perhaps that is what we mean by 'traditional'. The systems which will interest us in this book, however, are principally the 'non-traditional' systems, in which the bulk of basic instruction is taken over by resources other than the teacher. Such systems, as Taylor points out:

> are made from the same cloth frayed out into threads or, in the case of the computer, overlaid with the dazzle of electronic millinery. For brevity, we can group all these systems together and, since they rely on collections of learning situations and materials, call them 'resource-based' or, alternatively, 'package-based'.

2.3 The system of control: the prescriptive/democratic/cybernetic controversy

Many of the various viewpoints on teaching may be classified as being either highly 'prescriptive' or highly 'democractic'. The prescriptive approach (characterized by both Ausubel and Gagné) supports individualization on the basis of a comparison between the individual student's profile and some ideal model. Such a comparative diagnosis leads to an individual prescription of learning activities for the student.

The democratic, or student-centred, approach (favoured by the Discovery Learning school) supports individualization for the student's own sake — to adapt the course to his needs, to give him responsibility and to develop him as an individual.

There is a certain amount of partisan warfare between these two points of view, on philosophical grounds. An alternative to both of these opposed camps is being constructed by the cyberneticians. Work (for example, that of Pask) suggests that machine-based systems can be constructed which can learn from the learner, can adapt to the learner's strategy for learning, and can redesign the presentations (on a conversational/tutorial pattern) in ways superior to those achieved by human tutors. This was obviously the case with machines such as the SAKI keyboard trainer for complex high-speed sensori-motor skills. Recent work in the field of computer-assisted learning (CAL) is beginning to achieve similar results in the conceptual and problem-solving area. Pask (1972), in an article setting out his views on the State and prospects of computer-assisted instruction, states:

> Most people in the educational profession (teachers, psychologists, university professors, curriculum designers, ETV producers, graduate students and CAI merchants) have a sense of vocation. Many of these practitioners owe their vocations to having at least glimpsed some moment of excellence; the power of evolving symbolism; the sheer joy of comprehension. The phenomena in question are varied. A child suddenly learns to learn, and you account for it by some sort of neurophysiological change; but you know that the explanation is phoney and really you saw a miracle. A culture is engendered by a project; sometimes by an idea; or an adult who seems to have died in his twenties comes alive again. A design class in California, where the students were ignorant of electronics, gets, uses, and innovates

with laser technology; all in a week. Von Foerster has over 100 well-documented examples, Illich more than 1,000. Papert has legions of instances, my own students have many.

In general life, the phenomena dubbed 'moments of excellence' are rare; a circumstance that is only in part attributable to the dissonance established by conventional training in scientific techniques. The chief reason for their rarity can be uncovered and represented formally; I shall gloss a lengthy argument by saying the world of learning and knowledge does not contain enough situations that count in a valid, non-trivial, very profound sense as 'conversations'.

That, I think, is CAI's important role: to foster conversation which is coupled to a corpus of wisdom (some of it encoded no doubt, but some of it not) and thus to increase the frequency with which moments of excellence occur.

If I did not believe that CAI could do that (it is a belief, though a reasonably founded one), I should not be in the field.

This strongly stated point of view may lead us into a brief consideration of society's view of the individualization of instruction.

2.4 The basic educational viewpoints on individualization

The views expressed so far have all been concerned with alternative concepts of improved learning:

☐ The task-analysis-oriented prescriptive view, as expressed in the mastery learning model.
☐ The individual-development-oriented democratic view, as expressed in the free discovery learning model.
☐ The moments of excellence, creativity-oriented view, as expressed in Pask's computer-based conversational model.

Two other viewpoints supporting individualization are the 'humanist' view, as expressed by Gagné and Briggs (1974) and by O'Daffer (1976), and the 'cultural push' view, expressed by Davis (1972).

The humanist view supports individualization as 'the only way to treat humans'. People are all different and should be treated as such. O'Daffer therefore argues that individualization is not simply methodology, or a psychological position. He contends that: 'the basic issue in any individualized programme is not which modes of instruction should we use but rather at which time, with what types of content shall we use which mode with which students.' It appears that this view is not necessarily at odds with any of the three approaches outlined above.

The cultural push view (Davis, 1972) sees individualization as a step toward building a more vital and viable sub-culture within the school (and, where possible, within the community). From this point of view, the student working by himself is important mainly because he can report his discoveries and accomplishments back to his friends; and small group collaboration between students is even more important.

This last view is, in a sense, a sociological argument for individualization, interesting if only because it is from the sociology camp that most of the strongest opposition to individualization has come in the past. Jackson (1968) has, for example, criticized individualization on many counts, but in particular he regrets any loss in student-teacher contact:

> When the teacher is in constant attendance, he is available not only to call attention to errors and to affirm correct responses, but also to beam with pleasure and to frown with disappointment . . .

and then again:

> . . . although a computer can store almost countless pieces of information about a student, it cannot know him as one person knows another. Only humans care about humans, machines never do.

Finally, Nichols (1972) also attacks programmed instruction on sociological grounds. He states:

> Completely individualized systems of instruction are based on the differences between individuals. Perhaps we should attempt to find out in what ways individuals are alike, rather than different, and capitalize on that to bring them together. Isn't this what the world needs today?
>
> [Machine-based, programmed instruction] systems are basically dehumanizing. They successfully eliminate the direct interaction of the mature and the disciplined mind with that of a novice attempting to master basic skills and concepts of a given discipline. Because of this, these systems, while they succeed in teaching students some basic skills, may impoverish them intellectually and socially.

2.5 A practical view: supply and demand

The dehumanization that Nichols attacks can, however, be overcome. It is becoming possible to computerize the heuristic, conversational tutorial. Excessive drill and practice routines, to the exclusion of problem-solving activity, should be avoided, but not only computer-assisted instruction is guilty of developing courses which concentrate on drills. Many teachers administer courses which are as operations-oriented and as rote learning-oriented, as the most outdated of linear programmed instruction. They do this because they learned in that way, and because they do not have the skills necessary to use a 'conversational tutorial' mode of instruction (even if class numbers allowed them to attempt it).

This failure on the part of individual teachers is the greatest justification for the study and development of teacher support systems — perhaps even teacher replacement systems. We have no alternative. The traditional approach to teaching has been singularly unsuccessful, more so as mass educational opportunities expanded.

It is not the function of this chapter to investigate or comment upon the quality of teachers in detail. It will suffice to observe that quality and quantity are inextricably linked, by the laws of supply and demand, to the value that society appears to put on education. As long as priorities, as expressed by salary levels, remain as they are, educational systems will continue to be short of highly qualified teachers, particularly in certain key areas such as mathematics.

For the past few years I have worked in Brazil. There, the answers are perhaps clearer to see. The Federal Ministry of Education has repeatedly stated that there is no way in which the country's current educational needs, at any level but particularly in technological and scientific subjects, can be met by traditional approaches to teaching.

The alternatives being tried include the mass media. Two States, each bigger in area than the UK, have primary and secondary educational systems entirely based on radio, television and print — they use no teachers, as we know them. Other projects use para-educational staff (the Keller Plan, using proctors/ monitors, was after all conceived in Brazil), programmed correspondence courses for in-service teacher training (60 per cent of practising teachers are untrained), and the chain reaction multiplier approach, in which every course graduate leaves the course with a 'kit' to enable him to repeat the course in his locality. ('Every trainee a trainer'.)

Most of these large and ambitious projects are working reasonably well. That they are working at all, given the low budget, rapid way in which most of them have been set up, is incredible. That they may be improved further by better design of the basic systems of control and of the instructional materials used is beyond doubt. That there is need for further basic research in order to facilitate the design and improvement of such systems is indisputable.

Such systems are of paramount importance to developing countries, but they are also of growing importance in the developed world. They will be of particular importance at post-secondary levels of education, especially in the training and retraining of adults, and in continuing (or recurrent) education (see Romiszowski and Biran, 1970).

It is for these reasons — on the grounds of both quantity and quality — that I see a bright future for the continued development of mediated individualized instruction. The current economic problems and the resulting cutback in expenditure on education and training have perhaps slowed down the process. However, in the long run these same economic difficulties will lead to the search for more cost-effective means of instruction. In large-scale applications, this will generally imply an increase in the use of carefully prepared mediated instruction, both in the mass media mode of distance education and in the individualized mode of learning packages.

With the current spread of microcomputers, local networks and national systems of videotext, the probable future application will be some form of total fusion between these two modes resulting in the individual learning package administered at a distance. In the words of Roy Jenkins (1983) such systems will shortly 'allow the contents of all the world's great libraries to flow through every living room in the land'.

The problem is how to channel the flow and how to use it with great effect. We shall return to this question in later chapters.

3. Some Individualized Systems: An Evaluative Review

3.1 Introduction

In Chapters 1 and 2 we have attempted to redefine the basic concepts of individualization more clearly, and to identify the principal aspects of the structure of individualized systems. We have argued that individualized instruction is a good thing, if properly implemented, and have attempted to show that this inevitably leads to the mediation of at least some aspects of the instructional system.

Purposes of the review We will now examine the overall structure of some existing innovatory systems of instruction. The systems chosen all have one thing in common: they employ media other than the live teacher for a sizeable proportion of the instruction. They differ, however, in many other characteristics. An analysis of the structure and the differences and similarities will, therefore, bring together most of the concepts that we shall be using in this book.

Being at least in part media-based, these systems would normally require a deeper level of design for at least some of their components. We shall, therefore, consider these same systems in later chapters, when we study some of the micro-level techniques used in their design and production.

Organization of the review This review is organized in terms of the principal media that the system uses to communicate with the learner. The three main categories into which I have divided the examples quoted are:

1. Print-based instructional systems.
2. Multi-media-based instructional systems.
3. Computer-based instructional systems.

The instructional processes used by the examples quoted are not always easy to describe in a few words. Thus, the structure of some of the processes can only be outlined. Indeed, some are so varied in terms of the methods of instruction employed that they would merit whole chapters for a full discussion. Detailed analysis is left to later chapters.

However, one characteristic of any instructional system that is almost as easy to identify as the media being used is the control strategy. Again, some systems vary their control strategies, but there is usually a principal strategy applied most of the time. We shall, therefore, use this factor as another parameter for the classification of our examples. We will attempt to place our examples in their correct position in the matrix illustrated in Figure 3.1 (see p18).

3.2 Print-based systems

3.2.1 Programmed instruction as product or as process

The systems described in this section are print-based instructional systems. The principal medium of instruction is the printed word, in the form of books, workcards, etc. These systems do not all necessarily use strictly programmed materials, in the sense of linear or branching programmed texts.

Although they do not all use programmed instruction materials, these systems have incorporated many of the principles of programmed instruction.

	Print-based systems	Multi-media-based systems	Computer-based systems
Prescriptive control			
Democratic control			
Cybernetic control			

Figure 3.1 *A simple classification scheme for mediated instructional systems*

Thus, if one were to adopt the wider definition of programmed instruction, given by Biran (1974), we would well include these systems within one class, as products of the same general programming process. In the words of Susan Markle (1970), 'programmed instruction is a process' capable of producing a variety of products.

3.2.2 Individually Prescribed Instruction (IPI)

The IPI system was devised at the Learning Research and Development Center (LRDC) of the University of Pittsburgh. Development work began in 1963 (Scanlon, 1970). It is applied to most subjects of the American elementary school curriculum.

The prescription   A unique feature of IPI is its requirement that each pupil's work be guided by a written prescription, which is devised to meet his individual needs and interests. The prescription is a link between pupil and teacher. The teacher communicates to the pupil the choices made to achieve an objective. Information about the pupil and his progress is communicated to the teacher. The data to be used for prescription writing should include:

1. General ability level in the given subject.
2. The degree of mastery or lack of mastery in each skill in the particular learning unit to which the pupil is assigned.
3. Information on progress in previous units directly related to the skills in the current unit.
4. Detailed information on pupil progress, including test results, in his current unit.
5. General learning characteristics of the pupil as they relate to specific assignments.

The procedure   The pupils proceed through the prescribed curriculum with a minimum of teacher direction and instruction. The teacher gives assistance only when requested. This frees the teacher for instructional decision-making, tutoring and evaluation of student progress. The marking of tests and the tabulation of student data are done by teacher aides, or by the pupils themselves.

Inherent in the IPI design is its capability for progressive adaptation. In this respect, the availability, accuracy and format of the prescriptions are crucial. With the information they contain, the teachers can organize the classes for small/large group instruction or for individualized tutoring, and can strengthen the instructional procedures, as required, in relation to each individual.

3.2.3 Personalized System of Instruction (PSI)

The Personalized System of Instruction derives its name from the fact that each student is served as an individual by another person, face-to-face and one-to-one, in spite of the fact that the class may number 100 students. It is suitable for courses from which the student is expected to acquire a well-defined body of knowledge or skill. The PSI teacher expects almost all of his students to learn his material well, and is prepared to award high grades to those who do, regardless of their relative standing in the class. He accepts the responsibility of meeting this goal within the normal limits of manpower, space and equipment.

Origin This method of instruction is associated with the name of Fred Keller, who, together with J G Sherman, R Azzi and C M Bori, devised it in 1963 to meet the needs of a new psychology programme in a new university in Brazil.

The main features of the Keller Plan include:

Main features

1. Individual study units, usually written matter, which may, but need not, be specially produced for the course, and may, but certainly need not, be in the form of programmed instruction.
2. Self-tests, which the student attempts and then discusses with a proctor or monitor.
3. Study guides in the form of detailed objectives, cross-referenced to the reading and practical assignments.
4. Individual and/or group practical work and discussion, controlled by specially written guide notes.
5. The role of the teacher is mainly that of a manager of the system. He has monitors to help him assess and tutor the students. The monitors may be special staff, but are often more advanced students who are given responsibility for the progress of the slower ones. They usually have a monitor's guide book to help them. The teacher evaluates overall progress and revises the course materials, and takes on monitoring when necessary.
6. The teacher also gives a certain number of face-to-face classes, but these concentrate on enrichment of the course, and students have to 'earn' the right to attend these classes by reaching proficiency in certain sets of objectives.
7. Proficiency in most Keller courses is taken to mean 100 per cent on each study unit test. Only when the student achieves this can he move on to the next one. (Keller, 1967; Keller, 1968.)

Utilization The system was first introduced experimentally in the psychology department of the University of Columbia in 1963, and in 1964 was installed at the University of Brazilia (Azzi, 1964; Azzi, 1965). Since then, use of the Plan has spread to other universities and institutions throughout the world and has been applied to subjects other than psychology.

Although the Keller Plan is the name now in vogue, other similar attempts were being made to overcome some of the shortcomings of early programmed instruction courses. For example, in the UK, Croxton and Martin at the University of Aston were attempting to increase the adaptive nature of programmed courses by roughly similar methods, although at the same time using a computer as a diagnostic aid (Croxton and Martin, 1970). There are many other examples which have some, though not all, of the characteristics of the Keller Plan.

The Plan has been used in several thousand college courses. Conferences on it are held regularly. A newsletter circulates among users. Workshops are being held to help new users learn the details of the method and avoid its pitfalls. The literature about the method numbers several hundred papers. (Sherman, 1974; Ruskin and Hess, 1974.)

3.2.4 The Kent Mathematics Project

Structure of the system This started as a small one-school project at the Ridgeway School in England (Banks, 1969). A course of about 20 to 25 hours' work was first organized to start in November 1966. The course was arranged so that the students selected their own path through the material, conditional only upon the availability of equipment and the sequencing of some of the topics. At the start, the course used programmes, both written and taped, worksheets for structural work, exercises on the desk calculator and post-programme exercises.

The students were supplied with a sheet of general instructions and a 'record of work' sheet. The course was organized into tasks which were identified by a cross-reference of a letter and number on a master matrix displayed on a wall board. Each student was supplied with a blank form of the matrix, to be completed as each task was finished. This was used as a record of work sheet and kept in the student's folder.

Use of the system   The task allocated to each cell in the master matrix was designed to take from between 40 and 75 minutes to complete, and the students consulted the matrix to select their next task. When the task was completed, the student's record of work sheet was written up by the student with the title, date and time taken, and then submitted to the teacher, who would check and initial it and update the progress chart. Each programme carried a test, and each task was only approved by the teacher when it had been completed to his satisfaction.

3.2.5 The IMU project in Sweden

Origins   The IMU project is perhaps the best documented and most intensively researched system of individualized mathematics instruction in Europe, certainly at the secondary level. The project began in 1964 on a pilot basis, and was extended to many schools during 1968-71 (Larsson, 1973).

In the autumn of 1963, a study commissioned by the Swedish National Board of Education was set up to compare the effects of completely individualized teaching and conventional teaching in mathematics in Grades 7 and 8. The results of the first year of the experiment were such that it was considered worth while to follow up the work. So, in the following year, the National Board of Education launched the IMU project. The original study was incorporated into the project in the form of a preliminary study.

Aims   When the project started, the aims were:

1. To construct and test self-instructional study material in mathematics.
2. To test suitable teaching methods and schemes for the use of this material.
3. To try out different ways of grouping the pupils and making use of the teachers.
4. To measure, by means of the material constructed, the effects of individualized teaching.

Developments   Various versions of the materials used in the project were prepared between 1964 and 1968. The third version (referred to as the IMU Upper Level, version 3) was extensively tested in a series of thorough studies. Revision of materials has continued, and today most materials are in a fifth version. The materials are programmed texts and printed tests. No manipulative materials have been prepared, although, because of the flexibility and high level of individualization of the scheme, there is nothing to prevent individual teachers from introducing such additional materials if they so desire.

Structure of the modules   The principle behind the model for IMU Upper Level is that there should be no grade differentiation and no division into general and special courses. Instead, the material is built up out of nine units, which together cover the upper level course in mathematics. Starting with a common curriculum for all pupils, the subject material is then structured according to the degree of difficulty within each module. Figure 3.2 (see p 21) outlines the principles on which a module is based.

Each module comprises four components, the first three of which belong to the basic course. They are called components A, B and C. Component A is common for all pupils. The B and C components are divided into levels of difficulty, hereafter called booklets. For the B component, there are three booklets, called B1, B2, B3. The C component comprises three booklets, C1, C2 and C3. The degree of difficulty is easiest in the B1 and C1 booklets, while B3 and C3 are the most difficult.

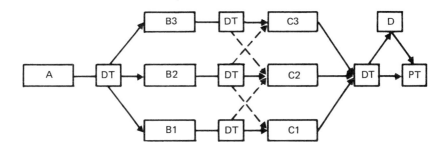

Figure 3.2 *Diagram of the structure of a typical module of the IMU programmed mathematics materials (adapted from Larsson, 1973)*

The different booklets cover roughly the same material, but the way in which the instructions are presented, and the number of extra tasks, vary. The D component is not part of the basic course. It exists only on one level, and comprises both revision tasks and certain tasks of a more independent nature. Each component, except the D component, is completed with a diagnostic test (DT).

Using the modules   The material is individualized in both the rate of work and the 'degree of penetration'. As a result, pupils within one grade can reach different points in the material. The intended normal rate of study is three modules per year.

In principle, the pupils are free to choose which booklet they like. The idea is that the pupils should, together with their teacher, go through what they have achieved earlier, and on the basis of this and other experiences choose a suitable level. It is possible and permissible to change level both within and between modules.

3.2.6 Information mapping (TM) *

This example is not a specific project or system, but rather a methodology for the production of print-based informational and/or instructional materials. A later chapter is devoted to the analysis of this methodology, so we do not go into great detail here. At this point, it is sufficient to understand the overall principles of the structuring of the pages, or 'maps', of a text prepared using this methodology.

Structure of the material   Each page of the text is reserved for one unit of information, which can be clearly titled to indicate the contents of the map. Thus, the reader may easily decide whether he needs to read a particular page. Furthermore, all the information on the map is organized in separate paragraphs, or 'blocks', each with its own sub-title in the margin, and again making it easy for the reader

* The terms 'information mapping' and 'Infomaps' are now registered trade marks of
   Information Resources Inc, Lexington, Massachusetts.

to be selective. Various organizing and cross-referencing devices make it very easy for the user of the texts to identify the maps that interest him and locate any more detailed explanations that he may need, etc.

The texts also provide feedback questions for self-checking one's comprehension of the information presented. Again, these are presented in separate maps, and may be studied or omitted at the user's discretion.

All this makes a system of information which is suitable for:

1. Initial learning, as a self-instruction text
2. Review and revision
3. Reference

Using the system

The system is also very easy to update by the substitution of the occasional map, as the information changes.

Many industrial organizations have adopted the methodology for the production of all their informational and training literature. The methodology was developed in the late 1960s by Robert Horn (1969), and continues to be refined and updated. Interest has grown recently, because it can also be used for the preparation of computer-based informational and instructional systems.

3.2.7 Structural communication

This example, like the last one, is a methodology for the production of individualized textual material that offers specific advantages in certain situations. We deal more fully with structural communication in later chapters. At this stage, our main interest lies in the special way that the methodology attempts to individualize instruction.

Programmed instruction with open-ended responses and feedback

Unlike linear or branching programmed instruction, which allows only one, or a very few, alternative student responses to a question to be taken into consideration, the structural communication methodology allows the student to compose a very large number of possible different responses, by the selection of key concepts, or response components, from a set of between 20 and 50 alternatives. As any number of components may be selected and combined to form the learner's personal best solution to the problem posed in the text, there are literally thousands of different responses that may be submitted.

By means of a keyword search performed on the learner's responses, the text may direct him to any number of clarifications, comments or items of extra information. Generally, about 15 to 20 alternative comments are formulated, to cover the most likely alternative solution types. However, each learner will read different combinations of two to five of these comments, selected in relation to the keywords in the response he made.

The technique is interesting and useful because it extends individualized textual materials design into the less well-defined areas of the curriculum, where there are no unique 'right' or 'wrong' answers. The technique can be used for the writing of self-instructional texts and for correspondence courses at a distance. It may also be used as one technique for the preparation of computer-assisted learning materials (Hodgson, 1971).

3.3 Multi-sensory instructional systems

3.3.1 Concrete materials and learning laboratories: the learning lab

Learning lab concept

The learning lab concept grew out of the trend towards concrete operations and discovery learning, fostered by the researches of Piaget and the development work of such innovators as Dienes, Cuisenaire and Bruner. Although this approach is most common at the lower primary 'beginning mathematics' stage, there have also been some attempts to implement laboratory-based learning systems at secondary and even post-secondary levels. A good example of laboratory material applied at the post-secondary level are the experimental kits on basic statistics developed at the Cranfield Institute of Management in the UK. These kits have been used with great success to overcome conceptual difficulties experienced by undergraduates on social science degree courses when first confronted with statistics.

haracteristics
a
arning lab

Depending on the resources available to a school and the usage level, a learning lab may be a temporary affair — equipment brought into the normal classroom — or it may be a permanently equipped special-purpose room.

Models for the usage of concrete materials vary in terms of the proportions of time spent on laboratory and other classwork. However, in general, they follow Bruner's stages of enactive-iconic-symbolic operations (Bruner, 1966). Thus, the laboratory work comes first in the learning of a new concept. However, in order to maximize teacher usage and save on equipment duplication, it is common to break down the class into smaller groups, some groups working with the materials, others performing follow-up activities with the teacher or his assistants.

he teacher's
le

Kessler (1972) describes the teacher's role as follows:

> The instructor sets the learning atmosphere for his students. The classroom emphasis shifts from teacher-dominated to child-centred. It is up to the teacher to know when to question, when to be a silent partner and when to withdraw completely.
>
> Instruction in the lab should start slowly and easily. The teacher who uses this approach in a self-contained classroom might begin with one small group of students. Some teachers start the whole class with one hour a week; some start with 10 minutes a day. Once these students are involved in their projects, he may start a second group, etc. Warning: don't set up more groups than you can comfortably handle!
>
> All pupils must be allowed to play freely with the materials. The questions the children's undirected explorations generate can be used by the teacher to guide them to further interest and activities.

3.3.2 The Fife Mathematics Project

aracteristics

Unlike the IMU project, the Fife Mathematics Project does not use programmed instruction. The materials are Workcard Booklets, worksheets and manipulative equipment — a sort of laboratory.

The project did not set out to construct a total system. It was designed to form part of the mathematics activities of the first year in the comprehensive school. Normal classroom teaching activities play a significant (in most schools, the major) part in the mathematics curriculum. The degree of involvement of the participating schools in Fife, in Scotland, varies: of the total time allotted to mathematics, from 10 per cent to 60 per cent is devoted to the individualized scheme.

rposes

The project was designed as an answer to the problem of teaching mixed ability groups. The claim made for the individualized aspect of the project is that it helps pupils to understand basic mathematical concepts by using concrete apparatus. Many textbooks still contain mainly verbally-based material; children must possess a high standard of literacy both to interpret the information given and respond to the questions asked. When pupils are using concrete aids (or manipulatives), it is possible for the teacher to assess their understanding of the subject simply by observing how they handle these aids.

3.3.3 Learning packages, packets and activity packs

Many individualized projects are based on the use of multi-media packages, which may include self-instructional and group-instructional materials. The use of the materials may be teacher-prescribed as in the IPI system, or student selected, as is often the case in resource-based learning.

One popular system in the USA is called the Learning Activity Pack (LAP).

The LAP is a booklet on a given topic, containing objectives related to this topic, diverse activities to reach these objectives and evaluations to determine if the objectives have been met. The components of the LAP are:

☐ Topic   ☐ Pre-test
☐ Sub-topics   ☐ Activities and self-evaluations
☐ Rationale   ☐ Quizzes
☐ Behavioural objectives   ☐ Post-test

Topics and sub-topics The student's initial introduction to a LAP is the statement of the topic and sub-topics. The extent of coverage depends on the individual teacher, the typ of student using the LAP, and how long he has been using such systems.

Rationale The topic and sub-topics are usually followed by the rationale. This rationale is aimed at providing the student with a reason for studying this topic. The rationale can take a variety of forms: a film to stimulate interest, a large-group presentation, a challenging experiment, an explorative study or written rationale which explains the relevance of the topic within the framework of the total curriculum, the student's everyday life, or his future life.

Behavioural objectives After a brief introduction to the topic, the student reads the objectives fo the particular LAP. All objectives are stated behaviourally. The completeness of these objectives depends on the level of development of the student involved. Within the LAP the function of the objective is to communicate goals to the student, and it should thus be written in his language.

Pre-test For some LAPs, the teacher may determine that the pre-test is at the student's discretion. In such a case, when the objectives unveil a topic or concept with which the student is totally unfamiliar, his decision might well be to omit the pre-test and immediately begin the LAP.

Activities The activities of the LAP attempt to provide the student with a multi-media, multi-modal, multi-level road to reach the objectives of the LAP. The multi-media activities, in directing the student to readings, transparencies, tapes, filmstrips, demonstration models, etc provide for the learning style of the individual student. The multi-modal activities include within the flexible programme large group, small group and independent activities. The multi-le activities provide the pupil with the opportunity to start at the base of his particular weakness.

Quizzes Frequent quizzes give the student feedback on this progress and correct his errors by re-routing him or her to remedial activities.

Post-test The post-test evaluates student fulfilment of all objectives of the LAP.

3.3.4 The audio-tutorial system

Characteristics Audio-tutorial instruction was first proposed and developed in 1961 by Sam Postlethwait at Purdue University, primarily to meet the challenge of teachin biology to large numbers of students (Postlethwait, Novak and Murray, 1972 Since that time, the method has been adapted to many different subject area class sizes and institutions.

The chief characteristic of the audio-tutorial method in its original form v individualized audiotapes as the main medium of communication, with print materials taking a supporting role. Over the years, however, the system has taken over most of the key characteristics of programmed instruction, and h tended to rely less exclusively on the audio medium. Indeed, Green, in comparing various instructional systems which have roots in programmed instruction, includes the audio tutorial among them (Green, 1976). He describes the system's presentation of instructional content through a variety of media available in a self-instructional carrel equipped with the necessary hardware. The method's strength lies in its attempt to present instructional activities in the sensory mode preferred by the learner and to integrate experiences from various modes into a meaningful whole.

3.4 Types of computer-based education

The impact of the computer on education is being felt in several areas, for example, administration, research, computational aids and the learning process. We shall concentrate our attention on this last area, an area often referred to as computer-assisted learning (CAL). However, even within this area, there are several distinct categories of systems. We can usefully subdivide CAL into three main categories:

- ☐ Computer-managed instruction (CMI)
- ☐ Computer-assisted instruction (CAI)
- ☐ Computer-based learning aids (CBLAs)

These can be further subdivided, as shown in the following schema presented in Figure 3.3:

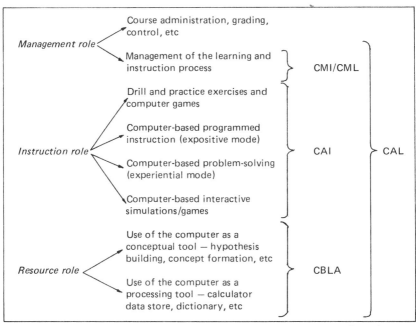

Figure 3.3 *A schema of types of computer-assisted learning (CAL)*

3.4.1 Computer-managed instruction

CMI encompasses a wide range of computer uses in education that involves the gathering and management of information necessary to develop flexible and individualized learning strategies. CMI uses the power of the computer to solve many problems of individualized instruction. These include diagnostic testing, test scoring and instructional prescription management. Management functions of CMI may include test item analysis, scheduling of instructional resources and student record-keeping.

CMI can be implemented in many ways. The computer may process information that students have coded on machine-readable answer sheets. Student-generated information (answers to test items) may be encoded in punched (Hollerith) cards, or students may interact with a computer terminal to enter information into a CMI system. Regardless of the method used to enter information into the CMI system, CMI uses the capability of the computer to manage the progress of a student through a programme of instruction, testing that progress at several points.

In general, the functions of CMI are:

☐ To administer student tests.
☐ To score student tests.
☐ To store data from student tests.
☐ To analyse data from student tests.
☐ To provide feedback to students, instructors and administrators.

Applications A simple example of CMI is the remedial mathematics centre for undergradua
in the social sciences, which was organized at the Middlesex Polytechnic in
London in 1969 (Hamer and Romiszowski, 1979; Romiszowski, Bajpai and
Lewis, 1976). This project included a small CMI element. At the beginning o
the year all students take diagnostic tests. These are marked and the results f
into a computer. The computer identifies each student's areas of weakness an
depending on the pattern of these weak areas, prepares an individual
prescription for study. In addition, it performs item analysis and error
analysis to supply information for the improvement of the diagnostic tests
and the instructional materials. The students progress at varying rates throug
different units of self-study materials, which are not computer based. Once t
initial prescription is prepared, the management of the course is carried out ▮
the tutors responsible.

A more sophisticated 'terminal-oriented' CMI system (as opposed to
'batch-oriented' CMI) is in use at Florida State University. When a student is
ready to be evaluated over a particular unit he may sign on to a computer
terminal and respond to the randomly selected test items by typing his answ
on the terminal keyboard. When he completes the test, the computer scores
his answers and displays a diagnostic learning prescription based on his
performance on the test. This prescription will direct the student to proceed
on to another unit or to perform specified remedial activities. After complet
the prescribed remedial activities the student may return to the computer
terminal to make another attempt, or take a new test composed of randomly
selected items over the same unit.

Perhaps one of the largest projects to use CMI was the project PLAN in t
USA, which set up a computer-based instructional management system for
all the primary curricula of American schools. The participating schools, in
various locations throughout the USA, have direct access to a Westinghouse
computer in California, which marks and comments on all the standardized
tests developed to control the progress of the learning process. Each child,
when ready, is tested and evaluated individually.

The test results are posted into a special computer terminal in the
classroom. Almost immediately, the child gets feedback on how well he has
done and guidance on what to do next. The teacher also receives help with
administrative and troubleshooting tasks, as well as guidance on how to plan
the future learning for each individual and for the group as a whole. He can
obtain data on typical difficulties in the curriculum, on how his students are
doing in comparison with the national norm, and much other information —
even career guidance for the students.

With this guidance, project PLAN makes use of a database established for
the earlier project TALENT — which contains data on several million school
children, how they performed at school and what they did in later years. Th
is an example of a very special application of computers in education, not
just assisting learning but providing a complementary service that was
hitherto carried out very haphazardly.

3.4.2 Computer-assisted instruction (CAI)

Instruction may be administered by a computer in several different ways, or
modes. The instruction provided by 'drill and practice' is supplementary to
the regular curriculum taught by the classroom teacher. The latter introduce

ill and
actice: a
pplement to
nventional
struction

each new topic or concept. Students work at the computer on exercises or review material previously introduced in class. Skills are maintained at a high level and difficult exercises are mastered through daily interaction with an eternally patient and tolerant instructional system. Often the drills may be presented in the form of games. Competition can be between individuals, between teams of learners, between the computer and an individual, or between performances of one individual at different times.

A simple computer-presented instructional game might involve the presentation to a student of 10 simple addition problems, one at a time. The computer records the amount of time the student required to give correct answers to these problems and displays this time to the student. The student is then asked to solve 10 more problems similar to the first 10, and to try to beat his former time. Games of this kind are useful in providing motivation for students to practise a repetitious activity.

In CAI's drill and practice mode, the aim is to take over the main responsibility for developing a learner's skill in the use of a given procedure or concept. Drill and practice lessons typically lead learners through a series of examples, whereby they can practise material already learned or can have the examples worked out for them step by step by the computer.

torial CAI:
sophisticated
rm of
ogrammed
struction

The tutorial mode is intended to provide as much actual instruction as possible. A tutorial system assumes the major burden of instruction, rather than playing a supplementary role like a drill and practice system.

In tutorial CAI applications, the computer functions like a very sophisticated programmed textbook, but allows a more complex network of instructional pathways through the material than a book could provide. The purpose of the computer in this mode is to present instruction that is simple, straightforward and individualized for each learner.

Tutorial CAI lessons are quite difficult to design and develop if there are to be more than just a few pathways through the instruction. Computers can provide the facility to branch to an appropriate set of materials, depending on the student's current response. Such a facility cannot be provided in any way other than with one instructor for each learner. However, the success of tutorial lessons depends heavily on the creativity and careful planning of the instructional designer.

In our classification, we shall reserve the tutorial mode for describing materials that follow on expositive strategy, that is, present (expose) information to the learner and control the learning process by eliciting answers from the learner to questions or problems posed, thus evaluating the reception, memorization and comprehension of the information presented.

alogue CAI:
basically
periential
ode of
struction

The dialogue/conversational mode of CAI describes attempts to use the computer to administer instructional sequences that implement an experiential strategy. In contrast to the tutorial mode, the computer does not present the information to be learned, but sets up a problem situation which should enable the learner to *discover* a new principle or relationship through his interaction with the problem.

The term dialogue is appropriate, because the learner or the computer may pose questions or supply answers. Typically, the computer can set up a problem situation for the learner to analyse and attempt to solve. The initial data given may be incomplete and the learner may ask for further data, which may or may not be available in the computer. The learner may offer solutions, which the computer will analyse and use as a basis for the decisions on what information to present next to the learner. This analysis could be performed on the basis of a keyword search of the learner's response, or on the basis of executing the learner's suggested solution and evaluating the results. In either case, the learner's response is used by the computer to generate useful comments or hints which will help the learner to solve the problem.

One early, and obvious application of this mode of CAI was in teaching computing. The trainee programmer would work at the computer terminal, attempting to solve computer programming problems, under the guidance of the computer itself.

Another early attempt to develop programming techniques which would allow the computer to engage in a dialogue with the learner led to the development of structural communication — a technique since applied both in CAI and in printed textual form. We shall be studying this technique in depth in later chapters.

More recent attempts to use this mode of CAI have used the heuristic programming approach. In such systems, the computer, by interacting with the learner, 'learns about' the learner and diagnoses his learning difficulties, using this information to select appropriate problems and formulate appropriate guidance.

Simulation: a form of experiential learning

Simulation techniques use the computer to simulate (or model) the behaviour of real systems. The learner may investigate the potential impact of alternative actions that would be too costly, too dangerous, too time consuming, or, for some other reason, impractical to experience in the real situation.

In essence, the learner behaves just as he would in reality, in terms of the decisions he must take. These decisions are, however, used to manipulate the simulated model of reality and are stored in the computer. The results of this manipulation are fed back to the learner by the computer, and in this way the learner discovers how the system under study — the reality which is simulated — behaves under certain conditions.

However, the computer does not analyse the learner's learning — it is up to the learner himself to analyse the insights he makes, form hypotheses concerning the system's behaviour, test out these hypotheses by further manipulation of the system and thus discover the basic principles or concepts that govern its behaviour.

Alternatively, the simulation may be built into an instructional package in which the teacher is responsible for observing the learner's progress, or organizing periodic debriefing sessions, with a view to guiding the learner, if necessary, to the discovery of the principles involved. The teacher then provides the Socratic dialogue that supplements the feedback obtained by manipulating the simulation.

If, on the other hand, the computer were programmed to carry out such debriefing dialogues with the learner, then we would have crossed the boundary to the dialogue/conversational mode of CAI, in which the simulation was being used as the problem situation under study.

3.4.3 Computer-based learning aids (CBLAs)

CBLAs use the computer as a supportive tool in the learning process, but do not use the computer either to perform the functions of a CMI system or to provide the primary instruction required for the student to master the instructional goals.

Use of the computer as a 'processing tool'

The use of the computer by a student in physics to perform numerous calculations required to find the answer to a problem would be a type of CBLA. Another example is the service of a computer-based information retrieval system available in many libraries.

Other uses of the computer that would be classified as CBLAs include the capability of storage and retrieval of user-generated data; demonstration by an expert of some natural phenomenon that could not otherwise be shown; and communication between users of a computer system by means of the system itself.

One more use in this category is the growing trend towards computer-generated tests and examinations. A teacher, or indeed a student, may call up a battery of test questions to satisfy stated requirements, taking into consideration the questions used in previous tests, students' past performances, etc (Lippey, 1972; Toggenburger, 1973; Romiszowski, 1976b).

All these can be considered as examples of the computer being used as a processing tool, in order to reduce the amount of data processing or number crunching that the learner has to carry out. To use Nick Rushby's phrase, the computer is being used in an *emancipatory* role by 'reducing the workload of the student' or facilitating access to organized data stores and thus promoting 'serendipity learning' (Rushby, 1979).

se of the mputer as conceptual ol

The computer can also be considered as a learner's conceptual tool when it is used to help the learner to structure his ideas about a subject and to form new hypotheses and theories. In this sense, the computer is a tool to assist thinking rather than a tool to reduce the need for thinking.

When a scientist or engineer, grappling with a new problem, attempts to formulate the problem in a form capable of being entered into a computer, he has to organize the problem, and the stages of the proposed solution, in terms capable of being translated into the computer language he intends to use. In doing this, he often obtains insights into the nature of the problem, and learns a great deal about that class of problem and sometimes about problem-solving in general. This effect has been put to good use in education by using computer programming as a means of developing logical thinking and problem-solving skills.

This approach is not new. Half a century ago, some mathematics teachers used slide rules not only as a handy way to multiply and divide, but also as a tool that could teach students the principles of logarithms, of exponential scales and of trigonometrical functions. More recently, a strong movement has grown up among mathematics teachers to use calculators in the classroom, not merely as processing tools that take the drudgery out of routine calculations, but principally as conceptual tools that may help students to understand the basic principles of arithmetic.

It is, therefore, no wonder that the use of computers in schools may be a powerful tool for the teaching of the principles that make computers work and the principles of the languages used to communicate with them. If these languages are carefully designed, so that they are similar to logical thought in other areas of problem-solving, we may indeed expect a transfer of learning from the computer context to these other areas. This is what has been attempted by researchers such as Seymour Papert in the formulation of computer programming languages, such as LOGO, designed to transform the computer into a tool for thinking. The research results of Papert and others working along similar lines are very promising (see Taylor, 1980).

We shall return to some aspects of this and other categories of CAL in later chapters that deal specifically with the production of computer-based learning materials.

3.5 Summary of the systems reviewed

In Chapter 2 we identified three characteristic positions regarding the control of an instructional system:

1. The prescriptive approach, which attempts to measure students' individual differences, and match instructional strategies to them, according to a predetermined algorithm.
2. The student directed, open, or free learning approach, which attempts to give the student maximum control over the choice of learning strategies and media and even sometimes of content and objectives.
3. The cybernetic approach, which attempts to set up an interactive system, adaptive to the student's needs in an online manner, based on what the system has learned concerning the student's needs, learning styles, difficulties, etc.

Figure 3.4 below is an attempt to classify the main systems of instruction discussed in this chapter. The classification, according to the primary media used, is combined with the above-mentioned classification, according to the main type of control adopted.

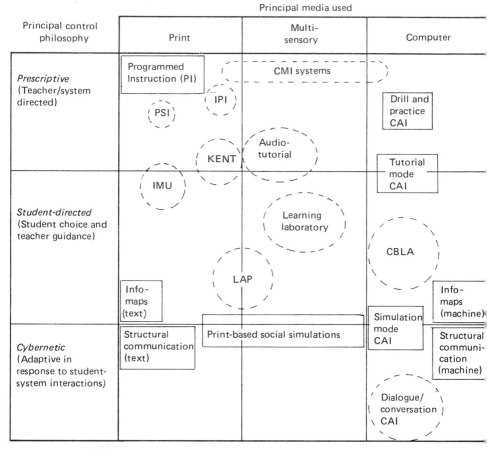

Note:
1. *The circles and ovals are not drawn to any scale, they simply indicate approximately where into the suggested classification, the systems described fit.*
2. *The items in the rectangles refer to techniques of materials preparation (programming) which will be discussed more fully in Volume 2.*

Figure 3.4 *Schema comparing the systems discussed*

This comparison is necessarily rather crude, as many of the systems can be prescriptive or student directed to greater or lesser degrees, often depending on the personalities of the teachers and learners involved. No quantitative implications should be read into the chart.

However, it does help to illustrate certain general trends. There appears to **Apparent** be a general trend, at least so far as print-based systems are concerned, **differences** for a concentration of prescriptive projects in the USA and student-directed **in approaches** projects in Europe. The big growth projects in the USA have been IPI at the **between the** elementary level and the Keller Plan (PSI) in higher education. Both of these **USA and** systems are directly descended from the programmed instruction movement of **Europe** the late 1950s and early 1960s and have abandoned many of the early PI characteristics, but have not abandoned the highly prescriptive nature of PI.

The computer-managed system, project PLAN, is somewhat less prescriptive, in that the teacher or the students are free to choose from a limited range of suggestions generated by the computer. In Europe, on the other hand, systems based on programmed instruction, such as IMU in Sweden or the Kent Mathematics Project in the UK, have attempted to build in a strong element of student-directed learning. The Kent project has organized its learning materials on a matrix structure, specifically to facilitate student choice of pathways. The Fife project is even more student directed, as well as using a greater quantity of manipulatives and multi-sensory learning aids.

In the multi-sensory area, once again, the Audio-Tutorial system (Postlethwait *et al*, 1972), which has become very popular in many North American universities, is highly prescriptive. The more student-directed LAPs and mathematics laboratories, although much publicized, are reported to be declining in some parts of the USA (Fitzgerald, 1974). In the UK, however, to judge from the literature on mathematical education and from the curriculum materials produced by such projects as SMP, Nuffield and Mathematics Applicable, the learning laboratory is a growth area.

Applications of prescriptive and student-directed modes in adult education The various systems which have been developed specifically for use at the university level have generally been prescriptive (eg PSI and Audio-Tutorial). This is rather surprising, considering the lip service paid to the need for greater student responsibility for the learning process. It is perhaps true that these systems have not caught on to the same extent in the UK as they have in the United States. Also one should remember that higher education has a long tradition of individualized teaching based on the tutor, on projects and essays and on small group seminars — methods which can be much less prescriptive and much more student directed, if handled in the right way.

There seems to be a need for both types of model in higher education. There are bodies of knowledge to be mastered, techniques to be practised, opinions to be formed and intellectual curiosity to be satisfied. Systems such as PSI have an obvious value in enabling certain basic prescribed goals to be reached rapidly and with the minimum of teacher contact hours, thus releasing more teacher time for goals that cannot be prescribed in advance.

The promise of the computer in instruction The area of greatest promise for the future, would appear to be the use of adaptive cybernetic strategies of programming. In the conversational or dialogue mode, the computer is programmed to learn from the learner as well as to teach him. The computer learns to interpret the individual, perhaps idiosyncratic, learning strategies of each learner, and his preferences for teaching style, media and so on.

The need for a theory of individual differences is thus eliminated. One no longer needs to develop *general* rules for matching learner characteristics to methods and media. These rules are developed online for each individual learner. They do not have to be generalized to groups of learners. Mary learns to solve equations better if they are explained step by step in an expositive manner, and needs many examples, while Johnny learns better if he is prompted to discover the rules for himself. However, Johnny needs geometry theorems explained and drilled, while Mary discovers such rules almost without prompting. The computer learns these individual learning styles and adapts the presentation accordingly. There is no need to classify the differences between Johnny and Mary according to some theory of learning, of cognition of personality, or of aptitudes.

The simulation mode of CAI is also particularly promising, in that it can compress a great amount of 'lifelike' experience into a short period of learning time and can present the learner with opportunities to gain this experience in the 'safe' setting of individualized study on a computer terminal.

The game aspect is also highly important as a motivating factor, whether used in more complex, experiential simulation/games, or in the simpler context of drill and practice exercises. Drill and practice, though much maligned, has its place, and will always continue to have its place for the learning of routine skills, standard procedures, facts (eg language vocabularies) and so on. The use of the computer as a base for such exercises offers a careful, error-free, tuition service of infinite patience and the injection of a gaming aspect can do much to relieve the dullness of such learning. Although curriculum changes may reduce the sheer bulk of the memorization content of school learning, they will never eliminate it completely. The more that can be transferred to interesting computer-based games, the better.

It is the programmed instruction tutorial mode of CAI that is the most widely used in current applications. But this, in fact, offers the least innovation. This mode, as currently practised, is not much more than the branching programmed instruction of the 1960s or the multi-media audio-tutorial of the 1970s. However, the presentation of the material can be somewhat more slick and sophisticated, and indeed, as computer prices fall and availability increases, it may become both cheaper and more convenient to use microcomputers than any alternative audiovisual device.

The use of computers in the management of learning has, in some respects, become indispensable. The use of computers as a tool in the classroom is also fast becoming essential. It is vital that the children of today leave school computer literate, and are thus prepared to live and work in the society of tomorrow. And from another viewpoint, the potential of the computer as a tool to think with, which is only just beginning to be explored, may become the strongest, most educationally-based argument for its use in schools.

PART 2.
Strategy: Macro Instructional Design

Overview

This book is, in many respects, a continuation of *Designing Instructional Systems.* Whereas that work dealt with the theory and the overall or 'macro' planning of instruction, the present work is devoted to the more detailed planning and preparation of individual lessons and exercises and materials necessary to implement them.

The approach and techniques described in the chapters that follow are based on ideas and techniques developed in the former book. However, not all readers of this book will have read *Designing Instructional Systems.* Some may, indeed, be principally interested in the micro levels of instructional design — lesson planning and materials production — and be only marginally concerned with the macro levels of overall instructional systems design.

However, certain concepts already developed in the previous work are essential for continuity at the micro level. The basic technical language of systems thinking, and the systems approach itself, are also common at all levels in the instructional design process. Finally, certain models and schemata developed previously will now be used as starting points for the more detailed aspects of instructional design.

Therefore, Part 2 presents, in a condensed form, many of the main ideas developed in *Designing Instructional Systems*, to give readers easy reference to all the necessary concepts and techniques. Chapter 4 presents a summary of knowledge and skills analysis, together with the principal concepts on which our instructional design model is based. Chapter 5 reviews the principles of the systems approach to instructional design (ID) and the four-level ID model adopted, and summarizes the procedures of macro ID — which are the first and second levels of the model.

Chapter 6 presents some practical examples of instructional systems planned at the macro level, together with guidelines on how to evaluate the macro design before passing on to the development of lesson planning and materials production. This chapter provides examples of the concepts discussed earlier and serves as a spring board for the detailed treatment of the third and fourth levels of ID that follow in Part 3 of this book and the second volume in this series, *Designing Auto-Instructional Materials.*

4. The Analysis of Knowledge and Skills: A New Model for Instructional Design

4.1 Introduction

Given the large number of models and systems for classifying learning and the development of instruction that have appeared in the past 20 years, the author of any new model owes his readers an explanation of why yet another model is needed.

In my case, this need has grown over many years of using (and teaching others to use) some of the best-known models as tools to assist in the planning of instruction. Most of the well-known models have proved to be useful and usable up to a point. I suppose that is what has led to their becoming well known. However, none of them has proved to be applicable in every situation that may be encountered in education or in industrial training. Also none of the existing models has proved to be easy to teach to the novice.

These two drawbacks have led me to attempt to construct a new model, based, to a large extent, on existing concepts, but more all-embracing in its applicability and easier to communicate and to use in practice. The model presented here has evolved over several years, and has been outlined, in part, in previous publications (eg Romiszowski, 1979b and 1980b). It is also fully described in *Designing Instructional Systems*, in which it forms the backbone of a methodology for the design of instruction in both educational and industrial training contexts (Romiszowski, 1981a).

This chapter analyses the limitations of present models, suggests a new, more complete model for the analysis of knowledge and skills, and illustrates how this model can be used for the macro design of instructional systems.

4.2 The missing domain — interactive skills

It is probably fair to blame Bloom and his associates for setting the division of learning into three domains, even if they were not to blame for their invention. The great impact of the work of Bloom and his collaborators in producing taxonomies for the classification of educational objectives has rendered it difficult for successive generations of educational thinkers to break away from the tripartite division of education (and, often, training) into:

1. The cognitive domain — intellectual knowledge and skills.
2. The affective domain — feelings, attitudes and values.
3. The psychomotor domain — physical skills.

A basic distinction between skills and knowledge

However, the training sector has not always agreed to be bound by the 'education' view. In the first place, many trainers have traditionally preferred (and still do prefer) to use a basic division between knowledge and skills as a basis for classification. In the second place, training has for some time distinguished between a variety of different types of skills. These include physical skills, intellectual skills (with various subdivisions such as perceptual skills, sensori-motor skills, planning skills, procedural skills, problem-solving and troubleshooting skills) and a further very important category of interpersonal or interactive skills.

This does not imply that the education sector has habitually ignored these types of skills. On the contrary, many curricula stress the social aspects of education as perhaps the most important elements in a general education. It is all the more surprising, therefore, that the most widely known classification of educational objectives should omit this category of skills altogether. The amount of research and development that has gone into management development in the interpersonal skill domain and into group dynamics techniques for developing interactive skills has demonstrated that this is indeed a domain of learning with its own characteristic problems and its own type of solutions.

Interactive skills: a separate category

It is not easy to classify these types of skills into Bloom's tripartite classification. Most interactive skills would seem to have some elements of attitude (affective domain) and would require some basic knowledge to be applied (cognitive domain). They may even call for some physical action at times. Thus, at some very detailed level of breakdown, one could perhaps classify the elements of an interactive skill into Bloom's three categories. However, an interactive skill is essentially concerned with interaction between people, just as a psychomotor skill is concerned with physical action, a cognitive skill with intellectual activity, and an affective skill with reacting appropriately (to objects, events, phenomena, people, etc).

4.3 The affective domain — feelings or skills?

We began the previous discussion of interactive skills by observing that it was not easy to classify many of these into the three domains identified by Bloom. However, we saw a certain affinity between these skills and the affective domain. It is difficult to separate the way we react to people or events from the way we feel about them. The difficulty for the sales woman learning that 'the customer is always right' reflects this problem of separating feelings from reactions: she must behave as if the customer is right, pleasant, intelligent, etc, when really she may be scornful of his lack of intelligence, angry at the unpleasant way in which he treated her and exasperated because she knows that the customer is wrong.

The skills element in an 'attitude'

The extent to which we should teach the sales woman not to feel scorn, anger or exasperation in situations which would naturally raise these feelings in any normal person is a moot point. Rather we are concerned with teaching her to control her emotions and not to show her feelings. When we do this we are attempting to develop certain skills of self-control.

The type of experiences that she has undergone, either in training or in real life, may have formed a specific attitude towards customers (or different attitudes towards different types of customers). This will have occurred through some form of conditioning process, either planned or accidental. The attitude of the sales woman will certainly influence how easily we can train her to treat all customers with civility, but whatever her attitude, however negative, it is still theoretically possible to train her to behave *as if* she had a positive attitude to all customers. This would imply that she had mastered a type of skill. In practising this skill she controls her feelings in order to achieve certain objectives she has set herself, in this case to improve sales and the company image or perhaps simply to hold on to her job.

Whatever the nature of the goal, the problem for the individual is the same, namely to control his or her own behaviour to achieve a long-term goal, despite short-term difficulties and unpleasantness. Those who do this well may quite justifiably be said to have developed the skill of self-control.

The main characteristics of a skilled activity

Does this sort of behaviour exhibit the characteristics of a skill? It certainly requires practice and repetition to acquire, as do skills in general. It certainly may be acquired to varying degrees of perfection, as can skills in general (unlike knowledge, which one either has or does not have). Finally, the type of behaviour we have described exhibits the typical stages of a skilled activity:

☐ *Perception* of one's own options.

□ *Decision* involving the planning and selection of actions.
□ *Action* directed towards a clear purpose.
□ *Evaluation* involving perception of results, further decisions, actions, etc.

There is a similar set of stages in the case of interactive skills — perceptions of other persons' behaviour, decisions on how to react and the actual reaction, etc — and we shall meet similar stages in the physical and intellectual skills areas. Thus, the affective domain seems to be composed of two different types of behaviour:

1. *Reflexive, conditioned* reactions to certain specific stimuli (situations); we can call these attitudes.
2. *Voluntary* reactions and actions, planned to lead to certain goals and involving the exercise of skills of self-control.

A contrast with the Krathwohl and Bloom taxonomy

These two distinct types are not clearly shown in the list of major classifications used in the Krathwohl and Bloom (1964) taxonomy.

Attending to specific phenomena may be considered a conditoned approach behaviour, but it may also conceivably be voluntary effort to attend to something uninteresting, but potentially useful (which requires a certain amount of self-control).

Responding could similarly be reflexive or planned.

Valuing the phenomenon appears more to be a voluntarily planned behaviour, but the man with a drinking habit obviously 'values' his whiskey to the extent of the best part of his salary, yet may not consciously include drink in his value system — what he lacks are the self-control skills.

Organizing one's values and establishing a personal value system are quite clearly planned voluntary activities. However, it is one thing to do the organizing (an intellectual activity) and quite another to live by one's values (a skill).

The categories of the affective domain's taxonomy are not different types of attitude, but different stages of development of an attitude. As such, they may be useful for evaluating progress but not for the prescription of instructional methods. The division into reflexive reactions and planned lifestyle may be more useful as a means to selecting specific instructional techniques.

4.4 The neglected domain — physical skills

The analysis and training of physical skills (or psychomotor skills) seems to have had a history quite divorced from the mainstream of educational research and development. This is probably because for a long time educators tended to look down on the physical skills domain as unworthy of their attention. Practical skills seem to be learned by simply 'watching and doing'. Anything that can be learned without the aid of the skilled human teacher must surely, it was argued, be so easy to learn that it would not warrant close analysis. In any case, training in most skills, apart from sports and some 'recreative' manual skills such as home carpentry, were traditionally the domain of industrial schools and technical and trade colleges outside the mainstream of the formal educational system.

Thus, in 1956, when Bloom's taxonomy was published, it dealt with the cognitive domain. It was not until 1964 that the second handbook, dealing with the affective domain, was published, As its preface says:

'The success of *Taxonomy of Educational Objectives, Handbook I Cognitive Domain* has spurred our work on the affective domain . . . we found the affective domain much more difficult to structure . . . our hope is, however, that it will represent enough of an advance in the field to call attention to the problem of affective domain terminology' (Krathwohl, Bloom, *et al*, 1964).

not a word concerning the psychomotor domain!

However, the taxonomies of Bloom and Krathwohl are essentially hierarchical descriptions of levels of competence or levels of mastery. *Handbook 1* suggests that cognitive development follows a sequence, from knowledge (of specific facts or procedures of classifications, etc) through comprehension of the knowledge, its application in particular situations, to the higher order mental skills of analysis, synthesis and evaluation, all of which are involved in the problem-solving process.

In the affective domain, the categories of attending to specific phenomena, then responding to them, then learning to value them, then organizing one's values in relation to each other, and finally creating a generalized personal value system to guide one's life, have a definite sequential and 'developmental' flavour about them.

An early 'taxonomy' of the psychomotor domain and the best to date

If we take this view of the taxonomies as 'stages of development' or 'milestones on the road to mastery', it can be argued that a taxonomy of the psychomotor domain existed even before Bloom's and Krathwohl's work was published. However, this was overlooked, because the work behind this taxonomy was performed in a different area (work study) and in a different country (the UK).

The myth of the relative unimportance and simplicity of training in physical skills was shattered by World War II. The sudden need for large numbers of workers in highly mechanized industries focused the attention of all countries involved with the problem of more effective and more rapid training. In the USA this led to the formation of the 'training within industry' (TWI) service (see McCord, 1976).

In the UK, on the other hand, the Seymour brothers, while following similar lines of development (including investigations of alternative instructional tactics — 'parts to whole', 'whole to parts' and 'progressive parts') went further in the study of the nature of physical skills and developed a much deeper approach to analysis. This was originally christened 'process analysis', but is now known almost universally as 'skills analysis' (Seymour, 1954; 1966; 1968).

The original work study basis of practical observation, documentation and breakdown of jobs and tasks was supplemented by a theory drawn from psychology and physiology. The original practical decision to observe and analyse both the detailed steps of each operation and the perceptual cues which control these steps was a direct parallel to the stimulus-response analysis of behaviour advocated by the behavioural psychologists. However, the characteristics of skilled behaviour — its apparent automatization and the number of different functions that seem to be performed in parallel (for example, planning, initiating actions, controlling actions and evaluating the results of actions) etc — led Seymour also to consider the special psychological aspects of skilled physical behaviour.

The observed stages in the development of a physical skill can be summarized as follows:

1. Acquiring knowledge of what should be done, to what purpose, in what sequence and how.
2. Executing the task in a step-by-step manner for each of the steps of the skilled operation. The characteristics of this stage are: (a) that there is a conscious application of the knowledge — the 'what and how to do?' aspects of the operation are controlled by the conscious thinking out of each step; and (b) the perceptual information necessary to initiate and control action — the 'when to do and how well done' aspects of the operation — is supplied almost entirely by the eyes.

   The observable result of these two characteristics is that the execution of the action is erratic and jumpy. Each step is performed as a separate unit before the next is attempted. The time taken to perform a given step may vary considerably between attempts.

3. Transfer of control from the eyes to other senses. For example, in car driving, the signal that triggers off the decision to change up a gear becomes the sound of the engine turning at the requisite rpm (which is heard), whereas originally it tended to be the reading on the revolution counter or the speed registered on the speedometer (which are seen). The reaching down to grasp the gear lever in order to change gear, which initially is a movement controlled by the eyes – the driver glances down to locate the position of the gear lever – becomes increasingly controlled by the kinaesthetic sense – the hand automatically finds the gear lever, being guided by the 'feel' in the arm muscles of the correct position. This transfer of control releases the eyes to attend to other aspects of the skilled task, in particular to the planning of subsequent actions. The observable change in this stage is a marked increase in the fluidity and regularity of action.

4. Automatization of the skill. This stage is characterized by a reduction of the need for conscious attention and thinking through of the actions. The skill becomes almost a set of reflex actions, one triggering off the next without conscious effort being called for from the operator. Of course, he must continue to pay attention to perceive the information necessary to plan, control and evaluate the activities, but the planning, control and evaluation occur unconsciously.

The observable result of this stage is that the operator may perform skilled activity and, at the same time, be thinking or talking about other matters. He may even, to some extent, perform things not related to the skill, without this having any appreciable effect on the quality of execution. Thus, a skilled motorist may discuss other matters or may appreciate the passing scenery without detriment to his driving.

5. Generalization of the skill to a continually greater range of application situations. This last stage only really applies to non-repetitive skilled activities. Car driving is a good example. No matter how well one has learned the basic rules and procedures of driving and the application of this knowledge to specific components of the skill (eg to gear changing), and no matter how efficiently these components have been automatized and subjected to unconscious control, the driver continues to learn and to improve his skill in dealing with unusual and unexpected road situations. It is still possible to discriminate between more and less skilled drivers, although they are both equally proficient in the basic manipulative skills of driving a car, by the 'road sense' which they exhibit in dealing with a variety of situations.

This last stage has in recent years been called the development of planning skills or strategy skills.

The importance of planning skills in non-repetitive activities

The wording of the five stages in the development of physical skills, outlined above, is my own. However, the stages themselves are based on well-documented work. The first four are based on the observations of Douglas Seymour from the 1940s onwards. These were published at about the same time as Bloom's taxonomies (Seymour, 1954 and 1966). The fifth was only hinted at in Seymour's work, which was concerned primarily with repetitive industrial 'operative' skills (generally requiring only a low level of planning skill). It is largely based on observations made by a research team at Perkins Engineering in Peterborough in the UK, during the late 1960s.

In his book on physical skills training, John Wellens (1974) emphasizes the importance of this research in formally identifying the 'planning' or 'strategy' skill (or experience) element in complex skilled activities. The importance of formally identifying and measuring this element is that it leads to considerations of how to teach planning skills.

4.5 The cognitive domain — knowledge or skill?

We have already indicated the limitations of Bloom's taxonomy, and similar taxonomies, as aids to the design of instruction, however useful they may be as aids to the evaluation of learning (ie test construction). There have been many attempts to develop categories of learning or objectives which are more directly linked to specific instructional tactics, so that the identification of the category of a given objective leads more or less automatically to a specification of the way the instruction ought to be organized.

A common confusion between 'skill' and 'knowledge'

The best known of these systems for instructional design is the one devised by Robert Gagné and his colleagues (Gagné, 1965; Gagné and Briggs, 1974). These approaches have been with us for more than 20 years, and have been very widely publicized, but, to my knowledge, they have not resulted in sweeping revolutions in any national educational system. Indeed, they have spawned as many opponents as they have converts.

Let us consider why, in 1977, Williams felt forced to suggest a new approach to topic analysis and the stating of cognitive objectives. He though it necessary to move away from the 'intellectual capability' statements of Bloom's taxonomy, but did not see the categories of learning defined by Gagné as sufficiently clear in behavioural terms. He saw them more as categories of information, on which certain operations have to be performed.

Operation refers to the way in which the information or content is used. 'A stitch in time saves nine' is an often quoted principle or rule. As such, it is content which is often learned. Once learned, this content may be used in various ways. It may be recited verbatim (memorization). It may be restated in different words (summarization). Cases where the rule has been applied may be identified (instantiation). The rule may be used to anticipate the consequences of certain acts, eg sewing or failing to sew up small rips in clothing (prediction). The rule or principle may also be used to arrange conditions so that a desired outcome results (application). Finally, knowledge of the rule may be used in conjunction with values to select the most desirable action in a given situation (evaluation). These same intellectual operations may be applied to almost all types of content.

Williams' approach illustrates an interesting and current 'back to information' trend in considering the types and patterns of information that should be supplied for effective learning. The four types of information content listed by Williams — facts, procedures, concepts and principles — could act as a basis for classifying information.

We headed this section 'the cognitive domain — knowledge or skill'. It should by now be obvious that it is both. Facts are information, but the learning and memorization of facts may involve certain specific cognitive skills. Concepts are in themselves a class of information, but the learning of a concept, thus turning it into part of one's personal store of knowledge, may require the use of certain cognitive skills, such as the skill of restructuring one's cognitive schemata in order to accommodate the new concept and store it in a way which relates to other knowledge.

This skill may itself be composed of several sub-skills, such as the skill of analysis of the concept and of one's existing conceptual schemata, in order to see whether and how the new concept 'fits in', the skill of evaluation of one's existing conceptual schemata to decide whether they are adequate to the task of assimilating a certain concept or explaining a certain phenomenon, and the skill of synthesis of new schemata that give a better explanation of reality.

Procedures are in themselves information and the learning of the steps of a given procedure leads to the acquisition of knowledge. However, the execution of the procedure may require the application of a variety of skills physical co-ordination, dexterity, visual acuity, etc in the case of practical procedures; tact, empathy, listening, speaking, leadership and persuasion skill in the case of interpersonal procedures.

Rules and principles are information and their acquisition implies the creation of new knowledge in one's personal store. However, the application of this knowledge requires the use of certain cognitive skills, which one might term 'problem-solving skills'. However, we have already noted that there are many types of problems and that the ability to solve one type of problem successfully does not necessarily imply that other types of problems will be solved equally successfully.

This difference is due to the specialist knowledge that each type of problem requires. The knowledge is of two types: knowledge related to the content of the problem (the facts of the case and the concepts and rules that are involved); and knowledge of how to get to grips with the type of problem (the problem-solving strategies or heuristics that generally lead to a rapid solution of a given class of problem).

Certain cognitive skills are also involved. These include the ability to see the problem in its true light, and to distinguish between what is relevant and what is not relevant to the solution. Both of these involve the sub-skills of analysis and evaluation. Often, the required solution is novel and depends on the application of certain creative skills, or 'productive thinking' skills, which probably involve the sub-skill defined by Bloom as 'synthesis'.

In our analysis so far, we have made reference to many authors and their models for classification of types of learning. Particular reference has been made to the work of Bloom and of Gagné. These two authors have been very influential over the past 20 years in shaping the thinking of instructional designers. I have made a point, however, of emphasizing the limitations, the gaps and the conceptual fuzziness that, despite their basic usefulness, exist in these two models. The time has now come to make constructive suggestions, in the form of a new model, which knits together some ideas from the authors mentioned and adds a few original ones.

4.6 Analysis of knowledge and skills — a modified approach

4.6.1 Basic concepts

The following approach to knowledge and skills analysis is based firmly on systems thinking. We start with our learner represented as a 'black box', receiving information inputs and outputting certain behaviours which are indicators that learning has taken place. The two tangible things that we can analyse are: (i) the information we feed the learner, and (ii) the behaviour he emits.

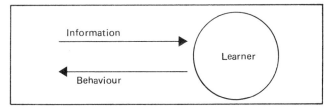

Figure 4.1 *The learner as a 'black box'*

Now let us define knowledge and skill.

ne basic
inition s

1. *Knowledge* refers to information stored in the learner's mind.
2. *Skill* refers to actions (intellectual or physical) and to reactions (to ideas, things, or people) which a person performs in a competent way in order to achieve a goal.

In practising a skill, one uses certain items of knowledge that are stored in the mind. One uses perception — of the situation/problem/object — to gain new information. This is combined with existing knowledge to form a plan of action and provide the basis of these planning decisions. Any skilled action may have four component activities — perception, recall of prerequisite knowledge, planning and the execution (or performance) of the action.

Factual knowledge can take two forms:

(a) Knowing facts, objects, events or people (either directly as concrete experiences, or as verbal information).

(b) Knowing what to do in given situations (ie knowing the procedure).

Conceptual knowledge can also take two common forms:

(c) Specific concepts or groups of concepts (being able to define, etc).

(d) Rules or principles which link certain concepts or facts in specific ways (enabling one to explain or predict phenomena).

Thus we have four categories into which we can classify knowledge:

1. Facts
2. Procedures
3. Concepts
4. Principles

These are the four categories of information used by Williams (1977) in his suggested improvements to the taxonomies of Bloom and Gagné. They are a not so different from the categories of information used by Horn *et al* (1969 as the basis of information mapping.

Skills are divided into a wide variety of categories by various writers and are given various names. We shall adopt a basic division into four categories:

1. Thinking or cognitive skills.
2. Acting: physical or motor skills.
3. Reacting: to things, situations or people in terms of values, emotions, feelings (self-control skills).
4. Interacting with people in order to achieve some goal, such as communication, education, acceptance, persuasion, etc (skills in controlling others).

4.6.2 The knowledge schema

Let us now expand the basic concepts presented above into a more comprehensive schema, which can act as the basis for our system of classifying types of learning. First, let us consider the 'knowledge' domain.

The 'structure' of knowledge The schema presented here (see Figure 4.2, p 45) subdivides our four bas types of knowledge (facts, procedures, concepts and principles) in order to illustrate several aspects of knowledge:

1. The information stored — the knowledge — may have been gained directly through concrete experience (observation of the outside worl by any one of our senses) or it may have been gained from some form of message, usually by means of the spoken or written word but also through the use of other symbolic languages. (This implies mastery of the language in question.)

2. The information may be stored as discrete items — individual facts, concepts, rules, etc — or it may be combined into information system (or schemata) which relate the discrete items to each other in particul. ways. The form of these systems or schemata may have been received from outside, as part of the way in which the information was communicated in the first instance, or it may have been constructed internally by the student himself when he tried to relate new informa received to information previously stored, which is the process of assimilation and adaptation described by Piaget.

3. Knowledge of a particular topic is seldom of one type but is usually a

combination of several types of factual and conceptual knowledge, both concrete and verbal, some stored as coherent schemata and some as discrete unrelated items. The circular diagram is intended to emphasize the non-exclusive, non-hierarchical nature of the categories.

The two tables laid out below present definitions and examples of each of the subdivisions in our knowledge schema.

1. *Factual information.*

1.1 *Facts* (knowing objects, events, names, etc).

1.1.1 *Concrete facts* (concrete associations; things observed and remembered). This category includes all knowledge that has been gained by direct experience, exemplified by the ability to recognize objects or people or places. The name of the object, etc is usually associated with it by the teacher and is used as a means of verifying that recognition has taken place, but the verbal element is not an essential part of the learning process.

1.1.2 *Verbal (symbolic) information* (including language such as logic, maths). This category includes all knowledge of a factual nature that has been gained by means of a symbolic language: statements of fact, descriptions of events, specifications of a motor car part by means of a code number, etc.

1.1.3 *Fact systems (or schemata).* This category includes the more complex interrelated factual knowledge that one acquires. The symbols of Morse code, the conventions of geography maps and the international road signs are examples of fact systems.

1.2 *Procedures* — knowing how to proceed in specific situations.

1.2.1 *Chains* (simple step-by-step procedures). This category includes the type of learning described exhaustively by Skinner in his work on the training of rats and pigeons. The training procedures of 'shaping of behaviour' which he describes are of particular relevance to this category. Note that Skinner was concerned with the study of behaviour rather than of knowledge. Our contention here is that an organism, whether rat or human being, that exhibits the ability to perform a procedure, carrying out all the steps in the correct sequence whenever it is called upon to do so, has stored certain information regarding the steps and their sequence. Thus we are quite justified in talking about the 'knowledge' of a procedure. The performance of this procedure may, in practice, involve more than the knowledge of the steps; it may also involve specific skills necessary for its performance. The separation of these two aspects is considered a valuable aspect of the model we are presenting.

1.2.2 *Discriminations* (distinguishing similar information). This category equates to the 'multiple discrimination' type of learning referred to by Skinner, Gilbert, Gagné and many other writers. Whereas a chain is built up of a series of stimulus-response associations, joined 'end on', a multiple discrimination is built up of a set of associations 'in parallel'.
   Whereas picking up and speaking into a telephone is a simple chain, the decisions on how to connect the phone call to the correct extension depend on the presence of a stored multiple discrimination (a set of associations linking the correct extension number to the correct person/department). This example illustrates why we are justified in labelling such discriminations as knowledge.

1.2.3 *Algorithms.* Most procedures are not simple chains or discriminations, but a combination of step-by-step actions, leading to decision points, where some discrimination has to be performed. It has become common to use the mathematical term 'algorithm' to describe any procedure, however, complex, that is nevertheless fully definable by a pattern of chains and discriminations. An algorithm is a 'recipe' for execution of a procedure. It is thus a form of knowledge that may be communicated, often by means of flow-charts of various types.

Table 4.1

2. *Conceptual information.*

2.1 *Concepts* (name of classes of items or ideas that can be exemplified).

2.1.1 *Concrete concepts* (primary concepts). This category includes concepts which are classes of real objects or situations, etc. Thus red is a concrete (or primary) concept as it is a word which defines a particular class of real objects (objects which are red in colour). A child can learn this concept by direct experience of a variety of red objects and other objects which are not red. The word 'red' is a useful learning aid (in order to check that the concept is being learned), but it is not essential to the learning process. Such ideas as 'higher', 'bigger', 'same', 'different', 'first' and 'last' are also primary concepts, because they too can be developed entirely through direct experience, without the need of a language.

2.1.2 *Defined concepts* (secondary concepts). This category includes concepts which are classes of other concepts. These cannot be learned without the use of a suitable language. Whereas one can demonstrate one's possession of the concept 'red' or 'bigger' by pointing at appropriate real objects, one cannot do this to demonstrate one's understanding or 'colour' or 'size'. The examples that make up the class described by these words are themselves concepts. Every real object has a colour and a size.

One needs language, and previous mastery of simpler concepts, in order to communicate to the learner the meaning of 'colour'. 'Red' is a colour, and so is 'blue' and 'green'. By quoting such examples of colours, one can communicate the concept of 'colour'. But if the learner does not have the concepts of 'red' and 'blue' the sentences we use to communicate the concept of colour will be meaningless to him.

2.1.3 *Concept systems (schemata).* This category includes sets of related concepts which, it is hypothesized, the learner stores in his memory in such a way that the relations between the concepts, as well as the concepts themselves, are remembered and can be recalled. The concept 'physical properties', together with the properties themselves, may be thought of as a system of interrelated concepts. Thus such physical properties as mass, weight, density or size may be stored in such a way that the interrelationships between them are also remembered, or alternatively they may be stored as separate concepts. In the former case, the observation that one object floats while another sinks would lead (apart from the direct conclusion that one is more dense than water and the other is less dense) to other, correct, conclusions about the relative masses of the objects in relation to their apparent volume. In the latter case, it is less likely that such secondary conclusions would be made correctly.

2.2 *Principles* (rules that guide action or explain change).

2.2.1 *Principles of nature* (rules that govern the behaviour of our environment). This category includes all principles or laws that we can see to be in operation in the world around us, either by direct observation or by inference from the effects. A rule is a statement of a relationship that exists between two or more concepts or phenomena. For example, the statement 'metals expand when heated' is a rule or principle of nature. It is an explicit statement of an interrelationship which exists between the concepts 'metals', 'heat' and 'expansion': '*if* it is a metal and *if* it is heated *then* it expands'. The 'if/then' type of rule is the most common form.

2.2.2 *Principles of action* (rules that govern the principle-holder's behaviour). This rather clumsy expression is intended to include the knowledge that one acquires regarding appropriate actions or reactions in specific situations, whether they be real-life or purely reflective (conceptual) situations. Thus such rules as: 'if I identify a problem situation I should also examine the wider system to establish whether the problem is "real" or whether it is a symptom of a more general problem' is a rule that one may use to guide one's actions in a problem-solving situation. These are the type of principles that Polya (1945) refers to as heuristics for problem-solving.

Table 4.2 *(continued)*

2.2.3 *Rule-systems* (theories and strategies). Just as discrete facts combine to form fact systems, or as discrete but related concepts combine to form concept systems (or schemata), so discrete but related rules combine to form rule systems. As an example, heuristic strategies for geometrical problem-solving are a combination of specific knowledge of geometry (in my classification, the individual geometry theorems are rules or principles of nature) and knowledge of how to search for solutions to maths problems (in my classification, general heuristics, or principles of action). The result is a set of highly specific problem-solving strategies, suitable for a given class of problems. Similarly, the combination of certain observed principles of physics, together with the application of certain general principles of thought (scientific inference, etc), might lead to the formulation of a new, highly specific, theory of hypothesis.

Table 4.2

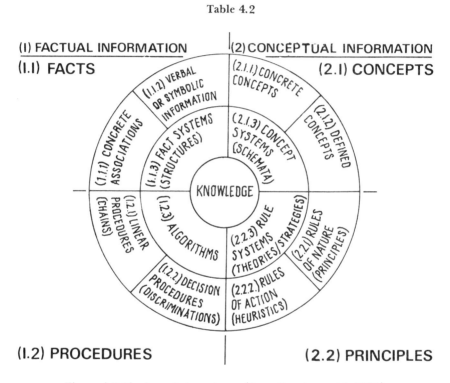

Figure 4.2 *The knowledge schema* (from Romiszowski, 1981)

4.6.3 The 'skills' schema

A second schema may be developed for the skills area. This postulates four domains of skilled activity, rather than the commonly accepted three domains of Bloom *et al*. Within each of the four domains, one sees a continuum of skills, from the fully automated 'reflexive' actions that make up sensorimotor skills, attitudes, habits and the following of algorithms, to the more complex types of skilled activity, based on a high level of planning and heuristic decision-making (see Figure 4.3, p 46).

We shall call the first type 'reproductive' skills and the second type 'productive' skills. I use these terms in the sense in which several educational psychologists have applied them in the context of learning and instruction. Briggs (1970) used the terms 'reproductive learning' and 'productive learning'

	Reproductive skills	Productive skills
Cognitive skills	Long division Writing a grammatically correct sentence	Proving a geometry theorem Writing creatively
Psychomotor skills	Typewriting Changing gear Running fast	Page layout design Driving with road sense Playing football
Reactive skills	Attending, responding, valuing (Krathwohl/Bloom) Approach/avoidance behaviours (Mager)	Developing a value system (Krathwohl/Bloom) Self-actualization (Rogers)
Interactive skills	Good manners Pleasant tone Verbal habits Etiquette	Leadership Persuasion Discussion Salesmanship

Figure 4.3 *The skills schema*

as the two grand categories of educational objectives. Bloom's main categories of cognitive objectives can be classified into these two groups with a high degree of accuracy (knowledge, comprehension and application being 'reproductive'; analysis, synthesis and evaluation being 'productive').

A little reflection on the types of test items that one would use to test for these categories of objectives should illustrate the difference. In the first case, one tests whether the student can reproduce what he has learned, either verbally exactly as learned (perhaps put into his own words) or as applied to standard types of tasks. In the second case, the tests should seek to establish whether the student can apply what he has learned to novel situations and tasks — ie whether he can produce a novel solution to a novel problem. Covington and Crutchfield (1965) have used the term 'productive thinking' in exactly this sense. Different tasks require different strategies for their 'productive' execution and the complexity of the necessary strategies also varies. For example, the painter requires very little knowledge in order to apply paint to a wall uniformly. He needs to know the recommended procedures for mixing paints, for laying on the paint and for spreading it out without leaving brush marks. He does not need to know any general principle or problem-solving strategies.

When wall papering, however, the decorator needs to know not only the procedures for measuring up the room, cutting the wallpaper, mixing and applying paste, etc, but he must also be aware of certain aesthetic principles concerning the positioning of patterns and joints in the wallpaper to obtain a pleasing effect. These principles combine into a decision-making strategy that enables him to decide, for a room of any shape or size, which parts of which walls to paper first, which corners to use as references points, how to balance the pattern around features such as doors and windows, and how to accentuate or hide such features as excessive height, asymmetry, irregularity, etc. This example illustrates the interrelationship that exists between knowledge and skill.

The terms 'reproductive' and 'productive', when applied to the classification of skills, should not be taken as two watertight compartments. Most relatively complex skilled activities are partly reproductive and partly productive. One could place a given activity at some point on a 'mainly reproductive-mainly productive' scale.

A more detailed analysis of the skilled activity will, however, identify the sub-skills, or component skills, involved. At this more detailed level of analysis, some of the sub-skills may appear to be purely 'reproductive', while others will appear as very much 'productive'. Such a level of analysis is useful as the techniques of instruction for the development of these two categories of sub-skills are quite different.

In Chapter 5, we shall show how this model for the analysis of skills and knowledge is used at the macro levels of instructional design.

he
oductive/
productive
mension of
ills analysis

5. A Review of Instructional Design: The First Two Levels

5.1 Defining problems in 'systems' terms

Problems exist in the eye of the beholder, when he expresses dissatisfaction with things as they are. One man's problem may be another's panacea. The raising of the school leaving age from 15 to 16 may have helped to reduce problems of youth unemployment (a source of dissatisfaction to society in general), but it created problems for schools starved of resources, a source of dissatisfaction to many teachers. The poor performance of students in, say, mathematics, may be a source of dissatisfaction to the teacher, but not necessarily to the students who have a different set of priorities. The non-observance of safety regulations is seen as a problem by the company's safety officer, and he may propose solutions such as training or tighter supervision or fines, but the staff, being paid on a piece-work basis, do not share his dissatisfaction. Indeed, they may view his proposed solutions as problems, and seek counter-solutions.

Problems as discrepancies between two states of a system: the actual and the desired

Serious problems are those that generate enough dissatisfaction to justify action to reduce them. Someone is sufficiently dissatisfied with what is, in order to pay the cost of achieving what should be. This cost may be simply the inconvenience caused by a small change, or it may be a combination of real costs: time, money and other resources required to develop and implement a solution. The amount one is prepared to pay is a measure of the worth of a successful solution. One may sometimes be able objectively to calculate this worth, from the value of changing what is into what should be.

In industry and commerce, a productivity increase, reduction in waste or overtime, or increased turnover can all be quantified to establish the worth of a successful solution. In education, it is generally more difficult to establish the worth of an innovation, but this is no excuse for not attempting such an evaluation. One way of setting about it is to use our black box concept.

First it is necessary to identify the system which best defines the problem in input-output terms (see Figure 5.1 below).

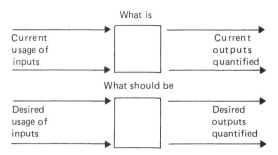

Figure 5.1 *Stating the problem in input-output terms*

Second, define the problem as a discrepancy between the *current* state of the system and the *desired* state. Do this in input-output terms only. If you find this difficult, you are probably looking at the wrong system.

Third, attempt to quantify the worth of the change which you would accept as a measure of a successful solution.

Notice that we have not mentioned any specific solution — nor should we at this stage. Indeed, we must avoid this at all costs, lest we fall into the trap of mixing up problems with solutions and confusing aims and means. All too often people make premature decisions about the form of the solution before they have really come to terms with the problem. Worse still are those who believe they have a mission or those who are selling an idea, for they have a vested interest in clouding the problem and concentrating on the solution. The education and training field has been plagued by more than its fair share of solutions looking for problems.

5.2 The systems approach to problem-solving

There is a time and a place for solutions seeking problems. Much research concerns itself with searching for new practical applications of a given phenomenon or product. The results of such research generate possible solutions to as yet unstated problems. But effective problem-solving is concerned with the selection of the best solution from amongst alternatives. The criteria for such a selection to be made must spring from the specific problem. Hence the emphasis on first defining the problem. Thinking in systems terms helps us to define the problem as clearly and as completely as possible. It also helps us to analyse the problem in order to identify possible alternative solutions. It helps us to select from among the alternatives and to develop the most viable solution mix. Finally, it helps us to implement the solution, to evaluate its effectiveness and real worth and to re-think if necessary.

Characteristic stages in applying a systems approach to problem-solving
This approach to problem-solving has been termed the systems approach. It has been used successfully in vastly different areas. These include electronics engineering, product design, economics, military projects, ecology, education and training. The one thing these areas have in common is that they are concerned with complex systems. Hence the systems approach is essentially a way of thought — a tendency to think about problems in systems terms. But it is also a methodology — scientific method applied to complex systems. It follows the general stages of:

1. Problem definition in systems terms.
2. Analysis to generate alternatives.
3. Selection and synthesis of an optimal solution.
4. Controlled implementation.
5. Evaluation and possible revision.

Many problems can be solved by either algorithmic or heuristic approaches. The motor mechanic or TV repairman may be taught an algorithm — a step-by-step procedure for fault finding. This logical procedure should guarantee that he locates a fault in a reasonable time, compared with, say, random checks. But, as his experience grows, he develops heuristic approaches. He forms conceptual models of certain types of car or TV set, made up of sets of principles like 'in this car this type of symptom generally means this fault'. These heuristics do not guarantee a solution. But once a sufficient number of such heuristic principles have been learned, the repairman jumps to conclusions, and more often than not is correct, thus reducing the average fault-finding time. Although algorithmic procedures are easier to learn and apply initially, heuristic procedures are more efficient in the long run.

The systems approach is primarily an heuristic procedure. Step-by-step procedures exist for certain activities (eg for task analysis), but these only apply at the level of collecting or organizing information. What to do with the information is not governed by an immutable algorithm.

5.3 Instruction: a definition

To limit our area of interest, it is necessary to define our use of the term 'instruction'. Not all education or training is necessarily instruction, but instruction is a necessary and an important part of educational and training systems. We shall use the term 'instruction' to mean a goal-directed teaching process, which has been pre-planned and tested. Whether the goal has been established by the learner, or by some external agent such as a teacher or a syllabus, is immaterial. What is important is that a predetermined goal has been identified. Whether the routes to the goal are unique or various, and whether they are prescribed by the instructor or chosen by the learner, is also immaterial. What is important is that pre-planning has taken place regarding the routes available to the learner and an end route has been pre-tested, to ensure that it is indeed likely to lead the learner to the desired predetermined goal. Figure 5.2 summarizes this definition.

Instruction is pre-planned objectives-based teaching

		Specific objectives exist?	
		Yes	No
Pre-planned study resources exist	Yes	Instruction	Visits to theatre/ museum, study tours, library, etc
	No	Projects, apprenticeships, research, etc	Incidental learning

Figure 5.2 *A definition of instruction*

It is thus the presence of precise goals or objectives (however they are arrived at), and the presence of careful pre-planning and testing that are the main characteristics of our use of the term 'instructional system'. Instructional systems design is, therefore, a three-phase process of establishing precise and useful objectives, planning study methods and testing them. We are concerned with *analysis*, *synthesis* and *evaluation*.

5.4 The four levels of instructional design

5.4.1 The four levels of analysis

We can define four levels of analysis. These can be summarized as follows:

Level 1. Defines the overall instructional objectives for our system, as well as certain other non-instructional actions that should be taken to ensure success in resolving the initially defined problems.
Level 2. Defines (a) the detailed intermediate objectives that have to be achieved to enable us to achieve the overall objectives (hence the term 'enabling objectives'); (b) the interrelationship between these objectives (in terms of prerequisites); and (c) the level of entry, or the knowledge and skills which will not be taught but which the learner must have mastered before entering the instructional system we are developing.
Level 3. Classifies the detailed objectives according to some system or taxonomy of types of learning and assigns specific instructional tactics to each objective or group of similar objectives. Thus, typically, one might find that the objectives of one lesson were all the same category or type (say, 'verbal information'), so one would dip into one's bag of tactics, pull out a set labelled 'for teaching verbal information' and use it in our lesson.
Level 4. Does not take the objective 'as found' from Level 2, but (a) analyses

it further in order to discover exactly what is entailed in achieving this objective (in terms of basic motions for physical skills, in terms of basic behaviour patterns or in terms of basic mental operations for other skills and for knowledge); and (b) matches instructional tactics at this micro level, generally in order to develop and produce special-purpose instructional materials or exercises.

These four levels are in a sense arbitrary, but they do help to define four levels of instructional design which correspond more or less to the four levels or system with which the instructional designer has to deal.

5.4.2 The four design levels

The four system levels are:

Each level of analysis is related to a level of design

Level 1. The project level — final objectives, principal measures and constrain
Level 2. The curriculum or course units level — detailed objectives, sequence and content.
Level 3. The lesson plan level — the 'instructional events' that should take place at each stage in a lesson.
Level 4. The learning step or individual exercise level. This implies that a given lesson is planned in detail and written out in some form of script or self-instructional material.

This structure is summarized in Figure 5.3 below.

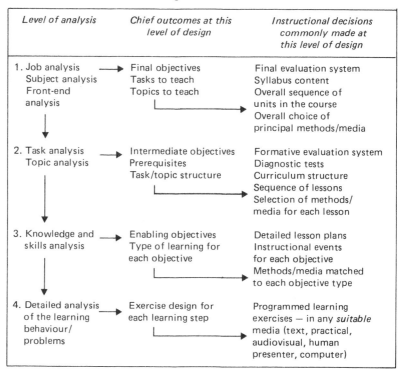

Figure 5.3 *The four-level design process*

Each level of design leads to a greater level of 'transparency'

At Level 1 we will treat the course more or less as a black box, concentrating on the specification of the outputs, inputs and control mechanisms for the course as a whole. At Level 2, the course structure will become apparent in terms of the sequence and interrelationship of the lessons that will make up the course and each lesson will be specified in terms of its outputs, inputs and control mechanisms. However, the lessons themselves — their internal structure and sequence and the detailed events which take place during each lesson — will remain to a large extent black boxes. At Level 3, the structure of each lesson becomes apparent in its overall detail. We will have a specification of the sequence of instructional events which should take place, however, we will not necessarily know exactly how each instructional event will take place. For example, the planned event may be 'recall previously learned relevant concepts', and it will be clear from the sequence of the objectives in the course. However, it is not specified exactly how the instructor should get the learners to recall these prerequisite concepts, what questions to use and in what order, whether to do it in group activity or by an individual test, etc. Thus the instructional events are specified in terms of their intended outcome but the internal structure of each remains in general terms a black box.

At Level 4, the instructional events themselves become 'transparent', allowing us to see exactly how they will take place.

5.5 Macro design

At the first and second levels of design, the prior steps of analysis define:

1. What should be achieved? — the desired outputs, or objectives.
2. With what? — the principal inputs (content, learners, resources).
3. In what context? — the environmental climate and constraints.

The main questions the designer must answer are:

1. When? — the sequence of units and lessons that should occur.
2. How? — the strategies, methods and tactics that should be used.
3. Who? — the structure and grouping to be used.
4. With what? — the instruments or media to be used.
5. How well? — the tests and control mechanisms needed.

This chapter examines the four questions referring to the instructional process — the questions of sequence, methods, grouping and media. Figure 5.4 shows some of the considerations that will be discussed. We shall examine each of the four key questions in turn.

	The question of sequence	The question of methods	The question of grouping	The question of media
Level 1	Overall curriculum structure	Overall philosophy and general strategies	Overall grouping decisions	Overall media options
Level 2	Sequence of units and lessons	Specific strategies and methods to be used	Grouping for each lesson	Essential media characteristics

Figure 5.4 *Macro design decisions*

5.6 The question of sequence
5.6.1 Decisions at Level 1

Already, at the stage of Level 1 analysis, the main instructional objectives can be seen to be interrelated. The relationship may be a strict sequential dependence, one objective being impossible to achieve until another has been learned, or it may be a thematic relationship of a looser nature. For example, some objectives cohere because they deal with the same general topic.

Thus, the instructional designer will already be able to make certain decisions concerning the overall sequence and structure of the course. His decisions will be influenced by the type of instructional course he is planning. For example, is it part of a programme of general education, destined to develop certain skills or habits in the students up to the limit of each student's ability, or is it part of a programme of job-related or professional training in which each student should achieve mastery of all the key objectives? A further factor will be the instructional designer's theoretical or philosophical views on the nature of the learning and instructional processes.

Plan the overall curriculum structure

An overall curriculum structure may begin to emerge at this stage. Often a 'linear curriculum' structure is adopted. A linear structure is most justified in the case of objectives which are closely related to each other sequentially and which constitute obligatory learning (as in the case of job-related training)

In another case, the overall structure of the main objectives may suggest that there is no one sequence. Some rules of sentence construction must be taught early, while others can wait and indeed depend on prior teaching of some rules of punctuation. Thus, one wishes to treat a topic at a relatively shallow depth, then study another topic and come back to the original topic later. This gives rise to the concept of the 'spiral curriculum'.

It is useful, early in the design process, to identify the overall structure that the course will probably require, as this will influence later analysis and design decisions. In the case of adopting a spiral curriculum model, for example, one will need, at the Level 2 analysis, to examine very closely the interrelationships between the objectives in different topics, to ensure that all parts of topic A that are prerequisite to the teaching of topic B are included at the correct point on the overall sequence.

Another curriculum 'shape' is the pyramidal structure. This is designed for courses that have a common core which all students study, and that allows specialization in one or more specific areas later. This shape is perhaps not as useful in conceptualizing a whole curriculum. It communicates the type of path that one particular student may follow.

Yet another type of curriculum design is often referred to as the 'inquiry-centred curriculum'. The basic idea is that the curriculum should be structured around questions which the student has in mind.

Mager and McCann (1961) showed that even in quite complex subject areas such as electronics, it is possible, and in many cases more efficient, to let the student choose the order of learning a subject. Their students tended to choose to start learning from the complex rather than the simple by immediately asking questions about actual pieces of home equipment with which they were familiar (for example radios and televisions). The answers to these questions immediately led to the discussion of the main components (valves, amplifiers and transformers, etc). Questions raised about these led in turn to more detailed questions and eventually the students were led to ask questions about the basic principles of electricity flow, electric current, potential difference and electron theory, usually the starting point of most courses on this subject.

Tom Gilbert, in an article extending his mathetics approach to the information-based part of education, shows how an inquiry-based, integrated social science curriculum could be presented as a matrix that relates the separate subjects which comprise the social sciences at school level (Gilbert, 1969).

There are many other possible approaches to establishing a flexible sequence. Gordon Pask and his colleagues (Pask and Scott, 1972) have worked on the mapping of subject matter in ways similar to those described above which they term 'knowledge structures', and have discovered that learners can use these structures in order to follow their own effective learning style, as far as sequence is concerned.

Others, among them Wyant (1973) and Vaughan (1972), have developed the use of network diagrams (drawn from the 'network analysis', or PERT, technique of project planning and control) for the mapping of course curricula. The application of this technique to curriculum plans is not a full use of the power of network analysis which has its uses in the overall planning and implementation of instructional systems. However, the use of a network diagram of this type to map a curriculum is an excellent visual guide to the course structure, as it clearly shows all the interrelationships between the topics.

5.6.2 Decisions at Level 2

Much of what has been said above concerning techniques of sequencing course curriculum is equally applicable at Level 2. The grain of detail at which the techniques are applied will, however, be much finer at this level as we are now working with all the detailed objectives of the course rather than only the key terminal objectives.

Plan the detailed instructional sequence

Techniques which help to examine the sequence and dependence of the individual objectives are of particular use at this point. It is at this level of detail that one might use the hierarchical approach to analyse the main objectives and identify the intermediate and 'enabling' objectives (as suggested by Gagné, 1965). Once the hierarchy has been constructed it is an immensely useful tool for deciding sequence, dividing topics into lessons and identifying the prerequisite entry behaviour.

Alternative sequences are still encountered in most analyses. At the Level 2 stage of analysis we have little concrete evidence of the best way to organize the instruction of a group of generally related objectives which are not sequentially related. There are, however, a number of rules of thumb or general-purpose heuristics which are often brought into play. Examples of such heuristics are:

1. From simple to complex, implying that the subject matter which is easiest to learn should be taught first, or that new ideas should initially be introduced by simple examples and applications.
2. From known to unknown, implying that learning should be so planned as always to begin from a concept or procedure which the learner has already mastered and to expand his abilities by carefully building on this base.
3. From particular to general, implying that general principles should initially be introduced by means of examples.
4. From concrete to abstract, overlapping in one sense with the previous rule, but also being taken in the sense implied by Piaget, Bruner and their followers concerning the 'learning cycle': concrete experiences followed by analysis, followed by generalization in abstract terms, and then referred back to more concrete experiences.

In addition, there are some general tactics for instruction in practical tasks (the above points refer more to intellectual learning). These include:

1. The 'progressive parts' method.
2. The 'cumulative parts' method.
3. The 'backward chaining' method.

Consider a three-stage task, involving steps A, B and C, normally executed in that order. The instructional sequences would be more or less as follows:

1. *Progressive parts:* practise A, then B, then A and B, then C, then A, B and C.
2. *Cumulative parts:* practise A, then A and B, then A and B and C.
3. *Backward chaining:* practise C, then B and C, then A and B and C.

To decide between the options, the instructional designer uses his judgment to structure the course in a certain way. At Level 1, the designer is establishing the overall structure and philosophy of the course and will therefore be strongly influenced by the particular theories of instruction that he happens to agree with. However, at Level 2, he will be bound more by the interrelationship of the detailed objectives, in terms of learning prerequisites, difficulty, familiarity to the learner, ease of explanation and similar factors which affect learning in a general way.

5.7 Strategies, plans and methods

5.7.1 Level 1: Overall instructional strategies

Overall instructional strategies are the translation of a philosophical or theoretical position regarding instruction into a statement of the way in which instruction should be carried out in specific circumstances. Among current theoretical viewpoints, we can identify two more or less opposed positions related to the process of learning and instruction.

1. *Reception learning:* the strongest open supporter of this position is Ausubel (1968), but the behaviourist camp also largely favours this position.
2. *Discovery learning:* the strongest supporters of this approach are Piaget (1965) and Bruner (1966), together with most of the cognitive school of psychology and the humanists.

Both groups have tended to support their position in preference to the other for all, or most, learning. Hence, they would tend to translate their view into a global strategy of instruction, to be applied whenever possible.

Two basic instructional strategies An intermediate position has been adopted by Gagné and Briggs (1974) and writers such as Landa (1976). They argue that for some types of learning the reception learning position (leading to expositive strategies) is more effective and efficient, while for other types the discovery learning position (leading to experiential strategies) is better. Such intermediate positions tend to lead to the adoption of differentiated strategies, the choice of which often requires more information than is available from Level 1 analysis.

The two strategies that spring from these processes of learning would have the following main steps:

Expositive strategy (for reception learning):

1. Present information. This may be achieved through explanation or through practical demonstration.
2. Test for reception, recall and understanding. Repeat or rephrase the message if it proves to be necessary.
3. Present opportunities for learners to practise applying the general principle to a range of examples. Test for correct application. Modify the quantity and difficulty of the examples when necessary to ensure correct performance.
4. Present opportunities for the application of the newly learned information to real situations and problems.

Experiential strategy (for discovery learning):

1. Present opportunities to act and observe the consequences of one's actions.
2. Test for understanding of the cause-effect relationship. This may be done by questioning or simply by observation of the reactions of the learner. Present further opportunities to act, if this proves necessary.
3. Either by questioning, or by observing further activity, test for the formation of the general principle underlying the cases presented. Present further cases as required until the general principle has been learned.
4. Present opportunities for the application of the newly learned information to real situations and problems.

There are many variations on these two basic strategies. It is possible to construct a continuum of discovery/expositive strategies, ranging from totally free discovery to totally controlled expositive rote learning (see Figure 5.5, p 57).

Impromptu discovery	Unplanned learning: no instruction (eg free use of a library/resource centre)
Free exploratory discovery	Broad learning goals are fixed; otherwise the learner is free to choose (eg resource-based learning systems)
Guided discovery	Objectives are fixed: learner is guided as to appropriate methods, conclusions, etc
Adaptively programmed discovery	Guidance and feedback correction is given on an individual basis (eg computer-based learning systems)
Intrinsically programmed discovery	Guidance and feedback according to a pre-planned programme, based on the 'typical student' (eg some programmed instruction materials)
Inductive exposition	Also called 'reflective lecturing': the teacher 'talks through' the discovery process
Deductive exposition	The 'meaningful reception learning' process favoured by Ausubel (mostly lectures; mostly PI)
Drill and practice	Rote reception learning: instructor demonstrates what to do and provides practice. No conceptual understanding is necessarily involved (memorization)

Figure 5.5 *The range of instructional strategies*

The discovery-expositive continuum is perhaps the most important group of strategies concerned with the actual process of instruction. Other important strategy decisions concern the overall sequence and structure of the course. In the last section we discussed the rationale behind linear, spiral, pyramidal and inquiry-based curricula. Choosing a particular overall curriculum structure is a strategic decision. This decision is sometimes influenced by one's knowledge of the subject. For example, the pyramidal and common core curriculum structures are dictated by the structure of the content we wish to teach and the use that the learners will make of it. At other times, however, the sequence strategy is related to one's choice of instructional strategy. For example, the spiral curriculum is particularly well suited to the application to a free exploratory discovery strategy. The inquiry-based curriculum is ideally suited to adaptively programmed discovery. Linear curricula are not so well adapted to discovery strategies but are ideally suited to expositive strategies.

It is the presence of such interactions between strategy decisions that makes it difficult, indeed undesirable, to adopt one overall strategy from the beginning of the instructional design process.

5.7.2 Level 2: Strategies for the teaching of knowledge

A course of instruction usually has a variety of aims and objectives. We would, therefore, expect to see both discovery and expositive strategies used. The question is: when should each strategy be used?

There are no hard and fast rules, but, on the basis of existing research and our conceptual schemata of knowledge and skills, it is possible to establish some guidelines. Let us first consider the learning of knowledge.

The information to be learned falls into four basic categories: facts, concepts, procedures and principles. Remembering the definitions of these four categories given in Chapter 4, and the use that is made of these types of information in subsequent skilled activity, we can delineate the areas of application for discovery and expositive strategies (see Figure 5.6 on p 58).

he 'best'
rategy
pends on
e type of
owledge
be taught

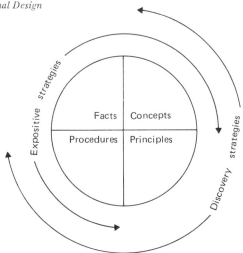

Figure 5.6 *Strategies for teaching knowledge*
(from Romiszowski, 1981)

The rationale for this division is as follows:

1. *Facts.* It is possible to discover facts. We discover all sorts of facts every day and this constitutes a large part of the unplanned incidental learning that goes on throughout life. We need to know a great number of facts in order to survive. There are others, which we do not need to know in order to survive, but need to know where to look them up when they are required. (Compare the need to know the meaning of road signs with the need to look up telephone numbers in a diary.) Facts, by definition, do not have examples — they exist independently. Thus, the learning of one set of facts does not greatly help the learning of another set. There is little transfer value, and what there is relates to the development of memorization and recall skills. They are not as highly valued in education today as they once were.

2. *Principles.* Just as facts can be learned through discovery, principles can be learned through exposition. However, there is overwhelming evidence that principles learned through discovery are remembered more efficiently, and applied in transfer of learning situations with more success, than those learned through reception learning. The price one has to pay for this is an increase in the initial learning time.

   Furthermore, the principle learned through a process of discovery is more easily rediscovered if it is forgotten through lack of use. Finally, the learning of principles by discovery, which employs the solution of problems as an instructional method, exercises the learner's problem-solving skills. In addition to mastering a new 'principle of nature', he is using and developing his 'principles of action' or heuristics. Thus he is likely to become better at the solving of other types of problems related to other sets of concepts and principles. For all these reasons, it would seem reasonable to use discovery strategies for the teaching of principles whenever this is practically possible and economically justifiable.

3. *Procedures.* By our definition, procedures are algorithmic, composed of associations and discriminations of discrete stimuli. As such they are a category of fact systems that answer the question 'How do I do it?' in a unique and unambiguous way. It would seem, therefore, that, like facts, procedures should be taught by expositive strategies. This is, in fact, usually the case. Most industrial procedures are taught through the method of demonstration, followed by imitative practice (unstructured, as in 'sitting next to Nellie', or structured, as in the TWI method). So

are most procedures in school subjects (eg long division or the rules of grammar). One often hears the complaint, however, that children can carry out a long division sum correctly, but that they do not 'understand the concept of division'. This is important, as they need to have a working concept of the operation in order to decide, in 'open' problem situations, whether they need to divide or not and which number they need to divide by which other. They also need a working concept in order to visualize the result of a division and thus to be able to assess their computed answer as 'reasonable and probably correct', or as 'obviously incorrect'.

It is possible to teach long division by a guided discovery approach in which the teacher asks the learner to deduce the next step, by applying the concepts and principles of number and basic operations. Thus, the learner constructs the algorithm for himself during the learning process. Subsequently, he simply recalls the algorithm 'from store', when required, and applies it mechanically. There is no long-term advantage, in terms of the performance of long division, as long as the algorithm remains completely remembered. However, if it is seldom used, it may be partly, or completely, forgotten with time. As in the case of principles, this is less likely to occur if a process of reflection and construction takes place during the initial learning. Also, if forgotten, the conceptual schema used in the original construction may still be 'in store', allowing the learner to reconstruct the forgotten steps. The process of construction during learning strengthens the conceptual schemata and the problem-solving schemata (heuristics) used in the proof of the algorithm. This not only aids the reconstruction of that particular algorithm, if forgotten, but also helps the solution of other similar future problems, say, the construction of the algorithm for calculating the square root of a number.

However, not all procedures are based on concepts or principles that are worth building into one's schemata and strengthening. This is the case with many administrative and bureaucratic procedures, which have no real logic. Such procedures are best taught by expositive strategies.

4. *Concepts.* These come in two forms: (i) primary (or concrete) concepts and (ii) secondary (or defined) concepts. The situation is slightly different for each type.

Concrete concepts can, up to a point, be learned without verbal communication. Skinner's laboratory animals can learn simple concrete concepts, such as 'red', 'circle', 'biggest' and 'different from'. They do not, of course, learn these verbal labels, but they demonstrate that they 'have' the concept by exhibiting correct 'classifying behaviour'. For example, the pigeon pecks at a red object, but not at other colours (including near-reds such as pink or orange), or it pecks at circular objects, but not at oval objects. The monkey learns to expect food under the biggest container presented, whatever its shape or colour or absolute size, or, alternatively, under the container which is different in shape from the rest, irrespective of other properties such as colour or size. The operant conditioning method used in such animal training, though based on the principle of reinforcement by food, is nevertheless an example of a discovery learning strategy. Mastery of the concept depends on experiencing sufficient numbers of instances of the concept to enable the learning organism to generalize the classifying principles involved.

Human beings learn primary (concrete) concepts in exactly the same way. We also learn verbal labels as we go along. When a child is presented with a coloured disc it helps greatly to establish the context of the exercise by verbal questions such as 'What's the colour?' or 'What's the shape?' (At an earlier stage of learning, when the secondary, defined, concepts of colour and shape have not yet been learned, we would say 'Is it red?' or 'Is it round?') However, language only establishes the context. The child needs a range of examples similar to those presented to the pigeon in order to classify red objects with precision.

In the case of concrete concepts, therefore, we would probably apply discovery learning strategies. The case of defined concepts is, however, rather different. A defined concept is, in a sense, a rule for the classification of simpler concepts. Let us examine an example.

'Red', 'blue', 'green', 'pink' and 'yellow' are examples of the concept 'colour'. It is impossible to learn this concept without first learning at least some colours and their respective verbal labels. Given that prior learning, it is possible to learn the concept of colour either by expositive means (eg by the presentation of the definition in the first sentence of this paragraph) or by discovery strategies (eg by presenting a large set of concrete examples of objects of a variety of known colours and, instead of associating the specific labels of the colours, associating the generalized label 'colour' every time). (The latter procedure will be more time-consuming and more likely to confuse the student.) In the case of 'defined concepts', therefore, the use of clearly worded definitions, and thus of expositive strategies, is indicated.

5.7.3 Matching instructional strategy to skill category

Are we dealing with productive or reproductive skills?

We shall now consider a little more closely the causes of poor performance by the learner. His performance deficiency may be the result of a knowledge deficiency or a skill deficiency, or a combination of both. All skilled performance involves the execution of a cycle of activities which can be summarized as:

1. Perception of the relevant stimuli.
2. Recall of the relevant prerequisite knowledge.
3. Planning of the appropriate responses.
4. Performance of these responses, followed by perception of the results, etc.

Some skills are highly dependent on the planning element — strategy skills, planning skills or, preferably, productive skills — while other, similar skills involve very little original planning, simply requiring the recall of a standard procedure — reflexive skills or reproductive skills.

Reproductive skills are always much the same in their execution. Once the basic procedure involved has been learned, there is little need for further learning of knowledge. Reproductive skills improve in time because of improvements in the performer's skills of perception and of performance (dexterity, speed, precision, etc).

Productive skills, on the other hand, involve an element of novel problem-solving in the planning of a response. There is a great deal of variety in the stimuli that present themselves to the performer. Although the basic principles of planning may always be the same, the examples which present themselves are always different. Thus the performer's experience grows with practice, both in terms of knowledge (the variety of different problems that may present themselves) and skill (in perceiving and interpreting the problem, deciding a course of action and executing it).

The approach suggested for matching instructional strategies to skills is based on the nature of the skill, and on two other considerations:

(a) Skilled activity is useful; and
(b) skilled activity is enjoyable (once a reasonable standard of performance has been reached).

One should, therefore, attempt to get the learner to perform at a reasonable (though not necessarily exceptionally high) standard of performance as quickly as possible. In order to achieve this, the procedure outlined below is suggested. (See Figure 5.7 on p 62 for a summary.)

1. Teach the knowledge necessary for reasonable performance. In the case of reproductive skills this may well be all the knowledge necessary. In the case of productive skills it will be basic knowledge required to start at a reasonable level of proficiency. The choice of strategy at this stage should be governed by considerations presented in the previous section on the matching of instructional strategies to knowledge categories.

2. Apply an expositive strategy to aid the learner's initial performance of the skill (mainly because it achieves results faster). This strategy would follow a three-stage procedure:

   (a) Demonstrate the skill that is required, both in its entirety, and in its main parts or key points. This may, on occasions, be done concomitantly with the teaching of the essential knowledge — demonstration plus explanation.

   (b) Arrange simplified, or prompted, practice of the skill by the learner: the prompting may be achieved by guidance, by simplifying the task artificially, by dividing the task into stages or parts to be practised one at a time, or by other tactics.

   (c) Arrange supervised 'free' practice of the complete skilled activity by the learner, supplying feedback in the form of knowledge of results, appropriate praise or other reinforcers. The feedback should be in a form capable of interpretation by the learner so that he may correct any errors.

3. Once the learner is performing at a reasonable standard, the strategy will depend on whether the skill is basically reproductive or productive:

   (a) In the case of reproductive skills, no third stage of planned instruction is called for, as far as the knowledge content is concerned. Often, the continuation of step 2(c) is all that is required for the skill to be developed to the required standard. In some cases, when performance depends on exceptional levels of perceptual acuity, dexterity, strength, stamina, patience or persistence, etc, special training exercises, quite apart from the practice of the actual skilled task, may accelerate the process of skill development.

   (b) In the case of a productive skill, a discovery strategy should be adopted in further instruction. Rather than leave the learner to develop his skill as best he can, the instructional system should: (i) arrange as wide a variety of problems as are likely to be encountered in real life. This should be done in the shortest possible time, thus concentrating the variety that may, in reality, be met over a period of years into weeks or months. This can be achieved by various techniques of simulation (it may not be necessary to simulate reality if the requisite variety of real-life experiences can be arranged in a reasonable period); and
   (ii) arrange for the analysis of these situations by the learner in such a way that he demonstrates the growth of his conceptual schemata to encompass the ever-greater variety of problems that he has encountered. He should demonstrate that he is applying the principles he has learned, and, in the light of new experiences, is modifying, complementing, or reorganizing these principles. As we are dealing here with conceptual learning an element of verbal interaction between teacher and learner is almost inevitable at this stage, even if the skilled task itself does not call for verbal responses. The verbal communication is necessary for the learner to demonstrate to the instructor the processes of analysis (of new situations), of synthesis (of new principles or schemata) and of evaluation (of the new principles in yet further situations). The instructor, by observing the learner's performance on new and

The vital importance of verbal interchange and reflection in the learning of productive skills

increasingly difficult problems, can assess whether the learner is developing his skills satisfactorily. But only through discussion can he hope to get 'inside the mind' of the learner in order to assess why a skill is not developing and what should be done to help it to develop.

	Reproductive skills	Productive skills
1. *Impart the knowledge content*	Expositive or discovery methods (dependent on the type of knowledge)	Discovery methods (principle learning is always involved)
2. *Impart the practical application*	Expositive methods (demonstration and prompted practice) *Note:* Imparting the knowledge and skills content may be combined	Expositive methods (demonstration and prompted practice)
3. *Develop proficiency*	Supervised practice of whole task and/or special exercises Continuing feedback of results	Discovery methods (guided problem-solving) Continuing feedback of results

Figure 5.7 *Instructional strategies for the development of skills*

5.8 Grouping

5.8.1 Decisions at Level 1

Overall considerations that affect group size

The data that we have available after a Level 1 analysis may help us to make some overall decisions on the group structure of the instructional system that we plan to design. It may force us to adopt certain decisions, because of the existence of immutable constraints imposed by the wider system in which our problem is embedded. The information we now have would include the following:

1. The tasks or topics to be learned. Job analysis (or subject analysis), together with a gross analysis of the target population, its needs and present level of preparation, lead us to define the tasks (or topics) that are 'worth teaching'. The nature of these tasks and topics may suggest that certain methods of instruction and certain forms of learning group structure should predominate in the final instructional system. One may see the need for individual self-instruction, or for 'group dynamics' learning methods, or for a mixture of approaches to cater for different types of learning.
2. The quantitative aspect of the target population analysis also provides a good deal of information regarding the geographical location of the target population (concentrated or scattered), distribution according to needs (large groups at a given time of year or a constant dribble of trainees) and the lifestyle and preferred (customary) study styles of the potential students.
3. The analysis of the wider system should have given a clear picture of the scale of resources that are available for the design and implementation of the system with which we are concerned. This may impose obvious constraints on the approaches that we may economically adopt. Large-scale use of pre-prepared materials may be out of the question, because of cost limitations or insufficient time for development. There may be limits on the minimum staff/student

ratio to be employed in our system, imposed either by economic or by legal factors.

4. The philosophical viewpoints, and traditions, of the wider system may create obstacles to the adoption of certain course structures. For example, the limits of the staff/student ratio could be ameliorated by the use of other, non-traditional human resources in our system (eg parents, teachers' aids, the students themselves through a monitorial system, etc), but cultural, legal or trade union objections render these options difficult or impossible to implement.

5.8.2 Level 2: Grouping decisions for knowledge content

There are four main categories of knowledge in our classification schema: facts, concepts, procedures and principles. The areas for which individual and group learning are favoured are indicated in Figure 5.8 below. The arrows in this diagram should read as suggestions, not as immutable rules. After all, any item of knowledge may be learned either by individual or group learning methods.

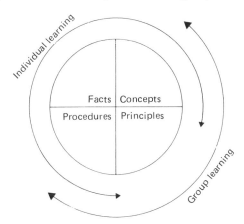

Figure 5.8 *Suggested areas for the use of group and individual learning methods*

The critical factor is not so much the group structure as the form in which the information reaches the learner. Is it clear? Can he perceive it? Can he interpret it sufficiently to store it in a sensible way, related meaningfully to other information already in store?

In some situations, however, the presence of a group of learners may help the individual to perceive what is important, to interpret and store it, and to reorganize the schemata already in store in order to accommodate the new information.

In the learning of discrete facts, or of simple factual information, there is comparatively little to be gained from group learning, as opposed to self-instruction. The learning of facts is very much drill and practice. Different learners require different amounts of practice. The more individualized and personal this practice, the quicker will be the learning.

The learning of principles, on the other hand, has much to gain from well-organized group learning. In order to learn a principle, and be able to apply it effectively in the future in a variety of situations, the learner must experience as wide a variety of situations as is possible during the actual learning. He must also reflect on the relations that exist between the new principle and previously learned principles and concepts in order to forge meaningful links and store the newly learned principle as part of a wider schema of conceptual knowledge.

To encourage this process of reflection, recall and restructuring, the instructional system should provide the maximum opportunity for analytical conversations. The lone student must have some form of conversation with himself, reflecting internally on the relationships between what he has learned before and what he is learning now. He will be stimulated to do this by his own curiosity as a learner and by the structure of the learning materials which he is using. Some learning materials can be quite effective in stimulating the appropriate form of reflective activity (eg the 'structural communication' technique). However, the mutual sharing of insights between a group of learners and the mutual overcoming of misconceptions can enhance the richness of the reflective processes and hence improve the quality of the conceptual learning taking place. A learning group, through discussion, ensure that the individual learners cooperate, helping each other to form and reform their conceptual schemata in order better to accommodate the new principles being learned.

In the case of concept learning consider the 'level of abstraction'

Much of what has been said concerning the learning of principles also applies to the learning of concepts. However, a fair proportion of concept learning is at a lower level of difficulty than the learning of principles. In the case of primary (concrete) concepts, learning depends on exposure to a sufficient quantity and range of concrete examples of the concept. There is little to discuss in this case. Each learner has to observe and classify the examples. It matters little if he does this on his own or in a group. Group methods may be more fun, but there is no reason for them to be more efficie than individual methods.

There is not that much difficulty with simple defined concepts either. A defined concept that is only one step removed from the concrete (eg the concept of 'colour', which is classification of concrete concepts — 'red', 'blue' 'green', etc) is easy to define clearly and leaves little room for fruitful discussion of its meaning. As we climb up the ladder of abstraction, however (eg from 'red' to 'colour' to 'property' to 'physical property' and 'chemical property'), the room for misunderstanding increases, as does the web of interrelationships between the concept being learned and other previously learned concepts. The need for analytical reflection grows and so, therefore, does the need for instruction that stimulates and encourages such reflection. Hence, as the degree of abstraction of conceptual learning increases, so does the need for group learning techniques that capitalize on the communal store of insights and experiences, and share them in cooperative group discussions and activities.

Group learning of procedures is indicated only when an experiential strategy is to be used

The case of procedures is governed by a different consideration. The knowledge of a procedure simply implies that the steps of the procedure (the algorithm) have been learned and stored in a usable manner (ie they can be recalled correctly and in the right sequence). The algorithm may have been acquired through reception learning (eg by observing the procedure being performed), or through discovery learning (eg by a problem-solving approach We saw that the discovery approach was favoured when the steps of the algorithm were deducible by the application of previously learned concepts a principles. We may argue, therefore, that when a procedure is learned through reception learning techniques, without investigation into the reasons, individu learning is quite adequate. When, however, the procedure is to be learned through discovery, deducing the steps of the procedure from the reasons for the procedure, group-based problem-solving strategies may be superior, as, once again, they provide greater opportunities for reflective discussion and th sharing of difficulties and insights.

5.8.3 Grouping decisions for the skills content

The most influential factors on the grouping of learners for the teaching of skills are probably the task/topic factors. Tasks that are performed in groups

r skills
evelopment
mulate
e real-life
uation

are usually taught much more easily in groups, because the post-training situation can be simulated. Some categories of skills, in particular interactive skills, rely on the presence of other people as sources of the stimuli that control the skilled activity. Such skills can only be learned and practised effectively in a certain kind of group. In the training of salesmanship skills, for example, it is necessary to provide experience of interaction with customers (the source of the controlling stimuli). This experience may be difficult to provide in real life practice, in a controlled manner. Hence the importance of various simulation and gaming techniques in the development of interactive skills.

Similarly, it is often only possible to teach tasks that are practised on one's own in an individual learning situation. A lathe operator could receive a part of his training in a group — the basic theory (knowledge) content of his job and perhaps a demonstration of the basic operations to be carried out. But, since in the practice of these operations the task will eventually be the responsibility of one man, even the instructor takes a background role, restricted to providing guidance and feedback. The main learning occurs through the interactions of man and machine itself. The task is a one-man task, and so is learning.

When the characteristics of the task do not dictate the type of learning group, one can follow the decisions made with regard to instructional strategy. When an expositive instructional strategy is used, there is less value in group learning. The interchanges on the whole occur between the teacher (or some substitute medium) and the learner, either as an individual or as one of the mass in the lecture hall. No significant learner-learner interchanges occur.

When discovery learning strategies are employed, however, there is always something to be gained through exploratory and analytical discussion and reflection. This can be promoted in the small or medium-sized group. Furthermore, as much of the work of such a group is made up of learner-learner interchanges, it is usually desirable to reorganize a large group into several smaller groups for discovery learning.

5.9 The question of media

5.9.1 Media selection decisions at Level 1

formation
instruction;
rge or small
edia; fixed
flexible
esentation?

Analysis at Level 1 gives little insight into how to teach. We are primarily concerned with what to teach. One decision which can be made is whether we require instructional media or informational media. The difference is important and is quite simple. Instruction requires two-way communication between the transmitter and the receiver. This entails the use of two-way communication media, or a combination of one-way media that effectively provides the necessary two-way communication. Hence one-way media, such as television, may be used for instruction, if supported by the necessary feedback media (eg correspondence in distance education systems, or discussions in normal schools or practical application exercises in vocational training).

The 'gross' analysis at Level 1 also tells us quite a lot about the quantitative aspects of the target population (eg how many people are to be taught, with what frequency, in what size groups, how dispersed geographically, etc). This leads to the identification of many constraints and also of certain factors related to effective communication. Our choice of media must be able to reach the learners and to do so at reasonable cost. We are naturally led to consider the alternatives of distance education — mass media are the principal media — and face-to-face education, with teachers as the principal media, supported by teaching aids. This distinction was nicely put by Wilbur Schramm (1967) when he referred to 'big media' and 'little media'.

Finally, at Level 1, we form an overall view of the final objectives of the course we are about to design. These objectives may be obligatory, in the sense that all learners should achieve mastery of all objectives — this is the case in most vocational training and also in educational courses that apply the master learning model — or they may be optional, with room for individual students to choose which objectives they wish to master and to what degree of proficiency. (This is the case with many non-vocational educational courses.) We may at this level be led to decide, for practical or philosophical reasons, between media that are capable of presenting a fixed message, thus controlling the uniformity of learning, and media that are capable of presenting information in such a way that it is easy for teachers or learners to modify the content or the sequence of the message, thus allowing freedom of choice and a measure of 'individualization'.

To summarize the media question: the first level of analysis would lead us to consider

1. *Learner factors:* big or little media?
2. *Content factors:* one-way or two-way media?
3. *Objectives:* fixed or flexible?

5.9.2 Media selection decisions at Level 2

An eight-factor analysis schema

Unless, at Level 1, the constraints were such as to define completely the medium (or media) of presentation, we now have the opportunity to select our media with more precision, or to allocate different learning objectives among the selected media.

Analysis at Level 2 involves, in the training context, the analysis of the tasks to be taught or steps that must be executed. In the educational context, it concerns the analysis of topics to be taught or elements of information that must be learned. In each case, the sequence and structure of the tasks or topic should be identified, giving insights into the way they should be taught, the prerequisite knowledge or skills that the learner should possess and the intermediate objectives that must be attained during the course as stepping stones to the final objectives.

We now also gain some insights into how to teach, at least to the extent of establishing the content of individual course units and lessons, and of determining the possible sequence (or alternative sequences) in which the lessons should be learned.

Analysis of the schema

Let us now look at the factors indicated in Figure 5.9 on p 67.

1. *Objectives, communication and content.* If you expect a certain behaviour from the learner after instruction, you should give him opportunities to practise that behaviour during instruction. Thus, if the learner is expected to be able to give examples of a certain concept, he should be presented with examples during instruction. If he is expected to perform a procedure after training he should practise performing the procedure and not just observe it or hear it described, though both of these may be steps to getting him to perform correctly.

    Use the most appropriate sensory channels for communicating the information to be learned. Attempt to match the sensory channels to the message. Often this is not a significant factor, as the information to be communicated is verbal, and the only choice open to us is between the spoken and the written word. However, in other cases, a wider variety of sensory channels may be involved.

2. *Cost, market and availability.* We are now likely to have more precise data on which to make cost estimates. We have specified our media, lesson by lesson, objective by objective, so we can now make quite accurate estimates of the proportion of our course that any given medium will present. We could derive a fair estimate of the study hours through television, the study hours in direct contact with the teacher, the study hours on self-instructional materials, etc. Given the standard

costs for the preparation of each of the types of media to be used, one can estimate the costs of media production with a fair degree of accuracy.

One should not forget to question, in terms of cost-effectiveness, whether a particular presentation should be developed. Are there suitable materials already available on the market, which can be bought in at a fraction of the production cost and incorporated into the course?

3. *Practicality, time, resources and facilities.* One can now estimate production times for each group of lessons, or for each specific presentation. Thus, in the case of time constraints, one might assign priorities so that the media most important to the effectiveness of the course are produced early and without delay.

These can now be allocated on an item-by-item basis, giving a method for the control of media production. Once again, if resources are scarce, it should be possible, taking effectiveness into consideration, to establish priorities. We can then prune down our ambitions to the size of our pockets, by opting for less problematic and more easily produced media for the less essential objectives.

4. *Human factors.* At Level 2, detailed consideration should be given to ways of preparing teachers to accept and use any novel instructional medium that we plan to adopt.

Media presentations that are not absolutely essential, and that demand significant changes in practice, or substantial learning to use, on the part of teachers, should be avoided. Particular care should be taken to allay any fears or negative attitudes that complex gadgetry sometimes produces, as these attitudes may easily be transferred from the specific item to whole classes of methods and media, thus increasing future difficulties for innovation.

Any learner factors which might produce fears of negative attitudes should also be taken into consideration. These would be particularly important considerations when planning individualized or resource-based courses, in which learners come into direct contact with the hardware, having to load their own projectors, recorders or videocassettes. If the learners are not adequately prepared, apart from possible operational difficulties and consequent rejection, the breakdown rate will be high. This will be both expensive and disruptive.

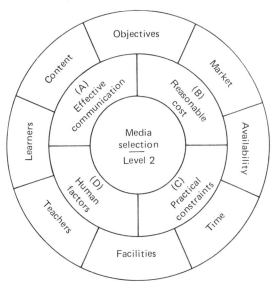

Figure 5.9 *Factors involved in Level 2 analysis*

5.10 Developing a plan of the proposed instructional system

Analysis of the task or topic leads to the development of a hierarchy of intermediate objectives, or a network of sub-topics, which allow quite detailed decisions to be made regarding the sequence of units and individual lessons in the proposed training system. This sequence may be now transformed into a plan of the overall structure of the instructional system. This may be a linear, pre-ordained plan which defines the exact sequence of lessons that will be given, or it may be a flexible plan allowing for alternative routes, for student choice of certain objectives, for elective topics complementing a common core or for many other variations. A further aspect of the system that this plan would specify is the method, or combination of methods, that will be used to achieve each of the intermediate objectives.

A suggested planning sheet for the 'macro' design decisions

A record of the decisions being made will be built up. This may take the form of a list of the objectives, in sequence, and other aspects of the design in columns alongside (see Figure 5.10 below). Assuming that the first two columns have been more oŕ less completed, we shall consider the third column – instructional methods. We have already considered in some depth the basic instructional strategies that we may be led to consider, partly through our philosophical predispositions, but mainly (we hope) through an objective consideration of the overall objectives and content of the course, the general characteristics of the target population and other important factors that we have identified in our analysis of the wider system.

Objective	Test items	Methods	Grouping	Media	Material and equipment

Figure 5.10 *Suggested form for Level 2 instructional design*

Armed with the more detailed breakdown of the instructional objectives, a more precise idea of the necessary content, and a more thorough analysis of the existing levels of knowledge and skill in the target population, we are in a position to turn our views regarding appropriate strategies into more detailed suggestions of the methods that should be adopted to put these strategies into operation. The procedure to follow is outlined below:

1. Determine from the objectives whether we are dealing with: (a) an information problem (the need to instil knowledge); (b) a performance problem (the need to develop skills); (c) a combination of information and performance problems. Each objective should be considered in turn.
2. Consider, for each objective, the basic category of knowledge or skill that we intend to teach: (a) if knowledge, is it factual information, concepts, procedures or principles (or what combination)?; (b) if skill, is it basically a simple reproductive skill, or a combination of both reproductive and productive skills?
3. In the light of considerations 1 and 2, decide whether expositive or discovery strategies are indicated.
4. Now consider the practical constraints that have already been identified at Level 1 as 'immutable'. These might include such factors as: (a) resources: what quality and quantity of teachers, books, audiovisual equipment, etc can we expect?; (b) target population: what is the geographical distribution of our student population, its level of study

skills and social habits?; (c) wider system: what are the political decisions or social pressures that affect our system's design?; and what restrictions do these constraints impose on the selection of specific instructional methods?

5. Select a method (or several alternative methods) that is (are) both appropriate and viable, in the light of the considerations outlined above. At this stage, we are working at the level of overall recommendations and there is no need to describe exactly how the method will be put into practice.

6. The decisions relating to method selection create certain constraints or requirements that should be taken into account when specifying the group structure and the presentation media to be used. These should be considered in combination with the theoretical selection factors that were discussed earlier when specifying the structure of the course.

7. The practical requirements for implementing the course design should be taken into account in specifying the materials and equipment that must be made available. This list should include both available and as yet unavailable resources, perhaps indicating by some code which are and which are not ready for use.

There is nothing sacrosanct about the form of the suggested chart (Figure 5.10 on p 68). It is possible to increase or reduce the number of columns to better suit specific projects. We shall see some possible variations in the examples presented in the next chapter.

The resulting chart, whatever its form, is a useful map of the proposed instructional system. One can look at it critically, as a whole, evaluating the individual decisions that have been taken earlier, in relation to each other. This enables the designer to maintain the systems view, and to identify decisions that are too ambitious in relation to the development time and resources available, or that will necessitate some special training for the instructional staff. It also makes possible the identification of alternative sequences that will make better use of resources, or alternative divisions of the objectives into lessons that will be more coherent, more varied in the method used, more stimulating or more simply implemented and executed.

Any modifications that spring to mind can be noted on the chart before the detailed development and production work commences. Indeed, when working in a team, it is a good idea to build up the planning chart as a collection of ideas written on separate cards arranged on a wall in appropriate rows and columns. The instructional plan then grows as a dynamic wall display, to which all the team members contribute and which can be easily modified at any time. This approach also maintains a flexible decision-making process, and communicates progress clearly to all concerned, with a minimum of those formal reports which give to each stage of the project the appearance of finality and tend to stifle the evaluation and rethinking of earlier decisions.

Once the chart is more or less complete, it can be used as a basis for the planning of production schedules, detailed lesson plans, instructor training or orientation sessions, pleas for extra resources, etc. It is an all-purpose control document for the later stages of instructional systems development.

ng the
rt for
ject
nning,
lysis
control

6. Some Typical Instructional Plans – An Evaluation

6.1 Introduction

This chapter examines instructional plans that have been prepared along the lines suggested in the previous two chapters. Our intention is to indicate how, in practice, an overall plan (or map) of an instructional system is prepared, how it may be used to evaluate the macro decisions taken in the initial planning stages, and how it may guide the further, micro design stages of lesson planning and materials development.

We present two plans in detail. The first is a design for an in-company training system to be installed in a large real estate company, which has over 20 offices that handle the sale and rental of property of all types: apartments, houses, land for building, development sites, farms, factories, etc. The company also handles its own development projects, having built several dozen apartment blocks and having undertaken other property development schemes in the past year. Naturally, the company has a large staff, employed on a variety of tasks. The training system presented here is a simplified version of one planned by the author for this company. The part presented is designed to train secretaries/receptionists.

The second example is adapted from an instructional plan for a scuba diving course, prepared as a course project by a student of the author, Madeleine Morin, during an instructional design course given at Concordia University, Montreal. The plan presented here has been adapted from the original, in order to emphasize certain aspects and to shorten it — only four out of a total of nine lessons are included in this extract.

The overall approach in the two plans is similar, but there are many small differences — in layout, in columns omitted or added and in depth of detail. These differences are discussed later. They are included, however, to dispel any impression that the approach suggested is rigid or authoritarian. The approach is in fact quite flexible and it is possible to modify the details of layout or depth of analysis to suit particular preferences or needs.

6.2 Secretary/receptionist training

The example of secretary/receptionist training (presented in chart form as Exhibit 6.1 on pp 80-86) is an adaptation of a larger plan that was prepared for a real estate company in Brazil. The company employs about 180 secretaries/ receptionists in its 20 branches. The turnover is quite high, so about twice a year a training programme is organized for new entrants. Apart from this, the various branch managers and department chiefs are expected to perform on-the-job training of their own staff. The company was not satisfied with the twice-yearly courses, which were just 'chat and theory', nor with the on-the-job training, which for the most part just did not happen (as no one was sure what to teach or how to teach it).

The secretaries/receptionists who are the target population for our training are the first link between the company and its clients, so their performance is of vital importance. A job description reveals that secretaries/receptionists divide their time between attending to clients, in the office or on the phone, and acting as general secretaries to their bosses. They recieve clients and make them comfortable, often attend to their requests for information directly, and at other times take them to see the appropriate person or make an appointment at a suitable time. They keep their boss's appointments diary up to date, exercise tact and courtesy, both personally and on the phone, and, in general, make themselves indispensable. They also do the typing and filing.

Job analysis as a basis for training needs assessment

A full job analysis was carried out, which revealed the tasks listed in Figure 6.1 (see p 73). This chart lists the principal tasks performed and notes the specific items of knowledge and skill that the trainees should acquire in order to perform adequately. The skills have been subdivided into job skills (or professional skills) and social skills. This is a first step in the definition of skill and knowledge and will be taken to a more detailed level of analysis later. At this stage, however, we identify those items that normally need training and those that are looked for in the recruitment and selection procedures. In Figure 6.1 we have indicated the probable training content with boxes. Those items not in boxes are evaluated at the selection stage and can be considered as prerequisites for the planned training programme. The comment in the right-hand column help to explain how we reached our decisions.

Specification of training objectives and sequence

On the basis of this job analysis, we were able to prepare the training objectives. These are listed in the first column of the overall instructional plan presented in Exhibit 6.1 (see pp 80 - 86). Seven terminal objectives are identified. These are expressed in behavioural terms, complete with given conditions and expected criteria. They are listed in the intended order of mastery. As there are many possible sequences for teaching these objectives, we shall explain how the order was determined. A close study of the seven objectives reveals very little sequential interdependence. Objective1 is, indeed, the only one that is a prerequisite for any of the others. Almost all the objectives depend on the trainee's knowledge of the company, its structure and the work that is performed. It seems most apt to put the objective that direct uses this knowledge at the beginning of the training programme.

Thereafter, there seem to be many alternatives. For example, objectives 2 and 3 could be taught in the reverse order. Also, objectives 4, 5, 6 and 7 could be taught at any point after objective 1. To select an appropriate

Overall selection of methods and media

teaching sequence, we therefore applied another criterion – the usefulness of the trainee to the company. We were planning to shorten the introductory training so that it could be given more often than twice a year. The ideal would be training in small groups whenever new staff were admitted. We did not choose wholly individualized self-instruction, as some of the skills to be mastered are social skills and must be practised in a group. One other important factor taken into account was that the critical tasks, where most damage can be done by poorly trained staff, are those concerned with the reception of clients, when social skills and knowledge of the company count most. We therefore drew up a network, on the lines of a PERT critical path network, showing the possible alternatives for teaching sequence, taking care to put the reception tasks at the beginning. This network is presented in Figure 6.2 on p 74. Objectives 1, 2 and 3 are taught during the initial small group training session. If a person joins the company at a time when no training session is available, he or she may master objective 1 by individualized self-instruction while waiting for the training course.

The remaining objectives are to be treated mainly through on-the-job training, under the supervision of the trainee's boss, but organized largely in the form of self-instruction, from manuals and other specially prepared materials. The objectives can be mastered in any order, or indeed in parallel. The training programme for these objectives is carefully laid down in a control manual used by the managers and supervisors who are responsible for overall results. The programme has no fixed time for this second stage, being entirely competence based.

| Tasks | Knowledge | Skills | | Comments |
		Professional	Social	
1. Compose and edit letters	Grammar Special company norms and standards	Ability to express ideas in writing	—	Company selects trainees with good levels of basic education
2. Type letters, forms	Norms and standards of layout, conventions, etc	Typing skill at 50 wpm and low error levels	—	Company selects fully trained typists to these standards
3. Plan and keep up to date the boss's appointments diary	Principles of time management Knowledge of the boss's work, commitments and priorities	—	Tact in all contacts with clients and other employees who wish to make appointments	The trainee must learn how to set priorities and how to negotiate or refuse meetings without upsetting clients or boss
4. Give and receive telephone calls on all aspects of company business	Knowledge of the work performed in the office, and the job of each employee in the office. The extension numbers of key personnel	Operation of telephone switchboard of type used in company	Pleasant voice, clear diction, courtesy, patience	Company selects candidates with adequate levels of the required social skills. An internal directory of extension numbers is used
5. Receive and attend to the needs of clients visiting the office	The work and organization of the company and one's own office Company rules and standards	Ability to express ideas in speech Form-filling skills; interviewing skills	Courtesy, good manners, pleasant voice	See comments 1 and 4 above
6. Plan, organize, execute and control the routine work of office	Norms and standards of the company. Work executed by the office. Principles of planning, delegation, control	Organizing skills. Work management skills	Persuasiveness, tact and courtesy in relation to colleagues and subordinates	We will probably have to give training in all these skills, as candidates do not normally have experience of supervising work of others
7. Plan, organize and update filing systems	Principles of office filing. Types of work performed in the office	Analytical skills used to correctly classify documents, etc	—	Candidates do not normally have relevant experience of filing systems

Note: Items in boxes are the identified training needs

Figure 6.1 *Job analysis of secretaries/receptionists in a real estate company*

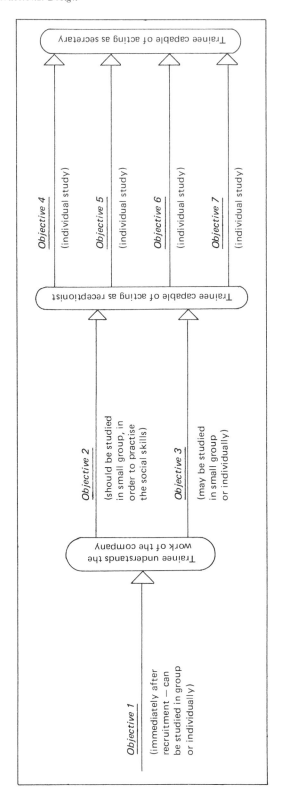

The decisions outlined so far all form part of what we have called Level 1 instructional design. These are the macro decisions taken on the basis of the initial analysis of the problem. We now proceed to Level 2 design. This involves more detailed analysis of the tasks that comprise the job, the planning of suitable methods for the evaluation of training results, the deeper analysis of the knowledge and skill content of each objective in turn and the classification of this content as an aid to the later selection of appropriate methods and media. The decisions taken are documented in the second, third and fourth columns of Exhibit 6.1 (see pp 80 - 86).

At this point the reader should study the detailed decisions presented in Exhibit 6.1 In general, they are in agreement with the earlier decisions. However, there are some deviations. For example, some parts of the teaching for objectives 4 and 5 are now included in the initial group training. This decision is the result of the more detailed analysis of the knowledge and skill content of these objectives.

The planning of methods has been divided into three stages: (i) the selection of the intended general strategy; (ii) the specific techniques to be used for each objective; and (iii) the group size and structure to be employed. It is possible to use other ways of mapping and descriptions of the decisions taken, but the chosen one is the most apt for the present case. We have specified the strategies, techniques and group structures in some detail. This was done because the map was used to communicate the details of the instructional plan to people who were not involved in its preparation. It must therefore be sufficiently complete to make sense.

Finally, we come to the last main section of our map — the specification of resources. Once more, we have opted to subdivide this section into three columns: (i) instructional media/materials (the 'software' that must be obtained in order to put our plan into operation); (ii) equipment/tools/job aids (that is, everything else that must be provided to make the training system work); and (iii) time (an estimate of the time trainees will need to achieve each specified objective).

Note that only now can we estimate total training time, by adding up the individual time estimates for each objective. This indicates one advantage of using a map as a layout for the instructional plan. The map shows the structure and interrelationships that exist in the proposed plan. The sum of the time estimates in the last column can be checked against the time available. If there is a mismatch, steps should be taken to adjust the methods, or even the objectives, to the available resources. It is better to cover less ground efficiently than to skim over everything.

The totals of the resources columns can be transformed into costs, which can then be compared with available budgets. The totals of the group and technique columns give an idea of the variety of teaching methods to be employed and these can be compared against available teaching expertise. The totals of the skills and knowledge columns give an idea of the quantity and type of information that will have to be included and these can be matched against available subject matter expertise.

The variety of content, techniques, media and materials, and the sequence in which they occur in the plan, give a clear picture of the amount of variety or repetition that is built into the plan. Steps, at this stage, can be taken to enrich or to simplify the plan.

As well as looking for structure and 'vertical' coherence in this way, we may also use the map to assess 'horizontal' coherence. Are the proposed evaluation systems and instruments compatible with our objectives? Are the skills and knowledge identified compatible with the objectives? Can they be adequately evaluated, in sufficient detail, by the tests proposed? Are the general strategies selected compatible with the category of the objectives aimed for? Are the techniques selected capable of implementing the preferred strategies? Is the group size and structure well chosen, in view of the type of objectives to be achieved and the techniques to be adopted? Are the media and materials well chosen, in relation to the objectives and strategies? We can ask similar questions of every entry on the map in relation to every other entry (see Figure 6.3 on p 77).

Use of instructional map as a visual representation of our decisions This process, which might be called 'coherence analysis', takes place duri the actual decision-making process, and the visual layout of the decisions as a two-dimensional grid (for that is really what our 'map' is) is enormously helpful in keeping track of all decisions taken so far and verifying whether t cohere reasonably well. The visual layout also enables other people — traine media experts, project managers, even financial controllers — to understand the project better and helps in the identification of defects.

The plan presented in Exhibit 6.1 (see pp 80 - 86) was prepared in quite large parts; some of the objectives are estimated to need eight or more hours of training. The next example is rather different in this respect.

6.3 Scuba diving course

A modified form of map The second example is an extract from a student project on an instructional design course. The author of this plan has followed the same basic approach illustrated in the previous example but there are some marked differences as can be seen by studying Exhibit 6.2 on pp 87 - 94.

First, we note that the division of the map into columns is slightly differe The separate columns for knowledge and skill elements have been combined into one. The time estimates column has been eliminated. There is no great significance in these modifications, especially the first one. They probably both spring from another characteristic of the plan — the level of detail of the objectives.

Different level of analysis of objectives A comparison of the objectives listed in Exhibit 6.1 (pp 80 - 86) and Exhibit 6.2 (pp 87 - 94) reveals that, in the first example, the plan lists only the main or terminal objectives of each task, whereas the objectives listed in the second example are at a finer level of detail. Perhaps for this reason, it makes sense to combine the knowledge and skill columns, as there is much l to say about any given objective.

We also note that the objectives in Exhibit 6.2 have already been groupe into lessons — there are four lessons included in the plan shown. If this lesso is a fixed period of time on a timetable, we do not need a separate column f time estimates.

A more significant difference between the two plans is in the degree of analysis of the objectives. In the first example, it is still necessary to break down the terminal objectives into their component intermediate objectives this may conveniently be left to the lesson planning stage. In the second example, the intermediate objectives are already identified, thus making it possible to derive a lesson plan from the overall plan, without need for furth analysis of the objectives.

Different level of detail of description Another important difference is in the amount of detail that has been pu into the descriptions in the various cells of the plan in Exhibit 6.2. These are much more condensed, based on keywords and technical terms, without mu effort to explain or illustrate what the author meant. This aspect makes the plan much less useful to outsiders, who may have difficulty in making sense some of the comments. However, the comments listed may be of sufficient clarity to the author of the plan. In that case, if the plan is to be used only t the author and perhaps other members of the work team, there may be no need for further explanations. The detailed decisions would already have be discussed in the planning sessions, and the 'shorthand' descriptions in the map may be sufficient to remember those planning sessions and the decision taken.

Thus the exact layout of the instructional plan is not critical, and variatic may, indeed, be justifiable in particular circumstances. There is, of course, n

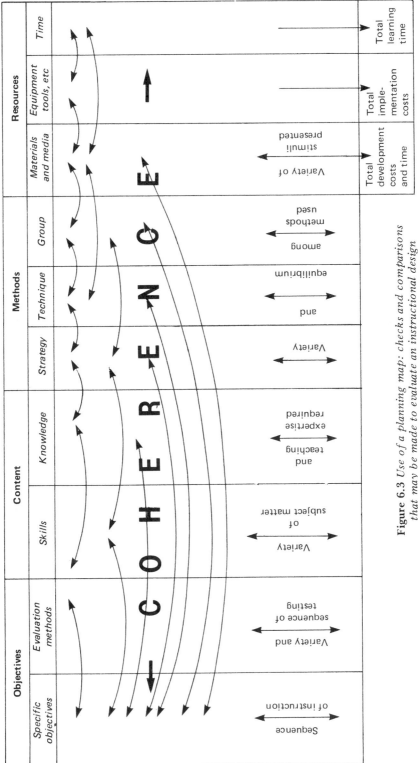

Figure 6.3 *Use of a planning map: checks and comparisons that may be made to evaluate an instructional design*

obligation to organize one's instructional plan in any form of map or chart.
It could be written out as text, or as a series of numbered items. However, th
layout suggested helps with the evaluation of the plan.

6.4 Checklist for evaluating instructional plans

Twenty
questions
for the
evaluation
of an
instructional
plan

In order to assist the task of evaluating an instructional plan for coherence it
useful to ask some basic questions. Most of these have been mentioned earlie
and the layout suggested for our plans makes it easier to perceive the answers
However, it may be useful to write down these key questions in the form of a
checklist, that may be used to evaluate *any* instructional plan, whatever layor
is used to document it (see Figure 6.4 below).

Question	Yes	In part	No	?
1. Are the instructional objectives presented clearly, specifying *conditions, behaviour and criteria?*				
2. Were the terminal objectives analysed sufficiently to reveal the hierarchy or sequence of intermediate and prerequisite behaviours?				
3. Do the resulting decisions concerning instructional sequence seem reasonable?				
4. Are there evaluation methods or instruments or test items prepared for every one of the objectives included in the plan?				
5. Are the suggested tests and evaluation instruments compatible with the objectives? Do the tests measure exactly what the objectives specify?				
6. Are all the necessary forms of test already prepared and included? If not, are there good reasons for not including some form of test in the evaluation system — we may not need pre-tests or tests of prerequisites?				
7. Have the objectives been analysed and classified according to some model of categories of learning?				
8. Was some such classification used as a basis for the selection of appropriate strategies or techniques of instruction?				
9. However selected, are the strategies to be used suited to the objectives and content of instruction proposed?				
10. Is there a specification of the content or the subject matter to be included for each of the objectives?				
11. Is this content reasonably selected in relation to the category of objectives proposed?				
12. Are the specific techniques (methods) to be used for each objective clearly specified?				
13. Are the techniques selected for each objective reasonably appropriate?				

Figure 6.4 *(continued)*

Question	Yes	In part	No	?
14. Do the techniques incorporate all the characteristics of the training strategy to be implemented?				
15. Does the plan include clear media and materials specifications for each of the objectives?				
16. Are the materials and media selected compatible with earlier decisions regarding strategies and techniques?				
17. Are the materials and media selected adequate for the content to be transmitted?				
18. Do the materials and media help students to reach the objectives set for the course?				
19. Is there a specification of the supplementary equipment and materials necessary to carry out the project?				
20. Is there an estimate of the amount of teaching time that will be required? Is this estimate reasonable?				

Figure 6.4 *Checklist for evaluation of instructional plans*

Each of the questions in the checklist can be answered in one of four ways:

☐ *Yes:* the plan seems to satisfy the criteria specified.
☐ *In part:* the criteria are partly satisfied (like the curate's egg).
☐ *No:* the criteria are not satisfied.
☐ *?:* it is impossible to tell whether the criteria of the question in hand are satisfied or not, as the plan contains insufficient information, ie the plan is incompletely defined.

A well-designed instructional plan should give a majority of positive answers — about 70 per cent or more is quite commonly achieved by students on instructional design courses given by the author. Occasionally, owing to the special characteristics of a given problem or project, not all the questions in the checklist are relevant and some adjustment has to be made for this when attempting an evaluation. The evaluation is, of course, rather subjective, relying on what appears 'reasonable' to the evaluator. However, experience in using the checklist as an aid in controlling this author's own instructional design work, as well as an instrument for the evaluation of student projects on instructional design courses, has shown that a considerable degree of consistency in evaluation can be achieved.

	Objectives
Specific instructional objectives (in the sequence of instruction)	
1. Given requests from clients concerning the rental or purchase of property, and all the lists of property duly updated and manuals/tables of reference that are normally used on the job, the trainees should be able to: ☐ give the addresses and characteristics of all properties still available; ☐ give the costs of rental or purchase and any special conditions that may apply in a specific case; ☐ prepare all necessary documentation in order to process the rental/sale. The information given and documents prepared should be 100 per cent correct.	
2. Given any form of contact with a potential client (visits to the office or telephone calls etc) that involve personal contact and verbal exchange, the trainees should be able to: give information, explain procedures, resolve clients' doubts or complaints, always maintaining a pleasant tone of voice, a sense of respect, tact and politeness, patience, etc.	
3. Given any incoming telephone call, the trainees should be able to use the firm's switchboard and connect the call to the person/department best able to deal with the query. Trainees should connect 80 per cent of calls correctly at the first try.	
4. Given instructions on the content of a letter, verbally, by one's boss, the trainees should be able to compose an appropriate form of letter or other missive, obeying the company standards for official correspondence, and produce a grammatically correct and well-constructed text.	
5. Given a normal office workload, the trainees should be able to plan, distribute and organize the work of the office staff, establishing realistic deadlines and using the skills of junior staff to the best advantage.	
6. Given a normal workload and a typical flow of requests for meetings, the trainees should be able to plan the boss's daily schedule and keep his diary up to date allowing an adequate time for each type of meeting arranged, taking into account the current work priorities, etc.	
7. Given a normal workload and a typical flow of correspondence, reports, lets and sales, new properties, new building projects, etc, the trainees should be able to plan, organize and keep updated an adequate filing system, which is easy to maintain and capable of allowing any document to be located by any person with the minimum of training.	

Exhibit 6.1 *Instructional plan for the training of secretaries/receptionists for a large real estate company*

Objectives	
Proposed system of measurement and evaluation of learning	
One should present a series of typical cases of requests for information, covering all the types of situations normally encountered in the working environment. These cases may be evaluated 'live' when used as the basis of group discussion in the classroom, or may be used as the basis for written tests, as a form of final examination. Both modes will be employed — the observation of group discussion exercises as a means of formative evaluation and a final written test for summative evaluation.	
This type of objective can only be evaluated through the observation of the trainees' behaviour in real or simulated contacts with the company's clients, the analysis of this behaviour followed by feedback, more practice if required, until a satisfactory level of performance is demonstrated, even in trying circumstances.	
One should prepare simulation exercises of the principal types of requests and other messages normally received by telephone. The set of exercises should be sufficiently representative of the real work to *guarantee at least 80 per cent correct performance* on the job.	
Present a variety of typical letter-planning exercises. Analyse the resultant letters and feedback corrections or suggest extra practice if necessary. Practice the company standards to 'perfection' and the letter style and structure to a 'reasonable' standard as judged by secondary school teachers.	
Evaluate the planning and distribution of work by analysing written plans to be prepared by trainees. Evaluate the execution of the plans by later observation of on-the-job performance.	
Final evaluation must be performed in-service as the constraints to be taken into account are different in each department and for each boss. One may use some simulated planning exercises during initial training stages (an opportunity for formative evaluation).	
During initial training, the principles of filing systems may be tested by verbal questions and simple filing exercises. Final evaluation should take place in the real job situation by means of job performance evaluation techniques, as each department's filing requirements are somewhat different.	

	Content
Skills content	
The skills of analysing a request for information, to identify the exact data to be given to a client: this is a relatively standardized, reproductive, intellectual skill.	
Skill in the use of tables and charts, such as interest tables, to extract the correct information from the table: this is a reproductive, intellectual skill, based on the practice of reading a variety of tables.	
Personal and interpersonal skills of tact, self-control and polite behaviour: these skills fall into the reactive and interactive categories and are, in general, reproductive in the case of this objective. The receptionist is not a creative problem-solver of client complaints; she must merely follow the rules of normal, polite behaviour.	
Skills of handling and operating telephone switchboard equipment: *reproductive, psychomotor* skills. Skills of classifying/interpreting the incoming calls according to types of request/types of action to be taken: *reproductive, intellectual* skills.	
Skills of authorship and composition of written communications that really say what they mean: productive, intellectual skills. Skills of writing/typing grammatically correct communications: reproductive, intellectual skills — we regard the typing skills as prerequisites.	
Skills of planning and organizing work: productive, intellectual skills. Skills of control and motivation of the work of subordinate staff: productive, interactive skills.	
Skills of evaluating the priority of a given meeting in relation to the boss's current work deadlines/priorities: productive, intellectual skills. Skills of dealing with requests politely: reproductive, interpersonal skills. Skills of time estimating/planning: productive, intellectual skills.	
Skill in planning and organizing filing systems: productive, intellectual skills. Skills of self-discipline required always to file documents at the earliest opportunity — on arrival or as soon as reference to them has been made: reproductive, reactive skills.	

Exhibit 6.1 *(continued)*

Content	
Knowledge content	
A schema of concepts used for classifying requests into categories that require different information, different documents, etc. Knowledge of the procedures to be followed when completing specific documents or using specific tables or reference manuals.	
Knowledge of the procedures of polite treatment of clients, including any special procedures laid down by the company. Also requires the above mentioned schema of concepts for classifying requests, in order to avoid upsetting the client through incompetent interpretation of his request and inappropriate action or information.	
Knowledge of the procedures for operating the specific telephone equipment installed in the office. A schema of concepts relating to the way the company operates, how it is organized and which department does what. Also the names (facts) of key people in the office.	
Cognitive schemata composed of the concepts and principles of creative, persuasive and clear writing. Knowledge of the rules of grammar and punctuation. Knowledge of special norms for business letters, or special company standards/rules.	
Knowledge of the skills and capacity for work of each staff member (job-specific facts). Knowledge of procedures of work planning (time charts, PERT, etc). Concepts of human relations, motivation, principles and strategies for motivation and control of fellow workers.	
The boss's work schedule and priorities (job-specific facts). Identification of work/project that a given meeting is concerned with (conceptual schema of work in progress). Proceedings for diary updating. Principles of time planning, of human relations, of negotiating with superiors.	
The types of work performed in the department (facts and concepts). The principles of filing systems. Knowledge of the problems that might arise for the company if filing/data systems are out of date or poorly organized (knowledge and conceptual understanding).	

Methods	
General strategies to be implemented	*Specific techniques/methods to be used*
Part expositive, part experiential: definition of basic concepts, followed by skills practice on simulated cases.	Case studies (written). Orientation by *instructor*. Work in *small groups*. Final discussion/*debriefing*.
Expositive strategies for the use of tables, etc: demonstration followed by drill and practice exercises, until error-free performance is achieved by all trainees on all the job aids used in the office.	Study of a self-instructional manual which presents worked examples of the use of all job aids and then supplies practice exercises and feedback for self-correction by the trainee. (Could be in the form of information mapping.)
Expositive strategy at first; demonstration of the required procedures. Experiential strategy later; simulation of the client/receptionist interaction.	Demonstration of models of good receptionist behaviour. Explanation of procedures. Role-playing: simulation of problems between client and receptionist and how to handle them.
Expositive strategies for the operation of equipment.	Practical demonstration and individual practice, guided by the operator's manual.
Expositive strategy for the explanation of company structure/organization, followed by experiential strategy for the matching of requests to actions taken.	Classroom exposition with visuals/charts, followed by group analysis of taped incoming telephone calls.
Experiential strategy for writing skills; composition and analysis of letters on simulated work topics. Expositive strategy for the company rules. (We hope we do not need to teach the rules of grammar.)	Practical exercises of composition of letters from given short notes. Analysis of the letters produced. Self-instruction from a manual of company rules and examples of their use.
Expositive strategies for the procedures and the principles of work planning. Experiential strategies for the skills of planning, motivating, delegating, etc.	Classroom instruction on the procedures and principles of planning/organizing. On-the-job training for the development of skills, specific to the work actually done.
Expositive strategies for the facts, concepts and procedures that are to be learned. Experiential strategies to develop skill in dealing with actual job situations.	On-the-job training for all aspects of this objective. The boss must explain his work, priorities and must keep this knowledge updated as work changes. He must set appropriate tasks and monitor trainee progress.
Expositive strategies for the facts, concepts, procedures and basic principles to be learned. Experiential strategies to develop the skills and attitudes required.	On-the-job training for most of this objective. General principles and procedures of filing may be given in introductory classroom instruction. Department-specific knowledge and skill development under the boss's control.

Exhibit 6.1 *(continued)*

Methods	Resources	
Group size and structure and methods of working	*Instructional media/materials*	
Large group (12 trainees) subdivided into small groups of three or four for the case study analysis.	10 - 15 case studies each one prepared on separate sheet of paper — to be selected from real examples of company work.	
Individual study in the class or at home, aided by the instructor when difficulties arise (trainee seeks help from the instructor only when the feedback supplied in the self-instructional text proves to be inadequate).	Self-instructional text (70 pages estimate) — to be specially written to accompany a typical set of tables and manuals as used on the job. The text presents the problems and refers the trainee to the job aids.	
Demonstrations to the whole group of 12.

Role-playing in pairs, or in some cases threes or fours (to complicate the problem situations). Rest of group act as observers and evaluators, until their turn comes to act. | A set of demonstration videotapes, showing good and bad examples of client treatment.
It is also possible to record on videotape the performances of the actors in the role-play exercises. The roles of these actors must be printed and available beforehand. About eight sets of roles. | |
| Demonstration to pairs, then practice in pairs (one practising on the equipment; one evaluating his partner's performance).

Whole group initially, followed by three groups of four trainees. | Programmed introduction on the use of the telephone switchboard equipment used by the company. (To be written — 10 pages.)
30 simulated telephone calls, recorded on audiotape, based on a frequency analysis of the most common types of requests. | |
| Work on groups of four. Each member prepares a version of the letter and then four are compared.
Individual study of the manual. Feedback by analysis of written work. | 12 different boss's notes, giving three exercises for each member of a group of four trainees.
Programmed text of questions and exercises on company standards and business norms in letter writing. (To be produced — 80 pages approximately.) | |
| Whole group of 12. Possibly some small group work.

Individual training under one's immediate boss. | Overhead projector transparencies to accompany the classroom instruction (12 sets artwork).

Printed training plan/checklist for controlling on-the-job training (for the boss). | |
| Individual learning, adapted to the real job content and controlled by trainee's immediate superior. | Self-study and reference materials on procedures for office meetings, etc (these already exist, but should be updated). Checklist for controlling the trainee's learning on the job (to be used by boss). | |
| Initial classroom study in whole group of 12 and some small group filing exercises.
Later on-the-job training as individually adapted to the department's needs controlled by boss. | Learning and reference material to be used in class and on the job, on the principles/procedures of file organization. Checklist for controlling the trainee's learning on the job, to be used by the boss and then returned to training department. | |

Resources	
Equipment/tools/job aids, etc	*Time estimate*
Classroom organized for small group discussion.	Four hours
Comprehensive set of the tables, manuals and other job aids actually used in the office.	Four hours (Total of eight hours for this objective.)
Videotape, or cassette, recorder/player and television. Compatible video camera, if recorded video feedback is to be used in the role-play debriefings. A set reminiscent of the office may be necessary, if training in a classroom setting.	Initially allow two hours for the demonstrations. Then, one hour for each play and ensuing debriefing. (Total of 10 hours if eight role-plays are run.)
Operator's manual (supplied by manufacturer). Access to the switchboard (or a simulator) for practical training. Three tape recorders.	One hour initially, plus six x one hour for practice on switchboard. Four hours classroom instruction and two hours group work. (Total eight hours.)
Classroom arranged for small group work. Writing materials or typewriters, as preferred. Printed copy of the company norms and standards (already exists) for reference.	Four hours — one for each exercise and one for analysis/comparison. Two to four hours of individual study. (Total six to eight hours.)
Overhead projector. Classroom arranged for flexibility — small/large group. Standard forms or charts used on the job for the planning and control of office work.	Six hours of classwork for the group. Individual on-the-job training for one to two months.
The boss's diary and a similar dummy one for practice exercises.	Continuous in-service training for one or two months, until an adequate standard of performance is maintained.
Empty files, file cards, labels and all other materials needed to organize a filing system of the type used by the company. Adequate variety of real job filing requirements to give necessary practice to trainees.	Four hours class instruction initially, followed by in-service training for one or two months, as necessary.

Exhibit 6.1 *(continued)*

Specific OBJECTIVES of each lesson	
Lesson 1(a): Objectives 1 to 6 (theory) Given a test on the theoretical aspects of diving, the student will score over 80 per cent as evaluated by the instructor	
Lesson 1(b): Objectives 2, 3, 4, 5, 6 (practice) Given a mask, fins and snorkel, the student will (2) Clear a flooded mask completely (self-evaluation) (3) Clear a flooded snorkel to enable easy breathing (self-evaluation) (4) Enter the deep end of the pool, demonstrating at least three of the methods correctly as judged by the instructor (5) Swim at least two lengths of the pool demonstrating the four leg strokes to the satisfaction of the instructor (6) Equalize properly to prevent any pain or damage to the ear (self-evaluation)	
Lesson 2: Objective 1 Given a tank and regulator, the student will correctly attach the regulator to the tank in 30 seconds so that the regulator comes over the right shoulder *Objective 2* Given a mask, fins, snorkel, tank, regulator and weight belt, the student will put on the equipment correctly	
Lesson 3: Objective 1 Given a flooded mouthpiece, the student will clear it and resume breathing *Objective 2* Given a tank and regulator, students will 'buddy-breathe' calmly for two lengths of the pool to the instructor's satisfaction	
Lesson 4: Objective 1 Given scuba gear, the student will demonstrate mastery of the basic scuba skills in a pool to the satisfaction of the instructor	

Exhibit 6.2 *Objectives, tests and instructional plan for a practical training session on scuba diving, organized in four lessons*

	Evaluation system and TEST ITEMS to be used	
	A written test composed of multiple choice, true/false, short answer questions	
	In the pool, the student will perform all the basic skin diving skills correctly in the presence of a qualified instructor	
	The student will explain and execute the correct procedure in attaching the regulator to the tank. Instructor checks the procedure The student will put on the scuba gear in the proper order in three minutes	
	The student will successfully perform the task in 30 seconds The two students will swim two lengths of the pool while 'buddy breathing'	
	Review test of all the required skills, in the form of a checklist to be marked by the instructor observing the diver	

Exhibit 6.2 *(continued)*

Principal CATEGORY of knowledge/skill	
Factual knowledge ⎤ Concepts ⎬ Procedures ⎬ See the Principles ⎦ ⎦ test attached	
Psychomotor-reproductive skills, based on the application of the knowledge identified above (mainly the procedures)	
Knowledge of procedure. The necessary physical (psychomotor-reproductive) skills are probably already mastered by the trainees Knowledge of procedure. (Psychomotor-reproductive) skills required are no different from those met in putting on other gear or clothes	
Knowledge of correct procedures. Psychomotor-reproductive skills (new breathing techniques) Reactive and reproductive skills (of self-control when short of air)	
All procedures introduced in earlier lessons Psychomotor-reproductive skills, being the sum of all prior lessons	

	Proposed STRATEGY	
	Expositive-inductive/deductive	
	Expositive-demonstration, practice, feedback	
	Expositive — explanation, demonstration, practice and feedback	
	Expositive — explanation, demonstration, practice and feedback	
	Expositive — learning by practice of the clearing procedure	
	Experiential — learning by finding out what it feels like	
	Expositive/experiential — free practice under observation	

Exhibit 6.2 *(continued)*

	Instructional METHODS to be used	
	Presentation of transparencies with discussion in a normal classroom setting. Optional presentation of a film about scuba diving	
	Demonstration by instructor. Practice of each task by the trainees. Correction, feedback and repetition until adequate performance standards are maintained	
	Lecture with visuals followed by demonstration/practice session	
	Transparencies presentation of each step (overlay) Demonstration/practice on dry land, or in classroom	
	Objective 1: Demonstration by instructor, followed by: practice ⟶ mastery ⟶ confidence ⟶ calm breathing

Objective 2: Free practice of 'buddy breathing' (two divers sharing one mouthpiece) to discover the best way to perform the task. Final de-briefing discussion | |
| | *Practice* — under observation of instructor and other trainee divers
Test evaluation — checklist completed by instructor and other observers
Analysis of performance in a de-briefing session
New practice if required, repeating the cycle | |

	Ideal GROUPING of trainees	
	Group of eight to ten trainees	
	Small group/individual exercises	
	Whole-group at lecture Small group/individual practice Small or large group presentation Small group/individual practice	
	Individual and small group work	
	Work in pairs, followed by whole group discussion	
	Individual practice and group discussion	

Exhibit 6.2 *(continued)*

	Instructional MEDIA	
	Overlay transparencies, instructor, film (if available)	
	Master performer (the instructor)	
	Lecturer and transparency presentation	
	Instructor, overlay transparencies	
	Master performer and 'Buddy'	
	Instructor and fellow trainees	

	MATERIALS and EQUIPMENT
	Overhead projector, screen, 16mm projector transparencies (detailed sketches attached)
	Mask, fins, snorkel, pool (one set for each learner)
	Overhead projector, screen, transparencies Regulators and tanks for each learner Overhead projector, screen, transparencies Masks, fins, snorkels, tanks, regulators, BCs, weight belts (two sets)
	Full scuba gear for each learner
	Full scuba gear for two people

Exhibit 6.2 *(continued)*

PART 3.
Tactics: Micro Instructional Design: Lesson Planning

Overview

This part of the book descends to a deeper level of analysis, leading to more detailed instructional design — what we earlier called 'level 3 instructional design'. We shall be considering the development of detailed lesson plans for various types of lessons, including conventional classroom-based expositive instruction, various types of small group learning activities and the planning of simulations and games.

Chapter 7 is a short introduction to level 3 design. It identifies the need for deeper analysis of objectives, content and target population, in order to be able to select appropriate tactics. Tactics are seen to be the lesson-specific decisions that the designer must take — the choice of appropriate examples and non-examples to define completely a certain concept, the use of appropriate vocabulary or a meaningful analogy, and so on.

Chapters 8 and 9 present a methodology for the performance of this deeper analysis, by means of identifying the structure of the knowledge and skills content of the proposed lesson. In analysing the knowledge content, we use as our basic conceptual tool the knowledge schema which we developed in Part 2. To analyse the skills content, we use the previously developed four-domain skills schema and our model of the skill cycle. This identifies up to 12 possible sources of learning and execution difficulty in a given skilled activity.

In Chapter 10, we pass from analysis to synthesis, developing a general model for lesson planning. This is a two-dimensional model which takes into consideration both the critical aspects of an instructional system and the important stages in the sequence of delivery of a lesson. We give several examples of lesson plans prepared for expositive classroom instruction.

Chapter 11 considers group learning situations, both from theoretical viewpoints of basic advantages and limitations and from the practical standpoint of how to select, prepare for and use a variety of group learning methods. We also show that our general lesson planning model may be used for designing group activities.

In Chapter 12, we analyse the role and the possible range of applications for simulations and games in both education and training. We present a compendium of games and simulations, selected to illustrate the variety and scope encompassed in this category of instructional methods. We see that they can be used at all levels of education and training, with all manner of target populations and, depending on the content and objectives of the lesson, they may adopt both expositive and experiential strategies.

Chapter 13 deals with the evaluation of individual lessons. A systematic model of evaluation is adopted and practical techniques and instruments are presented for the evaluation of lesson outputs, of the instructional process itself, of the inputs (both material and in the form of planning) upon which the success of the lesson may depend and of the overall context which may often disrupt the best laid plans. The chapter ends with a case study.

The structure of Part 3 of the book is thus seen to take us, systematically, through the analysis, synthesis and evaluation aspects of the tactical level of instructional development.

7. The Third Level of Analysis: Selecting and Planning the Tactics of Instruction

7.1 Introduction

In Part 2 we reviewed the instructional design decisions that should be taken regarding the overall structure of the system we are planning. We considered decisions on sequence, methods, group size and structure, media and other resources required to implement the instructional plan. These decisions can be taken either at the 'project' level, for the course or course unit as a whole, or at a more detailed curriculum level, that considers each major terminal objective individually. We referred to these as the first and second levels of instructional design.

We now proceed to the third level. This chapter examines some of the further analyses that we may need to perform to plan the detailed *tactics* of a lesson or training exercise.

Level 3 design

The third level of instructional design is concerned with the individual lesson. Very often, the basic data needed to decide the question of sequence within a lesson is already available from Level 2 analysis. If a hierarchy of all the intermediate objectives has been prepared, this can serve equally well as a basis for the sequencing of the lessons in a course or for the internal sequencing of the objectives in a given lesson.

We saw in Chapter 6 that the overall instructional plans prepared as a part of the macro design may be developed to a greater or lesser level of detail. In the case of a less detailed instructional plan, which lists only the principal instructional objectives, it will be necessary to analyse further objectives at the lesson planning stage in order to uncover the prerequisites or the 'enabling objectives' that must be mastered before the 'end of lesson' instructional objectives can be achieved. In the case of a more detailed instructional plan, or 'curriculum map', which already lists the intermediate or enabling objectives, it may be possible directly to extract the sequence of the objectives of individual lessons from the overall map.

general lesson planning model

However, apart from the sequence of instructional objectives to be dealt with, a lesson also follows some general plan, or model, which governs the way that it is organized and presented. What are the activities that the learners should perform in order to learn effectively? What are the activities that the instructor should perform in order to facilitate learning? What are the 'instructional events' that mark the key stages in the lesson? The most common form of lesson planning model is a list of stages that should be followed in executing the lesson. A typical example of such a model is:

- ☐ Open the lesson and motivate the learners.
- ☐ Review past work related to the current lesson's content and objectives.
- ☐ Introduce the lesson topic and explain the objectives to be achieved.
- ☐ Present new information and demonstrate, explain or illustrate, as required.
- ☐ Reinforce the new learning by questioning, repetition, practice, etc.
- ☐ Assess the learning and repeat, or practice further if necessary.
- ☐ Summarize the lesson and close, indicating opportunities for further study.

An approach similar to the one presented above is suggested by Gagné (1976), though it is couched in somewhat more technical terminology. A much simple variation on the theme is the approach said to be used by some army instructors: 'You tell them what you're going to tell them, then you tell them, and then you tell them what you've told them'.

Matching tactics to objectives

The techniques of Level 3 analysis to be studied here classify the intermediate instructional objectives and then match them to specific instructional tactics. This approach forms the basis for a rather more rigorous method of lesson planning. A general sequence of events, somewhat like the list presented above, is followed, but within this overall sequence each objective receives individual treatment. For example, we suggested earlier that expositive strategies are more appropriate for teaching simpler types of knowledge and skills, whereas the learning of general principles is enhanced by using the discovery approach. One might therefore use an expositive technique in one part of the lesson and an experiential technique in another, if the lesson contains a variety of types of objectives. In a Latin lesson, for instance, one might teach to discriminate between the parts of speech — subject, verb, object — by means of expositive demonstrations and drill and practice exercises. Later in the same lesson the learners may use their newly gained knowledge as a means of discovering the rules that govern the position of the principal parts of speech in a correctly formulated Latin sentence.

7.2 Influence of lesson content on the selection of instructional tactics

Why talk of 'tactics'?

As we are now at a very detailed level of analysis, dealing with specific items o information to be transmitted to the learner and specific learning activities to be performed with this information, it is appropriate to use the term *instructional tactics*. The difference between strategies and tactics is not only one of size; it is principally one of specificity. Whereas the general learning category of what is to be learned suggests the adoption of a particular overall strategy, the detailed structure and the specific content suggest specific tactic to be employed in order to put the preferred strategy into effective operation.

What are tactics?

When analysing content in order to select instructional tactics, we are faced with a series of questions similar to the following examples:

Example 1. 'OK, so we wish to use an experiential strategy to lead our student to discover what it feels like to be discriminated against. This might be achieved through some form of simulation, role-play exercise or game. But *exactly what* situation shall we simulate? What situations will the students relate to? What situations will be too complex or too sophisticated for them t understand? Of the possible situations, which ones can be simulated with ease in the classroom setting? How can we do this in practice?'

Example 2. 'OK, so we wish to use an expositive strategy to teach our student the concepts associated with the flow of electricity in circuits (potential difference, current, resistance, etc). These are 'defined concepts', but we know that mere definitions are rarely sufficient in order to communicate such concepts clearly and completely. We must use examples to illustrate the concepts and relate them to other, previously learned, information, by means of analogies, contrasts, comparisons, etc. But what examples shall we use? What level of difficulty? How many examples will be required in order to establish the concepts clearly in the minds of all our students? Are there any significant exceptions, or 'non-examples', that might lead to confusion in the students' minds? How can we best overcome or avoid possible sources of confusion? Can we strengthen the ties between the new concepts and prior learning by means of suitable contrasts or analogies? What analogies will be meaningful to the students?'

The instructional designer's expertise in the content and his experience in teaching it to particular types of students are of great value in seeking answers to such detailed questions. He may, however, supplement his expertise and experience by reference to the work of others. He may study how the topic has been taught in the past and with what measure of success.

If successful lesson plans already exist, there may be no point in attempting to 'reinvent the wheel'. For example, taking the first case, the knowledge that Gary Shirts' game STARPOWER has been successful in giving students of various age groups the experience of being discriminated against may lead the instructional designer to incorporate the game into his own lesson plan, or to adapt it to his own objectives while maintaining the basic structure of the game. In the second example, knowledge that some teachers have successfully taught the concepts of electricity flow by means of analogies to the flow of water in a system of household pipes may lead the designer to adopt the same tactic. However, as in the previous case, he should carefully analyse the content in relation to the students and their present levels of knowledge and skill. The water flow analogy may be an extremely useful instructional tactic to use with students who already have some notion of plumbing systems and the pumping of water through pipes. But for other, less well-prepared, students the analogy may be meaningless, or may even increase the level of learning difficulty through the introduction of apparently irrelevant content. However, the basic principles of the water flow analogy may be adapted to create a more familiar comparison — and thus a more useful instructional tactic for the learning group in question. Instead of comparing the diameter of electrical wires (and therefore their resistances) to the diameter of water pipes, the instructor might draw a comparison with the width of streets in a city centre. A narrow street offers more resistance to the flow of traffic than does a wide street. We can, for example, force fewer cars per minute (current flow) through the narrow street. Two narrow streets in parallel can double the flow (halve the resistance), and so on. The traffic flow analogy may not be as technically exact as the water flow one, but at a certain point in the instructional process, with certain groups of students, it may be a much more powerful instructional tactic.

7.3 Conclusion

The selection of appropriate tactics for specific lesson content is thus a process of creative design or adaptation of:

☐ Explanations and definitions.
☐ Illustrations, examples and analogies.
☐ Learning activities, drills and games.
☐ Feedback questions, tests and exercises.

All these should be appropriate to the *content*, the proposed *objectives* and the particular *target* population. The instructional designer's expertise in the content, and his experience of the target population, are of undeniable importance. However, at this stage his analysis of the objectives is also important, and should be performed to a level of detail that is sufficient to define and select truly appropriate tactics. This means that the instructional designer should look very carefully at the structure of his objectives.

8. The Structure of Knowledge – and its Analysis

8.1 Introduction

In Chapter 4 we presented a schema of knowledge categories, in which the four basic types of knowledge — facts, procedures, concepts and principles — are further subdivided. These sub-categories, listed in the outer ring of our circular schema, are a useful framework for discussing the influence of the detailed, intermediate objectives on the selection of instructional tactics. We shall take the categories one at a time and consider some of the factors that influence our lesson planning decisions. The basic definitions and short descriptions of each category and sub-category of our schema may be found in Chapter 4, Table 4.1 on p 43. It may be useful to refer to this diagram while reading this chapter.

8.2 Tactics for teaching facts

Our schema divides facts into two principal sub-categories: *concrete* facts (or concrete associations) and *verbal* (or, more correctly, *symbolic*) information. It also indicates that factual knowledge may be structured in the form of schemata that organize a large number of specific items of information into a coherent and complex 'message'. An example of structured symbolic information is a geographical map. A person who reads the map uses the knowledge of the individual symbols on the map to form a mental image of the terrain it represents. Similarly, being able to find one's way about in a dark room during a sudden power cut, for example, indicates that the physical layout of the room and its furniture has been memorized as a mental 'map' of the concrete structures that surround us.

Appropriate tactics for the communication of facts are generally based on the presentation and repetition of information, whether concrete or symbolic, in a *form*, *sequence* and *frequency* conducive to efficient rote memorization. With concrete facts, learned through direct observation of one's surroundings, it may be sufficient to arrange the opportunity to observe the relevant information only a few times. For example, it would not need many presentations of the neighbour's dog, in the context of the neighbour's garden, to establish the simple fact that the dog belongs to the neighbour. However, more than one presentation would be necessary to exclude the possibility that the dog was just visiting. As the information to be learned becomes more complex, the frequency of presentation necessary to establish learning increases. A reasonable amount of practice is needed to learn to move about a given environment in the dark, without bumping into the furniture. Several repetitions of an exercise designed to encourage the learner to form a mental map of the room will be necessary.

Experiments with KIM'S GAME — which is used widely for visual memory training, and involves the listing of objects exposed briefly for observation — show that the learning difficulty increases rapidly as the total number of objects is increased. These experiments also illustrate the possibilities for improving one's performance of such visual memory tasks by 'thinking structurally', that is, classifying the objects into some arbitrary categories as an aid to learning. It is easier to memorize three sets of four objects than 12 apparently unrelated ones. The invention of useful — although arbitrary — classifications and structures for the organization of large bodies of information is part of the development of a general memorization skill, if the learner has to invent his own structures. If, however, the teacher takes it upon himself to invent useful structures as memorization aids, the activity becomes part of the instructional design process.

The reader may at this point be feeling that all this is interesting, but not particularly relevant to the main body of education and training, the objective of which stretch far beyond the mere rote memorization of factual information especially of concrete and observable facts. This is true, but it is useful to start with this very simple category of learning as it illustrates distinctions which we shall also encounter in the higher order categories of learning. We now proceed to the consideration of verbal or symbolic information.

Tactics for teaching symbolic facts

The case of verbal or symbolic information is somewhat different. The effective communication of a verbal or symbolic message depends on the ability of the receiver of the message to understand the 'language' being used. This generally implies prior conceptual learning of the meaning of the words or other symbols used and the learning of principles that govern the syntax and structure of the language. For example, to communicate verbally the previously observed fact that 'my neighbour has a dog', the person receiving my communication must have sufficient language expertise to first understand the words 'neighbour', 'to have' and 'dog' (these are all concepts) and, second to understand the rules of grammar that govern the structure of the sentences used to communicate the message (these are general principles). If these conditions are not satisfied, the listener might yet learn to repeat a string of (to him) meaningless sounds, but we would not consider that he had acquired the knowledge that I am attempting to communicate to him.

Given the necessary language expertise, the mere statement — once only — of the message is generally sufficient to establish meaningful communication. However, though the message might be understood at once, it may be necessary to repeat it several times to establish efficient learning. Repetition may be necessary to reinforce the learning against the danger of being immediately forgotten — the more lengthy or complex the message, the more frequent must be the repetition. People vary considerably in how many times they must listen to, or read, a message to memorize it. Some people appear to be 'visual' learners, while others learn better when listening. Certain groups, such as actors, develop the ability rapidly to memorize large tracts of text. This indicates that specific memorization skills exist and there are probably several different types. These can be developed by means of appropriate training exercises. However, it is also possible to promote more efficient learning by organizing the material to be memorized and the practice sessions devoted to learning. Practical experience and laboratory research suggest several useful tactics. One is the 'spaced repetition' of the reading or listening task, as opposed to end-on or massed repetition on the same occasion

Several models exist for the planning of spaced repetition. These include the repetition of the whole learning task at progressively increasing intervals; the splitting up of the task into parts to be learned separately and only put together after the last of the parts has been mastered; and the progressive part tactic, which involves learning one part and then practising what has been learned at the same time as learning the next part.

There is no conclusive evidence that any one of these tactics is generally superior to the others. It seems to depend on the particular learner's preferences and, to some extent, on the type of content being learned. Some learners prefer to attempt to learn whole poems all at once, while others find easier to learn one verse at a time. The learning of a sequence of steps is generally easier to achieve by the progressive parts approach, while the learning of a set of names is usually facilitated by presenting sets of similar names together as a whole learning task. However, in all cases, some form of spacing of the learning and practice sessions does appear to lead to more efficient learning.

8.3 Tactics for teaching concepts

e of
mples
non-
mples

Our schema subdivides concepts into two classes — *concrete* concepts and *defined* concepts. Appropriate tactics for the teaching of concepts are, in general, related to the generalizability of the idea which the concept communicates — in other words, what is included and what is excluded when we use the concept. This raises the issue of the selection of appropriate examples to be used during the instructional process. Appropriate examples are not necessarily the most obvious ones. The importance of the examples is to illustrate the limits of the concept: When is an object to be classified as 'red' and when is it some other, near-red colour?; Which examples best illustrate the difference between the concepts 'long' and 'big'?; Which examples of governments that call themselves democratic would be considered to be true democracies and which do not fit into our concept of democracy (that is, act as contra examples or non-examples of the concept)?

To establish a given concept with precision, the instructional designer must therefore present the learner with a sufficient number of appropriate examples and non-examples, particularly the 'borderline' examples and the 'near-miss' non-examples. What is a 'sufficient number' may depend on the characteristics of the target population, but what are 'appropriate' examples are identified by the analysis of the concept itself and of other related, but different, concepts. This concept analysis is extremely important at the lesson planning stage of instructional design, because it is the key to effective teaching of higher order intellectual objectives — it is difficult to develop principles and theories from woolly concepts that lack clearly defined boundaries.

tics for
ching
icrete
cepts

With concrete concepts, the instructional design problem is to present the 'sufficient number of appropriate examples' to the learners in a convenient manner. As the examples are concrete — that is, real objects, people, etc — the instructional design task is one of planning the instructional environment to make the necessary objects available to the learner. This may be done by taking the learners to the examples (by, for example, visits to museums and practical projects), or by bringing the examples to the learners, through the use of appropriate objects, pictures and other types of learning materials. Most concrete concepts are learned in the early years of childhood. Teachers who work in the pre-primary and early primary levels, especially those who use well-designed concept development methodologies, such as the Montessori method, are very familiar with the sort of planning that is needed. The building up of concrete concepts may require a considerable period of time, partly because the children in a particular age group may not all have reached the required stage of intellectual maturation (as shown by the work of Piaget) and also because of the large number of examples and non-examples that must be presented to the child in order to refine his understanding of the concept to the necessary level of precision.

The learning of concrete concepts is not, however, restricted to the primary school. It is a common component in the learning of industrial inspection tasks, such as the checking of the surface finish of machined components or the quality of a paint job on a motor car body. Some such inspection tasks are based on the application of verbal definitions and should therefore be classed as the use of defined concepts. Many tasks, however, depend on the general quality of the finished product, which is not totally definable in words but

tics for
ching
ined
cepts

which the experienced worker 'recognizes when he sees'. He has a concrete concept of the required level of quality.

With defined concepts, the task of planning the learning environment is supplanted by the task of planning the learning sequence. A defined concept is (by definition) one which can be expressed verbally, or by some other form of symbolic language, such as mathematical notation. However, many of the words or symbols used in the definition themselves represent other, perhaps simpler, concepts. If these have not previously been adequately learned, the definition may be ambiguous or even totally meaningless to the learner. Thus it is particularly important for the instructional designer to perform a thorough concept analysis of the topic to be taught, in order to identify the structure of interrelationships that exists between the various concepts. It is necessary to ensure, in the sequence of the lesson plan, that prerequisite concepts are mastered adequately before they are used in later teaching. The mastery of these prerequisite concepts should be systematically tested.

Any lesson that aims to teach new defined concepts should incorporate a 'prerequisite testing and revision' stage. This testing must be carefully designed. It is all too easy to fall into the trap of testing superficially or inappropriately. It is common, for example, to use a certain set of examples in the teaching of a concept and then to use the same examples when testing it in a later lesson. A teacher might ask: 'How would you define democracy, and give me an example of a democratic government currently in power?' The learners might answer with a standard definition and a string of examples mentioned by the teacher in the previous week's class. What the teacher has tested is, of course, *facts* — verbal information memorized by the students. The test has not proved that the students have only learned factual information. They *may* have formed an adequate concept of democracy, but the test used has not proved this beyond doubt. To be a valid test, the students must *apply* the definition to create or identify new examples. The teacher might describe several governments and ask the students whether they consider each of these to be democratic or not and to explain why they think so. The important point is that the situations must be new to the students, not previously discussed in the context of the concept currently being taught.

Tactics for developing conceptual schemata

As the learners progress, they build conceptual schemata, interrelating the concepts previously learned and incorporating the newly learned concepts into ever more complex structures. This is a continuous process of structuring and restructuring the knowledge stored in the mind. The instructional designer may apply several tactics to assist this process. They include the use of analogies, schematic or diagrammatic representations, graphs, tables, comparing/contrasting charts, etc. What tactics the instructional designer chooses will, in part, depend on the specific subject matter being studied. However, an important factor that will guide his choice of tactics is his earlier choice, made at the Level 2 design stage, between expositive and experiential strategies. We saw in Chapters 4 and 5 that both these strategies may be used for the teaching of concepts and that each offers specific advantages and limitations. Depending on the choice of strategy, the specific tactics will be substantially different. When following expositive strategies, the instructional designer should attempt to present models of a possible conceptual structure, to assist the learners in organizing their own minds. He may do this verbally or, more effectively, by means of visual representations of the interrelationships that exist between the various concepts being taught. The various schemata used in this book, such as those for classifying knowledge and skills, are examples of this tactic being put into practice.

When planning to follow an experiential strategy, however, the instructional designer will attempt to get the learners to form their own conceptual schemata. He will not present ready-made structures and learning aids. Instead, he will create learning situations that force the learner to examine his existing conceptual understanding of a particular problem, identify inadequacies and restructure his ideas in order to explain, or cope with, the situation better. This may be achieved by verbal questioning (as in the case of Socratic dialogue), by posing problems that require a novel approach, or by creating situations, whether real or simulated, that take the student by surprise (in the sense that he cannot understand them or adequately relate to them unless he restructures his views).

role of
ation
e
ation of
eptual
nata

The major proponents of the discovery approach argue that the learner should *always* form his own conceptual schemata. Piaget, when discussing the processes of 'assimilation' of new concepts and the 'accommodation' of existing conceptual schemata, stresses the very personal nature of these learning processes. He suggests that one learner's conceptual schemata may well be different from another's, without necessarily resulting in errors of comprehension or differences in performance. We, as teachers, may have substantially different conceptual models of the learning process, yet be equally effective as teachers. Scientists may differ in their conceptual understanding of the origins of the solar system, yet be able to use these different schemata adequately to explain some newly observed astronomical phenomenon. The very existence of rival scientific theories illustrates that quite different conceptual schemata may exist in peoples' minds in relation to the same body of observed facts and phenomena. The variety may be even greater in less well-defined subject areas than science: in philosophy, for example.

It is not easy to define the extent to which the educational system should promote certain specific 'views of the world'. To what extent should teachers strive to form specific, pre-defined, conceptual structures in the minds of their students? This is a central question relating to the discussion on the aims of education. However, there is no doubt that in some areas of study, certain conceptual schemata are not useful problem-solving tools, are incomplete, or even downright wrong. The view that students should discover and restructure for themselves the interrelationships between the concepts they learn is not an adequate excuse for the teacher to abrogate the responsibility for checking that the resulting conceptual schemata are indeed useful to them. One must distinguish between schemata that are plausible alternatives and ones that are incorrect. Particularly in the case of instruction, when we are attempting to lead the student to the achievement of specific, predetermined learning objectives, we must be sure that the conceptual schemata the students are forming will help them to meet those objectives.

to
uate
en
eptual
ma

Thus, whether the basic strategy of instruction is experiential or expositive, the instructional designer should plan to evaluate the conceptual schemata that exist in the minds of the learners. This requires the arrangement of some form of activity that will expose the effectiveness of those schemata in particular types of situations. The tactics may vary, from the solution of pre-set problems to the free discussion of an experience and its causes and implications.

In the first case, the instructor looks for evidence of correct interrelationship between key concepts in the method of solution adopted by the student. Has he followed a path that indicates full understanding of the structure of the subject, or has he shown a poor grasp of the interrelationships that exist?

As an example, one might quote two brain teasers recently published in the *Sunday Times*. The first concerned trains leaving at hourly intervals from two stations at a certain distance apart and travelling at a certain fixed speed. The reader had to calculate how many trains he would pass going in the opposite direction during a journey on one of the trains. The second problem concerned a chain of buckets, attached at fixed intervals to a belt and used to extract water from a flooded mineshaft, one side of the belt carrying full buckets up to the surface where they would empty and then descend again on the other side. The reader had to calculate how many buckets would enter the water at the bottom of the mineshaft during the time that one full bucket travels up to the surface. A reader might correctly solve both problems by writing out all the steps of his calculations, making small diagrams of the mineshaft or maps of the train journey, and yet never realize that the two problems are essentially one and the same — two sets of equally spaced poir travelling at the same speed but in opposite directions. The reader who reali that the same solution serves for both problems — only changing the data o distances and speeds given in the two cases — shows that he has a more powerful, or better structured, schema of the concepts involved. The instructional designer should seek out such 'transfer situations' which can demonstrate the power of the learner's conceptual schemata.

The second tactic mentioned above — the free discussion of the results o project or the implications of an experience — also requires careful planning The instructor leading the discussion must have a clear idea of the types of conclusions or observations that he is looking for in the comments made by his students. Once again, a more powerful, or more useful, conceptual scher can produce insights that transcend the immediate boundaries of the proble under discussion.

Gilbert (1969) quotes a good example of this type of transferability of a concept across subject and discipline boundaries in his reference to the 'carg cult'. A student was presented with information about an event during Worl War II. Troops on a Pacific island were being supplied by parachute drops. Many of the drops were going off target and were being received, in error, b tribes living in the interior of the island. The question under discussion was: What would be the probable effect on the lifestyle of the natives of these unexpected deliveries of provisions? The student came to the conclusion tha the tribes would stop their usual food gathering activities and would come t incorporate the supplies into their religion as 'gifts from God' which must b sought by means of special religious rituals. When questioned on his reasons f his opinions — which in fact were very close to what actually happened — tl student, who had previously studied behavioural psychology, gave the following explanation: the cargo drops were a form of reinforcement; they occurred at irregular and unpredictable intervals not associated with any specific activity of the tribe; they therefore constituted a 'random reinforcement schedule'; this type of schedule leads to ritualistic — what Skinner called 'superstitious' — behaviour in rats, pigeons and other experimental groups; ritualistic and superstitious behaviour in human group generally takes the form of cults or religions; the random drops of cargo wo therefore almost certainly lead to the creation of a cargo cult among the natives. In his paper, Gilbert argues that this type of interdisciplinary transf of concepts is one of the chief objectives of an integrated social sciences curriculum and goes on to suggest how such a curriculum could be planned. The story serves as an excellent example of the type of free discussion problems that should be designated and incorporated in a lesson plan to evaluate the transfer power of the conceptual schemata that our students have formed.

8.4 Tactics for teaching principles

We have analysed at some length the chief considerations that influence the choice of tactics for teaching facts and concepts. We will be able to move a little more quickly when dealing with procedures — a form of factual knowledge — and principles — a form of conceptual knowledge. We begin b considering principles, which are the 'cause-effect', and other relationships which explain how we, or the environment in which we live, behave in certa circumstances. In our discussion, we will find it useful to distinguish betwee principles that govern our environment — called 'rules of nature' in our sche of categories of knowledge — and principles that govern our own actions in certain circumstances — referred to here as 'rules of action'.

The use of experiential and expositive strategies

We have seen that the preferred general strategy for teaching principles is experiential, though this is not always possible, because of time restrictions practical difficulties in arranging the appropriate experiences needed to 'lea by discovery'. Fortunately, human beings have the faculty of imagination, which enables them to learn abstract principles, through discussion and visualization of particular situations, without necessarily experiencing them at first hand. Thus, expositive instructional strategies may also be used successfully for teaching principles. However, research findings show that principles learned through experience are more easily transferred to other similar situations and are less likely to be forgotten.

ics for
xpositive
egy

The detailed tactics that should be applied depend very much on the specific content to be taught and on the present state of knowledge and learning skills of the particular students. However, the category of principle to be taught also exerts some influence on the choice of tactics. As in the case of concepts, principles are taught by means of definitions and examples. If an expositive strategy is used, the principle (a particular cause-effect relationship, perhaps) is first defined and is then illustrated by applying it to specific cases or problems. The learner then shows his comprehension of the principle by applying it to yet other situations.

ics
in
riential
egy

If, however, an experiential strategy is to be implemented, the examples come first — in sufficient quantity and variety to enable the learners to 'discover' the general relationship that explains or governs the phenomena observed. The learning may be further reinforced by discussion of the relationship (or principle) discovered and its application to the prediction of the results of other similar situations in the future. This third stage of the experiential learning strategy, often called 'debriefing' when performed in case studies or simulations, is of great importance in ensuring transfer of learning.

Some authors have used the following labels to describe the two alternative sequences of instruction that may be adopted in the teaching of principles:

RUL-EG	and	EG-RUL
(rule followed by example)		(example leading to rule)

These terms were used in the early days of programmed instruction to describe specific ways of sequencing and writing 'frames' of self-instructional materials, but now they are in more general use since they summarize the main difference in tactics dependent on the initial choice of general strategy.

ics for
s of
re

In relation to rules or principles of nature, we see the contrast between these two tactics in the 'traditional' textbook-based approach to the teaching of sciences and the more 'progressive' experimental laboratory-based approach. In the first case the principles come first, to be learned from reading or through exposition by the teacher. If a laboratory is used, it is first used by the teacher, to demonstrate the principle that has been presented. Sometimes, the students then perform an experiment to verify the truth of the principle. More commonly, they pass straight on to the application of the principle in problem-solving. Often, this does not really step beyond the drill and practice of what has previously been presented by the teacher or the textbook, but in better planned systems it does lead to the transfer of the principle to an ever wider range of examples.

In the second case, the examples come first, usually in the form of a simulated research project, in which the students are required to observe and study certain phenomena until they manage to formulate the principle or principles that explain them. Then, in later discussion with the teacher, they refine their definition of the principles and apply them to other similar phenomena in hypothesis building exercises aimed at reinforcing the conceptual schema being formed and transferring the new learning to a wider range of examples. These discussions also serve to enable the teacher to evaluate the power of the conceptual schemata being formed by the students so that decisions may be taken concerning the next learning exercise.

Tactics for rules of action

With rules or principles of action, the tactics are similar to the case just described. Rules of action, or heuristics as they are often called, are even more dependent than rules of nature on learning through experience. We seldom seem to learn what is the right thing to do in certain circumstances simply by being told. It seems that we must be convinced of the soundness of the advice we receive, by experiencing the consequences of the correct, and incorrect, actions that we take. Thus, experiential techniques such as role-playing and all manner of simulation games are of particular value in this case.

There may be some exceptions to this general rule. For example, in the case of heurstics that govern our approach to the solution of certain categories of intellectual problems, we may learn quite effectively by receiving the rules ready-made, by means of some expositive technique, and then practise the application of the rules to given problems. If this were not the case, a book such as this one would be of little use to the teacher or the instructional designer, dealing as it does with the application of the systems approach, which is no more than a bundle of heuristics for planning and troubleshooting in large and complex human activity systems. *How to Solve It* (Polya, 1945) is an expositive account of the heuristic principles and strategies which may be used to facilitate creative problem-solving in mathematics. However, as Polya points out, such a book can only outline the principles and communicate a superficial understanding of how to put them into practice. A fuller understanding of how the principles apply in reality is gained through experience in attempting to apply them in real problem-solving situations.

Similarly, it is unlikely that anyone would master the full implications of the systems approach simply from reading about it. It is necessary to gain some experience in its application, at least by means of case studies, but preferably by experiencing real projects in which the approach is being applied.

The structure of a strategy

These examples — Polya's 'heuristics for mathematical problem-solving' and the 'heuristics for instructional design' outlined in Part 2 of this book — are examples of sets or schemata of interrelated principles. We may refer to them as *strategies*, that is, sets of organized principles that guide one's approach to certain classes of problems. One may develop a strategy for certain types of mathematical problems, for administrative problems, for certain types of human relations problems, etc. These strategies may be interrelated, thus forming complex conceptual schemata in the mind of the learner and creating more powerful, more general approaches to problem solving. The systems approach is one such complex schema, relating to so many areas of human activity.

We can conceive of strategies as being structured mainly from rules of action. For example, 'living a good Christian life' implies that the person concerned has adopted a set of principles that guide his activities and has welded them into a general approach, or strategy, to life.

The structure of a theory

When we attempt to explain phenomena, however, we are said to have a theory, that is, a certain way of welding together, or interrelating, a given set of relevant principles, or laws, of nature. We can therefore conceive of theories as being structured mainly from rules of nature.

Just as one Christian's life strategies may be somewhat different from another's, so two men's theories may link the same basic principles to form two quite different cognitive structures. For example, the theory of the propagation of light is based on a small set of observed principles: the laws of reflection, refraction, diffraction, etc. The cognitive structure in which the principles are embedded creates a powerful problem-solving tool, capable of transferring and applying the knowledge of the principles to a wide range of different problems. However, although the laws of reflection, refraction and diffraction have been known for centuries, the theories that interrelate these laws have changed several times. Once it was imagined that some substance or particles were emitted by the eyes, enabling us to see the objects on which they impinge. Later, the analysis of a wider set of phenomena showed the inadequacy of this theory and supplanted it by a theory which postulated the emission of a stream of particles from incandescent objects, which impinge on objects and are reflected and refracted, etc enabling us to see when the particles impinge on our eyes. Still later, the analysis of yet other phenomena uncovered principles that did not fit this theory, so scientists adapted their cognitive schemata, reorganizing the same, well-known, principles into a new schema – the 'wave' theory of light. The age of nuclear physics revealed yet other phenomena which could not be adequately accommodated in this view of the world, so still another adaptation occurred – the 'quantum' theory of light, which is in fact not that different from the older 'particle' theory, though constructed in a much more complex, mathematically sophisticated manner. Nowadays, the wave and quantum or particle theories of light coexist, since it is easier to explain certain phenomena in relation to one or other of these alternative views of the world. Thus, the two (once rival) theories have merged into one, more sophisticated and more powerful, schema of interrelationships.

The example reinforces our earlier comments concerning the teacher's role in the development of cognitive schemata. In a subject area such as light, there are certain generally accepted theories that structure the knowledge currently available. As new knowledge is discovered, these structures might change. However, at any one time, the currently accepted, most useful, schemata should be developed in the learner's mind. It is not very useful for the learner to be left to form any theory of light, regardless of whether or not it bears any relationship to the phenomena that surround him. This is not to say that the learner should be brainwashed into accepting the teacher's views. He should be encouraged to question the schemata of others – an activity that depends on the development of his skills of analysis, synthesis and evaluation. (We shall consider this aspect later.) However, the learner cannot usefully question what he does not understand. He should therefore first master the knowledge available and this also implies mastering the theories that structure this knowledge into coherent and useful schemata. Then, on meeting new phenomena that are difficult to assimilate into the currently accepted schema, he should be prepared to restructure his schema in order better to accommodate the newly acquired knowledge. In order to progress, one needs an understanding of currently accepted knowledge structures and intellectual skills that enable one to question these structures. Having one without the other leads to conflict – the type of conflict in evidence in cases such as the Flat Earth Society, the recent debate over the teaching of Darwinism in schools, the acceptance or non-acceptance of parapsychology as a respectable area of scientific study, or the various clashes that have occurred between supporters of rival theories of learning.

Once again, therefore, we stress the tactics that we consider important for the effective development of cognitive schemata. We should take pains to establish the most useful schemata for the organization of the knowledge currently available in the minds of our students. This can be done through expositive techniques, presenting the students with models of the structure of the available knowledge (as we have attempted to do visually in certain parts of this book), or through experiential techniques that lead the student to 'discover' the interrelationships that exist and structure his own schema. The final stage is the debriefing discussion which should evaluate and reinforce or correct the schema, thus ensuring its usefulness.

8.5 Tactics for teaching procedures

Procedures, as we have defined them in our schema, are a form of knowledge –

knowledge of the steps and the sequence of their performance required in order to execute a given task. The actual execution of the task will usually also require a certain amount of skill, an aspect that we will return to later. It is useful to distinguish between the knowledge and the skill content in a given procedure, as this gives us a clearer view of what instructional tactics should be used. A supervisor or manager will require to *know* how a given procedure should be executed, although he may not need to develop the skil required for execution of the tasks he supervises. The subordinate who executes a given task will require knowledge of the steps in perhaps greater detail, but may not require to know so much regarding the relationship of th task to other activities in the organization. He will, on the other hand, need to develop the requisite skills of execution.

The difference between strategies and procedures
The difference between a *strategy* and a *procedure* is important. Whereas a strategy is a schema of interrelated general principles, a procedure is a fixe sequence of steps that should be performed to achieve a given aim. The step normally followed to divide two numbers constitute a procedure. The principles and concepts that define the properties of numbers constitute a general 'theory of number' and embody one or more strategies for the analy and solution of number problems. In the modern mathematics approach, for example, emphasis is laid on conceptual understanding, on the derivation of procedures from first principles. In such a curriculum, a student might use his number theories and strategies to devise a procedure for the division of two numbers. Once devised and learned, however, this procedure, although derived by the use of concepts and principles relating to numbers, is in itself an item of factual information.

Chains and discrimin- ations
We can conceive of procedures as a series of associations of an 'if-then' nature: if such and such occurs, then do so and so. It is convenient to subdiv procedures into execution procedures, or *chains*, of if-then steps, and decisic making procedures, or *discriminations*, between alternative if-then steps.

We are using here the terminology used by many writers on instructional design, including Skinner, Gilbert, Mechner and Gagné. Many of these writer refer to chains and discriminations as two classes of *behaviour*. We, however, consider them to be two categories of *knowledge* that must be learned in order to perform (or to supervise and control) a given task. The observable results are always behaviours. We see the performer executing a chain of actions, and, at certain points in this chain, he may take decisions based on his ability to discriminate between the desirability of certain alternative actions. However, in order to do this, he must *know* the steps to be taken an the factors which influence the decisions that he may have to make. It is this element of knowledge of a procedure which interests us at the present stage of our analysis.

Tactics for the teaching of chains
We have already mentioned the tactics that are most appropriate for teaching a chain of steps. Generally, it is advisable to divide the learning task into stages, teaching one step at a time. However, there are several alternative models for structuring this step-by-step instructional process. The simplest is the 'parts' method, which treats each step separately, leaving the learner to li them up during a final practice session. A more effective approach is the 'progressive parts' method, which includes spaced practice sessions of ever greater parts of the whole task. Yet another approach is 'backward chaining' which introduces the last step of the procedure at the beginning of the learni process, gradually introducing the other steps from 'back to front' in success practice sessions. This last method was developed for the effective teaching a chain of activities to laboratory animals, being the only sequence which guarantees that all steps in the task are related conditionally to each other ar to the end result. The use of this tactic in the teaching of human beings, whe we can always supplement any practical demonstration or any reinforcemen of end results by verbal communication, is more dubious. However, the technique has been suggested as theoretically more rapid and motivational b

authors such as Mechner (1965) and Gilbert (1961) and has often been applied with success in the teaching of simple procedures.

In the preparation of a lesson on 'how to verify your income tax deduction' to be given to car factory workers, I found the backward chaining to be the most effective technique. Starting with the first steps — the calculation of taxable pay from gross pay — made it necessary to introduce a number of new concepts and calculations right at the beginning of the lesson, such as gross pay, net pay, allowances and dependants. These new concepts were difficult to teach as they did not appear to be very relevant to the learners at that stage of the lesson. The alternative sequence (which began by verifying the calculation on the pay stub and proceeded with analysing the data needed to make this calculation) succeeded in introducing all the concepts and calculations at appropriate points in the lesson, where they made sense to the learners because they were indispensable steps in the overall procedure. The shift of tactic was so significant as to turn a lesson which was normally considered boring and a complete failure in terms of learning results into an unqualified success, both in terms of learning objectives achieved and learner attitudes.

tics for ching crimin- ns

The appropriate tactics for teaching a discrimination procedure are quite different. Whereas in the case of chains the emphasis is on subdividing the learning task into a sequence of stages, this has to be avoided in the case of discriminations. Discrimination means recognition of the differences that exist between two or more possible conditions that might present themselves. If these conditions are never put side by side, it is more difficult to learn the differences that exist.

Some years ago, when the UK was about to change its system of currency, much effort was put into planning the retraining of various groups of workers, as well as the general re-education of children in schools, to prepare them for the forthcoming change. Various audiovisual materials were prepared, among them a sound filmstrip about the new (and as yet unissued) coins. This filmstrip presented photographs of all the new coins, both the obverse and the reverse sides, explained their values in relation to the old currency and put forward many arguments in favour of the change. However, the photos of the new coins were each presented in separate frames of the filmstrip. One never saw the coins contrasted one with another, nor compared with the existing coinage. The result was that whatever the viewers learned from the filmstrip, they did not learn to *discriminate visually* between the coins. They could not say which of the coins was the biggest or which the smallest. They did not realize that the new 10 and 5 pence pieces would be just the same size and shape as the existing two shilling and one shilling coins. These weaknesses could have been avoided by the simple expedient of showing, in at least some of the filmstrip's frames, the new coins together as a set, and in other frames the contrast, or the similarities, between the new coins and the old. This was tried in an amended version, with great improvement in terms of the learning of the necessary discriminations.

rse Code a case dy in use of diators d ucture

When there are just two or three items or alternative courses of action to discriminate, it is quite simple to present the necessary information all at once, rather than in separate steps, or stages, of the lesson. When the number of different associations to be discriminated is very large, it is much more difficult to do this. The Morse Code is an example of a very complex discrimination learning task, involving more than 30 very similar symbols, all made up of different sequences of dots and dashes. It is very easy to confuse the symbols. The most common approach to learning the code — as an alphabetically organized list of symbols — has not been found to be very efficient. Much research has been done to improve the teaching of the Morse Code, most of it sponsored by military institutions. One approach tried was the use of mnemonics. I myself once learned the code by means of a mnemonic alphabet, devised by the Polish Army. The principle of this learning aid was the matching of a word to each letter of the alphabet, so that the number of syllables in the word corresponded to the number of dots and dashes in the relevant Morse symbol. Furthermore, each dash was represented by a syllable containing the letter O, while the other syllables — not containing the letter O — each represented a dot. For example:

Letter	Mediating word	Morse symbol
A	A-ZOT	· —
B	BO-TA-NI-KA	— · · ·
C	CZOR-NA-HO-RA	— · — ·
D	DO-LI-NA	— · ·
E	ELK	·
F	FI-LAN-TRO-PI	· · — ·

and so on.

I still remember this code, although I have not used it since I left the Polish Scouts at the age of about 15. It certainly seems to be a powerful learning and memory aid. However, in practice, it is not as efficient as it might seem. The prop functions well when one has to *send* a message — each letter of the message to be codified triggers off the recall of the appropriate 'mediating word', which can then be transformed into the correct pattern of dots and dashes. In the case of *reception* and *translation* of a message, however, the aid hinders rather than helps the execution of the task. In comes a symbol on the radio earphones and I try to match it with the correct letter of the alphabet. Is it A? (AZOT is a dot followed by a dash.) No, it's not A. Is it B? This process of matching in alphabetical order cannot be carried out in the time available to act on the job. The alphabetical mnemonic only works in one direction — from a given letter to its symbol. One must get away from using the mnemonic in order to learn to receive Morse Code messages and decipher them correctly.

If one has to forget the learning aid in order to learn, perhaps it is as well to do without it in the first place. Perhaps a better learning aid can be devised: one that will work both ways. Such an approach was used in the design of a later learning aid. In order to be efficient in the transmission or the reception of coded messages it is necessary to associate each of the symbols with the correct letter in a more or less random order and at high speed. The greatest difficulty for most learners is in discriminating the more complex symbols, especially ones that are very similar to each other. Nobody has trouble in learning that E is represented by a single dot, but many people have difficulty in remembering whether C is — · — · or (perhaps) · — · —. One tactic that may be used to assist learning is to impose some form of structure on the subject matter. In the case of the Morse Code, this has been done by organizing the symbols into groups, so that those symbols which are particularly easily confused are learned together (see Figure 8.1 on p 113).

The whole Morse alphabet may be arranged into a series of more or less symmetrical shapes, as shown in Figure 8.1. These shapes aid the visual memorization of the differences between the symbols most often confused. The diagrams act as a form of visual mnemonic, which can be used in the early stages of learning, both for the transmission and reception of messages. Another important aspect of the tactic employed is that it manages to break away from the alphabetical order of learning that is usually followed for no reason other than the fact that our alphabet happens to be always presented in a fixed order. However, letters of the alphabet occur in random order in Morse reception, and it is of no help to the learner to learn to recite the symbols in a particular order. On the contrary, he must learn them so that he can access the correct symbol-letter association rapidly and in any sequence. Furthermore, the use of the visual structures allows the information to be presented to the learner all at once, as previously recommended on p 104. In its unstructured form, the list of 26 letter-symbol associations

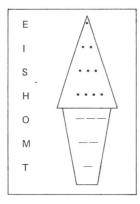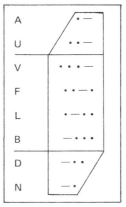

Figure 8.1 *Method of 'structuring' Morse Code*

and 10 number-symbol associations is perhaps too large to learn all at once. The structuring of the list, however, helps. A total of four or five diagrams can be presented, each composed of a set of similar and easily confused items that must be discriminated by the learner in order to perform the task of message codification/decodification effectively.

The instructional tactics embodied in the visual learning aid are thus much superior to the sequential mnemonic using mediating words which we illustrated earlier. Incidentally, the use of mnemonics, often referred to technically as mediators, is not to be frowned on for learning factual information. In later chapters we will see some examples of very effective use of this tactic. However, it happens that in this particular case the implied objectives of learning Morse Code condition the kind of tactics which are appropriate.

Most procedures are not pure chains of step-by-step, linear, progression. Nor do they generally consist only of discriminations. More often, they are a combination of chains and discriminations — actions to carry out and decisions to take. Such procedures are commonly referred to as algorithms. The characteristic of algorithms is that they are standardized procedures. As Landa (1976) states, *all people* using an algorithm for the solution of an appropriate problem will solve the problem *correctly* and *in the same manner*. There is no room left for doubt as to how to proceed. For this reason, we are justified in classing algorithms as a type of factual knowledge.

Generally, it is more appropriate to follow an expositive strategy when attempting to teach a particular algorithm. However, if the algorithm can be derived from certain general principles already known to the learner, it may be desirable to adopt an experiential strategy that leads the learner to construct the algorithm for himself. In the case of the example of long division discussed earlier, the instructional designer may well consider that it would be beneficial for the learner to derive the procedure from the basic concepts and principles of set theory, rather than receive it ready-made from the teacher. In deriving the algorithm, the learner will practise and reinforce his knowledge of set theory (benefit 1). Later, if through lack of practice he comes to forget some of the steps of the algorithm, he should be able to derive it again (benefit 2). It would not be so beneficial, however, to learn how to fill in an Income Tax form by means of an experiential strategy, as the algorithm involved is purely a man-made convention with no transfer value.

As all algorithms are combinations of chains and discriminations, the tactics we might use to teach an algorithm are the same as those discussed above. The decision points, which involve discrimination of at least two alternatives, should be so taught as to make quite clear the differences that exist. This usually requires the presentation of the alternatives in juxtaposition, as was mentioned earlier. If the actions to be executed are complex, made up of a chain of several steps, it may be necessary to break the instruction into parts, using one of the tactics mentioned earlier in our discussion of chains.

The use of an algorithm as a job aid

However, there are alternative tactics. When intending to use an expositive strategy with groups of learners whose study skills are reasonably well developed, it may be unnecessary to break the instruction into parts. A tactic that often proves effective is simply to give the algorithm to the learners as a form of job aid, to be used for reference during practice of the task to be learned. The learner, in due course, internalizes the algorithm, but in the meantime uses it as a memory aid whenever he needs to do so. This approach works best when the steps in the algorithm and the decisions to be taken are relatively simple and have already been mastered individually. Only the sequence of the steps is not known to the learner. For example, such an approach is sometimes used in teaching a doctor to diagnose certain groups of diseases. The doctor, from previous training, already knows how to apply the necessary tests, how to interview the patient and so on. What he must learn is the exact sequence of tests and questions that he should use in order to distinguish between similar symptoms and diseases. This information is contained in the algorithm, which he uses as a form of procedure guide. He may receive a whole manual of such guides. In time, he will memorize, through practice, those procedures that occur with reasonable frequency. In the case of rare diseases, which he encounters only from time to time, the doctor may never memorize the procedure, but may continue to use the relevant algorithm as a guide.

Breakdown of a complex algorithm to facilitate learning

When the actions and decisions that make up the algorithm are complex and not yet known to the learner, the 'whole presentation' tactic may not work. It may be necessary to divide the learning of the procedure into stages. Generally, these stages may be conveniently defined by analysing the main decision points.

It is usually easier to decide between alternatives if the alternatives are already known and understood by the decision-maker. For example, an engineer may wish to calculate the stresses in a given structure. He knows of four different procedures for calculating stresses in beams. In order to decide which of the four methods is most suitable for the given task, he should learn all four procedures, at least sufficiently well to understand how they work and what data they require. Similarly, a technician who is manufacturing a special component in a workshop may need to decide between the use of several available machines or several possible manufacturing procedures. To make a sound decision he must first have sufficient knowledge of each procedure, in order to match the characteristics of each procedure to the requirements of the project being executed.

For these reasons it is suggested that, in general, a complex procedure should be split at the key decision points, and the parts that follow a decision point should be taught before teaching how to make the decision. In Figure 8.2 (see p 115) the two chains 'A' and 'B' would be taught before teaching how to decide between them.

Figure 8.2 is a schematic representation of an algorithm made up of three chains, interlinked by one decision point, at which the performer must choose one of two alternative chains of action on the basis of the result of performing the initial chain of activities. At the decision point the performer must discriminate between the type of result that leads to alternative A and the type that leads to alternative B. In general, it is easier to make this discrimination once one has an understanding of the steps that make up the two alternatives. The suggested tactic for division of the learning task is, therefore, teach alternative A (or B, if this seems more convenient), then teach the other alternative chain and finally teach the initial chain that terminates at the decision point. During this last stage, the learner should go on past the decision point, practising the appropriate alternative, which was learned previously. Thus the training sessions always end with the completion of the task, with one or other of the possible outcomes as indicated on the algorithm. This has a beneficial effect on learning, as each training session is seen by the learner to have led him somewhere useful. This sense of achievement is not always present when a training session terminates midway through a procedure.

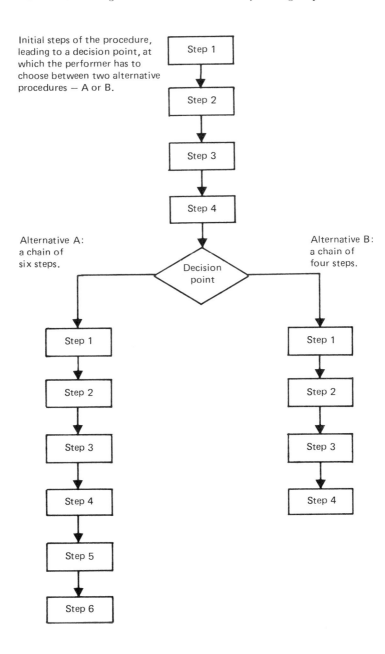

Figure 8.2 *Algorithm of a procedure with one decision point*

8.6 Conclusion

In this chapter, we have attempted an analysis of the structure of the possible knowledge content of a proposed system of instruction. As our basic analytic tool, we have used the schema of knowledge categories, which we developed earlier. This schema, based on the initial classification of knowledge as facts, concepts, principles and procedures, was extended and refined and several sub-divisions of each of the four basic categories were identified.

We observed, for example, that although one might use the same basic strategy for the teaching of any concept, the specific tactics might be quite different for concrete and for defined concepts. We also discussed how powerful cognitive schemata — theories and strategies — may be structured by the interrelation of relevant concepts and principles. We discriminated between *heuristic* problem-solving strategies and *algorithmic* procedures used for the resolution of standard problems and we have seen that the tactics of instruction are very different for each case.

However, the mere transmission of knowledge is rarely the ultimate objective of an instructional system. Generally, we also aim to develop certain *skills* in the use of this knowledge. Sometimes the knowledge is essential to be able to perform certain specific tasks, defined in the instructional objective. At other times, the knowledge may act as a 'store of experience' that enables general intellectual skills, such as problem analysis, hypothesis generation, or evaluation of alternatives, to be performed with success. In either case, however, the instructional designer should take into consideration the skills to be acquired when he is planning the detailed tactics for the teaching of knowledge.

For this reason, an analysis of the skills content of the proposed instruction should also be carried out. As an aid to this analysis, which should be appropriately detailed, we may use the skills classification schemata, developed earlier. This is the approach to the analysis of skills that we will discuss in the next chapter.

9. The Structure of Skilled Behaviour

9.1 Introduction

In Chapter 4, we presented a schema of skill categories. This divides skills into four major groups:

- ☐ Intellectual or cognitive skills.
- ☐ Physical or psychomotor skills.
- ☐ Reactive or self-control skills.
- ☐ Interactive or interpersonal skills.

Roughly speaking, these four categories deal with a person's abilities to:

- ☐ Control and use his mind.
- ☐ Control and use his body.
- ☐ Control his own emotions.
- ☐ Control or influence other people.

Reproductive
and
productive
skills

In addition to these major divisions, our schema suggests that skills can also be classified as:

- ☐ Reproductive or automated, reflex-type skills.
- ☐ Productive or creative, planning-type skills.

We suggested that, from the viewpoint of selection of overall instructional strategies, the productive-reproductive dimension is probably of greater importance than the basic four-category classification. There is more in common as regards the teaching of different creative skills, whatever their basic category, while there are marked differences between the teaching of creative and purely repetitive reflex-skills.

Effect of
skill content
on the
selection
of tactics

When we come down to detailed analysis of a skill, in deciding on the instructional tactics to be adopted, the specific content of the skill being taught assumes much greater importance, just as the specific nature of knowledge becomes more important when we investigate tactics for teaching it. The skills of dividing numbers rapidly, without making silly errors, or of typing with adequate speed and a low error rate, are both reproductive skills that may be developed by the same overall strategy — expositive teaching of the necessary knowledge content followed by plenty of 'drill and practice'.

The form and organization of the exposition will, however, be very different in the two cases. In the case of typing, practical demonstration of the various controls and the correct technique of 10-finger typing may be used. In the case of long division, we may choose one of the tactics mentioned earlier — presentation of the algorithm as a job aid to guide the drill and practice sessions, derivation of the algorithm from first principles by the learner, or demonstration of the process of derivation of the algorithm by the teacher in front of the class as a whole.

Long
division —
simple
cognitive
skill

The instructional tactics in the two cases will also be very different. A detailed analysis of long division reveals that problems differ both in complexity and in the level of difficulty. The content of the drill and practice sessions should be structured to include a range of problems that vary in both difficulty and complexity. The tactics of instruction should include some means of evaluating the level of a student's skill, and guiding him to new problems that gradually become more complex and more difficult. The instructional designer has the task of selecting or devising appropriate proble for the specific target students.

**Typing —
a simple
physical
skill**

In the case of typing skills, a different tactical problem faces the instructional designer. He needs to arrange graded practice at a series of spee levels, ensuring that the learner practises at a given speed until error rates are reduced to acceptable limits, only then proceeding to a faster speed of performance. There are, however, some further refinements that may be introduced. For example, in order to help the learner maintain a certain spee and a constant rhythm of work, some form of audible pacing may be supplie This is often done by means of music played in the rhythm that the typist should maintain. A more controllable pacing device, occasionally used in typing classes, is the metronome. Some sophisticated systems use specially recorded tapes of the exercises to be typed by the learner, together with the rhythmic ticking of a metronome, so that the learner need only listen to the tape and transcribe the content it presents without making any errors. Other aspects of the typing task may also receive special attention in the instruction design. For example, an analysis of skilled typists in action shows that they do not look down at the keyboard but use their eyes to monitor the results o their work and read the next passages to be typed. Poor typists, on the other hand, need to look down constantly to see what their fingers are doing. One training tactic often adopted is to use a 'blanked off' keyboard, either with th letters removed from the keys or with a screen interposed between the keyboard and the typist's eyes.

**Planning an
individualized
instruction
system**

These examples are sufficient to illustrate the importance of a detailed analysis of the specific skills to be taught, in order to incorporate all the essential tactics into the instructional design. The sophistication of the design depends on the available media and resources. The tactics mentioned in the examples above can easily be incorporated into normal classroom teaching. However, they may also form the basis of more complex instructional system The prerecorded typing exercises mentioned above may form part of an individualized course, of the type offered by the Sight and Sound typing schools in the UK.

Even more sophisticated systems may be developed, such as the SAKI keyboard trainer developed by Gordon Pask. This is a truly adaptive typing instruction system, developing individual sequences of exercises which relate to the learner's error pattern and response rate. The two-dimensional matrix of division problems may also form the basis of more sophisticated training systems. It was exactly on these lines that Patrick Suppes structured his first applications of computer-assisted instruction, in the drill and practice mode.

9.2 The skill cycle

**The four
stages of a
skilled
activity**

The previous section of this chapter illustrated the importance of the *content* of a skill for the selection of appropriate instructional tactics. Just as in the case of knowledge, the specific characteristics of what is to be learned must b considered and matched to existing characteristics of the target population. The difficulty level of a set of graded exercises is derived from an analysis of the content of the skill, and exercises are then selected to match the current skill level of the learners.

**The four
stages of a
skilled
activity**

We saw earlier that, in the case of knowledge, an analysis of the type of knowledge (using the categories of our schema) was a further aid to the selection of appropriate tactics. We shall now see that a similar approach may b used in selecting the instructional tactics to teach skills. We shall start by analysing, rather more closely, the structure of skilled activity. Any activity, whether intellectual, psychomotor, reactive or interactive, may be conceived as a *cycle* of up to four stages. These stages vary in importance, depending on the type and complexity of the skill.

The four stages are:

☐ *Perception* of the need to act.
☐ *Recall* of the necessary prerequisite knowledge of how to act/what to do.
☐ *Planning* of the necessary action.
☐ *Performing* the action as planned.

We can represent these four stages as a cycle, as shown in Figure 9.1 below. The dotted arrows show possible short cuts that may occur in certain categories of simpler skilled activity. For example, the fully skilled typist does not consciously recall the letter-finger associations every time she hits a key of the typewriter. The activity has become totally automatic — a *reflex* skill. The perception of the symbols to be typed immediately triggers off appropriate finger movements that lead to the performance of the task, as indicated by the direct arrow (from perception to performance). The proficient student, performing long division exercises, at high speed and with a low error rate, is following a somewhat more complex cycle of activity. When presented with a division problem (the stimulus to act), he *perceives* the problem, *recalls* the procedure — the algorithm — for long division, and applies it to *perform* the long division. His activity thus follows the dotted arrow in Figure 9.1.

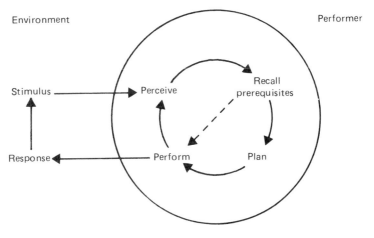

Figure 9.1 *The skill cycle: four principal types of internal activity may be involved in the execution of a skill*

Both these examples are *reproductive* skills, requiring little or no planning. The student confronted with a geometry or algebra problem that is new to him must, however, work out a specific procedure for solution. He will *perceive* the problem and the data given, *recall* appropriate concepts, principles and heuristics that appear to be relevant to the problem, use this recalled knowledge in order to *plan* an appropriate set of actions, and *perform* those actions to solve the problem. In this example, our student is proceeding full circle through all four stages of the skill cycle. This is a characteristic of the execution of *productive* skills. Such skills always require an element of creative planning.

In practice, however, people do not always perform an activity skilfully — the typist occasionally makes mistakes, although her overall performance shows that she has a full mastery of the keyboard; the student occasionally makes silly errors in performing long division, although it appears that he has learned all there is to learn; the mathematician does not solve all the problems

ᴜses of
ᴛning
ᴤciencies

presented to him with the ease and elegance that we expect from past performance. This leads us to believe that the performance of skilled activiti is somewhat more complex than might at first sight appear. It suggests that the instructional designer might do well to analyse the structure of skilled activity more closely, to identify the possible causes of error and of learning difficulty.

It appears that the old maxim that practice makes perfect is an over-simplification — mere repetition of the activity does not necessarily lead to higher levels of skill. Consider the foreigner who has lived in a country for 20 years but still speaks with a strong accent, despite full mastery of the new language and 20 years of practice. Compare his performance with that of his four-year-old son, who has had much less practice yet speaks with a perfect accent. Surely an analysis of such examples should reveal the causes of speci learning or performance difficulties, and should suggest appropriate instructional tactics?

Using the skill cycle as a basis, we may identify many possible causes of learning difficulty or poor performance. Some of these are presented in tabu form below:

(1) Perception	Inability to perceive the stimulus may be caused by a low level of perceptual acuity, as for example:
	☐ (Cognitive skill) — inability to 'see' a problem.
	☐ (Psychomotor skill) — inability to discriminate colour, tone, size, shape, etc to t degree necessary.
	☐ (Reactive skill) — inability to notice the signs and events occurring around one (a lack of attention).
	☐ (Interactive skills) — inability to notice the responses (including non-verbal responses) of other people.
	In all these cases the performer shows a low level of acuity in perceiving the necessary stimulus information even when that information is quite clearly presented. However, sometimes the information is not clearly presented. There are distractions. All manner other irrelevant information is being picked up as well (engineers call this 'noise'). Our performer may be adept at perceiving the stimulus when it is presented on its own, but may have trouble in picking it out in a 'noisy environment'. For example:
	☐ (Cognitive) — ability to notice punctuation error in a given single sentence, but inability to notice it when the sentence is part of a larger paragraph.
	☐ (Psychomotor) — the car driver who can identify danger signals in light traffic conditions but fails to identify them in heavy traffic conditions.
	☐ (Reactive) — the music lover who perceives opportunities to listen to good musi when directly invited, but fails to notice them in the general life of his communi
	☐ (Interactive) — the manager who can identify signs of employee insecurity in a specific interview situation, but fails to identify the same signs in a more general casual conversation.
(2) Prerequisites	Inability to recall prerequisites may be caused by a lack of these prerequisites. The performer simply does not know what to do in a particular situation. The relevant procedure has not been learned (or has been forgotten). The relevant principles that would enable him to invent or develop an appropriate procedure are not available from his memory store.
	Alternatively, the performer may fail to recall the relevant knowledge, although it i in store, due to a failure on his part to interpret the perceived stimulus information in the correct way. The new information is compared with the stored experience (knowle structures or schemata) and is misclassified. Thus the wrong procedure is recalled and applied:
	☐ (Cognitive skill) — a given Portuguese noun (the stimulus information) is misclassified as to gender; this leads to the recall of the wrong form of the adjec to be coupled to it.
	☐ (Psychomotor skill) — a given road sign is misinterpreted by the motorist, leadin the recall of an incorrect strategy.

	☐ (Reactive skill) — a student's examination errors are misinterpreted by the teacher as the result of laziness, leading to the development of an unduly negative attitude towards the student in question. This negative feeling (reaction) may later influence actions (interactions).
	
	☐ (Interactive skill) — the salesman who misinterprets a potential customer's reactions and as a result applies an inappropriate selling strategy.
	
	Thus we have two aspects involved in recalling prerequisite knowledge schemata, procedures or principles:
	
	    1. Ability to interpret the stimulus information in order to identify what knowledge is required.
	    2. Having that knowledge in memory store in a usable form.

nning	Inability to plan may also have two main causes. One is planning one's immediate actions. This involves considering the alternatives open to us and deciding among these. The causes of failure in the planning of an action, may be due to inability to generate the list of possible alternative courses of action, or to inability to make the best choice. The first implies inability to use the relevant principles in order to 'invent' alternative procedures (assuming of course that the relevant principles are in store). The second implies inability to evaluate the alternatives by thinking through the implications of each one. For example, the structural engineer may (or may not) come up with, say, four alternative solutions for the construction of a given bridge and he then may (or may not) select the most cost-effective solution. The manager faced with an industrial relations problem may (or may not) consider all the alternative courses of action open to him (eg sackings, warnings, suspensions, ignoring the problem, etc) and he may (or may not) evaluate correctly the hazards of each one (strikes, loss of productivity, etc).
formance	Inability to perform can also spring from two types of deficiencies — inability to initiate the necessary action or inability to 'see it through'. Assuming, once again, that the performer has perceived the stimuli, interpreted them correctly, recalled relevant knowledge, considered all the alternatives and decided which is the 'best' one, he may yet fail to perform. Examples: ☐ (Cognitive) — having 'seen' the problem (in, say, maths), the student works out the stages of the 'best' solution, but he does not actually work out the solution (due to lack of motivation, time, relevance, etc); alternatively, he begins to work it out, but gets bogged down in the detail of calculation and gives up (due to lack of persistence or mental stamina, etc). ☐ (Psychomotor) — the industrial operative responds as is expected, but his productivity/quality of work is below standard (due to deficiencies in strength, stamina, dexterity). ☐ (Reactive) — practical difficulties are encountered in attempting to live by one's values, leading to compromises. ☐ (Interactive) — a supervisor fails to initiate necessary disciplinary action (due to lack of moral courage) or fails to see it through correctly (due to lack of tact).

Table 9.1 *Some possible causes of learning difficulty or of poor performance of a skilled activity*

A study of the examples presented in Table 9.1 above leads us to construct a schema for the analysis of skilled performance. We may postulate four types of mechanism involved in the execution of any skilled activity (see Figure 9.2 on p 122).

    1. *Receptors* of stimuli to be perceived. In the case of most physical skills, these are principally the eyes and occasionally include other senses.
        In the case of intellectual activity, however, we must extend our notion of receptors to include the mechanisms inside the brain that enable us to perceive ideas and create visual images of abstract concepts — reason, logic, a sense of justice and many other intellectual 'senses'.
    2. *Memory:* the store of our current knowledge that may be called on to assist in the planning or performance of an activity. This store is organized in the form of structures that may be schemata for the

identification and classification of the stimuli perceived, algorithms f▪ execution of specific types of procedure or principles and heuristics for the planning of new procedures for new problem situations.

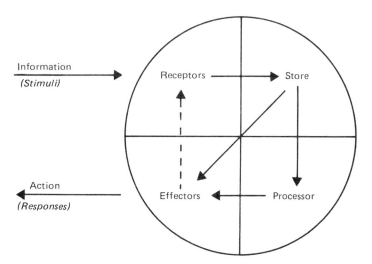

Figure 9.2 *A simple model of the performer: four principal types of internal mechanisms may be involved in the execution of a skill*

3. *Processor:* the intellectual mechanisms that enable one to think, analy▪ situations, generate or synthesize new ideas, evaluate the ideas and th▪ probable consequences of specific actions, devise new strategies, theo▪ and structures for our conceptual schemata.
4. *Effectors:* the mechanisms that actually carry out the actions require▪ In the case of physical skills these are our limbs and other parts of ou▪ body. In the case of intellectual skills we must once again extend our concept of effectors to include both the physical components of our brain and the psychological factors that occasionally inhibit our performance of certain actions (fear, lack of moral courage, low motivation, etc).

Basic abilities which may influence performance

Using this model of the performer, together with the observations listed in ▪ tabular form in Table 9.1 (see p 121), we may draw up a list of factors that may obstruct the efficient performance of a skilled activity. The 12 factors listed below may not all be equally important in a specific case, but researc▪ and experience show that they may contribute to learning and performance▪ problems and should therefore be taken into consideration when planning instructional tactics. These factors are valid for all four main categories of skill.

Receptors

1. *Attention.* Factors associated with the performer's ability to concentr▪ on the task in hand. Lack of attention will lead to vital information being missed.
2. *Perceptual acuity.* A lack of the necessary perceptual acuity will lead a loss, or a distortion, of stimulus information, even when the perforr▪ is fully attentive.
3. *Perceptual discrimination.* This refers to the ability to differentiate between what is and what is not important in the incoming stimulus information. In physical skills, it takes on importance when many things are happening at the same time and the performer should react to some but ignore others. In cognitive skills, it takes the form of

recognizing relevant and irrelevant information in a problem. In general, we may refer to this ability as being able to perceive what is relevant in a 'noisy environment'.

4. *Interpretation.* This ability implies that the performer has, within his memory, an adequate schema for the interpretation and classification of the information perceived. In the case of language and other symbols, this may be a factual schema. In the case of ideas, it would be an appropriate conceptual schema. The ability to interpret the incoming information thus depends on the present content and structure of the schemata stored in memory.

5. *Recall of procedures.* The ability to recall a specific algorithm suitable for the task perceived depends, naturally, on the prior existence of the algorithm, in a usable and recognizable form, in memory.

6. *Recall of a strategy.* The ability to select a suitable strategy for the resolution of a problem depends on the prior existence, in memory, of relevant principles — principles of nature and principles of action — which may be used in the planning of a procedure appropriate for the problem in hand. It is helpful if these principles are already related to each other, forming general theories and strategies that may guide the problem-solver.

7. *Analysis.* This ability permits the performer to break down a complex problem into its essential components and restructure it if necessary, in order better to understand it. It is essentially a form of general intellectual skill, used in any planning task.

8. *Synthesis.* This is the ability to create, construct or design new ideas, new structures, new strategies, etc, which enable the performer to generate alternative procedures to solve the problem in hand.

9. *Evaluation.* This is the general ability to choose between alternative courses of action and to foresee the consequences of a particular decision, etc. Evaluation, analysis and synthesis are general cognitive skills, necessary for all planning tasks, and are therefore involved in the efficient performance of any productive skill.

10. *Initiation.* This is the ability to act on the decisions taken. Analysis of a problem often results in the formulation of a plan, which is, however, not put into action because of some other inhibiting factor. The ability to overcome such inhibitions is referred to as 'initiation'.

11. *Continuation.* Once initiated, the actions required to perform the skilled activity may come to a premature halt, because of fatigue, boredom, growing opposition from other people, or some other negative factor. Continuation enables us to overcome these factors and to see the task through.

12. *Control.* Control closes our cycle. It is the ability to monitor the results of one's actions and correct any errors or shortcomings. This ability closes the cycle in the sense that it depends on constant attention to the progress of the task in hand, perceptual acuity and discrimination to identify potential difficulties as they arise, interpretation of the reasons for the difficulty, etc to recall of other relevant knowledge, further planning and, perhaps, re-initiation of action.

These 12 abilities may not be the only ones that influence the performance of a specific skill. However, they are the most commonly encountered ones, being present in all types of skilled activity, whether psychomotor, cognitive, reactive or interactive. Not all of the 12 factors are of equal weight in each case and the abilities of analysis, synthesis and evaluation are not relevant to the majority of reproductive skills.

It is useful to remember these 12 basic abilities when analysing the causes of learning and performance problems. We may structure the abilities in the form of an 'expanded skill cycle' (see Figure 9.3 on p 124).

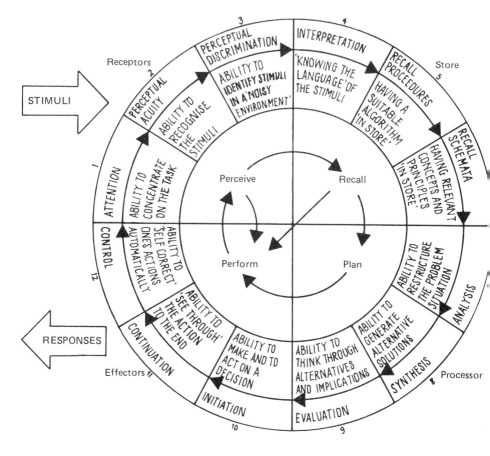

Figure 9.3 *The expanded skill cycle*

9.3 Using the expanded skill cycle — examples

The following section presents a series of sample analyses, which illustrate how the expanded skill cycle may be used as an analytical tool. We will also indicate how this analysis may be used as the basis for the selection of appropriate instructional tactics.

9.3.1 Typing

A reproductive psychomotor skill As we have already seen, typing is a reproductive, psychomotor skill. We shall now somewhat deepen our analysis, using the 12 basic abilities of our new schema as a basis for organizing our comments.

The importance of attention 1. *Attention:* highly critical. Good typing depends on a high level of attention to the task being performed, even though this attention may not be conscious. The good typist may carry on a discussion with a colleague about some matter totally divorced from the content of the material being typed, without any appreciable reduction in typing efficiency, as long as the conversation does not become so absorbing that the typist's eyes are taken away from the page being typed. Due care should therefore be taken in the training programme to develop adequate skills of concentration. The use of a fixed rhythm of work, imposed by music or a metronome, may help to develop a habit of concentrated rhythmical work which will assist in the maintenance of attention for considerable periods of time. Other tactics that may be used are teaching typists to set short-term goals (for example, a set number of pages per hour) and to execute the work as a form of competition with themselves. Of course, training is not the whole answer to this problem. The maintenance of attention on the job is influenced by many environmental factors, such as noise, lighting, working hours and external distractions.

2. *Perceptual acuity:* mildly critical. It is, of course, important for the typist to have good eyesight in order to be able to perceive the material to be typed. But this should be assessed at recruitment stage and it is something which cannot be rectified by training.

3. *Perceptual discrimination:* marginal. It is important that the typist can discriminate between similar but different letters. In the case of typed or clearly written material, this is a relatively simple matter. However, in the case of much handwritten material, the typist must have an exceptional level of ability in deciphering handwriting. Whether this is an aspect that should be included in a typist's training programme is debatable. Perhaps we should really train managers to write more clearly! However, there is no doubt that typists differ in this deciphering skill, so some effort to teach it might pay off. However, an analysis of this skill suggests that it depends to a large extent on the interpretation of the context of a particular word. We therefore enter the next sector of our schema.

4. *Interpretation:* generally not critical. With the exception of deciphering, it is not generally important for the typist to interpret what is being typed. It is for this reason quite possible for a copy typist to produce good typed copy in an unknown foreign language (which uses the same alphabet and keyboard). These comments refer, of course, to the pure skill of copy typing. This does not apply to the typist who must compose a letter, or plan an aesthetically pleasant layout.

5. *Recall of procedures:* not critical. Typing, being an automated reflex skill, does not rely on the recall of any specific procedures during its execution. The memory and the processor are not directly involved in the execution of the task. Once again, this does not apply to subsidiary tasks, such as changing the ribbon and lining up a set of columns in a typed table.

6. *Recall of strategies:* not critical. The recall of general problem-solving strategies is even less relevant in the case of a reflex skill such as typing. No planning is necessary to carry out the basic task of typing a given text. Once again, however, this may not be the case for some of the subsidiary skills that a typist must have. For example, laying out text depends on the application of some general principles that relate the ratios of margins to text and paragraphing. However, we are now talking of skills other than pure typing. These skills require their own analysis, in order to reveal the tactics required.

7. *Analysis:* not critical. For reasons already outlined, little or no planning is involved in the execution of typing. Therefore the ability of analysis is not critical.

8. *Synthesis:* not critical (see 7).

9. *Evaluation:* not critical (see 7).

10. *Initiation:* possibly critical. Nothing is 'threatening' in the task of typing, so we might expect the typist to get on with the job in a businesslike manner. However, in some working environments there may be hidden threats or hidden motivators that inhibit the typist's performance. For example, the norms and customs of work in a given office might discourage 'overproductive' work. Alternatively, the unwitting

ning
is not
vant

design
tors may
ibit good
formance

over-burdening of the best typists with extra work when the pressure is on may lead to a reduction in their productivity. Although this problem is not best dealt with through instruction, one might attempt to do something during the training to induce a level of 'pride in the profession' that may help the future typist to resist inhibiting factors encountered in the workplace. Tactics that may be employed in this context are similar to those used in any other case of attitude formation — the systematic reward of good workmanship (through internal competitions and points systems) and the setting of a good professional example. At least at the moment of completing training, it is hoped that the new typist has a sense of professionalism that is needed to initiate good workmanship.

The fatigue factor

11. *Continuation:* critical. In common with any other psychomotor skill, typing is an activity that may be tiring and it is therefore subject to a fall in productivity with time. The typist must build up the necessary level of stamina. This is one ability where, in general, it is true that practice makes perfect. However, the spacing and timing of the practice sessions have a considerable influence on the overall results. The instructor should plan the practice sessions carefully, to avoid undue fatigue in the early sessions, but with increasing frequency and extent, in order gradually to develop the learner's resistance to fatigue. Attention should also be given to correct posture and finger technique, to eliminate habits that produce tiredness at the beginning of training.

12. *Control:* highly critical. Good typing depends on the constant monitoring of the typewritten copy by the typist. Errors that are observed immediately after being typed are much easier to correct than those spotted when the page has been typed. Poor typing techniques use the eyes too much when studying the original being copied, or, worse still, when looking down at the keyboard, with the result that errors are not observed immediately. The instructional design should encourage the typist to look at the final work to spot any error as soon as it is made.

Tactics for the control of typing errors

Tactics that may help include the blanking off of the symbols on the keyboard, to reduce the habit of watching one's fingers, and the use of audio typing sessions. These may, in the initial stages of training, be made up of the dictation of a series of letters and other symbols (rather than words) presented in the rhythm that the typist is to maintain. Graded use of such prerecorded tapes may quickly develop a high level of rapid, error-free, typing.

9.3.2 Long division

A reproductive cognitive skill

This example has been discussed earlier. It is an example of a reproductive, cognitive skill. However, unlike typing, it is not a wholly reflex skill, as it depends on recall from memory and the correct application of a specific algorithm. This algorithm has to be applied with care, in order to solve any long division problem, whatever its level of difficulty and complexity.

Motivate and interest the learner to gain his attention

1. *Attention:* critical. The ability to concentrate on mathematical tasks is conspicuously lacking in some students, and this adversely influences their level of performance. Tactics that may be used to improve attention levels include the development of interest in mathematics, through motivational presentations of relevant problems, choice of difficulty levels that neither bore nor defeat the student, and the use of the game element in competitions or in interactive practice exercises now available for use on microcomputers.

2. *Perceptual acuity:* not critical. It is important that the student should have visual perception to see the problems on the page, but this is hardly a problem to be dealt with by instruction. The ability to recognize

numbers and mathematical symbols, whether written symbolically or expressed in words, is important and forms part of the prerequisite knowledge that must be in store in the learner's memory. The perceptual aspects of symbol recognition are usually learned some time before the student starts to study long division. It is rarely necessary to devise special instructional tactics at this point.

ach the
rner to
e the
oblem

3. *Perceptual discrimination:* of some importance. Although the signs and words that signify a division problem coming up may be well known to the student they may not always be easily perceived when embedded in the context of a problem, especially in the case of problems expressed in words. Expressions such as 'the three sons are to get equal shares of the money left in the will' may not immediately be perceived as a division problem, because of the 'noise' created by the irrelevant information given in its presentation. Exercises that give practice in perception of the nature of verbally stated problems should be included in the instructional design.

evelop a
hema of
e facts
d concepts
volved

4. *Interpretation:* highly critical. Perception skills are dependent on the presence of adequate schemata of facts and concepts related to division, multiplication, etc. The student must have the ability to interpret the problem as one of division, and, furthermore, must identify what is to be divided by what. He must have factual knowledge of the symbolic conventions used, for example that the number before the division sign is divided by the number that comes after. He also needs conceptual knowledge to interpret more complex problems.

ıpart
ıowledge
the
ocedures

5. *Recall of procedures:* highly critical. The skilful performance of long division depends on the error-free recall of the procedure. This procedure must be in store in a readily recallable form as a result of prior learning. The procedure may be taught by expositive or experiential means. At the stage of skill development, however, it must be in memory and retrievable. The tactics at this stage are concerned with verifying that the procedure is remembered and applied, correctly and quickly. A sufficient variety of graded problems should be arranged, to develop the necessary skill. Some of the recently introduced, microcomputer-based drill and practice arithmetic programmes are particularly well designed in terms of their tactics for skill development. (We shall examine some of these in later chapters.)

6. *Recall of strategies:* not relevant. In the case of a reproductive, algorithm-based skill, such as long division, there is no need to plan or use any general problem-solving strategy.

7. *Analysis:* not relevant (see 6).

8. *Synthesis:* not relevant (see 6).

9. *Evaluation:* not relevant. This may seem strange, as mathematics always seems to deal with the evaluation of various quantities. However, the sense in which we are using the term — to define a particular type of intellectual activity — is not the sense given to the term in mathematics. To calculate the value of — 'evaluate' in maths — is not the same as to assess the worth, validity or possible consequences of something — our meaning of the term evaluate. In the latter sense, evaluation is not used in long division. (Except, that is, in the checking of the validity of the result obtained. We shall, however, deal with this under item number 12 — control.)

void
xercises
hich are
unishing or
ıreatening

10. *Initiation:* of some importance. The student from the beginning may completely reject mathematics, or he may be inhibited because he fears making a mistake in the presence of his classmates, or being punished by the teacher. Whereas these fears are usually consequences of learning deficiencies, it is important not to increase anxieties by introducing punishments or other demotivating factors into the practice sessions.

11. *Continuation:* marginal. As in the case of physical skills, repetitive

intellectual activities can also be very tiring. If it is necessary for student to persevere for long periods, calculating large numbers of division problems (itself of dubious value in this age of cheap calculators), it would be worth planning some stamina-building exercises, based on progressively longer, timed practice sessions on long division. Few teachers, however, would now consider this type of activity useful, and the time is better spent on other aspects of the skill.

Teach methods for estimating the expected result

12. *Control:* highly critical. The greatest time-wasting aspect of some mathematics practice sessions is the repetitive practice of a wrong procedure. The most powerful instrument to avoid such useless and dangerous practice is the ability to see that the calculation is going awry. The ability of control, in this context, closes our cycle of activity. It depends on close attention to the results of each stage of the calculation, immediate perception of results that seem wrong, checking back to interpret the causes of the error and re-application of the correct procedure, if necessary. This ability to control one's own performance is critical. Tactics that may be used to develop it include the teaching of rough approximation techniques to assess the type of result expected.

9.3.3 Courteous treatment of customers

This example introduces a simple, mainly reproductive, interactive skill. To put it into a more specific context, let us imagine that we are involved in the design of training for telephonist/receptionists in a large organization. The skill that concerns us here is courteous treatment of customers which means that staff must use a pleasant tone of voice at all times, show a cooperative attitude and an interest in the customer's problem, arrange comfortable conditions in the case of unavoidable waiting, explain any delays, be polite and courteous, keeping an even temper even when customers are irritating or aggressive.

1. *Attention:* highly critical. In order to attend to the customer's needs, it is obviously necessary to pay attention to what he says and how he acts. Many receptionists do not pay sufficient attention. Training tactics might include quiz sessions, analysis of films, or role-plays of typical situations to identify the aspects to which the receptionist should react. Other tactics, more directly related to the job itself, should make it genuinely important for the receptionist to offer an attentive service.

Ability to recognize non-verbal signals of customer dissatisfaction

2. *Perceptual acuity:* highly critical. Some signs of customer impatience are not easy to perceive without some training in the language of non-verbal communication. This perception is strongly linked to the interpretation of a customer's state of anxiety or dissatisfaction. The skill often referred to as empathy depends on the perception of another person's unstated feelings.

Ability to deal with several people at once

3. *Perceptual discrimination:* often critical. When a receptionist has to deal with a number of people at the same time, the difficulty of perceiving signals of customer dissatisfaction increases. In such cases, the instructional design should include simulations of situations in which several people have to be attended to. These simulations may be recorded on videotape for later analysis and feedback.

Knowledge of the structure of one's organization

4. *Interpretation:* highly critical. If the receptionist is unable to interpret the customer's wishes, she is likely to displease him. In addition to the conceptual schemata necessary to interpret signs of impatience the receptionist must know the structure of the company, the principal departments and services, and, in particular, the structure, products and services, jobs and even individual employees of the department in which she works. This is prerequisite knowledge for the job. The minimum necessary knowledge should be derived from a task analysis performed in the department. The tactics at the skill development stage should

concentrate on giving the receptionist ample practice in using this knowledge in job situations. Once again, simulation exercises in some form are probably useful.

nowledge
standard
fice
ocedures

5. *Recall of procedures:* usually critical. Most organizations have specific procedures to be followed when receiving guests. These may include security procedures, form-filling procedures, even industrial safety procedures. These must be in store ready to be recalled and applied at the appropriate moment. Unusual, rarely used procedures may not need to be memorized, but may be recalled from a handbook. However, the need to follow the procedure must be recalled. In addition, such 'procedures' of good manners as saying good morning and offering a cup of coffee to a waiting customer, although not forming part of the official rule book, should also be recalled and applied at appropriate moments. While all of these procedures are knowledge that may be learned in classroom sessions, the correct application of the procedures at the correct moments constitutes an element of the receptionist's skill that should be practised in appropriate practical exercises.

ttle call
r creative
oblem-
lving

6. *Recall of strategies:* not critical. With the possible exception of some general principles of human relations that might help the receptionist to keep her cool, it would not normally be expected of the receptionist to master any general problem-solving strategies that might be used to persuade a difficult customer to cooperate, or to sell a product or service to a reticent customer. These are tasks which do not form part of the receptionist's job description. Her job is largely made up of repetitive activities which involve low-level, procedure-based skills.

7. *Analysis:* not relevant. For the reasons stated in 6, the intellectual capacity for analysis of problem situations is not relevant to the receptionist's job.

8. *Synthesis:* not relevant (see 6 and 7).

9. *Evaluation:* not relevant (see 6 and 7).

10. *Initiation:* not critical. Although it may be necessary to exercise a certain amount of self-discipline and moral courage in order always to start a conversation in a courteous manner, especially during a difficult day or with a customer who has proved problematical in the past, this does not generally require special training exercises.

eed for
e ability
resist
rovocation

11. *Continuation:* highly critical. It is much more difficult to continue to treat customers in a courteous manner when they become aggressive, make a pass or behave in some other objectionable manner. Under these circumstances, it is crucial for the receptionist to exercise self-control and to have the courage necessary to maintain a courteous manner. Training tactics should be devised to give off-the-job practice to develop this important ability. Such practice may be incorporated into well designed role-play exercises, devised to try to 'break the receptionist's cool'.

eed
develop
e capacity
r self-
nprovement

12. *Control:* highly critical. This ability is critical in almost any skilled activity. As seen in the earlier examples, it implies constant monitoring of the job and, in particular, of the receptionist's own behaviour, perceiving signals of poor performance, interpreting their causes and modifying actions as necessary. The chief tactic used to develop this ability is the regular analysis of problems that have occurred, either in simulated off-the-job exercises or in real-life on-the-job situations.

9.3.4 Manufacturing a one-off component

xample of
complex,
ulti-skilled
tivity

In order to explain the context of this example, we shall define the task in the form of a clearly defined performance objective:

Given a technical drawing of a one-off component to be manufactured in the workshop, together with all the necessary critical dimensions and material specifications, the student will manufacture the component, using the most appropriate processes and the most appropriate, convenient and efficient machine tools available, to the required criteria of dimensions, overall quality of surface finish, manufacturing time, economical use of raw materials and economical use of power.

It is obvious from this statement of objectives that this is a complex skilled activity, composed of several different types of skills. The operation of certain machine tools may involve reproductive, psychomotor skills, while the planning of the manufacturing process to achieve the criteria of speed and economy will require the use of productive, intellectual skills. The following analysis will necessarily be somewhat superficial, in order to be brief. It does, however, illustrate the analysis of a productive skill which is rather more complex than the examples studied so far.

1. *Attention:* highly critical. The ultimate quality of the work and also the safety of the worker depend in large part on the attention he gives to the work in hand. Tactics for the development of the capacity for attention to machine-minding tasks may have to be included in the training design.

Possible need for special perception training exercises

2. *Perception:* highly critical. Most work with precision and high-speed machinery requires high levels of perceptual acuity, usually visual, in order to read measurements, observe tolerances and control surface finish quality. In some cases, other sensory perception is also important, for example awareness of the sound made by a blunt cutting tool, or of the vibration of an out-of-balance machine. Other tasks require specially developed levels of kinaesthetic sense to perceive when the job is being performed correctly by means of the 'feel' of correct muscular coordination. All these special perceptual abilities need to be developed by means of appropriate exercises. These may often involve special off-the-job perception training exercises.

3. *Discrimination:* sometimes critical. Some machines are relatively simple and do not pose problems of discrimination between relevant and irrelevant information. However, some complex machines tend to create a 'noisy environment', with many things happening at once, making it difficult to identify the important signals. A full task analysis of such work would be required to identify the sources of confusion and devise suitable training tactics.

Essential to develop the necessary cognitive schemata

4. *Interpretation:* highly critical. In reading technical drawings, the student uses schemata of the symbols and conventions used (symbolic information). The interpretation of materials requirements, of machine defects, or of errors in the manufacturing process, may require the use of appropriate conceptual schemata. This necessary prerequisite knowledge will be learned through appropriate tactics. The skill of applying this knowledge correctly will be developed on the job, or, better still, by means of specially prepared training exercises – games involving the rapid reading of technical drawings, or simulations that require 'troubleshooting' to spot errors and defects.

Need to practice procedures of machine operation

5. *Recall of procedures:* highly critical. The operation of machine tools is based on following many fixed procedures – for starting up, setting up the work, etc. Some of them, when not practised regularly, may not need to be memorized, but may be looked up in job-aid manuals as required. Other, frequently practised, or high-speed, procedures should be memorized, and the skills of rapid recall and error-free application should be practised on the job.

Importance of developing job planning strategies

6. *Recall of strategies:* highly critical. In order to select the most economical sequence of manufacturing processes and the most effective machine tools, the student must apply various general principles, usually organized into specific job planning strategies. Once the basic principles are learned, by

means of tactics appropriate for the type of knowledge, the development of the planning skills depends on the critical analysis of the results of specific plans. This may be done prior to practice, by means of case studies, and immediately after practice, in special debriefing sessions with the instructor and other learners.

Essential to develop problem-solving skills

7. *Analysis:* highly critical. The intellectual ability of analysis comes into play at all stages of planning and controlling the manufacturing process.
8. *Synthesis:* highly critical. Also involved in the stages of planning of the manufacturing process.
9. *Evaluation:* highly critical. Essential for planning and control of the work.
10. *Initiation:* not very critical. Students who opt to study practical subjects are generally interested in practical work and are motivated to 'learn in order to earn'. No initiation problems are anticipated.
11. *Continuation:* may be critical. Some machine operation tasks are tiring and take a long time to complete. This may lead to boredom and a tendency for performance standards to drop. However, in the case being analysed here, the probability of continuation problems occurring is low, as the job is non-repetitive (a one-off component) and involves a variety of operations, as well as some intellectual and planning activity.

Develop the habit of checking work

12. *Control:* highly critical. As in all skilled activity, the ability to monitor one's own performance and perceive errors or defects before it is too late to correct them is of great importance. It is developed indirectly in briefing and debriefing sessions designed to develop the abilities of analysis, synthesis and evaluation and may be promoted directly by installing a systematic monitoring procedure to be executed as the job progresses. This may take the form of a checklist, to be completed as each stage of the manufacturing process is completed. This brings any defects to immediate attention.

9.3.5 The punctual executive

Good timekeeping — two skills in one

This last example is included to illustrate the analysis of a self-control or reactive skill, although other sub-skills are also involved in the execution of the activity. Once again we explain the activity to be analysed by stating its objective:

Given a series of appointments and other engagements to be kept, together with an estimate of the probable unexpected commitments that may arise, the trainee executive will plan and execute a personal daily workplan of activities, which meets criteria of feasibility of execution in the time available, sufficient flexibility to be adaptable to unpredictable events and compatibility with the workplans and commitments of other employees who will be involved.

This statement of objectives clearly indicates the need for two skills — the *planning* skills of preparing an adequate workplan and the *personal, self-control* skills needed to keep to the prepared plan. In the analysis which follows, we shall clearly see the differences in required abilities for these two basic skills.

Pay attention to the daily agenda and to the clock

1. *Attention:* not critical for planning. The task of preparing a workplan is an intellectual skill, involving a certain amount of productive planning. It does not require unusually high levels of attention. But attention is highly critical for execution. The task of keeping to the timetable specified in the workplan requires a considerable degree of attention to the passing of time. It is very easy, without noticing until it is too late, to let a given appointment eat into the time allocated to other activities.

Viable agenda depends on perception of time required for given tasks

2. *Perception:* highly critical for planning. The task of preparing a workplan requires the ability to estimate the probable time required for different engagements. Although some estimates may be made by calculation, many are 'guesstimates', or perception of time requirements. This skill is not

very critical for execution. It is necessary to 'perceive' the hour, but this only depends on adequate attention to the clock.

3. *Perceptual discrimination:* fairly critical for planning. In the intellectual sense of discriminating instinctively between more and less pressing engagements, this ability has some relevance in the planning of the day's timetable. It is not critical for execution — one merely needs to follow the predetermined plan.

4. *Interpretation:* fairly critical for planning. The executive may need to memorize some form of conceptual schema to assist him in the classification of commitments in order of importance. It is not critical for execution.

5. *Recall of procedures:* not critical. There may be a need to follow some procedures for the planning or layout of workplans, but these are likely to be simple and will not create learning problems for the typical executive. The procedure for execution of a workplan merely depends on the periodic checking of the time and the plan.

Planning a schedule involves some degree of problem-solving

6. *Recall of strategies:* critical for planning. The preparation of a viable and convenient workplan depends on the application of certain principles of time-planning. It is not critical for execution. No general principles are applied in order to execute a predetermined timetable.

7-9. *Analysis, synthesis and evaluation:* fairly critical for planning. As there are some planning principles to be applied, and a certain amount of creative adaptation to the commitments to be met, there is some need for intellectual abilities of analysis, synthesis and evaluation. However, the difficulty level is not very high, and is unlikely to be above the level of skill of most executives. These factors are not critical for execution. There is no creative planning involved in executing a time-plan.

Keeping to schedule requires some degree of self-control

10. *Initiation:* not critical for planning. Most executives, at some time or other, start to plan their time in a systematic manner. There is no great difficulty in getting them involved. Initiation is highly critical for execution, on the other hand, as all manner of factors may inhibit an executive when it comes to cutting short an interesting meeting, or dismissing an unexpected, but important, guest. The ability to close a meeting is of great importance to the effective execution of a time-plan.

11. *Continuation.* highly critical for planning. Although most executives start to plan their time, few manage to continue to do so on a regular and systematic basis over long periods. The intellectual 'stamina' necessary to continue a routine daily task such as work planning may need to be developed through appropriate exercises. Continuation is not critical for execution. Once, however, the necessary action to terminate a meeting on time has been initiated, it is usually fairly easy to see it through to the end. Sometimes, however, the executive may falter in the face of strong requests from the other participants for the meeting to continue.

12. *Control:* critical for both skills. The ability of self-control of one's performance supplies the feedback necessary to observe what caused problems in the execution of a given workplan, thus producing the data needed to improve both the planning and execution of future plans.

9.4 Conclusion

The examples presented above should be sufficient to illustrate that the skill cycle, in its extended, 12-ability form, may be used to analyse any category of skilled activity and to assess both simple and complex skills. The more complex and multi-faceted the skill being analysed, the greater the number of abilities that appear as critical for competent performance. This does not always lead to more complex instructional designs, however, as the same training exercise may serve to develop a number of different abilities. The main requirement is to incorporate tactics that help to develop all the essential, or critical, abilities.

10. A Model for the Preparation of Lesson Plans

10.1 Introduction: a lesson planning chart

In earlier chapters, we have stressed the use of instructional objectives as a means of ensuring quality control in the later stages of the instructional design process. We shall therefore base our lesson planning model on the systematic use of the instructional objectives defined at the first and second levels of the design process.

he three
ements in a
esson plan

We have characterized the instructional process as a two-way process of communication between the learner and the instructional system. This system may be just an instructor, with some communication aids, or it may be a complex and perhaps automated individualized package. Whatever the form of the system, it only merits consideration as a true instructional system if it is capable of activating all three channels of communication, as illustrated in Figure 10.1 below.

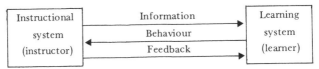

Figure 10.1 *The three channels of communication*

Our lesson plans should therefore specify:

1. What information should be communicated to the learner.
2. What behaviour or response should be exhibited by the learner to indicate that the desired learning has taken place.
3. What feedback or corrective actions should occur, if the learner has not learned as expected.

The majority of lesson planning systems emphasize the first of these three elements — the specification of the information to be communicated. They are content oriented. They make little mention of the instructional process to be adopted (usually a one-word label, such as exposition or discussion), and say nothing regarding the feedback or recycling activities that the instructor might need to perform.

In order to avoid what is in our view a distortion, which places undue emphasis on the instructor's actions, we suggest that lesson planners should use the following type of planning chart, divided into three columns:

Information	Behaviour	Feedback

The following alternative way of defining the columns is used by some psychologists:

Stimulus	Response	Reinforcement

These three columns are used to describe, in detail, each step of the proposed lesson. It may not always be necessary to write something in each of the columns for every step of the lesson, but the form of the planning sheet reminds the instructional designer to take into account all three components of the instructional process. If a column is left blank at any particular step of the lesson, it is because the instructional designer has deliberately decided tha there is no need to specify any special activity at this point.

Use of objectives as a basis for lesson planning

We should now recall the content of Part 2, especially the preparation of instructional objectives and their use as a framework for an overall, macro leve instructional plan. If this instructional plan has been prepared in sufficient detail, we may already have a list of specific, intermediate objectives for every lesson that we plan to give. These objectives may indeed already be sequenced so that an outline of the *intention* of each lesson already exists. When the overall instructional plan has been prepared in rather less detail, we may be able to extract from it only the terminal objectives of each lesson, and will need to perform further analysis and sequencing of the intermediate, or enabling, objectives at this stage.

Specific tactics for each specific objective

Once we have established the lesson objectives and their probable instructional sequence, we may begin to plan the details of the lesson — the tactics to be adopted to achieve the proposed objectives. Our overall instructional plan will be of some help here, as we have already considered the general strategies that should be employed in each lesson, the techniques that appear appropriate and the resources — instructional media, support equipment and time — to be devoted to each part of the plan.

In Chapters 8 and 9 we have seen how an analysis of the structure of the knowledge and skills content of the proposed lesson may lead to the identification of specific tactics that may be necessary to offer the right type of practice, guidance or feedback, or to overcome some specific type of learning difficulty commonly encountered by students. The knowledge and skills content required for each objective was defined in our overall instructional plan (see Chapter 6), so, using the ideas presented in Chapters 7 to 9, we are ready to plan our lessons.

When completed, the lesson planning charts will give a very detailed, step-by-step description of all the activities that should occur during the lesson — both the activities of the learners as well as those of the instructor. We shall have something resembling a script of the proposed lesson, specifying in full detail every scene in its correct sequence. The script falls short of specifying the exact words the instructor will use, but it is nevertheless a very detailed plan of the instructional events that will take place during the lesson.

Why plan lessons in such detail?

This approach to lesson planning may seem too detailed and too troublesome. After all, the majority of teachers survive on the basis of much less detailed lesson plans. Many enter the classroom with no written plan, but just an idea of the topic that they plan to teach. (Admittedly, with such scanty preparation, they do not always give very effective lessons.) It is, however, true that many instructors put in quite creditable performances in the classroom, with very little formal, written preparation. How, then, do we justify the considerable amount of time that must be spent to prepare lessons to the degree of detail suggested here?

The justification for such planning runs as follows:

1. Few people are 'born' teachers. Most of those who are good teachers had a hard struggle earlier in their career, when they learned either formally or through hard practical experience how to organize their teaching. The classes they give today are the fruit of much prior experience and much learning.

2. It is probable that in the early days these teachers did in fact plan their lessons carefully. If they do not need to do so now, it is because they have internalized the planning process, being able mentally to plan

appropriate instructional procedures, remember useful tactics employed in the past, and so on.

3. Although gifted and experienced teachers do exist, they do not form the majority of the teaching profession. Most of us need to set aside some time before the lesson to pull our thoughts together and decide on a plan. It is therefore useful to have some method of organizing this planning session.

4. The suggested planning chart, organized in three columns, may appear to be more complicated, or more time-consuming than other plans, but this is probably only because it is unfamiliar. In practice, it takes no longer to plan a lesson in this way than it does to prepare an equally detailed plan by any other means.

5. The basis for the design of the chart is the systems model of the instructional process. If we believe that this model has value, in paying equal or more attention to the learner learning than to the teacher teaching, then it would seem a good idea to base our planning tools on the model.

These arguments, taken together, suggest that the approach we are outlining is worth trying, if only for some lessons, or at some early stage in the instructor's professional career. With time, the instructor may devise a better planning system, more suited to his teaching style or his temperament. Also, he will internalize the planning system and be able to use a more condensed form of planning.

anning for dividualized struction   There is one other advantage to working with the planning system outlined in this chapter. The model of the instructional system on which it is based is an individualized system. In the first part of the book we defined individualization as the frequency with which the instructional system adapts to the needs or the capabilities of the individual. Our lesson planning system makes provision for the specification of some form of remedial or corrective tactic at every step. It is therefore a system for planning individualized instruction.

There is no reason why the same system should not be used for the planning of various forms of individualized instruction. We shall, indeed, illustrate how the same planning chart may be used to plan conventional classroom-based lessons, workshop-based training sessions, group-based learning activities, simulations, programmed instruction and modular training materials. It can even be used for interactive audiovisual materials, such as the recently introduced systems of interactive video, and for some forms of computer-assisted instruction.

10.2 Using the lesson-planning chart

1e three-lumn sson plan: example   To begin the study of this general lesson planning system, we present an example of part of a lesson plan prepared for a course that aims to train supervisors in a given organization to evaluate the performance of their subordinates, as part of the organization's efforts to introduce a standardized system of job performance evaluation (see Figure 10.2 on p 136). This plan is incomplete, as we shall see later. However, it presents the principal part of the lesson — the part which aims to teach the new knowledge and skills necessary to evaluate the performance of a subordinate. We suggest that, before continuing with the text, the reader studies this lesson plan and identifies its chief objectives.

The objectives of this lesson can be stated as follows:

Given a number of employees who are immediately subordinate, the necessary forms and other supplementary information, the trainees will be able to evaluate their job performance, on a five-point scale, for a series of factors defined in the evaluation forms, to criteria that will be judged

Information (stimulus)	Behaviour (response)	Feedback (reinforcement)
1. Explain the principles of the system of performance evaluation adopted by the company. Distribute copies of the forms that will be used.	Study the forms to identify the way that each one should be used. Ask for explanations of any aspects that are not quite clear.	Correct and explain any difficulty of comprehension of the principles and procedures on which the company's job evaluation system is based.
2. Distribute 10 descriptions of job performance. Demonstrate the use of a five-point scale for the classification of four of the 10 cases described.	In groups of three, study the other six cases and try to agree on the classifications of the performance described. Then each group should compare and discuss its results with the others.	Observe the work of the groups, helping them to classify the examples correctly. Distribute a checklist to assist the groups in the self-evaluation of their work.
3. Demonstrate how to complete the job evaluation forms for the four cases that were previously used as demonstrations.	Each participant should complete one or two forms, evaluating some of the other six cases and then compare his evaluations with those of other participants.	Observe the individual exercise and assist anyone with difficulties. After 10 minutes, distribute a completed form as a model to be used for self-evaluation.
4. Organize a practical exercise to be performed by each supervisor at his place of work. Explain that he should evaluate three of his immediate subordinates. Supply the necessary forms.	Each participant on returning to his job, should evaluate about three of his subordinates, each of whom has different jobs. He should then send the forms to the instructor, within one week of terminating the course.	Compare the evaluations made by the trainees with other evaluations of the same employees that were made as part of the routine job evaluations in the company. Identify any gross discrepancies between the two sets of evaluations and feedback results to trainees.

Figure 10.2 *Example of a lesson plan*

by comparison with evaluations of the same employees made by expert job evaluators — the trainees' evaluations should not diverge grossly from those of the experts.

Note that this is exactly what the lesson plan sets out to test in the fourth step. Note also the sequence of enabling objectives that are taught and evaluated in the preceding steps. Finally, note the instructional strategy and tactics that the instructional designer plans to implement in this lesson.

At the beginning of the lesson, the teacher plans to present the basic knowledge necessary for the task: the type of job evaluation system used in the company and its basic principles. In the second step of the lesson he plans to demonstrate the use of a five-point scale for the classification of performance. In the third step, he will demonstrate the procedure for completion of the evaluation forms that are used as part of the company's standard procedure for job performance evaluation. In each of these three steps, the instructor's demonstration is followed by relevant learning activities to be carried out by the trainees. And at each stage, the instructor observes the trainees' behaviour, corrects or reorientates their actions and gives fuller or simpler explanations, etc.

The general instructional strategy being implemented is obviously *expositive*, following the stages of *demonstration*, *practice* and *evaluation* in each step of the lesson. The division of the lesson content into three stages is an attempt to apply the principle of progress in small steps.

The three steps deal, respectively, with:

☐ Basic knowledge concerning job evaluation in general and the system used in this organization in particular.
☐ The basic skill of applying a five-point evaluation scale.
☐ The practical skill of operating the job performance evaluation system of the company.

In the structure of this lesson plan, we can see a certain amount of care exercised to ensure that the instructional actions really do lead to the achievement of the planned objectives. There are, however, several additional activities that might be added to make the lesson more effective, more motivational, better integrated into the course as a whole, or better able to promote the transfer of what has been learned to a wide variety of real-life situations.

10.3 General model for lesson planning

To plan the extra activities proposed above it is useful to follow, as a guide, a general model for lesson planning which, in addition to the main steps of the instructional strategy adopted, contains provision for certain 'opening' and 'closing' actions. The opening actions should motivate the learners to participate fully in the learning activities that follow, by making the lesson's objectives clear and establishing their importance to the learner. It is also important to ensure, at this stage, that the learners are ready to study the content of the lesson: for example, do they have all the prerequisite knowledge and skills? The closing events should evaluate the results of the lesson, but they should also ensure that the learning will be of real future use. We present an outline of our model below.

1. *Attention and motivation.* We should begin the lesson with some form of statement, quick presentation or initial activity, which will grab the attention of the learners and make them receptive to the lesson and ready to participate in the activities to follow. This may be a short story, a joke, a captivating visual, or some form of question to which the learners relate, but to which they have no immediate answer. This opener should leave the learners with the feeling that 'something worth learning' is about to be introduced.

'This is
where we
are going'

2. *Statement of the objectives.* Once the learners' interest has been awakene
it is usually a good idea to define more precisely what they are going to lear
The learners deserve to receive the lesson's objectives, clearly stated, right a
the beginning of the session. They may then use these objectives to self-
evaluate their learning progress during the stages that follow. They will
probably ask more relevant questions, tackle the learning exercises more
intelligently and avoid too many digressions into other topics.

'Do you
remember?'

3. *Recall and revision of prerequisites.* A lesson often requires the use of
certain knowledge or skills that the learners should have acquired in earlier
stages. These prerequisites are identified during the analysis of the lesson's
objectives and may include recent learning included in earlier lessons, or sor
basic skills which should have been developed at much earlier stages of the
learner's development. In both these cases, it will be necessary to include so
exploratory questions or diagnostic activities to verify that the prerequisites
really have been mastered by all the learners. This is of vital importance wh
sequentially structured topic is being taught, as in the case of any principle
learning, which depends on the previous learning of the component concept

When these diagnostic questions reveal incomplete mastery, it is necessar
to revise and reinforce this previous learning before going on. The lesson pla
should make provision for the revision of prerequisites, when necessary,
indicating how this revision may be carried out, how much time may be
required and what the effects will be on the execution of the later stages of
the lesson. If such revision is carried out regularly, there is less chance of th
creation of large gaps in students' learning.

**Instructional
actions**

'Here comes
the message'

4. *The instruction activities.* These are the activities carried out by the
instructor, or by some other component of the instructional system, with t
intention of transmitting new information to the learner, orienting him in h
studies or setting up a problem or situation for the learner to experience. In
case of expositive strategies, these activities are mainly explanations, or
demonstrations of what is to be learned. In the case of experiential strategie
they may take the form of data presented as a case study, the rules of a
simulation or game that the learners will participate in, or the arrangement
particular real-life experiences for the learners.

'And this is
what you
should do'

5. *The learning activities.* These are the activities that should be performed
by the learners, both to learn the content being presented in the lesson and
to show what they have learned. In the case of expositive strategies, these
activities are mainly composed of answers to questions posed by the instruc
or the performance of tasks previously demonstrated by the instructor. In t
case of experiential strategies, the learning activities may take many forms,
such as participation in group discussions, brainstorming sessions, games,
role-play exercises, simulations and projects.

'Oops . . .
let's try
again'

6. *The feedback activities.* These are the activities of online formative
evaluation — observation of the effects of each step in the lesson and
reinforcement of any weak aspects. Usually these activities are performed b
the instructor, even when the basic transmission of information is effected
by means of other media, such as videocassettes. However, in truly self-
instructional systems, these activities must be performed by the learner him
through his interaction with the material. This can be achieved up to a poin
in printed materials, by means of various questioning techniques as in
programmed instruction. A much more powerful and varied approach is
possible through the imaginative use of computer-assisted instruction.

In the case of expositive strategies, the feedback activities generally take
the form of formal tests or informal questioning and observation of the
learners by the instructor, followed by corrective actions, reorientation, ne
explanations, extra practice exercises and so on, until all the learners exhibi
an adequate mastery of the specific objectives of the lesson. In the case of

experiential strategies, the feedback activities take the form of analytical
discussions with the learners, debriefing sessions, individual discussions, or
presentation of the results of actions or decisions taken in simulation sessions,
etc. All these activities are so organized as to lead the learner himself to
recognize his errors or weaknesses, and to take appropriate action to overcome
them. The emphasis is on self-evaluation. The instructor takes on the role of a
catalyst, or acts as a source of data, selecting the questions he asks and the data
he supplies in such a way as to guide the learner himself to discover just what
it is that he has learned or failed to learn.

7. *The transfer of learning.* In many lessons, especially those which attempt to
teach general principles or problem-solving strategies, it is necessary to provide
ample opportunities for varied practice to ensure that the learners are capable
of transferring what they have learned in certain specific situations (used as
examples during the lesson) to other quite different situations, where the
same principles or strategies still apply. Often, transfer may be promoted
during the lesson, by deeper analytical questioning or by the presentation of
a wide variety of problems for solution by the students. Sometimes, however,
transfer may best be promoted after the lesson, through real-life situations,
either on the job or at home. Another way is through homework or individual
projects to be completed after the lesson. In all these cases, however, the
planning of these transfer activities forms part of the process of planning the
lesson. They should, therefore, appear in the lesson planning document.

8. *Evaluation of the lesson.* Although the formative evaluation of learning
progress is a continuous activity, forming part of all the lesson steps (especially
4, 5, 6 and 7), it is nevertheless usually necessary to arrange a final end-of-
lesson evaluation of the results of learning. This evaluation may be used for
summative purposes, as in the grading of students on a continuous basis, or
formative purposes, enabling the instructor to plan the next lessons of the
sequence better, or to replan the current lesson to improve its effectiveness on
the next occasion he has to give it. Generally, the final evaluation of the lesson
takes the form of a test of the lesson's objectives, by means of written or oral
questions or practical exercises. Often, an attempt is also made to evaluate the
learners' reactions to the lesson and its content by means of open discussion
or a formal attitude questionnaire. This does not have to be done at the end of
all lessons, but should occur with reasonable regularity. Sometimes, however,
the final evaluation can only be performed after the lesson, by observation of
on-the-job performance standards of certain tasks, or the behaviour of the
learners over a period of time after instruction. Affective objectives, for
example, must generally be evaluated by measuring the changes in the learners'
attitudes and general behaviour after completion of learning. In such cases,
follow-up activity must be performed. The plan of this follow-up should
appear in the lesson planning document.

9. *Summary and further study.* The last step in the lesson is a summary of what
has been achieved, and an indication of where the learners might proceed next.
At this point, there is the opportunity for the distribution of reference notes,
enrichment materials, extra, optional exercises, reading lists and suggestions on
how interested learners might extend their study of the lesson's topics beyond
the objectives that were pre-set for the lesson. This latter step, like the transfer
of learning, may not be necessary in all lessons. In rigidly job-oriented training,
for instance, there may be no need for wider study and no real opportunities
for the transfer of learning. Wider study and transfer of learning are, however,
of great importance in lessons dealing with general principles, problem-solving
strategies or productive skills.

We are not suggesting that all nine steps must necessarily appear in every
lesson plan. Some of the steps are of particular importance only in lessons
dealing with certain types of objectives. The list should be used as a general

model for lesson planning and should be adapted to the special characteristi
of each particular lesson. As an example, we shall apply the model to the
on-the-job performance evaluation introduced earlier (see Figure 10.3 on
p141).

10.4 Analysis of another example: sports training

The remainder of this chapter will detail two sample lesson plans produced b
students on an instructional design course given by the author. The first plar
follows the general suggestions specified in this chapter, but diverges on som
points. We have already seen the overall instructional plan in Chapter 6 — the
hypothetical scuba diving course. In preparing her detailed lesson plans, the
trainee instructional designer decided to give the objectives, exactly as stated
in the overall plan, to the students as a course guide. The section of this guid
that is relevant to the first two lessons is presented in Exhibit 10.1(a) on p 1
The course guide included not only the objectives but also a statement of the
tests that would be used to evaluate the achievement of the objectives.

A fundamental strategic decision: separate the theory and the practice into two separate lessons

Close study of the course guide, or of the overall instructional plan
presented in Chapter 6, shows that the instructional designer plans to give
two lessons — a theoretical and a practical lesson — with essentially the same
group of objectives. This can be seen even more clearly when the objectives c
lesson 2 are compared with the questions in the test that is to be used to
evaluate lesson 1 — this test is also presented in Exhibit 10.1 (see pp 143-150
The objectives of the first lesson are to impart the necessary knowledge, whil
the objectives of the second lesson are concerned with developing skills. One
may indeed consider the two lessons as parts of one lesson, aiming, first, to
impart the necessary basic knowledge, and, second, to apply this knowledge
to the practical tasks involved in scuba diving.

Two-column format of presentation — the pros and cons

First, we note that the lesson plan does not follow exactly the same layou
as suggested earlier in this chapter. It is based on a two-column layout, as
opposed to the suggested three-column model (we can ignore the time colum
on this occasion). The feedback activities to be performed by the instructor
have not been listed in a separate column. Nevertheless, the plan does indicat
at many points, that the instructor should ask questions to check the depth c
understanding. The instructional designer considered that, by implication, it
clear that when these questions show up learning deficiencies, the instructor
should take appropriate remedial action before passing on to new material.
This is quite a defensible position. There is nothing sacred about the suggeste
format for presenting a lesson plan. In this particular case, the lesson content
is simple and straightforward. There is perhaps no real reason for detailed
pre-planning of the remedial actions that may have to be taken. It would be
different in the case of complex theoretical content, when the instructor mu
enter the classroom prepared to confront learning difficulties by presenting
alternative explanations or different examples and analogies. In such a case,
these should be pre-planned and a third column in the chart is the best place
to note down these contingency plans. We therefore recommend that a three
column format be considered in general, although the third column may be
largely ignored when planning straightforward, easily learned lessons.

Analysis of the instructional activities that comprise the planned lesson

Second, we note that not all nine types of instructional activities suggeste
in our general model for lesson planning are included in this lesson. Our
analysis of the lesson's structure is as follows:

1. *Attention:* This is catered for in step 1 — the use of a film.
2. *Specific objectives:* These were distributed to the learners as a course
   guide, before the course began. It is, however, a good idea to call the
   attention of the learners to the specific objectives that will be dealt
   with in this lesson. Presumably the film, if well chosen, does this, so
   there is no need to specify a separate step in the lesson plan.

sson title: Job performance evaluation.
rget population: Foremen and supervisors at XYZ company.
umber of trainees: Maximum 20.
me: 1 ½ hours.

sson objectives: The trainees should be able to use standard company procedures and
cumentation in order to evaluate the job performance of their immediate subordinates, being
dged as competent by an experienced evaluator who compares their evaluations of certain
orkers with his own evaluations of the same workers.

quipment/resources required:
Documentation used for evaluating job performance (20 sets).
Handout, describing 10 performance case histories to be used in group training exercises
(20 copies).
Flipcharts, showing the structure of the documentation used and other summary information,
to be used as visual aids.
Chalkboard or overhead projector for other classroom work.

Information (stimulus)	Behaviour (response)	Feedback (reinforcement)	Time
pening actions			
Attention old a short discussion the use and mitations of job erformance evaluation, the departments of YZ company.	Trainees should demonstrate their attitudes, both positive and negative, to the use of job performance evaluation.	Observe the attitudes and attempt to form uniformly positive ones, by illustrating the possible uses of evaluation as a management tool.	10 minutes
Objectives xplain the lesson bjectives, as stated ove. Invite questions.	Trainees should clarify any doubts they may have.	All trainees should understand the objectives before continuing.	5 minutes
Prerequisites xplain importance of ecific criteria for each b in the department. et a criterion definition sk.	Each trainee should define the criteria for each job performed in his department.	Trainees may compare notes, or seek help from colleagues in their department. The criteria must be realistic.	20 minutes
structional actions			
Knowledge xplain the principles the system of erformance evaluation dopted by the company. stribute copies of the rms that will be used.	Study the forms to identify the way that each one should be used. Ask for explanations of any aspects that are not quite clear.	Correct and explain any difficulty of comprehension of the principles and procedures on which the company's job evaluation system is based.	10 minutes
. The scale stribute 10 descriptions job performance. emonstrate the use of five-point scale for e classification of ur of the 10 escribed cases.	In groups of three, study the other six cases and try to agree on the classifications of the performance described. Then each group should compare and discuss its results with the others.	Observe the work of the groups, helping them to classify the examples correctly. Distribute a checklist to assist the groups in the self-evaluation of their work.	20 minutes

Figure 10.3 *(continued)*

Information (stimulus)	Behaviour (response)	Feedback (reinforcement)	Time
6. The forms Demonstrate how to complete the job evaluation forms for the four cases that were used as demonstrations previously.	Each trainee should complete one or two forms evaluating some of the other six cases and should then compare his evaluations with those of other participants.	Observe the individual exercise and assist anyone with difficulties. After 10 minutes, distribute a completed form as a model to be used for self-evaluation.	20 minutes
Closing actions 7. Evaluation Organize a practical exercise to be performed by each supervisor at his place of work. Explain that he should evaluate three of his immediate subordinates. Supply the necessary forms.	Each trainee, on returning to his job, should evaluate three of his staff, each on different jobs. He should then send the forms to training department, within one week of the course ending.	Compare the evaluations made by the trainees with other evaluations of the same employees that were made as part of the routine job evaluations in the company. Feed back comments and corrections to the trainees.	This is to be done after the lesson.
8. Summary and further study Distribute checklist of procedure to be followed in evaluating staff. Indicate a reading list that may be used to learn more about performance evaluation and how to use the results.	—	—	5 minutes

Figure 10.3 *Application of general lesson planning model*

We may make a series of observations on this lesson plan:

1. The plan now includes an opening section that aims to gain the learner's attention, motivate and interest him in the content to be learned, explain clearly what is to be learned and prepare the learner for the ensuing learning activities.
2. The instructional strategy includes three steps, identical to those listed in the earlier, incomplete lesson plan.
3. The plan also now includes some closing events — the final evaluation (which also formed part of our original, shorter plan) and a summary/orientation for the future. We did not include the transfer of learning step as we are interested in training our foremen and supervisors to use one specific technique of job performance evaluation in one particular working environment. We are not seeking to train professional evaluators, capable of evaluating a variety of types of workers by means of a variety of techniques.
4. We have included, in a fourth column, an indication of the time that we feel will be necessary to devote to each step of the lesson. We predict it will take about 90 minutes, excluding the time to be spent by each trainee on his return to his department, to perform three specimen job performance evaluations.

   The total time for the lesson has been arrived at by totalling the time estimates for each of the lesson's steps. This is quite contrary to general practice, which tends to define the time to be devoted to a given lesson topic before a sufficiently detailed analysis of the topic has been performed and strategic and tactical decisions have been taken. The latter approach to planning the timing of lessons is quite wrong, and often leads to the non-achievement of the intended objectives, because of lack of time allowed at critical points in the learning process.

Objectives	Test items
Lesson 1: *Objective 1* Given a test on the theoretical aspects of diving, the student will score over 80 per cent as evaluated by the instructor.	A written test composed of multiple choice, true/false, short answer questions (sample attached).
Objectives 2, 3, 4, 5 and 6 Given a mask, fins and snorkel, the student will: 2. Clear a flooded mask completely (self-evaluation). 3. Clear a flooded snorkel to enable easy breathing (self-evaluation). 4. Enter the deep end of the pool demonstrating at least three of the methods correctly as judged by the instructor. 5. Swim at least two lengths of the pool demonstrating the four leg strokes to the satisfaction of the instructor. 6. Equalize properly to prevent any damage to the ear and/or pain (self-evaluation).	In the pool, the student will perform all the basic skin diving skills correctly in the presence of a qualified instructor.

Sample test (only a part of the test is presented here)

Lesson 1: Theoretical

1. Divers use a mask that fits over the exposed nose because:
   (a) Vision is greatly increased.
   (b) It is more comfortable and seals better.
   (c) The design can be adapted to a variety of face sizes.
   (d) It allows the user to equalize the internal pressure increase by exhaling through the nose.

   Answer _____

2. Since masks may be worn for long periods of time, proper fit is critical. List two things which determine good fit:
   (a) _____
   (b) _____

Exhibit 10.1 *Instructional plan for scuba diving course*

3. Two keys to mask clearing are sealing the highest point on the mask and creating more pressure inside the mask than outside to force out the water.

True _____
False _____

4. To prevent ear pain when you go underwater, you must:
   (a) Not go too deep.
   (b) Equalize the pressure in your ears.
   (c) Wear earplugs to keep the pressure from becoming too great.
   (d) Continue to breathe normally.

Answer _____

5. The easiest way to walk in fins is _____

6. Before climbing into a boat, the diver should first remove the fins.

True _____
False _____

7. The snorkel allows the diver to rest comfortably in a facedown position.

True _____
False _____

8. The diver must always wear the snorkel, even when scuba diving.

True _____
False _____

9. The best way to enter the water from a boat is the
   (a) Front roll.
   (b) Back roll.
   (c) Feet first.
   (d) Safest and easiest way.

Answer _____

Part of lesson plan for a theory lesson

Lesson 1 (a): Theory — expositive strategy

Equipment: Overhead and/or 16mm projector
Materials: Transparencies (1-1 to 5-4).
Film: Basic Skin Diving Skills — 10 minutes (if available).

Comments:

1. The use of a film focuses attention, gives a general overview and explains objectives more clearly.

2.1 The transparencies repeat content already presented in the film. At this stage, the learners must participate by showing what they remember from the film.

2.2 The instructor goes deeper into the specific procedures for clearing masks (Objective 2).

2.3 The instructor explains the procedures for clearing snorkels. This is Objective 3.

2.4 Now the instructor is seeking to analyse the depth of understanding that the students have gained. Have they learned the principles upon which the procedures are based? This is an opportunity for formative evaluation and reinforcement of learning.

3. A similar set of steps is included to teach the procedures and principles for Objectives 3, 4 and 5. (We have shortened the exhibit by omitting the remaining steps.)

Finally, the learning results are measured by means of the test included in this exhibit.

Teacher activity	Learner activity	Time (minutes)
Introduce the topic of skin diving. Show film, if available; if not, pass out masks, fins and snorkels.	View film or examine new equipment. Reactions should reflect interest.	10-15
Show transparencies 1-1, 1-2, 2-1 and 2-2 (see pp 147 - 148). Ask learners to describe or explain what is represented.	Learners state that the water in the mask and snorkel is being displaced by exhaled air from the nose or mouth.	
Show transparencies 1-1, and 1-2 (see p 147). Draw their attention to position of the head and hands, and the direction of the exiting water.	Learners comment that air bubbles rise to the top of the mask forcing the water out through the bottom lip of the mask.	15
Show transparencies 2-1 and 2-2 (see p 148). Ask the learners to compare illustrations.	Learners state the difference in head positions and relative depth upon exhalation.	
Prompt, if necessary, by asking: 'what property of air is being utilized?'	Learner should volunteer law: 'Under less pressure, air expands'.	
Discuss the relative merits of both methods to clear a snorkel: popping and expansion.	Learners participate in discussion by suggestion of what situation might warrant each method.	
Show transparencies 3-1, 3-2, 3-3, 3-4, 3-5 and 3-6 (see pp 149 - 150) of various methods of entry indicating in what situations each one is most suitable.	Learner labels drawings of entries and takes note of most appropriate use.	5
Administer sample test. Group correct and review problem areas. Assign further reading on the topic (sample test attached).	Learner does test. Indicates to instructor areas of difficulty. Does further reading at home.	30

Exhibit 10.1 *(continued)*

Lesson 1(b): Practical — expositive strategy (including group games)

Equipment: Pool mask, fins, snorkel (one set for each learner)
Materials: Prizes, can of defog, snorkel holders, scuba decals, case of beer

Part of lesson plan for a practical lesson

Comments

Step 1: a good idea to introduce the gaming element in the practice session. Not clear what happens to students who do not succeed at first. Do they get individual help from the instructor or must they rely on their friends? This could be specified in a third column of the planning chart.

Step 2: it may be a good idea to first hold a formal drill and practice session at the side of the pool, each learner practising (in shallow water) the procedures to be learned and then receiving immediate feedback from the instructor who is closely observing the performance of each individual. When basic difficulties are overcome on an individualized basis, the competition element is used to develop speed and efficiency.

Step 3: the lesson plan is not very detailed with regard to this step. How will the instructor judge and correct individual performances?

Step 4: once more, it may prove to be premature to launch into a competitive game before checking that the key points of each form of leg stroke are properly executed by each of the trainees. The game should be reserved for drill and practice aimed at perfecting the trainee's performance.

Step	Teacher activity	Learner activity	Time (minutes)
1.	Demonstrate two methods to clear a mask. Encourage practice by introducing game 1. Encourage learners to help each other. Class prize: can of defog.	Learner imitates the instructor and practises. Class wins prize when all learners are able to swim across the shallow end of the pool, retrieve their mask from the bottom, put it on and clear it before surfacing.	10
2.	Demonstrate two methods to clear snorkel. Encourage practice by introducing game 2. Individual prizes: snorkel holders. Class bonus: case of beer.	Learner imitates the instructor or master performer and practises. To win, learner must retrieve and clear both mask and snorkel in a set period. Successful learners receive a prize. Learners coach each other to win class bonus.	10
3.	Demonstrate different entry techniques (six ways).		
4.	Demonstrate different leg strokes. Instructor judges accuracy. Introduce game 3 — swim meet. Prizes: scuba decals.	Learner does each one correctly. Learner practises each leg stroke for a couple of lengths. Then learners who wish may participate in swim meet. Participants swim four lengths of the pool using a different leg stroke for each length against the clock. Winners are those who record the three best times.	10 15

Exhibit 10.1 *(continued)*

Transparencies for step 2 of the lesson

Transparency 1-1

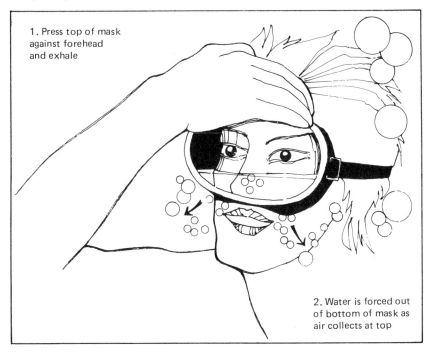

1. Press top of mask against forehead and exhale

2. Water is forced out of bottom of mask as air collects at top

Transparency 1-2

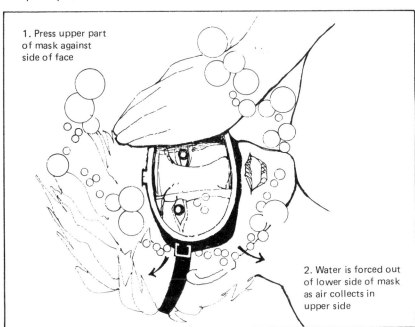

1. Press upper part of mask against side of face

2. Water is forced out of lower side of mask as air collects in upper side

Exhibit 10.1 *(continued)*

Transparency 2-1

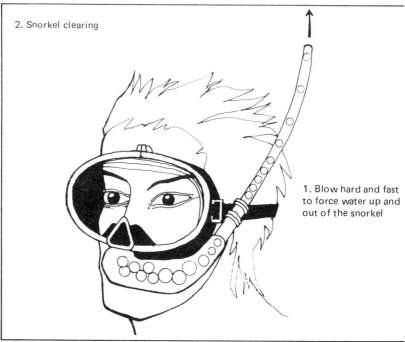

2. Snorkel clearing

1. Blow hard and fast to force water up and out of the snorkel

Transparency 2-2

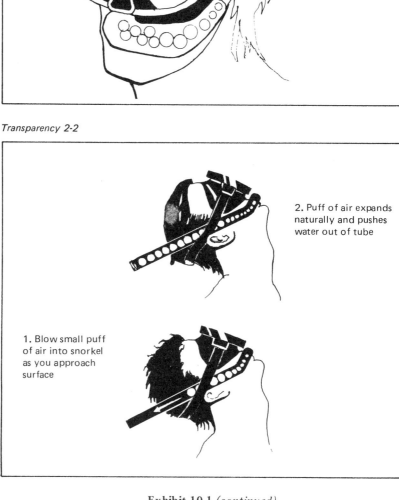

2. Puff of air expands naturally and pushes water out of tube

1. Blow small puff of air into snorkel as you approach surface

Exhibit 10.1 *(continued)*

Transparencies for step 3 of the lesson

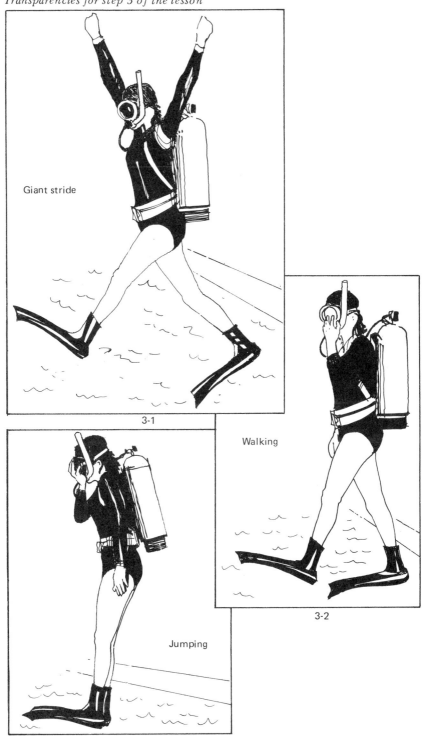

Giant stride

3-1

Walking

3-2

Jumping

3-3   **Exhibit 10.1** *(continued)*

Front roll entry   3-4

3-5   Back roll entry

Controlled seat entry

Exhibit 10.1 *(continued)*

3. *Prerequisites.* There is no separate step devoted to the recall of necessary concepts or principles that the learners should have gained from earlier learning. Perhaps the instructional designer did not identify any essential prerequisites, as this is the first lesson in the course. Perhaps the prerequisites were tested by means of an entry test to the course as a whole. Or perhaps the instructional designer preferred to test prerequisites later, at more appropriate points in the lesson sequence. This latter case is what actually happens in this lesson. In step 2.4, the learner should 'volunteer the law'. This law was not taught in our lesson. It was a prerequisite for the understanding of the principles that underpin the suggested procedures for clearing a mask and a snorkel.

4. *Instructional strategy.* This is obviously an expositive strategy in principle, although it has some experiential undertones in step 2.4, when learners discuss the suggested procedures and justify them in the light of other, similar, experiences they have had. The tactics of sequencing present first the whole job in the film, then one whole task in step 2.1 and finally analyse the parts in steps 2.3 and 2.4.

5. *Learner activities.* These are very clearly specified in the second column of the planning chart.

6. *Feedback activities.* As already stated, these are specified at several points, but it is not always easy to identify them as such as they are not in a separate column, and are sometimes mentioned by implication rather than explicitly.

7. *Transfer of learning.* No attempt has been made to include activities that would transfer the learning to other situations, because we are concerned here with the teaching of specific procedures to be used in specific situations. The principles on which these procedures are based may, indeed, be transferable to other situations, but here we are not primarily concerned with the teaching of these principles and their general application. It is quite reasonable, therefore, not to devote effort in the lesson plan to activities that promote the transfer of learning.

8. *Final evaluation.* This is specified quite clearly and illustrated by the specimen questions in the sample test.

9. *Summary and further study.* This lesson plan does not do very much in relation to this final step, although some further reading is to be assigned. As this is the first lesson in a series, and will be followed immediately by a practical lesson on the same content, it is probably acceptable to leave summary activities to a later stage.

lue of
uals
aids to
nning

Exhibit 10.1 also includes examples of some of the transparencies to be used during the lesson. When a lesson is supported by specially planned visual material of this type, it is possible to be less detailed in writing the lesson plan, as the visuals speak for themselves and remind the instructor of the examples and explanations that he should present at specific points of the lesson.

neral
aluation of
e theory
son

The lesson plan analysed seems to be adequate, given the original choice of strategy, that is, splitting the instruction into a separate theoretical and practical period. Some instructors would prefer to integrate the theory and practice. This has several advantages in relation to motivation, maintenance of interest and efficient use of study time. However, in this specific case, involving practice in a pool, under water, it is difficult to demonstrate all aspects of the task in the real situation, and an initial classroom session therefore seems desirable.

neral
aluation of
e practical
son

To complete our analysis of the lesson we include part of the lesson plan for the second, practical, part of the instruction. Again, the basic instructional strategy is expositive, consisting of demonstrations followed by practice. In this case, attention is not difficult to maintain, motivation is enhanced by introducing a game element into the practice exercises and various prizes are used as reinforcers. All these tactics are, in principle, good ideas. However, a topic like scuba diving, which is not usually an obligatory part of a curriculum and which is studied voluntarily by enthusiasts, is sufficiently self-motivating for many prizes to be unnecessary. The game element is, in itself, motivational and there may be other aspects of the course that could better use the financial resources.

We leave it to the reader to complete the analysis and to decide to what extent the modifications in the lesson planning model, as used by this particular instructional designer, were valid simplifications or were unjustified departures from a more elaborate model.

10.5 An example from the primary school

This lesson plan was prepared by a primary school teacher to develop the concepts of the seasons of the year. The lesson plan is presented in Exhibit 10.2 on p 155.

We shall concentrate our analysis on the interpretation of the plan, without commenting too much on the general strategy that has been adopted. This strategy is essentially expositive, the teacher taking a leading role in presenting new information, setting learning tasks, questioning and prompting in order to elicit appropriate responses, etc. It should be possible to adopt a more student-directed or experiential strategy if the teacher wishes. We will comment on these alternatives here, as in the next chapter we shall present alternative lesson plan for the same subject. Instead, at this point we leave the task of comparison and critical evaluation to the reader. In the remainder of this chapter we shall simply analyse the structure of the lesson plan, in order practise the interpretation of plans that are prepared in the three-column format. We suggest that the reader studies the analysis presented (and illustrated) below, at the same time making reference to the planning chart of this lesson presented in Exhibit 10.2 (see p 155).

Step 1:
Introduction

Attention and definition of objectives. The teacher plans to start the lesson by explaining what the children will learn and why it is useful for them to learn this. He plans to do this by explaining, in simple, non-technical language, the objectives of the lesson. He will follow this by giving some examples of the practical value of achieving them.

Step 2:
Preparation

Recall of prerequisite knowledge. On the basis of an analysis of the lesson's objectives, the teacher has identified certain essential prerequisites and so proceeds to check if the children all have an adequate grasp of the essential prior knowledge. This will be done by means of a question and answer session.

3.1:
ching
wledge

Develop the instructional strategy. The teacher presents the new information to be learned. In this case, he defines the concepts of summer and winter. The children demonstrate that they have understood and have learned the concept, by giving or identifying examples, eg the months of the year of the given season. The teacher evaluates the learning, checking that all the children respond to the questions and give some examples. Slow learners will be helped by new explanations and examples.

3.2:
eloping
ill

Apply the acquired knowledge in order to develop skills. The teacher shows, by examples, that there are many differences between the seasons. The children, in small groups, practise the task and prepare a list of differences between the seasons of the year. The teacher evaluates the task through observation of the group work, helping if necessary by hints, but not by giving the answers to the groups. A final self-evaluation session takes place at the end, when each group contributes to a common table of characteristics, to be prepared on the blackboard.

Step 3.2
(continued)

Step 4:
Closing
actions

Transfer of learning/final evaluation.
This is an optional step in the lesson.
In order to extend the experiences
of the learners and provide further
opportunities for use of the new
concepts, the teacher may ask the
children to perform a research
project, at home, on how family
life is affected by the seasons.

General
evaluation of
the plan

In the formal lesson plan presented in Exhibit 10.2 on pp 155 - 156 we can
all the steps illustrated informally in our analysis. The instructional designer l
in this example, used a three-column format for the presentation of the less
plan. In general, the steps of the lesson follow the suggestions made earlier i
this chapter, although they do diverge in some respects. For instance, the
explanation of the objectives and the gaining of the learners' attention are
both to be achieved by means of the first activity. There is an attempt to
promote the transfer of learning, although with concept learning of this kin
it could be argued that the homework task is not really transferring learning
but is merely creating an opportunity for further practice. Finally, there is
formal evaluation of the learning achieved. Presumably the teacher consider
this to be superfluous, as the observation of the group and individual work
assessment of the homework project would suffice.

We note that part of this lesson plan proposes to organize the children to
work in small groups. In this work, the children will learn from each other
(from each other's prior experiences of phenomena associated with the
changing seasons). Some people would consider this part of the lesson to ha
opted for an experiential strategy, although, without doubt, the main strate
being adopted is expositive. Others might say that, although the children
learn from the experience of others, they do not learn through experience - -
there is little difference between being told something by the teacher and b
told by a classmate. Some might, however, consider that there are greater
opportunities for experiential learning in the design of the final project. Th
could involve the observation of changes in nature, such as may be observec
on field trips, rather than the reception of more information, as might occu
in the suggested homework exercise if the child merely asks his parents and
receives additional information.

Lesson title: The seasons of the year.
Target population: 8- to 9-year-old children.
Number of students: Maximum 30.
Time: 1 hour + 15 minutes + 30 minutes.

Lesson objectives: The learners should be able to:
1. Define the four seasons of the year by name, by the months in each season and by the principal weather characteristics.
2. Identify and classify phenomena of nature, of society, of family habits, of school activities, etc, as typical of a particular season of the year.

Equipment/resources required: Some pictures or objects characteristic of each season; blackboard; paper and pencils.

Information (stimulus)	Behaviour (response)	Feedback (reinforcement)	Time (minutes)
Opening events 1. Attention/objectives State the objectives of the lesson. Explain the importance of knowing about the seasons for farmers, clothes makers, holidaymakers, children at school, etc.			5
2. Recall/prerequisites Recall the names and characteristics of the months of the year — 'in what month does Christmas fall?', etc. Recall the chief characteristics of each month — climate, etc. State that we are going to identify more characteristics.	The children must demonstrate knowledge of all the months and their characteristics.	Revise and complement the children's knowledge as necessary.	5
Instructional strategy 3.1 Knowledge Define each season in terms of hot, cold, warm, etc. Ask which are the hot months, cold months, etc. Give examples of other differences — rainfall, trees, flowers, etc.	Children should state the months of each season. Children should correctly identify the given examples.	Repeat questions involving different children, until all demonstrate a full knowledge of months/ seasons. Check that each child can identify the principal characteristics.	10
3.2 Skill Use the examples just presented, to form a classification table on the blackboard. Ask for some new examples to be classified on the table.	Children should help, by stating in which column to put a given characteristic.	Verify that the concept of a classification table is understood by all. Continue generating examples until the exercise runs smoothly.	10

Exhibit 10.2 *(continued)*

Information (stimulus)	Behaviour (response)	Feedback (reinforcement)	Time (minutes)
Form groups of about four or five children. Explain the task. Give two topic areas — sports practised in each season, tasks to be performed in the garden, etc.	Each group should prepare its own table of characteristics, for each of the topic areas defined.	Circulate and observe the group work. Give hints and comments, but do not suggest any specific examples. Judge how much time should be spent on this step before pooling the examples.	Approximately 15 (judge by the progress of the group task)
After a sufficient time, ask a representative group to contribute one example to a joint table, to be prepared on the blackboard. Write the contributions, or ask the children to come forward and write.	Each child, in turn, makes a contribution to the joint table. Children should question any items that they do not understand and criticize the items with which they disagree.	Observe and evaluate the level of participation and the contributions of each child. Encourage the weaker or shy child to participate more fully. Check and correct the logic of the comments/criticisms made.	15
Closing events 4. Transfer/practice Suggest a homework exercise based on the analysis of how the seasons affect the life of the family — the type of work, type of leisure activities, food, clothes, bedtime hours, etc.	Each child should prepare a table similar to the one prepared in class, based on the research to be carried out at home.	At the next class the tables will be presented and commented on by each child to the rest of the class. This will serve as a final evaluation of the lesson.	Approximately 15 at home; 30 in next class

Exhibit 10.2 *A lesson plan on 'the seasons'*

These questions of deciding between experiential and expositive strategies, the mixing of strategies, the basing of a whole lesson on group learning activities, or the division of a large group into smaller units for part of a lesson are assessed in more detail later. For the moment, we are principally concerned with the establishment of a general approach to the detailed planning and presentation of lessons. The examples we have studied so far are all classroom based with fairly conventional teaching, using mainly expositive strategies, and with typical groups of learners (about 15 to 30 in number). We will use the same basic approach for planning small group learning activities (Chapter 11) and for experiential exercises of the simulation/gaming type (Chapter 12). In all these applications of the lesson planning sheet we note a great concern for the progress of individual learners. The use of a three-column format forces the instructional designer to plan learner activities and on-line formative evaluation activities, which will enable the teacher to identify both general and individual learning problems and to take appropriate and immediate corrective action.

11. The Planning of Group Learning Exercises

11.1 Introduction

y should use group rning rcises?

The breakdown of a large group into smaller ones is one way of promoting individualization. The small group context makes it more difficult for any participant to remain passive, uninvolved in the discussion taking place or uncommitted to the achievement of the objectives of the task being undertaken. By breaking down the large group we also break down inhibitions and other barriers to communication, promoting a more intense level of interaction between students.

Group work often offers advantages over individual study. When we hear or read a message, we tend to gloss over slight misunderstandings, tend to neglect to use a dictionary or to ask someone to explain unfamiliar terminology or new concepts. In small group study, however, each member can voice his doubts and let everyone discuss them. This clarifies doubts and problems as they arise, and stimulates the other group members to be more critical in their study.

Another basic advantage of small group work is that it promotes a more systematic and goal-oriented study of a subject. In large group discussion, it is naturally much more difficult to prepare a coherent and comprehensive summary of conclusions, or indeed to come to any generally supported conclusions. In a smaller group, this is much easier.

eoretical nciples derlying up work

The nature and dynamics of group work have been studied by many psychologists and sociologists. These include Koehler, Kofka, Ehrenfels and other supporters of the Gestalt theory of group interaction, Lewin and his Field theory of group dynamics and Moreno in Sociometry. The contributions of these various lines of study may be summarized in two basic principles:

1. The group has its own 'being' or reality, with specific characteristics of behaviour, often quite different from the normal behaviour patterns of its members.
2. Individuals, when integrated into a group, are affected by the specific behaviour dynamics of the group, and often assume roles and attitudes that are alien to them as individuals.

The use of group work, therefore, is based on the following main considerations:

(a) *The possibility of a more diverse range of behaviour when individuals are placed in groups.* Normally shy people may be more outspoken, or normally aggressive people may adopt a passive role.

(b) *The forces or dynamics which the group creates.* Strictly speaking, group dynamics are the forces that act within a group. The practical application of group dynamics signifies the use of these forces to achieve specific goals. Sometimes, quite erroneously, all group work is referred to as group dynamics.

(c) *The role of the group leader.* To the extent that the leader identifies, steers and promotes the forces acting within the group, his effectiveness and efficiency as leader grows. This is what most distinguishes the natural leader. However, much can be done to learn and develop these natural group leadership skills.

11.2 Advantages of group work

Five main
advantages
of learning
in groups

Among the principal advantages of group work in the educational or training context we may list the following:

1. *Work in groups satisfies a social necessity.* Human beings are by nature sociable. Many aspects of modern life tend to diminish the opportunities for group interaction. Group work in education may offer opportunities for the development of social skills, such as cooperation, and strengthen social values.
2. *Work in groups promotes intellectual development.* According to Piaget, rational thought (as opposed to supersititious or 'magical' thought) only develops when individuals meet in groups.
3. *Group work humanizes the teacher learner relationship.* The substitution of authoritarian teaching by the orientation of study in the group situation leads to greater interest and motivation on the part of the learners.
4. *Group work promotes the development of personality.* The group is the appropriate environment for the personal development of the individual. Personality growth is largely the result of interaction between the individual and the group. According to Piaget, it is the result of cooperation. Thus we may argue that group work is truly individualizing.
5. *Group work promotes creativity.* The critical spirit engendered in group learning as a result of discussion, interchange and collaboration, tends to break down conventions, mental inertia and other barriers to innovative thinking.

11.3 The role of the instructor in group work

The instructor's role in small group learning is generally one of organizer, coordinator and evaluator of the work, rather than active participant, although in some group discussion activities he may participate as an equal partner, or occasionally as the group leader. However, in most types of small group learning, the leader should emerge from the ranks of the learners themselves.

The instructor
as organizer

In his role as organizer, the instructor may wish to structure the group according to specific principles, and he is always responsible for briefing the group. In order to structure the group, it is sometimes useful formally to study the group members and their individual characteristics. This may be done by direct observation, using questionnaires, drawing sociograms, etc. The information thus gathered is then used to divide the learners into balanced groups, according to certain predetermined principles of group structure — equal numbers of males/females, or extroverts/introverts, in each group; placement of personal friends in separate groups; equal distribution of natural leaders; simulation of the various strata of society in each group; etc.

Often, however, it is unnecessary to pre-structure the groups in any specific way. The groups may form spontaneously, as a result of the natural preference of the members. The best approach to group organization springs from the form and the objectives of the specific technique of group work being adopted.

The
importance
of briefing

The briefing function of the instructor is equivalent to the initial pre-instruction stage of any lesson. Just as in any other lesson, it is important at the beginning of the session to:

☐ Gain the participants' attention and interest.
☐ Explain the objectives of the work to be undertaken.
☐ Motivate the learners to participate fully in the work.
☐ Recall any prerequisite learning which will be necessary as input to the planned work.

In addition to these standard pre-instruction activities, the instructor may need to explain and illustrate the particular group work technique to be used, if this is new to the participants. For example, the first time brainstorming is used, it is necessary to explain the 'rules of the game', justifying the separate stages of ideas creation, ideas organization and ideas evaluation.

e instructor
coordinator

In his coordinator role, the instructor may need to carry out the following tasks:

☐ Keep the groups working productively.
☐ Plan timing of the stages and timekeeping.
☐ Distribute and control materials.
☐ Act as judge in disagreements between group members.
☐ Act as an information centre for the groups.
☐ Give advice or comments, when requested.
☐ Check, during the course of activities, that the objectives and rules of work have been understood.
☐ Check that the groups are not getting lost, or following totally inadequate problem-solving paths, or diverging from the planned activities.

In many cases, however, the instructor may delegate some of these tasks (for example, timekeeping or materials distribution) to the individual groups or their leaders. Once again, the instructor's role is dependent on the objectives and structure of the specific technique being employed.

e instructor
evaluator

e
portance
debriefing

Finally, at the end of a session of group work, the instructor may need to have a debriefing session. This is especially important in group work that attempts to promote experiential learning. In such cases, the results of the work of each group should include the formation of some new concepts or general principles that can be applied in similar situations in the future. The group members, or their spokesmen, should report back with their findings or conclusions to the other groups. The instructor should evaluate to what extent these reports demonstrate that the essential concepts/principles have been formed. In cases of doubt, the instructor should promote a general discussion of these principles, guiding the participants to a fuller understanding. He should do this by questions and dialogue which focus the attention of the participants on the general principles involved, but he should avoid formulating these principles for them.

This debriefing evaluation will sometimes lead the instructor to decide that the group activity should be repeated to deepen the learners' understanding of the principles involved.

11.4 Some techniques for small group work

vo types
small group
rning

Small group learning activities can be divided into two major types:

1. Verbal discussion techniques, involving two or more participants.
2. Role-playing, or case study-based techniques (including most games), which differ from the previous category in that they involve the study of a simulation of some real-life situations or phenomenon.

In this chapter we will deal with verbal discussion techniques, while role-playing and case study-based techniques will be dealt with in Chapter 12.

11.5 The 'dialogue' technique

11.5.1 Characteristics

scussion
diads

Two people discuss a given topic for a given period, in order to share opinions and reconcile viewpoints. The learners are divided into 'diads' — groups of two members — or into larger groups and sub-groups of two members. In the latter case, the sub-groups hold discussions in turn, in front of the other group members.

11.5.2 Organization

☐ Selection and definition of appropriate topics by the instructor or by the group members.
☐ Structuring of the groups and sub-groups.
☐ Allocation of topics to the sub-groups, in cases where different pairs of participants discuss different topics or different aspects of a topic.
☐ Allocation of preparation time to the pairs, to allow them to prepare a discussion plan.

11.5.3 Briefing

☐ Establish the principal aims or objectives of the discussions.
☐ Establish a timetable.
☐ Determine how, and at what points in the dialogue (if at all), the observers may question the pair holding the dialogue. Sometimes questions from the floor may be allowed to guide or stimulate the discussion. In other applications it is better not to allow such interventions.

11.5.4 Coordination

☐ Introduce the first pair of speakers and the topic (this may be done by the participants themselves).
☐ Execute timekeeping/chairmanship tasks.

11.5.5 Debriefing

☐ Evaluate the content and the style of the discussions in relation to the objectives of the exercise.
☐ Lead the participants in a final self-evaluating discussion. Get them to state clearly what has been learned.

11.6 The Phillips 6-6 technique

11.6.1 Characteristics

Discussion in groups of about six members

This technique was developed by Donald Phillips at the University of Michigan and takes its name from its principal characteristics — a group of six people discuss a given topic for six minutes. Naturally, this 6-6 format may be varied in practice without substantially altering the basis of the technique. However, the group size should be about six people (say four to eight), and the time of discussion should be about six minutes (say five to 10 minutes). Any greater deviations from the norm may lead to fundamentally different group interactions.

11.6.2 Organization

Generally, this technique does not stand on its own, but is integrated into a large group session at an appropriate moment. When a question for analysis or discussion arises, the instructor divides the larger group into small groups of about six members.

11.6.3 Briefing

☐ Define the topic for discussion clearly. Generally, all the sub-groups discuss the same topic.
☐ Establish the rules of discussion (see below).

11.6.4 Coordination

☐ Get the groups started on the discussion.

☐ After about five minutes, ask the group leaders or 'secretaries' to formulate the conclusions of the group members. Allow about one minute for this.

☐ Bring the groups together and ask the leaders/secretaries to report back. Allow about one minute for each group's report.

☐ Appoint a coordinator/secretary to note down, on a blackboard, the chief points made in every report.

11.6.5 Debriefing

☐ Evaluate the reports of the groups' conclusions in relation to the objectives of the discussion. Were all important aspects identified? Was the topic analysed adequately? Were the conclusions justified by the data given, etc?

☐ Encourage the participants to identify the strong and weak aspects of the reports submitted. Lead the participants to a clear identification of all the factors considered relevant or essential in the discussion.

11.6.6 Special value

The Phillips 6-6 technique is especially useful for promoting the active participation of all members of a larger group, by breaking it down into six-member groups for a limited period of time. It is useful for obtaining the opinions of all the group members on a given question in a limited period. It helps rapid decision-making and develops the skills of argument and synthesis of ideas.

11.7 Brainstorming

11.7.1 Characteristics

creative problem-solving discussion groups 10-15 members

This technique consists of the free discussion of a problem by a small group, with the objective of generating original ideas and novel solutions. The chief characteristic of the technique is to divide the discussion into stages. The first of these stages, which we may call 'ideas generation', involves the participants in free discussion of the problem posed, in an attempt to generate the greatest possible number of diverse ideas and views, some of which may lead to new solutions. To encourage diversity, it is usually forbidden to comment on or criticize the ideas of other participants at this stage. The instructor, or an appointed coordinator, makes a list of all suggestions on a blackboard or on separate cards which are displayed on a wall for all to see. Thus the creative ideas of one group member stimulate the other members to make their own insights and contribute to the list. This stage continues for a given time or until the ideas dry up.

Later stages of the discussion may entail classifying the ideas presented and eliminating duplications. This may be referred to as 'ideas organization'.

A further stage of discussion — 'ideas evaluation' — may allow the participants to comment on and criticize the suggestions of their colleagues. However, such criticisms should always be constructive, and should seek to refine the ideas and turn them into viable solutions for the problem under discussion.

When the technique is used for 'real' problem-solving, the discussion would proceed to a final stage of 'solution selection and formulation'. However, in the educational context, brainstorming is often used to explore possible solutions, without intending actually to implement a solution. In such cases, this last stage is superfluous or may be replaced by an extension of ideas evaluation to produce a shortlist of possible solutions in order of preference — 'solution evaluation'.

11.7.2 Organization

☐ Select an appropriate group size. This should be about 10-15 participants: very small groups lack the richness of ideas generation necessary to make the technique work and groups larger than 15 generally do not succeed in fully involving all the members.

☐ Organize the working space. Arrange the seating, preferably in a semi-circle facing the blackboard or other visual display to be used. The use of separate cards for the display of ideas is recommended, as they can be easily modified or reorganized in later stages of discussion, without the need for much rewriting of ideas.

11.7.3 Briefing

☐ Define the problem to be discussed. This may, for example, be a real problem, a predicted problem, or a challenge to invent something.

☐ Explain the rules of the game. Emphasize the function of each stage of discussion. Stress the importance of the following:

(a) no criticism of ideas when suggested;
(b) free association of ideas – the stronger and more outlandish the suggestions the better;
(c) large quantity of ideas – the larger the number of ideas generated, the more likely we are to produce an original solution;
(d) combination of ideas – contributions may be based on earlier ones.

11.7.4 Coordination

In this technique, the instructor generally acts as the coordinator/leader. However, he may need help to record all the ideas generated. When using cards, he may appoint two, three or more note takers to keep up with the flow of ideas.

The principal activities of coordination include:

☐ Recording the ideas and suggestions of the group participants.
☐ Stimulating the shyer, less productive, members to make contributions.
☐ Ensuring that the comments made obey the rules of the session.

11.7.5 Debriefing

The first two stages of discussion – ideas generation and ideas organization – form the main part of the brainstorming technique. The third stage – ideas evaluation – may be considered as part of the debriefing. The selection and/or evaluation of solutions also forms part of the debriefing. The role of the instructor is to:

☐ Evaluate the critical comments made by the participants at this stage.
☐ Comment on the comments, when necessary, in order to guide the participants to clearer insights and better selection of solutions.
☐ Summarize the conclusions reached.

11.7.6 Special value

Apart from its principal use for exploring, analysing and solving real problems, the brainstorming technique has several other positive benefits: the promotion of initiative, the breakdown of traditional linear patterns of thought, the development of lateral thinking approaches to problems, the development of group cooperation in problem-solving and the mastery of a general-purpose technique for the generation of creative ideas.

11.8 The integrated panel

11.8.1 Characteristics

Intensive participation by all group members in discussion and report back sessions

This technique involves two stages — discussion and report back. Each stage is performed in a small group. In the normal group discussion, or open panel technique, a large group is split into small discussion groups for a given period and a spokesman for each group then reports back the group's opinions in a plenary session.

In the integrated panel, the original groups are restructured in such a way that each new group contains one member from each of the original groups. For example, a group of 30 participants could initially be split into five groups of six members to discuss a given topic. Later, the participants are reorganized into six groups of five members, one from each of the original five groups. Within each new group, each member can report back on the findings of his original group. There is therefore no need for a plenary session. The advantages of the integrated panel are that all participants have to report back on the first stage, and the comparison of views at the second stage is performed in a more intensive, small group atmosphere. Both these characteristics make for more active participation by all members.

11.8.2 Organization

Organize the original groups to give a good mix of personalities or viewpoints, in order to extract the maximum benefit from the ensuing discussion. Alternatively, let the groups organize themselves. In the latter case, it is likely that members with similar attitudes or viewpoints will group themselves together. However, this group structure will inevitably get broken up at the second stage of report back and evaluation.

11.8.3 Briefing

☐ Define the topic or problem to be discussed.
☐ Define the objectives of the discussion.
☐ Explain the two stages and the structure of the groups in each stage.
☐ Explain that all participants will act as reporters at the second stage and must therefore take notes at the first stage of discussion.

11.8.4 Coordination

The task of coordination is limited to timekeeping and observation of the group activities in case any unexpected difficulties arise.

11.8.5 Debriefing

The integrated panel is a technique particularly useful for the reinforcement of previously learned knowledge and skills by applying them to given problems. As each aspect of the problem is likely to be discussed in at least one of the groups, and as, later, all the different conclusions of the initial group are pooled in the second stage of discussion, all participants are necessarily exposed to the whole range of views. It is therefore usually unnecessary for the instructor to plan a separate debriefing discussion. His observations of the group discussions are sufficient to evaluate whether the members are correctly using the knowledge and skills being reinforced. If at least some of the initial groups are on the right lines, then all participants will share their findings at the second stage of report back.

11.9 The seminar

11.9.1 Characteristics

The seminar promotes research, planning of presentations and critical discussion

This technique is very well known. Although the word 'seminar' tends to be used for almost any small or medium-sized group study, the classic seminar involves the preparation, by one student, or a sub-group, of a paper on a given topic, which is then presented to the group as a whole for analysis and discussion.

11.9.2 Organization

Depending on the size of the overall group, it should be divided into small groups of two to 10 people, to give a total number of sub-groups that can be accommodated in the time available for the seminar work. Remember that each sub-group will present a paper which will then be discussed, probably requiring about one hour for each group. Different groups generally present their papers in different sessions, over a period of several days or weeks. It is necessary, therefore, to plan the timetable in advance, allowing ample time for each sub-group to prepare its paper.

Generally, the seminar topics for each sub-group are different but related to each other, covering various aspects of the same subject. It is therefore necessary to plan the seminar topics carefully and to provide the resources required for study or research. This may take the form of bibliographies or other sources of information.

11.9.3 Briefing

☐ In the first session of the series, present the subject area to be studied, the views to be examined, the importance of the subject, etc.

☐ Divide the group into sub-groups and distribute the seminar topics among the groups.

☐ Establish the overall objectives of study and the specific objectives for each seminar group.

☐ If necessary, explain the methodology of seminar work, indicate the available resources for study and distribute and explain bibliographies.

11.9.4 Coordination

☐ Between sessions, it may be necessary to assist the groups in organizing themselves and dividing the tasks of study.

☐ During the presentations the instructor plays a minimal role, acting as timekeeper and resolving any problems that may occur. Generally, however, the groups are self-sufficient, taking over the coordination of their own presentations.

11.9.5 Debriefing

During the presentations, the instructor evaluates the performance of each group and the other participants in the ensuing discussions. Points to be evaluated include:

☐ The group's grasp of the topic being studied.

☐ The extent and the depth of the research undertaken by the group to prepare its paper.

☐ The quality of the arguments, views or analyses presented in the papers.

☐ The ability of the group to explain and defend its views in the ensuing discussion.

☐ The participation of the other members in the discussion, their perception of sound and unsound arguments, etc.

At the end of each session, a general discussion of the work should be held. This should focus on two aspects:

(a) The final conclusions reached on the topic under study.
(b) The methodology of research, presentation and defence employed by the presenting group.

In this manner, succeeding groups may build on the experience gained in earlier sessions, in order to improve their skills of research, organization and presentation of arguments.

11.10 Selection of appropriate techniques

Modify or invent techniques to suit instructional objectives

The five techniques described above are but a representative selection of possible group work techniques. It is, of course, possible to invent variations on the structure of these basic models to adapt them to one's needs. For example, the seminar model may be compressed into just one or two sessions, with several groups making mini-presentations during the same session. Each short presentation may be followed by a short discussion period, or, alternatively, there may be just one discussion, encompassing all the presentations given.

The form of group work should be appropriate to the objectives of study, to the level of the participants, to the overall size of the group, to the resources and space available and to the skills of the instructor. Rather than selecting a standard technique from a limited list, the recommended approach is to *design* the required characteristics of the group activity, taking into consideration all the factors just mentioned. Then, if a standard technique does not fit the bill exactly, an appropriate method may be invented or an existing one adapted to fit. This approach avoids the lamentable tendency to get hooked on one particular technique and to use it indiscriminately for all teaching.

11.10.1 Objectives

Two main types of objectives that may be pursued by the use of group learning exercises

Group work generally has two sets of objectives:

☐ Objectives related to the *content* of study – new concepts or principles to be mastered and applied, or specific problem-solving strategies to be practised, etc.
☐ Objectives related to the *process* of study – the interactive skills involved in group work, research skills involved in preparing seminar papers, productive thinking skills practised in brainstorming exercises, and so on.

Both types of objectives should be analysed in order to select the most appropriate group learning strategies. Indeed, we must decide whether group work is indicated at all for certain objectives. In cases where the content of the study is common to all the students, where the mastery of the content in minimum time is especially important and where there are no specific 'process' objectives to be pursued, more time-consuming and less directed group learning techniques are probably not appropriate.

11.10.2 The level of the participants

Consider the learning skills of the participants

The participants will vary in terms of their experience of working in groups, in their experience of autonomous learning, and in the level of their research and discussion skills. It is important not to select techniques which are too far outside the range of learning habits already present in the group. When working with less sophisticated groups, it is as well to begin with techniques that do not involve a very high degree of autonomy or participation, and slowly graduate to the use of more participative and more student directed techniques.

Consideration should also be given to the personal characteristics of the participants, their age, level of education, interests, motivations and expectations of the course of study. There is no point in engaging in lengthy discussion with groups whose members do not yet have the background knowledge necessary to discuss the topic intelligently, or who need to learn quickly a specific skill that you can demonstrate and teach. On the other hand, there is no point in lecturing or drilling students who already have considerable knowledge and views on the subject and are on the course in order to exchange ideas.

11.10.3 Size of the group

Consider size and structure of the groups

Smaller numbers permit the use of more informal methods, without a greatly organized structure or rigid rules of procedure. As the overall numbers grow, it becomes important to construct a formal structure for discussion, establish rules, have a strong chairman, etc.

A large group may always be subdivided into smaller, parallel groups, if space and other factors permit. It should be remembered that certain objectives, such as ideas generation in brainstorming, require a minimum number of participants. Other techniques can only be used with very small groups or with a certain specific number of members in each group.

11.10.4 Resources and space available

Make sure that all necessary resources and facilities are available

There should be ample space for each group to work in comfort, without interfering with the work of other groups. This may impose a limit on number or size of groups that can be used.

When the technique being considered requires bibliographic research or fieldwork the necessary study resources should be readily available, in quantities adequate for the number of groups competing for their use.

Finally, the time necessary for the group to complete these assignments should be assessed carefully. Larger groups might allow a greater level of delegation of the tasks, shortening the overall time needed for group work and reducing the number of report back and debriefing sessions. The use of a larger number of smaller groups may permit the subdivision into smaller tasks of the subject under study, requiring less time per group.

11.10.5 Skills of the instructor

Make sure that you are prepared to run the session

We should remember that none of the techniques mentioned above is an effective solution in its own right — 'it's not what you do, but the way that you do it' is a maxim worth remembering when considering group learning methods. This is particularly important in those techniques which require expert coordination (eg brainstorming) or which promote experiential learning thus requiring careful evaluation of the learning actually taking place and, with meticulous debriefing sessions, generalization and reinforcement of the principles being studied.

The instructor should himself master the skills necessary to lead group work. He may do this by the initial selection of simpler techniques, appropriate to his present level of skill and experience, slowly graduating to more complex designs which require a higher level of coordination and briefing/debriefing skills.

A complement, not a rival to other techniques

11.11 Group work in the context of other instructional techniques

The techniques we have studied in this chapter take their place alongside the more traditional techniques of classroom instruction analysed in the previous chapter and alongside individual tutorial or self-study techniques. All are tools to be applied judiciously by the instructor.

Group work should not be seen as a rival to the other techniques. Indeed, very often, a combination of techniques is needed, for example the use of individual study of certain basic material as a prerequisite for later group activities. In other cases, a series of conventional classroom lessons may establish the groundwork necessary to participate profitably in a group discussion.

We have already drawn the distinction between group learning techniques and group dynamics. Any group situation has a specific dynamic — a specific set of forces that act between the group members. The instructor, in his role as coordinator of the group learning activities, may benefit from his knowledge of group dynamics in getting the group members to work together more productively.

However, the systematic use of group dynamics (or, rather, the use of techniques for modifying a group's dynamics and thus modifying the personality or self-concept of the participants) is largely outside the scope of this book. Such techniques as transactional analysis, self-criticism sessions and even the T-group do not really fall within our concept of instruction, as generally there are no specific instructional objectives to be attained.

When, however, real-life situations are simulated and something specific about the real situation is taught, we are in the domain of instruction. Some simulations make conscious and systematic use of an understanding of group dynamics to reach their instructional objectives. We shall meet some examples of this in the following chapter.

11.12 Examples of lesson plans for group learning

We shall close this chapter by presenting some examples of lesson plans that set out to use group learning techniques. As in the last chapter, we present a series of examples, analyse them, and comment on aspects of their structure.

11.12.1 Example 1: The seasons

At the end of Chapter 10, we presented a lesson plan on the seasons of the year to be given to primary school children. The author of this lesson plan gave the lesson to several groups, with a good measure of success. However, as an exercise in the planning and use of group learning techniques, the same author prepared an alternative lesson plan, which we present here as Exhibit 11.1 (see page 169).

This plan opts for a strategy based on learning by sharing experiences. In a group of children of the age group proposed, there already exists a body of experience of a variety of phenomena associated with the changing of the seasons. It may be possible to harness this experience by using an appropriate group learning exercise. Perhaps a lesson can be devised which requires very little information input from the teacher, but which relies on the learners to share the bits of information that each possesses.

The various techniques described in the chapter were considered for this lesson, and evaluated in the following terms:

☐ The *dialogue* showed some promise, but was rejected because it does not guarantee that each child is exposed to all the communal experience of the class members.

☐ The *Phillips 6-6* method was likewise discarded, as it is more suited to the critical analysis of a problem than to the pooling of information on a topic.

☐ *Brainstorming* was considered initially, but it is a technique that requires a great deal of self-discipline which the age group in question perhaps lacks. Moreover, it is designed for creative, lateral thinking, and is not appropriate for the definition and application of simple concepts.

[marginal notes:]
e use group namics

relatively ple plication group rning in mary ools

ich type exercise uld we ect?

☐ The *seminar* technique was seriously considered. Why not get four groups to each prepare profiles of the seasons of the year? However, t would have consumed much more time than the original expositive lesson and could not therefore be justified in this case.

☐ The technique chosen was the *integrated panel*. It guarantees that ever child in the group participates actively in a small group situation, thin up a schema of seasonal characteristics and is then exposed to the idea of all the other children. The time taken for this technique is not likel to be much greater than that for the conventional large group exposit lesson.

The lesson plan . . . The tactics used for implementing the technique selected

The detailed structure of the resulting lesson plan is shown in Exhibit 11.1 c page 196. Note that some of the opening activities are exactly as planned in the earlier version and so are not repeated here in detail. The briefing stage (step 3) is, however, an important addition to the opening activities. Note tl this step has a structure very similar to the one used in the earlier plan to be the skill development stage of the lesson – the children learn to construct a compare/contrast table of the four seasons. It is probable that such tables ha already been used for other purposes in the past so the children should not find it very difficult to comprehend the 'rules of the game'.

As soon as the children show a reasonable understanding of what is expected of them they are split into structured groups and get on with the s task in their own way. From this point on, the teacher takes a secondary rol of observation and possible reorientation and the children themselves genera the information content and organize it into a comprehensive schema. The

Structuring the groups

groups are so structured that each one contains some brighter, more experienced children and some slower learners. In this way, the process of information and experience sharing is better distributed and will probably result in the 'product' from each of the groups being of a uniform quality.

When the groups are restructured, the teacher should again attempt to m the abilities in each group, as well as attending to the main principle of restructuring – one member of each old group in each of the new groups. However, it is necessary to avoid the best or worst of each of the original groups being put together in one of the new groups. If this were to happen, the discussions and insight-sharing in some groups will be less productive than in others. It is essential to have at least some live wires in each of the groups at all times.

The closing activities in this lesson plan are limited to a debriefing sessior in which the teacher leads a discussion comparing the findings of each of the groups and providing the class members with an opportunity to demonstrate that they can generalize what they have learned. They must state the concep learned in a clear and concise manner and show by the logic of their argume that they have formed adequately structured concepts and have integrated them appropriately with other related knowledge. If the debriefing session shows that the learners have indeed constructed a sufficiently powerful cognitive schema relating to the seasons of the year, then there is probably no real need for further transfer of learning activities.

11.12.2 Example 2: Solving human relations problems

Relatively complex application of group learning exercises in the training of foremen

Our second example is taken from a very different area – the training of adu (foremen and supervisors) in a range of highly productive, interactive skills - the resolution of human relations problems that may occur between membe of the workforce of an industrial organization. The sample lesson plan is presented in Exhibit 11.2 (see pages 170 - 171).

The reader will find this plan substantially more complex and the resultir lesson very much longer than the other examples analysed so far. In reality, the instructional designer is suggesting a series of about six brainstorming

Lesson title: The seasons of the year
Target population: Primary school children, aged 8-9
Number of students: 30   Time required: 1 hour 15 minutes

Lesson objectives: As in Chapter 10
Equipment/resources required: As in Chapter 10

Information (teacher activity)	Behaviour (learning activity)	Feedback (reinforcing activity)	Time (minutes)
Opening events			
1. Attention — as in Chapter 10			5
2. Recall of prerequisites — as in Chapter 10			5
3. Briefing Prepare a classification chart on the blackboard and locate about four example characteristics in the correct columns.	Children should demonstrate full comprehension by suggesting and classifying some other examples of seasonal characteristics.	Continue only as long as it proves to be necessary for most of the class to grasp the general idea of the chart.	No more than 10
Instructional strategy 4. Initial discussion Form six groups of five children each, mixing ability levels in each of the groups. Set a specific topic area for analysis by each group. The topics should be different, but may be related. Distribute a blank version of the classification chart to all learners.	Each group should analyse its topic and prepare a chart of seasonal characteristics. Each group member completes his own copy of the final chart.	Circulate among the groups, to observe their work and advise and direct the group members when necessary. But do not do the work for the group.	15
5. Report pool Reform the groups into five groups of six members, each group containing one person from each of the former groups.	Each member of the new group presents his chart to the others and receives comments, criticisms and additions. All six charts are displayed on the wall to give a composite picture.	Circulate and orient as before. Note the differences that appear between the charts of different groups and analyse them for future comment during debriefing.	25
Closing events 6. Debriefing Bring the children together into a large group. Comment on the differences observed between the groups. Ask for explanations. Seek to evaluate the learning that has taken place. Assess the conceptual schemata formed by the learners.	The children should comment critically on their own work and on the work of others. They should also be led to defend their opinions and justify the characteristics they have included in their charts.	Evaluate the logic of the arguments presented in discussions, as well as the list of seasonal characteristics compiled by the learners. The closing briefing may therefore act as an instrument of evaluation of the lesson as a whole.	15

Exhibit 11.1 *Sample lesson plan on the seasons*

Lesson title: Solving human relations problems in industry
Target population: Foremen and supervisors from organization XYZ
Number of trainees: 10-15   Time required: 8-10 hours

Lesson objectives:

1. Given typical human relations problems in an industrial setting, the trainees will be able to: (a) analyse the problems, identifying the principal causes; (b) apply known principles of human relations management to the problems in order to suggest appropriate forms of solutions. Both the analysis and the synthesis should be judged as 'correct and practically viable' by a skilled manager of human relations.

2. A subsidiary 'process' objective. Given a problem to be solved by a group of employees, organize the problem-solving session in the form of brainstorming and lead the session through its various stages, keeping to the rules of the technique and achieving, in a reasonable time (one hour) a satisfactory set of possible solutions (satisfactory in terms of the number of different solutions and the probable viability of at least some of them).

Equipment/resources required:
A minimum of six case studies of typical human relations problems of the type commonly encountered in organization XYZ. The cases described should be relatively difficult to solve, but should offer the opportunity to consider a number of different types of solution. Large blackboard or wall space suitable for cards or paper sheets. Writing materials suitable for the group to be able to see the charts and posters comfortably.

Instructor activity	Learner activity	Feedback activity	Time (minutes)
Opening events			
1. Attention/ motivation Tell the story of Solomon and the two women claiming the same child, or some other tale that illustrates the use of innovatory solutions to human disputes. Lead the group to analyse the human relations situation in organization XYZ.	Participate in the storytelling and draw parallels between the situations described and the reality of working in the company.	Observe the participation of the trainees in the discussion, and identify signs that indicate reluctance to solve human relations problems, or other motivational deficiencies. Try to correct attitudes before proceeding to the main part of the lesson.	5-15 (depending on the attitudes of the trainees)
2. Briefing Define the aims and rules of brainstorming. Explain how the technique will be used in the present exercise.	Suggest a list of advantages that brainstorming may offer in the context of XYZ.	Clear up any doubts that may exist concerning the aims or the methods of the technique.	5
3. Prerequisites By means of a question and answer session, recall the principles of good human relations management (these were taught in earlier lessons).	Reply to the questions, showing adequate mastery of the principles concerned.	Assess and, if necessary, reinforce earlier learning, by means of suitable revision exercises.	Depends on needs. If no revision is needed, 5 will suffice.
Main strategy			
4.1 Ideas generation Present a typical human relations problem as the basis for the first exercise. Ask for suggestions of possible causes. Write down all suggestions, and display them on wall.	Make suggestions of all possible causes of the problem, including unusual and improbable ones.	Control session, quashing any attempts at premature criticism of contributions. Encourage shy trainees to make suggestions.	About 15

Exhibit 11.2 *A sample lesson plan for problem-solving skills in the field of industrial relations*

Instructor activity	Learner activity	Feedback activity	Time (minutes)
4.2 Ideas organization Ask trainees to classify, improve or eliminate items in the list of causes. Identify the most likely causes.	Trainees may now comment and criticize earlier suggestions, as long as they are constructive.	Control any tendency to purely destructive criticism.	5-10
5.1 Generation — phase 2 Now ask for suggestions of possible solutions. Write down and display all the suggestions on the wall or blackboard.	Trainees should make as many and as varied suggestions as they can in the time available.	Control and encourage, as in step 4.1.	10-15
5.2 Organization — phase 2 Ask trainees to classify, improve or eliminate items in the list of possible solutions. Identify the most plausible solutions.	See step 4.2	See step 4.2	5-10
5.3 Ideas evaluation Lead trainees to the evaluation of the alternative plausible solutions and to selection of a solution to be implemented.	Trainees should discuss the pros and cons of each plausible solution previously identified. They should reach a consensus on the most viable one.	Evaluate the process of discussion and critical evaluation performed by the trainees. Evaluate the choice of solution.	15-20
6. More practice Repeat steps 4 and 5, using the other five cases of human relations problems. In each case, appoint a different trainee, or a team of two or three trainees, to organize and coordinate the session.	Each trainee has the opportunity of leading a brainstorming session, as well as ample extra practice in the analysis and solution of human relations problems.	The feedback activities that are listed in steps 4 and 5 above are now executed by the appointed trainees. The instructor observes the session as a whole and the performance of the leaders, in order to redirect them if necessary.	About 1 hour for each of the exercises (total 5 hours)
Closing events			
7. Debriefing Start a discussion on the solutions chosen. Question the theoretical bases for each solution. Question the practical viability. Invite analysis of the way in which the solutions were selected. Question the overall usefulness of brainstorming. Question the value of this particular exercise.	Trainees should demonstrate, by their arguments and comments, that they have formed sufficiently powerful and general problem-solving strategies and associated schemata of the principles involved. They should also describe how to implement the proposed solutions in the real-life situation of XYZ.	Evaluate the strategies and schemata of the trainees. Take decisions on whether more practice exercises are required to ensure transfer of the new skills to the job situation. Extend and/or replan the training sessions if necessary.	About 45
8. Transfer of learning Arrange for regular small group discussions, similar to the debriefing session described above, to analyse the real life decisions taken, after training, and to resolve problems occurring on the job.	Trainees should describe to the group how they came to make their decisions. The group analyses the decisions and predicts or comments on the end results.	As in item 7, the instructor attempts to evaluate the structures and strategies that are developing in the trainee's mind, in order to offer useful advice.	No prediction of the time needed

Exhibit 11.2 *(continued)*

sessions, each one lasting about one hour. In addition, some time will be
spent on initial briefing and a greater amount of time devoted to a final
debriefing/evaluation session. The total time for this training is thus estimate
to be seven and a half hours — a full working day if performed in one session
We would recommend dividing the training into two sessions of about four
hours each, or even more, shorter, sessions if possible, in order to reap the
benefits of spaced practice and avoid the tedium that might creep in if the
same type of exercise is repeated six times in succession.

In addition to this basic series of exercises, the planner suggests a phase
of on-the-job training, to ensure the transfer of the skills practised in the
classroom to the real job situation.

Why select brain-storming?
The instructional strategy is based entirely on group learning exercises,
specifically on the use of brainstorming sessions. The selection of this
technique is based on quite obvious considerations. Brainstorming is
specifically designed to promote the productive thinking that is necessary
to create solutions to novel and complex problems. Human relations
problems generally fall into this category. They are problems that cannot
be solved by the application of some standard algorithmic procedure, but, or
the contrary, require the application of general principles for the generation
of new problem-solving strategies. The particular example we are studying is
a rather more complex application of brainstorming than usual. The general
problem-solving strategy that is suggested has two productive thinking stages
first, the generation of ideas about possible causes, and, second, the generatio
of possible solutions. These two stages are reflected in the resultant lesson
plan (see steps 4 and 5).

The presence of 'product' and 'process' objectives
The instructional plan is further complicated by the inclusion of more tha
one principal objective. In addition to the skills of human relations problem-
solving, the lesson aims to develop the practical skills of running a
brainstorming session. This complicates the design somewhat, as all trainees
must be given the opportunity to lead a session. This is one of the motives fc
including as many as six cases to be solved. However,the development of the
problem-solving skills also requires repetitive practice on a variety of problem
The greater the variety, the more likely it is that the trainees will transfer the
new skill effectively to the job. For both these reasons, the training design is
lengthy and complex.

Modifications in detail but coherence in general
The design nevertheless follows the general recommendations for lesson
planning suggested in the previous chapter. A three-column format for the
presentation of the plan is adopted. The heading titles of the three columns
have been slightly amended — from information/behaviour/feedback to
instructor activity/learner activity/feedback. These are alternative titles that
are perhaps a little more accurate in describing the contents of the three
columns in designing group learning activities or experiential learning exercise
In such cases, the instructor is not always the provider of information. Very
often, information is generated by the learners themselves — from their past
experience or from the real-life or simulated experiences which the learners
are currently analysing.

The reader should compare the form of this lesson plan with the earlier
examples and with our basic 'three communication channel' model of the ide
instructional process, in order to satisfy himself that the lesson plans are
basically in line with our general lesson planning model. As with the other
examples, some of the suggested basic steps may not be apparent at first sigh
Some may be run into each other. Others may be omitted as superfluous.
However, the overall philosophy and approach to lesson design is the same in
all examples. We consider that this particular example illustrates very clearly
the value, at the planning stage, of reserving a separate column for feedback
activities. In this example, extensive and varied use is made of this column.

In later chapters we will meet further examples of the same basic approac
applied to other types of lessons.

12. Producing Educational Simulations and Games

12.1 Games and simulations — what and why?

Simulation has been defined as an attempt to 'give the appearance and/or to give the effect of something else'. This somewhat wide definition would seem to cover such things as play acting, disguise, models, even photographs and paintings.

There is, however, one further aspect of simulation which our definition should include. All simulations actively involve the learners in making decisions, playing roles, adopting attitudes or operating the simulator. The learner learns by 'manipulating the model'. If we use the word 'model' here in the wide sense (ie a model of an object, a process, or a complex system), then simulators are models which can be manipulated or operated in some way or other. We might therefore extend our definition of simulation to say that an educational simulation:

1. Requires a model (something giving the appearance and/or the effect of something else).
2. Requires that the learners operate or manipulate the model in order to learn.

The model is usually a simplified version of the real object, process or system under study. However, the extent to which one can simplify the model depends very much on the learning objectives. Those aspects of reality under study must be reproduced as faithfully as possible in the model; aspects not under study may be omitted from it. Thus when learners operate the model the effects of certain actions or decisions are similar to the effects one would obtain in reality.

Educational gaming is sometimes considered as a branch of educational simulation. However, there are some differences. Certainly the well publicized war games, in which army officers play out strategic moves against each other and a computer, or management games, which pit executives against each other, in similar battles concerned with production or sales, are examples of simulation. The participants make decisions and follow rules very similar to those which govern actions in reality. The computer, or sometimes a human adjudicator, acts as a store of the sort of data which may normally be available in reality and sometimes also as a generator of the type of chance events which again may occur in reality. The value of such games to the participant is in direct relation to how well the games simulate the decisions that have to be taken in real wars or in the real business world.

The main difference between these games and other simulations, such as computer simulations of a business structure or of an economy, is the element of competition which is introduced. Indeed, this is perhaps the main discriminating factor between games and simulations.

Among the usually quoted benefits of the use of simulation and gaming exercises are:

1. They can provide the student with experiences and practice which are much closer to the real-life situations he would encounter than might otherwise be possible in a training course. In particular, they can

reproduce the pressures and stresses under which students will have to work.

2. They can therefore be useful as methods of measuring how well studen are able to apply previously learned facts, concepts, or principles to real-life situations.

3. They allow one to simplify reality, controlling those aspects of a real-life situation to which a student should attend and respond.

4. They are often economically justified as a substitute for on-the-job practice when it would be difficult to arrange this, eg expensive, easily broken equipment (medical simulators), remote situations (space travel simulators or school geography games), and equipment used for day and night production (industrial process simulators).

5. They are often justified on safety grounds, in that they enable students to practise dangerous or threatening jobs without any danger (pilot training simulators, simulations of highly stressed personal situations such as dealing with discipline problems in the classroom, war games, et

6. A well-designed simulation or game usually involves students in the learning task, both intellectually and emotionally, more than other available techniques.

7. As a result of items 3 and 6, they have been found to be an extremely effective way of measuring, changing and reinforcing student attitudes.

8. Finally, simulation can of course be used as a research technique. The model being used in the simulation should reflect reality. If we understand the real-life phenomenon under study sufficiently, we shoul be able to construct a valid model. If, however, we do not fully understand the real problem, we construct a tentative model — a model which reflects our hypotheses about the problem. We can then operate the model and observe the effects, comparing them with the effects we obtain in reality. Any discrepancies are analysed, and, if necessary, the model is redesigned and our hypotheses changed.

12.2 The range of simulation and gaming techniques

Schema of the main categories

Several types of instructional techniques are commonly classified as simulatio gaming, or a combination of the two. They include case studies, role-playing, full simulations, educational games, instructional games and simulation games In order better to define and distinguish these categories, we shall give a brief description of each. We may interrelate the categories as illustrated in Figure 12.1 on p 175. The diagram attempts to show that all the techniques mentioned are based on the extraction of data or situations from the reality with which the learning is concerned.

Case study

Case studies are based on data extracted from a real case and adapted to illustrate better a specific phenomenon or to practise a particular decision-

Role-play

making process. Role-playing exercises may use some data about a real situation, but also include a specification of the characteristics, or roles, of the people involved, thus in some respects mirroring the reality more closely

Simulation

than a case study. A full simulation is even closer to reality, being based on a model of certain aspects of the real situation under study that the learners may operate in an interactive manner.

Educational game

On the other side of the diagram there are games. First there are education games, which aim at general educational objectives — basic skills, general knowledge. Then there are instructional games, based on specific objectives that the learners should achieve and are therefore more direclty based on

Instructional game

the analysis of a particular real situation. Games, whether instructional or educational, do not have to be full-scale simulations, as they may only practis isolated skills or specific steps of a much more complex real-life procedure. They do this in the context of *competition*, either between learners, or agains some standard of performance.

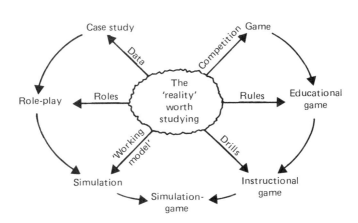

Figure 12.1 *Relationships between games and simulations
used in education and training*

At the bottom of the diagram is the simulation game. This is a learning exercise that combines elements of the full simulation exercise with the competitive element of games. This last category has become more generally used in recent years, at all levels of education and for all categories of objectives. We shall study several examples of simulation games later in the chapter.

A somewhat different view of the relationship between games, simulations and case studies is presented by Percival and Ellington, who conceptualize these three pure types of instructional techniques (see Figure 12.2 on p 176). This may be quite a useful way of classifying examples of the many types of games and simulations now used in education. However, it is important to emphasize the part that role-playing has as a technique in its own right and also as part of many simulations. It is also useful to draw a distinction between the 'educational' game, which has broad, general objectives, and the 'instructional' game, developed to lead students to the achievement of specific, often job-related objectives.

12.3 Applications of simulations and games

It is possible to use simulations and games across the whole spectrum of learning categories, although it may not always be desirable or particularly efficient to do so. We shall examine some specific examples of the application of simulations and games later. We will also discuss the factors to be taken into consideration when deciding whether to use them in particular situations.

As in all other cases, the particular application must be analysed from two viewpoints:

1. Analysis of the real phenomena, situations or skills that are to be learned, in order to be able to design an appropriately realistic model or exercise.
2. Analysis of the learning tasks and difficulties involved, in order to decide how much simplification of reality, or how much breakdown into simpler exercises, is appropriate.

Once this analysis is complete, the next steps will depend on the type and purpose of the proposed simulation or game. Using our four major skill categories as a basis, we can distinguish the principal uses of simulations and games.

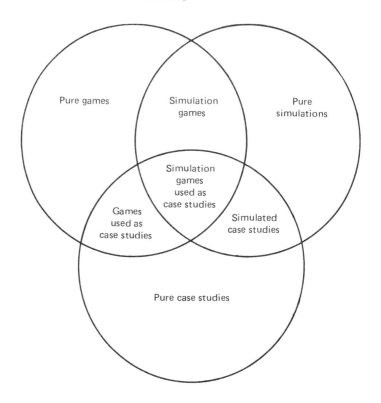

Figure 12.2 *Another view of the relationship between games simulations and case studies as 'overlapping sets' (Percival and Ellington, 1980)*

Use for cognitive objectives

1. *Cognitive domain.* The learners should demonstrate an understanding of the phenomenon being simulated, (the conceptual knowledge) and should use this understanding to explain the phenomenon, solve particular problems that involve the phenomenon and invent new ways of using the phenomenon, etc. Most simulations and games may have two separate functions in this domain:

(a) the transmission of new knowledge and/or the formation and restructuring of conceptual schemata;
(b) the development of logical thinking, memorization, analytical, creative and other cognitive skills.

Use for psychomotor objectives

2. *Psychomotor domain.* Any well-designed off-the-job training exercise is a form of simulation of the real job situation, or of a specific selected part (one sub-skill, for example). Occasionally, special exercises for the development of perception, or dexterity, or strength and stamina (which are of general use and not related to one specific job situation) may be organized in the form of games. The more complex, 'total' simulations in this domain, such as driving simulators, the 'Link' trainer for pilots or the simulated space capsule for astronauts, often involve the development of productive skills that require both the planning and execution of actions. In such cases, the simulation exercise may also help the learner to acquire and organize relevant knowledge into effective planning strategies.

3. *Reactive domain.* In many simulations and games the main objectives are

e for
itudes
d values

that the learners should emerge from the experience with a changed attitude, or with new values. Many so-called 'social' simulations fall into this category. Learning may involve the development of self-control skills, as in the case of a simulation of stress situations in business games, or the development of new knowledge structures, as in the case of a simulation such as TENEMENT, which aims to give an idea to middle class children of what it is like to live in a slum area.

e for
eractive
jectives

4. *Interactive domain.* In this domain, simulations are used to develop the learner's perceptions of other people's feelings and attitudes and their interpretation of other people's reactions and underlying motives. Some simulations in this category aim to develop the learner's skills in 'managing' others (leadership, selling, motivating, persuading), while other examples are more concerned with the knowledge structures that explain the behaviour of others. Again, it is not really possible to separate the skill and knowledge elements completely. The skills to be developed tend towards the 'productive' end of the schema so they incline to depend more heavily on the application of concepts and principles to construct specific strategies of action.

e for the
quisition of
owledge

Simple, drill and practice-type, exercises in simulated conditions are principally concerned with the development of reproductive skills. The more complex, 'full' simulations and simulation games may sometimes be concerned with imparting knowledge, by means of discovery, but very often are concerned with a mixture of objectives — development of productive skills and the acquisition of related knowledge, or the reorganization of existing knowledge, to accommodate new and more complex ideas. Finally, simple educational and instructional games are principally concerned with the transmission or reinforcement of knowledge.

We may imagine a continuum, with simple simulations at one end and simple games at the other, merging into more complex simulation games in the centre. On this continuum, we may map the principal categories of objectives that are usually achieved. This continuum (see Figure 12.3 below) will be used to develop a more complex schema, on which we shall hang the specific examples of simulations and games analysed in the next section.

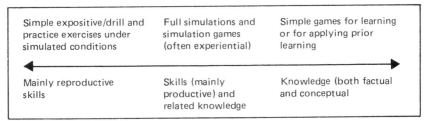

Simple expositive/drill and practice exercises under simulated conditions	Full simulations and simulation games (often experiential)	Simple games for learning or for applying prior learning
Mainly reproductive skills	Skills (mainly productive) and related knowledge	Knowledge (both factual and conceptual

Figure 12.3 *Visual representation of the relationship between categories of simulation and games and the principal categories of objectives*

12.4 A compendium of simulations and games

This section analyses a large number of examples of games and simulations. The selection has been made to illustrate the range of applications and the variety of objectives that may be achieved through the use of these techniques. Some of the examples may at first appear strange choices, as they are well known and very ancient children's games. Others may appear out of place in a book on instruction. However, the choice has been made in order to illustrate as clearly as possible the area of education and training in which games and simulations may be profitably used. Some of the examples are our own; others are the work of other well-known writers in this field; some are anonymous – having perhaps been invented by children sometime in the distant past.

In order to find our way around the compendium of examples which follows, we present in Figure 12.4 on p 179 a schema that attempts to place each of the examples in a part of a grid composed, along one axis, of the principal categories of objectives – reproductive skills, productive skills and knowledge – and along the vertical axis, of the four domains of learning that we defined in Part 2. In this way, we hope to relate our discussion of specific examples to the general schemata of learning categories and associated instructional strategies which have been the basis of much of our work so far. We suggest that readers use the schema which follows as a form of 'advance organizer' or 'conceptual index' while studying the games and simulations described later.

12.4.1 An interactive case study: FRONT-END ANALYSIS

This example is based on case study materials used on performance problem analysis workshops run by the author. Similar materials have been used by Praxis Corporation in the USA and by IDORT in Brazil. We shall not present the complete case study material here, as it runs to over a dozen pages, but shall limit ourselves to an outline of the case and the method of use.

This is not a 'classic' case study for several reasons. First, it is not fully open-ended. Although there is no unique correct solution, the components of the solution prepared by the learner are individually evaluated and a points system is used to assess and reward the participants. Second, the material is prepared in such a way that it may be used as a basis for group discussions or as a self-instructional text; the points system and the standard comments provided enable the learner to evaluate his own learning progress as he works through the case study.

1. *Initial situation.* the participants are briefed on their role as training specialists working for a large training consultancy organization. The case is introduced by a description of a client organization that has requested assistance in training its salesforce. The client organization imports and resells scientific equipment of a specialist nature to universities, research units and high-tech industries. Before this exercise, the participants have already studied the basic principles of front-end analysis, that is, the identification of where training can and cannot contribute to the improvement of performance. They are therefore already aware of the need for a reappraisal of the client's opinion that training of the salesforce is likely to improve sales and readily engage in the second stage of the exercise – the analysis of the sales situation in the client's company.

2. *Analysis of the problem.* This analysis may be organized in different ways, depending on the size of the learning group. The participants may be invited to interview the session leader to extract the information they consider important. In the self-study mode, this information is presented as a report of an imaginary interview. This report presents details of the size of the client company, its current sales, the salesforce and the sales record, together with reasons (based on comparisons with competitors) as to why the client thinks that sales could be much improved. It also gives an outline of how the typical salesman works, visiting his potential clients regularly to build up a technical and personal relationship. He eventually prepares a formal proposal of equipment items which meet the needs of the client's current and future projects. (Further data are included on how these official proposals are prepared at central office; how the salesmen are involved in the process; how they are paid; how they receive commission on sales; etc.)

At the end of the analysis of this report, the participants enter into the first round of decision-making. In the group study situation, this is organized as an

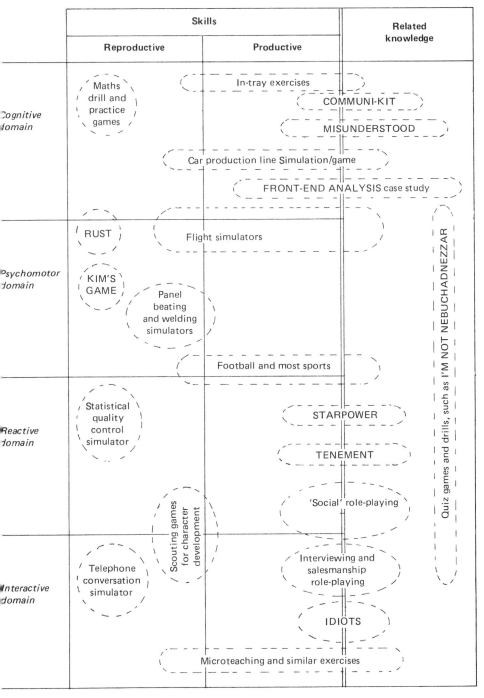

Note: The examples listed are those discussed in this section and in other parts of this chapter. The positions on the grid are only approximate. In certain cases, a particular form of exercise may step outside the bounds indicated here.

Figure 12.4 *A schema for the classification of games and simulations according to area of application/objectives achieved*

open discussion and presentation of decisions to the session leader, who is acting out the role of the client organization. The leader must, however, guide this process so that an appropriate decision is taken. Otherwise, the session simply grinds to a halt. In the self-study mode, the materials present a choice of decisions from which the learner must select that which most closely matches his own viewpoint at this stage. These choices include:

☐ Training is required – please give me more information on the tasks performed and the training objectives.

☐ Lack of motivation – please give me more data on payment systems and other possible motivators.

☐ Too early to say – please give me more information (specify) as it is not yet clear what are the real causes of poor sales performance.

The points system

The last of these alternatives is considered to be the most appropriate at this stage, and is duly rewarded by five points, whereas the other alternatives gain only one or no points. The points system is very useful in the self-study mode as it provides a means of quite flexible self-evaluation. With the group learning situation, it is not so necessary, especially when working with only one small group. When there is a large group of learners, it is, however, very effective to subdivide it into groups of three to five and use the points system as an inter-group competition element.

Stage 3: Further analysis

The second decision point

3. *Further analysis.* Having established that more information is necessary, the participants must define what information they require. In the group learning situation, this may once more be organized as open discussion. In the self-study mode, the learner must choose three from a list of 10 or more suggested questions, which he considers most useful to ask at this stage. Once the selection has been made, and the three questions recorded on a score sheet, the learners evaluate their choices with the aid of a comments sheet that analyses the strengths, weaknesses, hidden assumptions and pre-judgements of the questions. Each question choice is awarded a number of points that may vary from nought to 10. This scoring system produces the possibility of many different scores, and prompts the 'ideal' choice as only three or four of the questions are worth 10 points.

Stage 4: Design of a solution

4. *Synthesis of an optimal solution.* The case material now presents the 'answers' to the questions considered most useful. These answers are in the form of an interview report prepared in conjunction with staff from the client organization. The useful questions investigate the chief factors involved in a front-end analysis – the consequences of good or bad performance, the organization and structure of the work performed and any conflicting activities, the level of knowledge of the salesmen in relation to their job and to the performance standards expected and the extent of feedback of the results of a salesman's performance.

The third decision point

Using these reports as a basis, the participants must now engage in the third stage of decision-making – the planning of an optimal solution to the performance problems identified. Once more, this may be on the basis of guided discussion in groups, or, in the case of self-study, by selection of several alternatives from a long list. We use a standard score sheet that expects four different components of a solution to be selected from a list of about 15.

Stage 5: Debrief

5. *Debriefing.* The final stage begins with an evaluation of the solutions proposed. In the group learning mode this is done by confrontation between groups with alternative solutions, or by judicious prompting from the session leader. In the self-study mode, the learner receives a set of critical comments on each of the 15 types of solution suggested and a points system to be used in assessing his own selection. The comments sheets act as a form of debriefing as they include a final analysis, showing how the case illustrated all the typical aspects of a front-end analysis.

The ideal solution includes aspects of improved job information and job aids, the elimination of some hidden reinforcers of poor performance, the improvement of feedback of sales results to individual salesmen and the installation of a better system of reinforcement of expected performance. It does not include a training component. The final comments also emphasize that the case study was engineered to illustrate all these aspects, that in reality some training component may also be necessary and that yet other types of solution may be indicated, etc.

This debriefing can, however, be done much better in a group, when the instructor can assess the depth of comprehension of the basic principles and can ensure that a useful analysis schema has been learned.

al
mments

This description of the front-end analysis interactive case study serves to illustrate several important points:

1. The case study material, although doctored to illustrate the author's principal message, must be based on a real-life situation to which the learners can relate.
2. The task of creating and testing a set of case materials of this nature is time-consuming and requires a certain amount of practice.
3. The interactive aspect of this example transforms the case study into a step-by-step simulation of the training specialist's real-life task of deciding what the real training needs are.
4. The points system introduces an element of gaming into the exercise. This may be used to motivate individual learners or as a basis for competition between groups. The points system is not, however, an essential aspect of the exercise.
5. When used in the self-study mode, the exercise bears an affinity to programmed instruction, and even more so to structural communication.
6. The exercise may form part of an expositive strategy, as practice after a demonstration, or an experiential strategy, when a group has to discover the principles involved.

12.4.2 Microteaching as an example of role-playing

y
icro'?

There are many variations of exercises for the development of teaching skills that go by the name of 'microteaching'. The original system, developed at Stanford University in the USA could merit the label of 'micro' for two distinct reasons: first, the trainee teacher would practise only one or two of the skills normally used in a lesson during a session, and, second, the session itself was much shorter than the normal lesson. Thus, the microteaching session resembles a lesson, but is much less complex and very much shorter.

Other aspects of the session vary according to the application. Sometimes, the trainee teacher works with a small group of real students (the reduction in group size may be another reason for the label 'micro'), but often the other trainee teachers adopt the roles of the students — this mode of work is called peer teaching.

y
e-playing?

Some aspects of the real classroom teaching situation are simulated, but the microteaching sessions bear little resemblance to real lessons. They are more a set of separate exercises, which only at a later stage are welded together into realistic classroom teaching. However, the essential elements of a role-playing situation are present. The scenario is based on reality. Real topics from the curriculum are used as the vehicles for the exercises which are enacted in a realistic classroom environment, with all the necessary teaching aids available. The roles are based on real teaching behaviour, and the skills to be practised by the trainee teachers are derived from a task analysis of typical teaching.

e
croteaching
ocedure

The classical procedure for a microteaching session runs as follows:

1. The instructor demonstrates the skill to be practised. This demonstration

may be acted out by the instructor, but, more often, it is prerecorded on videotape (ready-made demonstration films may be bought or hired)

2. The group members select topics or situations from a list and prepare the session (of five to eight minutes), in which they will practise the particular skill that was demonstrated.
3. One of the group takes on the role of the teacher, while the others ado the roles of the students, and the session is enacted. (When real student are used, the other trainee teachers act as observers and evaluators.)
4. The progress of the session and the performance of the 'teacher' are evaluated. There are many possible ways of doing this. These include observations and comments by the instructor and observations and comments by the other trainee teachers, supported by notes made on pre-prepared evaluation checklists or a video recording of the performance, which can be analysed by all, including the performer being evaluated.
5. If the trainee's performance is not up to the expected standard, he may prepare a second topic and try again. This 'teach-evaluate-reteach' cycle may be repeated as often, within the limits of the time available, as is necessary to reach mastery in the skill. Usually, all the other traine will have a chance to perform once, before the reteach sessions are held
6. This procedure is repeated for each of the separate basic skills consider important for the teacher. Models differ: the original Stanford Universi model comprised 16 separate skills; other models are restricted to 12 or fewer.
7. When the separate skills have been mastered individually, further practi is arranged on somewhat more complex topics and in sessions that may be about 15 minutes long during which several of the skills are practise in combination.
8. Finally, when the instructor judges that the separate skills are sufficien well mastered and integrated, the trainees continue their practice in supervised real-life classroom situations.

Variations on the basic procedure

There are many variations on this basic routine. Although very commonly used, video feedback is not an essential element of microteaching. What is essential is the practice of real skills in simulated and simplified situations. Video feedback is most effective and tends to enhance the learning efficiency of the system, but we can get by without it. The custom of videotaping whol lessons in the real classroom and later analysing the teacher's performance is sometimes passed off as microteaching, which it is not. It may be a useful exercise, but there is no effort to simulate the essential elements of the proce and absolutely nothing 'micro' about its execution.

The greatest variety appears in the means of supplying feedback. Some instructors like to get all the participants to act as evaluators of each other; others prefer not to do this. Some use complex performance inventories or interaction analysis questionnaires; others use the minimum of instrumentatic Some rely heavily on video feedback; others do not.

Other applications of the principles

We have singled out microteaching because it is a representative example of a range of role-play exercises for the development of specific interactive skills. Other applications of basically the same methodology occur in the training of interviewers, bank managers, shop assistants, salesmen and many other types of professionals for whom interaction with the public is part of their job. In all such applications, the essential 'micro' elements of separating out the principal skills into separate exercises, thus reducing the complexity and duration of the exercises in the initial stages of training, are preserved.

Some applications may be more sophisticated than microteaching in terms of role-playing. For example, in one approach to training bank managers in the skills of interviewing clients seeking loans, the various clients were impersonated by professional actors, each with a well-defined character role and past history to guide him in his impersonation. It was up to the bank manager to break through any cover that the interviewee might put up.

All these examples are pure role-play exercises. There is no gaming element involved. They do not really simulate the real-life situation closely enough to be considered full simulations.

12.4.3 The in-tray exercise: a pure simulation

The in-tray exercise is used very widely in the training of executives and decision-makers. The documents placed in the in-tray simulate the flow of data that normally occurs in the trainee's job environment. The trainee simply works through the pile and takes decisions on how to deal with the situations that present themselves. These decisions are fed back to the exercise coordinator, who analyses them and, on the basis of this analysis, feeds other data and documents to the trainee, thus simulating the dynamics of the real working situation.

Almost any bureaucratic decision-making process may be simulated in this manner. The realism and the instructional effectiveness of the exercise depend on the care and accuracy with which the real process is analysed and its essential elements identified and included in the model that governs the decisions of the exercise coordinator.

It is essential that the consequences of the trainee's decisions are as similar as possible to those that would occur in real life. However, the danger element which may exist in real life is eliminated. The trainee may create situations that lead to strikes or to loss of contracts, without suffering the probable real-life consequences of such mismanagement. Time is compressed in the sense that, in a few hours of the exercise, the trainee may live through the stages of a problem situation that would take days or even months to develop in reality.

The in-tray exercise and its derivatives are examples of pure simulations. They do not include any gaming element, but to a high degree they do reproduce reality and the operational model that makes that reality work.

12.4.4 Simulators for psychomotor skills

The use of specially built simulators for the practice of practical skills is well known. These include driving simulators, flight simulators and the even more complex space flight simulators. However, not all simulators need to be very complex. As examples of the simplicity possible, we present some simulation exercises developed for the training of sheet metal workers in the motor industry.

The three diagrams below (Figures 12.5 on p 184, 12.6 on p 185 and 12.7 on p 186) represent, respectively, a simulation exercise to develop the correct use of a hammer in panel beating, a simulation exercise for developing the skill of using a 'dolly and spoon' (also for panel beating) and a somewhat more complex gas welding simulator. Each of the diagrams is accompanied by a short description of the objectives of the exercise, the analysis that led to the design of the simulator and the method of self-evaluation that the trainee may use to monitor his own learning. The examples are taken from a longer sequence of such simulation exercises that were produced to develop the necessary skills, one at a time, and then in combination, rather like microteaching in some respects. As the exercises are progressive and self-correcting, the approach also exhibits many features of programmed self-instruction. At the time of their development (1963-64) we called them 'programmed simulators'.

The first exercise in the series develops the skills of using a hammer to hit a given point accurately and squarely. Any error in the strikes on the real job may be identified by the fact that the dent in the sheet of metal, which should be vanishing, is instead getting bigger. However, the job only supplies

Margin notes:
w the tray ercise rks

en to an tray rcise

ulators — mplex d simple

plication sheet talwork ls

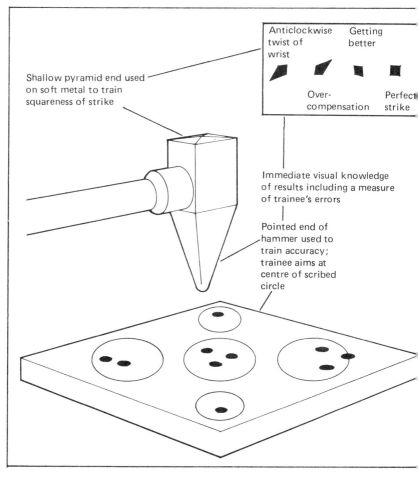

Shallow pyramid end used on soft metal to train squareness of strike

Anticlockwise twist of wrist   Getting better

Over-compensation   Perfect strike

Immediate visual knowledge of results including a measure of trainee's errors

Pointed end of hammer used to train accuracy; trainee aims at centre of scribed circle

Objective: To strike accurately and squarely.

Analysis: Points of difficulty to learner — no obvious feedback either on accuracy or squareness, as hammer rebounds too quickly. Only difficult-to-interpret feedback such as sideways jump of hammer is present naturally.

Training design: (a) Accuracy: soft workpiece, pointed hammer. Mark circles of decreasing size as targets. Aim for centre. (b) Squareness: soft workpiece, shallow pyramid point on hammer. Strike at a series of targets (eg along a line).

Evaluation: (a) Student judges progress by position of marks relative to centre of circle (knowledge of error). (b) Square strike leaves a square indented pyramid. Any irregularities in indent point to specific errors in strike. Student refers to sample errors (knowledge of error) or instructor corrects strike.

Figure 12.5 *A simple simulator used to enhance the feedback in the task of using a hammer correctly*

this feedback after many faulty strikes have been made and does not tell the operator why the dent is increasing or what he is doing wrong. The simulator enhances the feedback to the learner, enabling him to interpret his own errors and try to correct them.

Once the hammering skill is mastered, it is combined, in the second example shown, with another skill. The operator must now develop a degree of two-hand coordination, which will enable him to give support to the point being

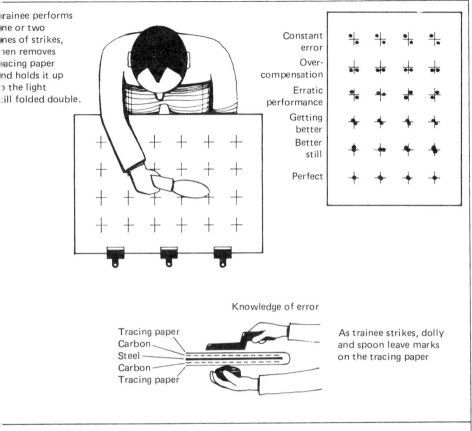

Trainee performs one or two lines of strikes, then removes tracing paper and holds it up to the light still folded double.

Constant error

Over-compensation

Erratic performance

Getting better

Better still

Perfect

Knowledge of error

Tracing paper
Carbon
Steel
Carbon
Tracing paper

As trainee strikes, dolly and spoon leave marks on the tracing paper

Objective: To beat out small dents in metal sheet.

Analysis: Difficulty in learning to strike so that 'dolly and spoon' are exactly at the right spot. Slight discrepancies can make the dent worse. This knowledge of error cannot be relied on in training as only several wrong strikes (ie practising errors) will make new dent appear obvious.

Training design: Sheet of steel for practice has carbon paper and tracing paper interleaved as shown. Target crosses marked on top sheet of tracing paper. Student strikes with spoon at a series of crosses in turn, holding the dolly below.

Evaluation: After exercise (say eight strikes) is complete, tracing paper is removed. Student can see the relative positions of cross, upper impact and lower impact (knowledge of error). He can attempt to correct error on next exercise. Several characteristic types of error exist (eg dolly always to left, or lines of motion of dolly and spoon always at a fixed angle).

Figure 12.6 *A later exercise, combining the hammering skill with others, in coordination*

hammered. Once again, the normal job situation does not tell the learner that he is making an error until it is too late. The simulated panel gives the operator visual feedback of error after every few strikes. He quickly develops considerable skill in coordinating the positions of the two tools.

Other exercises in this series give programmed practice in the localization of dents and defects, the checking of end results and the use of supplementary tools. The use of these exercises as an introduction to on-the-job training reduced the total training time for the creation of a new team of panel beaters

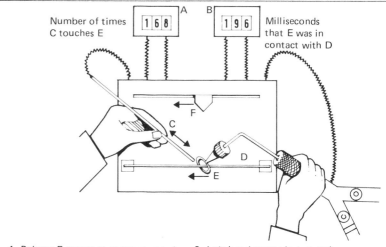

Number of times C touches E `1 6 8` `1 9 6` Milliseconds that E was in contact with D

1. Pointer F moves at constant speed.
2. Right hand moves welding torch in step with pointer, at the same time avoiding any contact between ring E and horizontal rod D.
3. Left hand moves in to touch rod C on ring E.
4. Object is to maximize score A and minimize score B.

Objective: To move torch smoothly at constant speed along seam, while other hand is irregularly feeding in welding rod.

Analysis: Coordination of uniform movement of right hand and jerky movement of left hand difficult to learn. Both speed of progress and distance from metal of the welding flame are critical.

Training design: As in diagram. Welding torch is moved right to left in step with the clockwork pointer. Loop on torch nozzle must not touch horizontal wire. The other hand feeds in the rod to touch the loop as often as possible. Each touch of welding rod on loop registers 1 on counter A. Time of contact between loop and horizontal wire registers on counter B.

Evaluation: Object is to maximize score A and minimize score B. Scores act as terminal knowledge of results, and as a measure of progress against pre-set standards.

This device is more of a full simulator than the earlier examples, as several skills are practised in coordination. One can in training break this down and first practise the right hand alone, then add the left. The scores can be used with some degree of objectivity, as a measure of the skill. Although the lowest scorers on counter B did not necessarily mak the best welders, it was found in practice that scores above a certain maximum ceiling indicated the futility of attempting to train the individual as a welder. The device has be used to aid selection as well as training.

Figure 12.7 *A more complex simulator, designed to develop the coordination skills needed by the competent gas welder*

from the 'traditional' estimate of 'two to three years on the job, supervised b a master craftsman' to a period of only four to seven weeks.

Application to gas welding skills
The welding simulator is rather more complex, in that several skills are bei practised at once. The operator is controlling the distance of the welding torch from the work, the speed of motion of the torch along the seam being welded (which should be constant and slow) and the motion of the other han which is feeding in extra metal, in the form of a welding rod, in rapid and erratic movements. Once again, there is a considerable coordination skill to master here and the real job situation does not provide adequate feedback on whether the skill is being satisfactorily developed. The simulator provides suc feedback by means of clocks and counters.

In the real job situation, the distance and speed of motion of the torch an the movements of the welding rod are all controlled by the operator's perception of the temperature of the work he is welding, the state of the molten metal below the torch, etc. If, at the time of trying to learn to interpret the real work and move the tools accordingly, the operator does not yet control the tools, no one can really say if his poor workmanship is the result of lack of coordination skills or lack of perceptual skills, or some combination of these. The simulator separates these two skills, providing practice in the coordination aspects of the task without the need for a high level of perceptual skills. Once a predetermined standard of performance is reached on the simulator, transfer to the real job gives practice in the perceptual aspects and makes the learner competent in his performance in a much shorter total learning time.

12.4.5 A simulator for changing attitudes

A problem often encountered in the training of adults might be called the 'doubting Thomas syndrome'. Trainees do not learn a given topic satisfactorily because they do not really believe that it has any relevance to their real-life situation, or that it is true at all. The proponents of andragogy — the science of adult learning — argue that it is much more important for an adult than for a child to see the relevance or the usefulness of what he is asked to learn. Otherwise, all manner of barriers to learning spring up.

Some years ago, I was involved in planning and teaching courses on statistics for industry, with particular emphasis on statistical quality control. Here, there was a case of 'doubting Thomases' with a vengeance. I was teaching orientation courses about statistical quality control to supervisors and foremen and was confronted with disbelief that the performance of some 'mathematical magic' on a small sample of a batch of products could be as effective a means of quality control as the traditional inspection of the whole batch.

To overcome this resistance, a simulated production line was constructed. A special batch of defective washers, with the hole in the middle punched a little off-centre, was produced. The defect could be easily observed by the naked eye. The production line was simply a motorized belt. A hopper at one end fed the washers on to the belt, and they moved past an inspector stationed along the line. The inspector had to identify and remove the defective washers from the belt as they came past. The hopper was filled with a mixture of good and defective washers. The proportions of defective washers in the total batch could be varied as required. The instructor, who prepared the mix, was therefore the only person who knew the real proportion of defects in the batch. Then the simulator was set in motion, with the most forthright 'doubting Thomas' as inspector. Another person took a handful of washers out of the hopper, put them on a side table and analysed the sample. The inspector busily checked the washers in the batch as they travelled past him and removed all the defective washers identified. Witness the inspector's surprise when his effort proved no more accurate than the statistical estimate, performed in a fraction of the time. Inspectors always miss some defective products, and sometimes also accidentally remove good washers. The simulator could be operated at various speeds, and a graph may be drawn showing how this type of human error increases as the working pace increases. By contrast, the statistical method gave consistently accurate results.

Some of our 'Thomases' accused the instructor of feeding data to the statistical quality controller, so we built in a sophisticated element. We magenetized the defective washers and constructed a magnetically operated automatic separation device at the end of the production line. As the washers came to the end of the belt, they fell down a chute and were automatically guided to separate containers for the good and the defective products. Any defective washer missed by the inspector would be caught by the magnets. We could now mix up batches blindfolded, so that nobody knew the real proportion of defects. That did the trick.

[margin notes] problem negative tude earning solution realistic ulator

12.4.6 I'M NOT NEBUCHADNEZZAR – a versatile knowledge game

One knowledge-quiz game that is not well known but which is worth discussin is I'M NOT NEBUCHADNEZZAR. It has the great advantage that it can be played anywhere, at any time, with any reasonable number of players (say two to 12), and can provide practice for and reinforcement of any body of knowledg It has sufficient appeal and simplicity to be adored by children and sufficient potential for complexity to be a don's delight.

Structure of the game   The game's structure is quite simple. One of the group of players is being interrogated by the others, who, in turn, ask questions of the type 'Did you u Jewish slaves to build the Tower of Babel?' The central player must identify the person to whom the questioner is alluding and reply, in this case, with the phrase 'I'm not Nebuchadnezzar'. The central player is, indeed, someone of his own 'choosing' (let us imagine he has chosen to be Moses), and if one of the questioners happens to guess who he is, by asking, for example, 'Were you found in a basket floating on the Nile?', he must admit that he is found out and change places with the player who posed the question. The central player usually selects the subject on which the questions must be based. The topic in the example above may have been people in the Old Testament. The object of the game is to remain the central player for as long as possible. The other players may gain this position by correctly guessing the current central player's identity, or, more often, by posing a question that the central player fails to answer correctly. Had the player in the example above replied 'I'm not Goliath', he would be challenged by the questioner to give up his central position in the game. Sometimes arguments arise. For example, if the reply given to the question 'Did you nearly conquer Europe but failed because your luck changed in Russia?' was 'I'm not Hitler', and the questioner had in mind Napoleon (the correct answer), a discussion might arise that would normally be put to a vote to decide whether the question was ambiguous or whether it was sufficiently precise to accept only the desired response. If the players are unsure, one resorts to encyclopaedias and other resources in order to resolve any differences of opinion.

The use of the game   The beauty of the game is that all players are constantly involved in recalling and reorganizing their knowledge on a given subject, and all players may learn new facts at any point in the game. The topics may be selected to suit any special interest and the complexity of the questions adapts to the intellectual capacities of the players. Though simple, the game is captivating.

The game has obvious educational value as a means of reinforcing areas of general knowledge. It can also be used in an instructional context, with the instructor defining the topic in the light of his teaching objectives. The topics are not limited to people, and the game can be used in the teaching of many different disciplines.

12.4.7 Card games for drill and practice

Flashcards   The use of flashcards as an aid to knowledge and simple reproductive skills is very common in primary schools. It is a simple game technique that can be adapted to many subjects and many types of learner group. A common application, now out of fashion, is the use of cards for the 'drilling' of multiplication 'facts'. The players turn up a card with a multiplication sum printed on it. The first player to respond correctly wins the card. The rules may be more complex, but this is the simplest structure and can be applied to the testing and drilling of many topics. More complex tasks, such as long division, can be handled with single cards. Even more complex tasks, such as constructing chemical equations, may be handled by using multiple cards. In the example of chemical equations, players must construct the formula of a given compound from a store of element cards. Thus, we have moved on from flashcards and have designed a fully fledged card game. Figure 12.8 on p 189 illustrates an example of games based on cards.

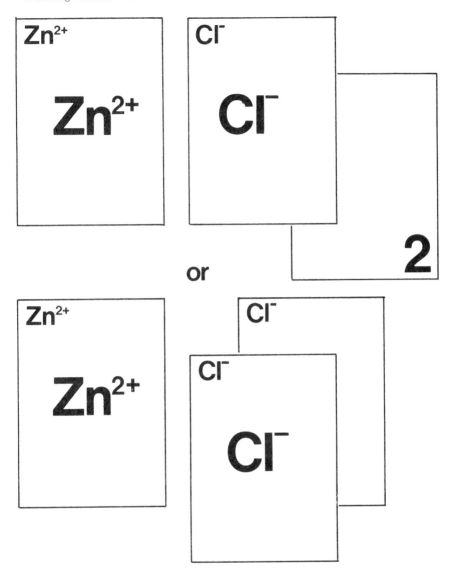

Use of cards in combination, in the game of FORMULON (Ellington, Addinall and Percival, 1982). The players must construct valid chemical formulae from the cards in their hand. Card exchanging may occur by any method used in standard card games.

Figure 12.8 *Some uses of cards in instructional games*

12.4.8 RUST — or is it 'snap'?

The card game of 'snap' can be adapted to many instructional purposes, by the preparation of special packs of cards. One popular application is in the drilling of foreign language vocabularies. One player turns up a set of cards with English words and another has a set of cards with the same words in another language, say French. Whenever two cards which are equivalent appear on the table, the first player to shout snap wins the cards.

The problem — rust

One practical teaching method based on 'snap' was developed by the autho some years ago as part of a project in Brazil. Brazil's coffee production is concentrated in the State of São Paulo. In the 1970s, the coffee plantations in that state were damaged by a disease called, colloquially, *ferrugem*, which means 'rust'. The name refers to the rust-like deposits that form on the leaves as the disease develops. Once rust takes root, the only cure is to burn the infected plants and start again. Whole plantations were wiped out at this time.

The initial plan...

The Institute in São Paulo where I was working was asked by the Coffee Research Institute to produce a series of television programmes to teach coffee plantation workers about rust and show them how to diagnose it in the early stages, when only individual plants might have to be destroyed and henc the plantation itself saved.

... and its inadequacy

Why television? Well, we needed to show the coffee plants and the symptoms of rust. We could not use books, as most of the plantation workers were illiterate or, at any rate, not accustomed to learning by reading. The medi experts and the instructional designers got to work, and it was soon obvious that the choice of media was not ideal. The photographers moaned that the quality of colour and picture on TV was not sufficient to show the fine differences between a healthy coffee leaf and one attacked by the early stages of rust. The media experts estimated that fewer than a third of the plantation in the state received television signals and that over half did not even have electricity. Complex plans were launched to produce slide/tape audiovisual programmes, which would tour the plantations in a truck with a generator. Costs were mounting and time was running out.

The game of RUST

It was at this point that suddenly 'snap!' — or rather, RUST! — the light dawned. There was very little, in general, that the average plantation worker needed to know about rust that he did not already know (from news programmes and the gossip grapevine that existed). The only important thing to learn was to *recognize* the early symptoms of rust reliably and fast. We searched through the photographs already taken and selected a collection of photos of coffee plant leaves, some at various stages of the disease, others with defects that had nothing to do with rust, and healthy leaves. This collection of photos was printed to form a pack of cards. Instead of shouting 'snap', the players had to roar 'rust' whenever an infected leaf was turned up in the game. (They roar because you can only roar out a word like *'ferrugem'!*

The packs of cards were circulated to the plantation owners, with instructions to put up the 'bank' money to get the first game started. From then on, the game took over. Everyone wanted to play, even after totally mastering the recognition skills involved. Months later, one would hear disembodied voices from amidst the coffee plants roar out *'Ferrugem*, I've won!', indicating successful transfer of skills to the job.

12.4.9 *KIM'S GAME — a perception training exercise*

Most readers will be familiar with KIM'S GAME, described by Rudyard Kipling in his writings about India and popularized by Baden Powell in his books on scouting. The game consists of exposing an assortment of objects for a short period of time, say a minute, and then covering them up again. The observers then make a list of as many of the objects as they can remember. The game is considered to develop visual memory and perception skills.

There is no clear evidence that KIM'S GAME aids everyday observation, but there is no doubt that practice in the game improves playing the game intself! With practice, it is surprising how many objects can be remembered from just a perfunctory glance. Players tend to develop memorization strategies, classifyin the objects into groups that have some common element — it is far easier to remember four groups of five objects than 20 unconnected items. Variation of this game may be used in many perception training and discrimination training situations.

12.4.10 Scouting games for character development

Baden Powell's writings are full of suggestions for games that have some educational or developmental purpose. Many are purely sporting games that develop strength, physique and agility. Others include those, like KIM'S GAME, which develop psychomotor perception and discrimination. Yet others are 'strategy' games that aim to develop problem-solving capabilities and those designed to develop character traits and reactive skills (such as perseverance, patience, resistance to pain, etc).

One example of a scouting game, which verges on a test of endurance, is called THE THREE FEATHERS. The player must, on three consecutive days, go one day without eating, one without speaking to anyone, and the third without being seen by anyone, all while staying in one's normal environment and with friends trying to catch the player out. This game is an example of the application of gaming to the development of self-control skills.

12.4.11 Group games and activities for communicating and analysing cognitive structures

Many exercises have been devised to promote introspection, analysis and the restructuring by an individual of his cognitive schemata. Perhaps the best known is brainstorming and its many derivatives. Brainstorming is not, however, a game or simulation; it is the organization of group activity for the analysis and solution of a given problem. Some practitioners, however, have injected a game element by organizing problem-solving competitions between groups engaged in brainstorming sessions.

One very useful way of controlling and documenting a brainstorming session is to write down all the comments and contributions made by the participants on separate cards. These cards can later be displayed on a table or wall, and the participants invited to organize and reorganize them into groups or structures that reflect the way that the ideas are organized in their minds. New classification concepts may emerge and new ways of viewing the topic generated, and a visual record is left of the deliberations of the group.

Another interesting approach to the analysis and communication of cognitive schemata is the kit of hexagons, called COMMUNI-KIT, developed by Anthony Hodgson and his colleagues. This consists of a set of hexagon shapes made of plastic, on which it is possible to write with a fibre-tipped pen. These are used in a way similar to the cards, but have the advantage of having many edges and can therefore be organized into more complex shapes, which better communicate the structure of the ideas being discussed.

One way to use the COMMUNI-KIT is to break a large group into working groups of four to six members, each with a set of hexagons. Each group then discusses and analyses a topic, presenting the results of the discussion in the form of a structure of ideas and related concepts, written on the hexagons and organized to highlight the important relationships identified between the elements of the topic. The groups then present their structures to each other, and discuss the differences in organization of ideas that the hexagons reveal. A competitive element is often injected by giving points for the various structures developed. A way in which this may be done is discussed in the next example.

12.4.12 MISUNDERSTOOD — a game of cognitive structures

The use of cards and hexagons to map out an individual's cognitive structures only becomes a game when some form of inter-group competition is organized. The activities themselves are fun and often very absorbing, but perhaps lack some of the competitive characteristics of gamers.

Terence Keen describes a similar sort of activity, which does have all the

ne three
athers

ne use of
rds to
cture
gnitive
ructures

ne
OMMUNI-
IT

aspects of a game (Keen, 1980). He calls the game MISUNDERSTOOD, as it is designed to highlight the different ways in which people may understand and organize the same basic set of concepts. The game is played in groups of three or four players. This number is critical, as the duration and appeal of the game vary with the number of players. The procedure is as follows:

How to play MIS-UNDERSTOOD

1. A topic for discussion is defined. This is usually some important area of discussion or difference in the work currently being performed by the participants.
2. A brainstorming session is organized to create a list of problems, examples, difficulties or other aspects of the topic under analysis that are considered important. The list is analysed and the 12 aspects of the topic voted most important by the group are written down on 12 separate cards. Each of the cards is numbered one to 12 on the back.
3. Each member of the group makes up his own set of 12 cards, copying the master set and numbering them in exactly the same way as the master set.
4. In the first stage of play, each player works on his own, taking the cards numbered one to three from his own pack and analysing the interrelationships that exist between the three aspects of the problem/top written on these cards. He thinks up a novel, but significant, way of classifying the three cards into two groups — two of the cards should be classified as having something in common which distinguishes them from the third card.
5. Each player now writes down a phrase which defines the *similarity* he perceives between two of the cards and another phrase which defines the *difference* between these two cards and the third card. He then picks up the other nine cards and analyses them, attempting to classify them into the two groups defined by the phrases he has written down. At the end of this stage, each player has two piles of cards, face down, alongside the two descriptive phrases that he has written down.
6. At this stage the players start to communicate their ideas to each other. One of the players is chosen to communicate his 'classifying phrase' to the others. He does this by reading what he has written down but *not* indicating which cards he has classified in each of the two categories. The other players may ask questions to clarify their understanding of the two classifying phrases.
7. Once all players agree that they understand the concept being used by the first player, they act as a group to classify the master set of cards according to this concept. This is done without reference to the first player's original classification. Any differences of opinion are discussed and, if necessary, a vote is taken. The result of this stage of play is two piles of cards placed alongside the two piles prepared by the player who communicated his concept.
8. The classification agreed on by the group is now compared to the classification originally prepared by the inventor of the concept. There are usually some differences. The player gains points for each card that was classified in the same way by the group and by himself. The other players gain points for the cards which were classified differently by the group and the concept's inventor.
9. The cards are separated out and the players start again, using the next three cards (four, five and six) as the basis for the invention of new and different classifying concepts. A different player takes the lead in communicating his concept to the group and the play proceeds as before.
10. With four players and 12 cards in the pack, each player gets the chance to invent four classifying concepts and to communicate one of these to the other group members. However, all the players indirectly communicate all their ideas to the others during the arguments that ensue over the classification of the cards.

Simple though this game appears to be, it reveals a great number of ways of looking at the same topic. In a group whose members are homogeneous and tend to view the topic under discussion in the same way, the minimum number of different viewpoints encountered is four, one in each round of the game. In a heterogeneous group, it is possible that all players will think up different classifying concepts at each stage, a total of 16 ways of organizing the topic under discussion.

12.4.13 A conflict simulation

Origins of
the exercise

This example is a simulation game used by the author on instructional design courses, in order to analyse and improve the relationships between the members of an instructional design team. The game was invented by Sivasailam Thiagarajan and published in *Improving Human Performance*, the quarterly journal of the National Society for Performance and Instruction. I am indebted to the author and the journal for permission to use and adapt the idea. The original name of the game, coined by Thiagarajan, was IDIOTS (Instructional Design in Ordinary Teaching Situations). We reproduce Thiagarajan's own description of the structure and rules of the game as Exhibit 12.1 on pp 194 - 5. We recommend close analysis of this Exhibit before reading on.

Using the
game in
practice

We have found it necessary, in practice, to modify some of the rules, in accordance with who is playing the game. For example, when we use the game with instructional designers who have a reasonable grasp of the subject, we find that they do not easily adopt the role of subject matter expert. They see both sides of the argument and opt for well-balanced choices which, in general, agree with their playing partner's choice. In such cases we have successfully used the instructor or 'actors' — ideally technical people, who may be subject matter experts (SMEs) in some project — to take on the role of the SME. When this is not possible, it is necessary to brief the players carefully and to exaggerate the game element introduced by the points system, so that the players forget their balanced view and really adopt the roles that will lead them to win. Only at the end of the game do they learn that they have been deceived into believing that the object of the game is to gain the maximum number of points.

When real subject matter experts are used, and the context of the game is based on a real project, these difficulties evaporate. The players enter into their real-life roles, with all their real-life motives and preconceived ideas, arguing heatedly for their own selection of action on each of the issue cards. In such cases, we abandon the points system and use only the issues gained or lost as a measure of the game's progress. The exercise really ceases to be a game and becomes a full simulation of the decisions that will actually have to be taken during the project.

Typical
issues for
debate

The issues that we have found most useful as means of encouraging discussion and the clash of opposing points of view include:

1. The choice of a suitable theoretical or practical model on which to base one's work. To what extent should a predetermined ID model be applied or hunches of the team members be followed?
2. How should the work and the responsibilities be divided among the team members?
3. Who should define the project objectives and from where should they be derived?
4. What procedures should be used for selecting/rejecting specific subjects?
5. What procedures should be used for selecting methods and media of instruction?
6. What is the best procedure for validating the quality of the instructional materials to be used?

IDIOTS is a simulation game designed to sensitize instructional technologists to various interpersonal aspects of working with subject matter experts on the systematic development of training materials.

Number of players. Two. The game is designed for parallel play by a large number of pairs.

Time requirement. About 30-45 minutes.

Materials. A printed scenario, issues-cards deck, poker chips, paper and pencil.

Play of the game

1. *Preliminaries.* Players are divided into pairs. Each pair is given a deck of issues cards and each member of the pair is given a copy of the background scenario and an unspecified number of poker chips (usually five to 15). The game leader also announces the time limit for the game.

2. *Providing the context.* Each player reads his/her copy of the scenario, which describes the context in which a series of interpersonal confrontations take place. This scenario outlines the mission for both players and the role of each, as in the following example:

> You and the other player are involved in an instructional development project in a university setting. The purpose of this project is to produce an instructional package to teach certain specific skills to undergraduate students.
>
> The professor involved in the project is a subject matter expert (SME). S/he knows very little about instructional design or media production. In addition to working on the project, s/he has a half-time teaching load.
>
> The instructional designer (ID) involved in the project has considerable experience in designing different types of training packages and producing mediated materials. However, s/he has very little knowledge of the curriculum. In addition to work on the project s/he has the regular duties of coordinating the learning resources centre in the school.

The winner of a coin toss chooses one of the two roles. The other player assumes the other role.

3. *Identifying issues.* One player turns over the top card of the issues deck. This deck contains about 30 cards, each describing an issue and five different positions arranged along a five-point scale, as in this example:

ISSUE: Working arrangements.

POSITIONS:

(a) The SME will initially outline the content and suggest different resource materials. The ID will do most of the actual development.

(b) The SME will provide initial guidance and periodic supervision as the ID develops the instructional material.

(c) The SME and the ID will share equal responsibilities and keep in close touch with each other.

(d) The SME will develop the instructional material with periodic suggestions and help from the ID.

(e) The SME will do most of the development. The ID will serve in consultative and editorial capacities.

Other cards deal with such issues as the use of behavioural objectives, sharing of credits, selection of media, need for evaluation, and hiring of the staff. Both players read the statement and the five positions on the issue.

4. *Indicating initial position.* Each player now individually writes down a number indicating his/her initial position on the issue. After both players have specified their positions, they compare them. If there is no difference, the players move on to the next card.

5. *Resolving conflicts.* If there is a difference between the positions indicated by the players, they hold a discussion session and try to persuade each other. Either player may ask for another round of secret voting any time during this discussion. Players may stick to their original positions or shift to new ones. After both have specified their revised positions, they compare them. The cycle of discussion, revision and comparison is repeated as often as necessary until players reach consensus.

6. *Scoring the round.* When consensus is achieved, each player compares his/her initial position with his/her final one and determines the difference. S/he pays the other player the number of poker chips equal to the number of intervals s/he has shifted in his/her position.

7. *Terminating the game.* After reaching consensus on each card, players move on to the next one. The game ends in any one of the following three ways:

> (a) *Mutual success.* If players reach consensus on all cards before they run out of time, game ends successfully. (This situation is analogous to the completion of the instructional development project before the deadline.)

Exhibit 12.1 *(continued)*

(b) *Pyrrhic success.* If either player runs out of poker chips at any time during the game, the game ends in an empty victory for the other player. (This situation is analogous to domination of an instructional development team by one of the two partners.)

(c) *Failure.* If players run out of time before all issues cards are discussed, the game ends in failure. (This situation is analogous to failing to meet the project deadline.)

8. *Determining the winning pair.* The situation simulated in the game does not permit a simple 'win-lose' outcome, since individual members in each pair are not competing against each other. The performance of a pair may be compared with those of other pairs. In this type of scoring, the game leader may use any or all of the following criteria:

(a) Relative status. A gain of large numbers of chips reflects attempted domination; a loss indicates submission. In the interdependent situation simulated in the game, the ideal is a co-equal status indicated by no difference between the number of chips held by either player at the beginning and at the end of the game. The pair which shows the least difference comes closest to this goal and wins an award on the co-equality criterion.

(b) Open-mindedness. Co-equal status in the pair could be due to similarity in thinking, acquiescence, or mutual give and take. The pair which had the most rounds of revising their positions wins an award on the mutual give-and-take criterion.

(c) Efficiency. The amount of time spent in resolving interpersonal conformations is inversely related to the task orientation of the pair. Hence, the pair which took the shortest time to reach consensus on all cards wins an award on the efficiency criterion.

Exhibit 12.1

The rules and playing strategy of IDIOTS | (reproduced from S Thiagarajan, 1976, with the permission of the author)

7. What should be done to evaluate the long-term effects of the project, and who should be responsible for carrying out such an evaluation?

8. Who should own copyright in materials produced?

9. Who should sign any official in-company reports on the progress of the project?

10. Who should sign and take credit for research or for any published material?

The scoring system   We have found the 'private vote' idea particularly useful, with three or more votes on the issue sometimes needed to reach consensus on an issue. For this reason, we developed the scorecard illustrated in Figure 12.9 on p 196). Each player completes his own card, vote by vote, calculating any points lost or gained by measuring the extent to which he was forced to change his own initial opinion (points lost) or to which he managed to influence his partner to agree with him (points gained). To make this system work, it was necessary to standardize a five-item choice for each issue card and to sequence these five items as a scale of graded viewpoints, extending from the extreme subject-oriented view to the extreme ID-oriented view. The number of positions moved on this scale is counted as the number of points lost by the mover and gained by the other partner. When the game is played without the use of a points system, it is possible to scramble the items on the issue cards. However, this has not been found to improve the game appreciably, as the players can easily identify the scale, despite the scrambling of the items, and can react to the issue cards in much the same way as to an ordered list of choices and a score sheet.

This quite simple simulation game has been found to be extremely useful in integrating new team members, analysing and overcoming real sources of friction and misunderstanding among team members, and as a team management training exercise.

12.4.14 STARPOWER — a simulation/game with a hidden message

On face value, STARPOWER appears to be a game of trading, not all that different in general terms from the game of Monopoly. However, there are two

Issue no.	Your choice of alternative				Number of positions moved by partner	Number of positions moved by you	Points lost/ gained by you
	First vote	Second vote	Third vote	Fourth vote			
1	4	4	4		2	0	2
2	5	3			1	2	− 1
3	5	4			1	1	0
4	3				0	0	0
5	4	3	2		0	2	− 2
6							
7							
8							
9							
10							
11							
12							
Totals							

Figure 12.9 *A score card developed for the IDIOTS game*
(partly completed)

quite distinct levels of simulation involved. On the simpler, more obvious level STARPOWER simulates the transactions of buying and selling goods and property, stocks and shares, etc. On a more subtle level, the game simulates the society in which we live and, in particular, the forces that lead individuals and groups to behave in specific ways. The stages of the game are outlined below:

Playing procedure

1. *Briefing.* The structure of the exercise is quite simple. The rules of the game specify that the objective is 'to become rich'. The participants are divided into three teams, usually denominated by squares, circles and triangles. Each participant receives at the start a 'personal fortune' comprising money and property. The quantity is different for each participant, simulating the actuality that some are better off than others. It is important that the participants should believe that the initial division of riches is fair, or at least that the distribution is random. But, in reality, the division is organized to favour the squares. On average, the squares are richest and the triangles poorest. The circles form a sort of middle class between these extremes.

The hidden social forces

2. *Play.* The game begins. A series of buying and selling transactions is completed. After a time, the session leader — the instructor — intervenes by saying 'Let's see who is getting rich'. The players declare their riches and (surprise, surprise) the squares are still the richest and the triangles poorest. The leader then says 'Let's establish some uniformity in the groups, in order to be a square it's necessary to possess at least X dollars . . .' Some promotions or demotions may now occur, a few circles becoming squares

and one or two squares dropping to the circles group. Triangles may be promoted to the circles group, and so on. These promotions appear to the players to be the consequences of success or failure in the commercial transactions being simulated. However, in reality, the principal factor is the unequal distribution of resources. Already at this stage of the game, some changes in behaviour occur. The players tend to identify themselves with their group more strongly and start to plan joint strategies. Each group develops an internal solidarity and cooperative spirit.

The game continues through several rounds of buying/selling transactions, until the leader, who is observing and judging the game, again intervenes and further promotions and demotions take place. He then says: 'The squares have performed so well that, as a prize, they may suggest and implement changes in the rules of the game, and, if they wish, may veto any suggestions made by the other two groups'.

e breakdown   At this point, it is difficult to predict exactly what will occur. Usually, the squares attempt to replan the rules of the game in their own favour, in an attempt to increase further their wealth. The other groups meet privately and make suggestions, usually vetoed by the squares, then voice their dissatisfaction with the direction that the game is taking. About two or three rounds of transactions under the new rules are usually sufficient to lead to the game breaking down, with the triangles refusing to play and the circles offering suggestions for compromise. Sometimes the circles unite with the triangles to protest, while at other times they may side with the squares in return for a modicum of preferential treatment in the game. Most often, the circles split, some adhering to the squares and others supporting the triangles. At an opportune moment, the session leader stands up and shouts 'We have a revolution!'.

e hidden
jective   *3. Debriefing.* Only now does it become obvious to all the players that the real object of the exercise is to simulate the forces that act in society to stratify it into classes, leading to dissatisfaction and class warfare. In the debriefing discussion the squares are forced to admit that, as a group, they have behaved in a way that, as individuals, they would consider to be reprehensible and unprincipled. They admit to having sought power and, once obtained, to having enjoyed exercising it over the other groups. The circles who supported the existing social system, in the hope of promotion, admit that they were prepared to sacrifice their friends for individual gains, and so on.

Without exception, the participants enter into a heated debate of the underlying forces within the group structure that led them to behave the way they did. They identify the general principles and relate what they have perceived to the real world. Often, the debriefing session lasts much longer than the game itself. It is during this stage that the really useful learning takes place. The participants form a comprehensive schema of concepts related to class structure and the session leader evaluates and guides the formation of appropriate concepts. This learning is experiential, based on the discoveries that the participants have made about their own behaviour and the behaviour of others. The participants also perceive the forces that lead to unrest and revolution and come to recognize the power of the group in subjugating the individual characteristics of its members.

ome
ecially
seful
spects of
e game   We have chosen STARPOWER as an example because it is an excellent illustration of a well-designed simulation/game in the social education field. It is a well-known game, and its designer, Gary Shirts, is the author of several successful simulation games. It has been on the market for several years, and has been widely used in various countries and with a very wide variety of learner groups — primary and secondary school children, university sociology students and managers in industrial and government organizations. At all these different levels, the game has proved to be popular and has led to useful

insights into social structure and group behaviour. Specific objectives and the nature of the debriefing session vary greatly according to the level and area of interest of the participants.

STARPOWER also illustrates the simplicity of an easily playable simulation game. It is essentially an adaptation of ideas that are used in many commonly available games. The one aspect of creative design that makes this game stand out is the idea to build in a second, hidden, layer of simulation, dealing with the forces within and between groups. This is the aspect that makes the learning truly experiential: the participants discover through their own action what it feels like to live in an unequal society and what this leads to in the long run.

The role of the session leader

This example also illustrates the critical role of the session leader, or instructor, in most simulation games. He does not teach in the traditional sense, but the success of the exercise depends in large measure on his skill in guiding the play sessions and directing the debriefing discussion. His roles in the three stages of the exercise may be summarized as follows:

1. *Briefing.* To present all the necessary data and roles in such a way that the participants understand clearly how they should play, *without* presenting or even hinting at the hidden objectives of the game.
2. *Play.* To observe each group and the individual participants; to evaluate their behavioural patterns; and to use these observations as a basis for 'online' decisions on how to direct the game, when to change the rules, what information to give to which player, etc.
3. *Debriefing.* To lead the participants to identify all the general principles of group behaviour that became apparent during play; to assist the participants in organizing and interrelating these principles into a useful comprehensive and transferable schema.

Some aspects of design

Finally, STARPOWER is an example of a well-chosen technique for tackling a learning problem. These characteristics may be listed below as an aid to the design or selection of simulation/games.

1. An open-ended situation, which provides opportunities for the choice of several avenues of analysis and several learning objectives.
2. An experiential learning situation, in which the participant learns through the analysis of the situation in which he finds himself and discovers new principles and relationships.
3. A simplification of reality, presenting only those aspects of the real-life phenomenon under study that help to identify the general principles that are to be learned, and exaggerating some aspects in order better to illustrate these principles.
4. A 'compression of feedback', so that the consequences of the decisions and actions taken are almost immediately apparent, thus enabling the learning process to be controlled by feedback of results.
5. A 'compression of time', so that in one or two hours' play, the participants can live through the various stages of a gradually developing problem, which, in reality, might take many years to develop.

12.4.15 A management game based on a physical simulator

Most management games are paper shuffling exercises similar to the in-tray exercise described earlier. The players make decisions on the basis of data presented and the results of these decisions are then received by the exercise coordinator. The latter hands out further information or poses new problems, following a conceptual model of how the real management decision process being simulated actually works. More sophisticated games use a computer-based model of the organization, which may enhance the complexity and the speed of reaction of the model to the decisions being taken by the players.

These games are, however, sometimes affected by the 'doubting Thomas'
syndrome (previously described in this chapter) when used with 'practical'
or 'down to earth' managers, because of the lack of realism that paper-based
data gives to what are often very practical decisions. Greater realism can
sometimes be injected by simulating the real working environment as part of
the game environment. In simple, Monopoly-type games, such simulated
realism is imparted by the use of boards that depict the work area — as in
NORTH SEA, which presents the players with a map of the oil prospecting
zones (as the board), by means of tokens or counters that simulate the money
or the units of production encountered in the real situation.

The author was involved in the design of quite a complex simulation of
this type, as part of the design of a course for production line managers and
supervisors in the motor industry. A large model of the real production shop
floor was constructed on a trestle table. The production lines were represented
by motorized moving belts, running the length of the table. The speed of these
belts could be adjusted to simulate actual production rates for different car
models and parts. Alongside the belts, the different production processes and
machines were indicated in their correct positions, by labels or actual wooden
models. Wooden blocks were used to simulate the units of production (say
50 door panels). These blocks would be placed at the beginning of a belt to
signify the decision to manufacture a batch of the given component
represented by the block. On reaching the end of the line, the blocks would
go into store or be re-routed to other lines where they would be used in final
assembly.

Trainees worked in groups of four players, dividing the normal duties of
shopfloor management, All normally used procedures and control documents
were employed. The speed of operation of the model was adjusted so as to
simulate, in two hours of play, a full day's production in the factory. The
session controller had at his disposal a protocol of critical incidents, such as
machine breakdowns, delivery failures by component manufacturers, strikes,
etc. These incidents would be brought into play at predetermined moments,
halting production on certain lines for predetermined periods of time. The
players had to deal with all incidents and keep an eye on the movement of
parts along the belts, while at the same time performing normal stock control
and production scheduling tasks. The simulation of reality was as complete as
possible.

Scoring was in terms of the production figures achieved in a session. Various
groups competed against each other during a course and could compare their
scores with the best results of other groups and of experienced production
managers who set the standards in early runs of the game. Several runs could
be attempted, working under different schedules of critical incidents, until
production rates approached the standards set by experienced managers.

12.5 Planning and developing games and simulations

12.5.1 Case studies

Although we have included the case study in our schema of categories of
simulations and games, many other authors would not classify case studies
as either a game or a simulation. Case studies do not usually contain the
competitive element of games, although it is possible for several groups to
compete against each other in solving the problems posed in the case. This,
however, is not very common, as the classic case study presents a situation
that has no unique correct solution. The aim is to examine, by discussion, all
the possible views or courses of action that may be taken. In such an open-
ended case study, it is rather difficult to arrange competition between groups.

As regards the simulation element, case studies can be considered as a
partial simulation of a real-life situation. They present data which are usually

extracted or adapted from the reality being studied. However, the case study is not based on an interactive model of that reality. The learners may discuss the consequences of specific decisions or actions taken on the basis of the data presented, but this discussion takes place at an intellectual, theoretical level. The opinions and past experience of the participants are brought to be on the problems posed by the case. What the participants learn from the discussion depends very much on what they bring to the discussion. The task of the author of the case is limited to presenting a static picture of the probl or situation being studied and the task of the instructor using the case is to guide and control the participants in the process of analysis of the picture presented and prediction of causes and effects.

The interactive case study
It is possible to write an interactive case study, in which further data are presented to the participants at specific stages of the discussion. If these data are made dependent on the decisions taken by the participants at the previou stage of discussion, then an interactive or dynamic situation is created. The data presented now depend on the decisions and actions taken by the studen They are now interacting with a model of reality, albeit a simple one, presen in written form. This sort of case study can, of course, be called a simulation

The simplification of reality
Another aspect that the author of a case study must take into account is the degree of simplification to be introduced. Real situations are often complex and the aspects to be studied are not always as obvious as they need to be for them to be identified by learners. It is possible to select, or to modify, the data of the real-life example which is being used as a source to emphasize those aspects of the case which the author considers particularly important, or to reduce the level of difficulty of the analysis necessary to understand the case. Such simplification should be undertaken with care, as it is easy to distort the case to such an extent that it bears little or no relationship to the reality on which it was originally based. It is possible, in such cases, for the learners to learn inappropriate problem-solving strategies or to form erroneous cognitive schemata which will in future hinder, rather than help, them.

The need for validation
This danger emphasizes the need to pre-test case study material in one or more validation sessions, using samples of typical students. The author shoul be present, even if he is not the instructor responsible for the session, as it is necessary to analyse the discussions that take place, in order to evaluate the usefulness and degree of difficulty of the case study material. These sessions also serve to plan the best way of leading the discussions, guiding the participants to appropriate decisions and providing feedback in the final debriefing. The case study should then be revised and an instructor's manual prepared.

12.5.2 Role-playing exercises

Peter McPhail (1974) suggests six factors which one should consider when planning a role-play exercise. A good role-play exercise should:

(a) have a clear purpose or purposes relevant to the needs of the participants;
(b) use a situation which is real to those participants;
(c) include only the number of people who can actively contribute;
(d) be conducted in physical conditions which make it easy for those role playing to accept the reality of the situation and identify with it;
(e) have enough time allowed to let it run as long as the motivation lasts; and, above all,
(f) be non-authoritarian in organization and practice.

McPhail then compares the procedures which one would use to build role-pla exercises, depending on whether one was attempting to establish a particular skill, such as selling a car, or to help people to take into consideration others' needs, feelings and interests. The procedure he suggests for specific skills and knowledge runs as follows:

w to plan
run
le-play

1. The organizer states the skill which the role-play is designed to improve. He may expand his introduction by showing a film or videotape to demonstrate skilled or unskilled performance.
2. The situation or situations to be role-played are selected for their relevance to acquiring the skill in question, preferably in consultation with the course members.
3. The course is divided up into role-play groups. For most situations small groups of five to 10 are best.
4. The amount of detailed information required by participants before they can respond to a situation will vary according to their experience and the particular situation. Nevertheless, classical role-play allows maximum freedom for those taking part and it reaps great motivational and learning benefit from doing so.
5. The participants play out their roles. Those who cannot have active parts are asked to observe the principal's solution, evaluate it and decide what they would do in his position.
6. As long as the participants are interested, and there is time, other members of the group can be asked to play out what they would do, rather than just talk about others' performances.
7. The organizer of the role-play discusses in detail with the participants their approach to the problem posed and the role-play solutions to it. If he has a tape recorder or, better still, a videotape recorder, a record of the proceedings will clarify exactly what individuals said and did.
8. When the role-play situations are simple dyadic (one-to-one) encounters — for example, where interview technique is practised by A interviewing B — a valuable feedback technique is to reverse the roles and try the whole exercise over again before further discussion.
9. Near the end of the course, it is useful to hold a plenary session, in which course members are encouraged to give their impressions of the course and to be uninhibited in their criticism.
10. After the plenary session, some role-play organizers talk to all the course participants about the insights which have been gained and the learning which has taken place.

For reactive and interactive objectives, particularly ones associated with teaching people to get on with others, McPhail suggests the following procedure:

e-play
conflict
ations

1. A conflict situation is chosen for role-play, preferably by the game members themselves.
2. The situation described, with support from cartoons, drawings or photographs, is read and seen by the group. To make the impact even more vivid, it can be acted.
3. Two participants naturally inclined towards the points of view in conflict are asked to play out what they would do, while the other group members watch and decide how they would react.
4. The conflict roles are reversed and each participant takes the place of the other and plays out what he would do.
5. Both participants then revert to their original roles and play out their 'final' responses. Wide experience suggests that the final responses are more considerate than the behaviour originally suggested and that the experience may affect the participants' life styles.
6. Other members of the group should be encouraged to criticize what they have seen, and to play out their solutions as long as they are interested.

12.5.3 Simulators for psychomotor skills

The complexity of a training device will naturally be a reflection of the complexity of the task being trained. The object of a flight simulator is to g the pilot every possible experience of flying without risking valuable lives an equipment. One therefore arranges for every possible relevant stimulus to be fed to the pilot. The ideal flight simulator would react to the pilot's respons in every detail — instrument reading, noise, vision through cockpit and the feeling of gravity changes. Simulators of such complexity are used in the training of astronauts, but the cost precludes their more general use. For ma purposes a partial simulation suffices.

Simulators for specific skills

When a full task analysis is carried out, certain skill elements are often found to be particularly difficult to master. Such elements should be isolate and trained separately. Very often, simulation can help in training these elements.

The learning problems associated with the difficult element must be identified. This may involve detailed observation and questioning of skilled performers and learners. The questions to consider are:

1. How is the element learned? What sort of a task is it? What senses are involved and how?
2. What is making the learning difficult? Lack of aptitude? Underdevelop motor skills? Conflict with previous learning? Fear of equipment?

If the difficulty is the result of certain defects of perception or muscular coordination, then the possibility of a special training exercise should be considered. This may take the form of eye focusing exercises for inspection skills, or a special bit of equipment for sensory-motor skills. For example, when tapping a screw thread in a hole, it is important not to put too much pressure on the tap. If you push too hard, the tap will break. The problem is to learn just how hard is too hard. One method is by trial and error, but this takes a long time and may be costly in replacement taps. If one can arrange for the tap to 'cry out' just before breaking point, one might expect learning to be more efficient. The number of breakages would certainly be reduced.

Another method might be by guidance. The instructor may guide the student's hand, or give him hints on what to watch for. In teaching a studen to use a file, the instructor first imparts the correct stance and the correct w to hold the file. He may demonstrate the motions and then supervise, correc and even guide, the student's actions. The golfer's swing is sometimes taught strapping the novice in a harness, which controls the extent and direction of his movements — a 'golf simulator'.

When designing training simulators, both feedback and guidance should b considered. They are not as simple as they appear at first sight. Any feedbac won't do. Some guidance methods are better than others.

Two types of feedback

There are two types of feedback which may be present in a task. One tell the learner how well he has performed — *knowledge of results*. The other tel him how he is performing right now — *knowledge of performance*. This seco type (termed action feedback) is of importance in continuous adjustment skills, like steering a car along a road. One is continuously using the visual feedback from the road to adjust one's actions. However skilled the driver, h is technically out of control if all his lights fail on a dark night. Knowledge o results, on the other hand, only becomes apparent once the action is comple Steering into a skid produces (generally) desirable results. Action feedback, i the form of visual and kinaesthetic information, tells us that we are skidding Previous learning tells us to steer into the skid. A comparison of the extent c our corrective action, with the result it produces, constitutes the basis for learning skid correction. Knowledge of results is therefore sometimes called learning feedback.

Learning feedback is vital for efficient learning. Action feedback does no

arch
e
tiveness
rning
ction
ack

help much at all. This was demonstrated by an experiment performed by Annett and Kay (1957). Subjects were told to press down with a certain pressure on a spring balance. If they were allowed to see the scale while pressing (action feedback) they performed perfectly. If they were only allowed to see the scale after they had applied pressure (learning feedback) they initially made errors, but improved with practice. When, after an equal number of trials, all feedback was removed, the group who received learning feedback performed adequately for some time, but the group who had received continuous action feedback immediately deteriorated. They had not learned the 'feel' of the correct pressure. The learning feedback group's performance also tends to deteriorate in time if the feedback is withheld, but this happens more slowly. We might say that the group is 'forgetting' the feel of a two-pound pressure. This finding is important as well, as it indicates the limitations from which some training devices may suffer.

If the knowledge of results a training device supplies is quite different in form from that found on the job the learning may not be permanent. Goldstein and Rittenhouse (1954) found that in training aeroplane gunners to aim on a simulator, performance could be vastly improved by supplying knowledge of results in the form of a buzzer whenever the gun was on target. When the aid was removed, however, performance rapidly deteriorated until it was much the same as people trained by normal direct methods. There seemed to be no long-term benefit whatever from using the extra artificial feedback.

Seymour (1954), on the other hand, used training devices successfully to teach the amount of pressure permissible in picking up fragile electrical insulators. He used dummy insulators which were spring loaded against micro switches and wired so that too much pressure gave a red light, the correct amount gave a white light and insufficient pressure gave no light at all. Other experiments have also given good results from the use of not normally available or 'artificial' knowledge of results during training.

The evidence is conflicting and more research is needed, but it seems that success may depend on what sort of artificial feedback one uses, and how one uses it. How similar is the artificial feedback to that actually present in the task? How is the 'transfer of control' from the artifial feedback to the natural feedback effected?

to use
oack in
lators

Several practical suggestions may be made on the use of feedback in simulators:

1. When training a skill, examine whether the normal method of training provides satisfactory knowledge of results.
2. When doing this, do not confuse action feedback with knowledge of results.
3. If the naturally present knowledge of results is not easily observable by the student (ie it uses undeveloped kinaesthetic or tactile senses), consider the possibilities of a training device which supplies more obvious feedback.
4. Try to produce a situation in which the artificial feedback supplies information of a similar nature to that supplied by the natural feedback.
5. Try to arrange training so that the trainees occasionally rely on natural feedback alone, and progressively withdraw the artificial aids.

e types
uidance

We might guide the student in a learning task in a number of ways. We may give verbal guidance — 'Use your body weight!' We may demonstrate an action visually. We may actively guide the physical responses of the student.

The first two types of guidance are really supplying pre-knowledge: what to do and how to do it. For example, when demonstrating an action it is best to demonstrate it as seen from the learner's viewpoint. Hence, the value of film or television in the training of skills. The decisions on what verbal knowledge is required to perform a task and how it should be taught spring from the task analysis.

Use of
physical
restriction
and forced
responses in
simulation

It is the third type of guidance, actual physical control that can be built into training devices or simulators, that concerns us here. This can be achieve in two ways. One can physically 'force' the correct movements out of the learner (forced response), or one can allow the learner to make his own movements but restrict the direction or extent of these movements (physical restriction). Both methods are used in training devices. We have already mentioned the harness used for training a golfer's swing. This is an example of physical restriction of the learner's movements. The learner makes his swing, but he cannot deviate from the correct path. Of course, he may still produce a poor swing. He may not follow through as far as he should. His movements may be even more restricted than the harness allows. Many golfir coaches therefore employ the forced response techniques, by standing immediately behind the learner, holding the learner's wrists or club, and physically guiding the stroke every inch of the way.

Such methods apply to motor responses, where the extent of a movement or its exact path are critical. Physical restriction is often employed in training devices and simulators, by the use of stops at the end of a machine bed, for example. Forced response techniques are more often employed by instructors. They are rarely employed in training devices, as it is difficult to construct a mechanism that would adequately simulate the required complexity of movement.

12.5.4 Designing and producing games

The design of games for educational and instructional purposes often involve the adaptation of a well-known format of entertainment game to the instructional designer's particular purposes. Typical formats are:

1. *Non-instructional games*: field games, such as football and hockey; indoor sports, such as table tennis and snooker; and group activity games, such as quizzes and charades.
2. *Instrumented games*: card games, such as Snap and flashcards; board games, such as NORTH SEA and Monopoly; equipment-based games, such as Lego and Cuseniere rods; print-based games.
3. *Electronic games*: video games; computer-based games.

Only the first two major groups of formats concern us here. We deal with electronic games in Volume 2 of this series, which assesses the application of computer-assisted instruction.

Before deciding on a format, the instructional designer should decide whether a game is really appropriate for the objectives of a particular lesson. Also, he must verify what resources (time and skills) are available for the design and development of a game. Ellington, Addinall and Percival (1982) divide the process of game design into three main phases:

1. Establishing the design criteria and the need for the exercise.
2. Developing the basic idea for the exercise.
3. Developing a viable package capable of meeting the design criteria.

The first of these phases is equivalent to the process of overall instructional design, our Level 2, which results in an overall plan that specifies the method and media to be used for every specific objective. The second phase is akin to lesson planning. In the case of most non-instrumented games (and some instrumented games that require very little in the way of special materials), this second phase will include all the planning that needs to be done before t actual playing of the game. The planning is a Level 3 instructional design exercise. The third phase, especially in the case of complex instrumented games, is a Level 4 materials design exercise.

In this chapter we will not enter into the intricacies of the design of specia materials. This would require a whole book on its own. There are several handbooks available which give detailed examples and case studies of game development (see, for example, Ellington *et al*, 1981; 1982; Megarry, 1978; 1979; McAleese, 1978; Race *et al*, 1980). Interested readers should study some of these before attempting ambitious game design exercises. We will restrict ourselves here to an overview of the process, listing some of the principles and procedures that are normally followed by game designers.

decision
se
ne

At Level 2, the main decisions hinge on the matching of instructional methods to the objectives and the target population. Our basic instructional design methodology will have already indicated the preferred overall strategy for a given objective. If this strategy is to be expositive, we may be led away from the consideration of specially designed games as initial teaching devices, but may consider the use of a drill and practice type of game as a means of reinforcing learning. Quiz-type games might also be suggested.

If, on the other hand, the preferred strategy is experiential, we may be led to consider games that furnish opportunities for learners to explore certain concepts or share experiences. Problem-solving games might seem appropriate. The game of MISUNDERSTOOD, described earlier in this chapter, might be appropriate for the development of new conceptual schemata, or a game like STARPOWER might be appropriate for making learners aware of certain social problems.

It may at times be difficult to draw the line between pure games and simulation/games at this initial design phase. The example of STARPOWER used above is a case in point. This is not important, however, as we are at the stage of designing the overall requirements of the exercise needed to achieve the proposed instructional objectives. The differences in design technique between simulation games and non-simulation games are only of importance at a more detailed level of design.

An important aspect to consider at Level 2 is the amount of time that playing the game will involve. Will the educational benefits of using a game be sufficient to justify this time investment? It is necessary to decide which of the objectives of the course can most benefit from the use of games.

planning
e game

Once the Level 2 decision to consider the use of a game, for a given objective with given students, has been taken, we come to Level 3 considerations. These may be considered under the headings of *content*, *format* and *structure*. These terms are used by Ellington *et al* (1981), whose description of the detailed design phase is summarized in Figure 12.10 on p 206.

ontent

The content may well be at least partly defined already, as a result of the overall instructional planning performed at Level 2. Further analysis of the content and selection of suitable examples may have to be made at this stage. In the case of knowledge objectives, the content must be carefully selected to mirror the knowledge requirements of the target population. For example, in the construction of a game I once developed for training telephonists to connect incoming calls to the correct department, it was necessary to make a detailed study of the types of queries usually received by the telephonists, in order to include similar types of queries on the flash cards used in the game.

In the case of broad, basic skills objectives, the content may simply be a vehicle for an exercise in which it is the process of handling the content that is really important. In a game such as STARPOWER, for example, the specific trading situation used and the types of commodities that can be traded are largely irrelevant, as long as they are realistic and interesting to the students. In such cases, the problem of content selection is treated more in terms of an analysis of the interests and motivations of the target population than in terms of what must be learned to achieve the proposed objectives.

ormat

The choice of format is a question of matching the basic criteria — the types of knowledge or skill that the exercise is to develop — to formats that appear appropriate and can be handled, in the particular course structure envisaged, by instructors. It would be inappropriate to use a field game format if the course is to take place in a city centre hotel, or an equipment-based format

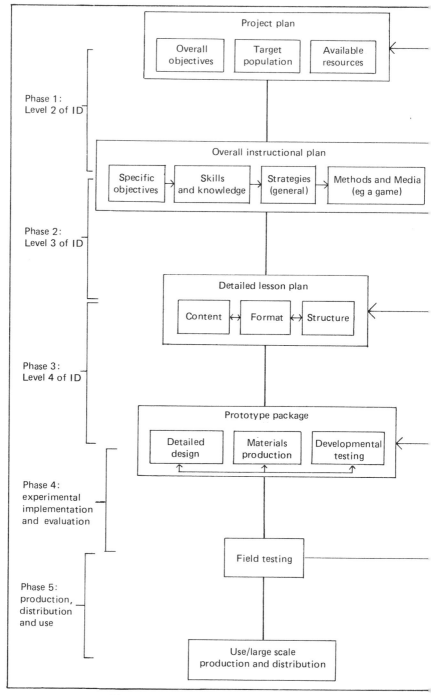

Figure 12.10 *The process of game design and development*

Note: In this chapter we are only concerned with phase 2.

if the equipment required is unavailable or the instructors are untrained in using the equipment.

The choice of suitable formats is usually a matter of common sense and partly inspiration. Remember the description of the events that led up to the selection of a card game format for the RUST game described earlier. In retrospect, the decision seems obvious. At the time, however, it occurred in a moment of inspiration. The best approach is to think of games that one has used before and draw up a list of their advantages and disadvantages in relation to the problem in hand; then to consider how the disadvantages could be overcome and the advantages exploited to the full. This leads the designer either to reject the format and begin an analysis of a completely different game, or to adapt the game being analysed to the exact requirements of the problem.

Structure
There are two possible approaches to the selection or design of a structure for the game:

1. The adoption of an existing structure in all its basic aspects. This means selecting a game with a structure that exactly suits the characteristics of our design problem, as in the game of RUST, which used the rules and playing strategies of Snap.
2. The development of a specific structure, specially adapted to the characteristics of the problem. This entails inventing a new game or drastically modifying an existing one. The game of IDIOTS described earlier is an example of such an adaptation.

Help in selecting existing structures may be obtained by reference to the various handbooks and case studies mentioned earlier. There, the reader will find many examples of educational and instructional games that have been developed, including detailed accounts of how they were designed and how they operate in practice. Browsing through such examples inevitably leads one to see similar possible applications to one's own subject.

of column ning et
When it is necessary to develop a new game from basic principles, the three-column format for lesson planning, described in Chapter 10, is a useful method. The 'teaching activity' column is used to describe any materials, instruments, equipment or situations that must be arranged by the instructor for the players. The 'learning activity' column is used to describe the rules and procedures of play. The 'feedback activities' column is used to describe how to handle the outcomes of the activities.

of ematics
We have found the three-column planning form adequate for the design of most simple or pure games. Some authors suggest the use of flow charts or other schematics to design and communicate the game's structure. In the case of very complex structures, this may be a useful addition to the three-column plan. However, it is a good idea to start by trying to keep the game structure relatively simple. Otherwise, it may turn out to be unplayable. If you cannot describe the game's structure adequately by means of the three-column format, ask yourself whether you are perhaps over-complicating the design. This is not a hard and fast rule. Sometimes, in games that have a cyclic, repetitive structure, it is much more convenient to use flow charts as a design tool.

In Figures 12.11 (see p 208) and 12.12 (see p 209), we present two versions of a hypothetical plan of the structure of the game STARPOWER. The schema is adapted from Ellington *et al* (1982), and the three-column plan is of our own manufacture.

veloping materials
The third phase of design depends to a large extent on the complexity of the game we envisage. In the case of non-instrumented games, there is perhaps no third phase, as a 'playing plan' of the type just illustrated may act as the teacher's guide to implementation, obviating the need for any other specially designed materials. In the case of instrumented games, however, the third phase may involve considerable development of special materials, design of special equipment, computer programming in the case of electronic games, etc.

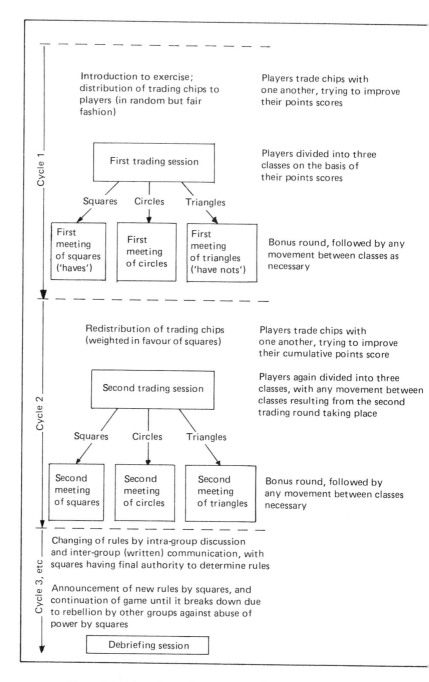

Figure 12.11 *A schematic representation of the game STARPOWER (from Ellington, Addinall and Percival, 1982)*

Instructor's activity	Learning activity	Feedback activity
1. Briefing Explain the game and the 'superficial' aims of learning to trade. Explain the method of play and the rules.	Participants should ask questions to clarify any doubts regarding the basic rules of the game.	Ensure that all the participants understand the rules.
2. Action Cycle 1 Distribute chips to each player. Lead the first round or two of trading to demonstrate how it works.	Play y rounds of trading, under the originally established rules.	After y rounds, divide players into three groups, on the basis of the number of chips held.
Organize a meeting of the three groups, in order to study the rules and the playing strategy.	Play a bonus round and comment on changes in rules that appear to be desirable.	Promote/demote any winners/losers and put into action any rule changes agreed democratically.
Cycle 2 Distribute more chips, following the schedule attached, to favour the squares (rich) and militate against the triangles (poorest group).	Play y rounds of trading under the modified rules.	Promote/demote 'big' winners/losers, as before. As a 'prize for good performance' give the 'power to veto' rules to the squares.
Organize a second meeting to analyse, and suggest modifications in, the rules of play.	Present all suggestions of rule changes in writing. Squares decide which changes to accept. Play a bonus round to test the new rules.	Observe the meetings and note signs of any dissatisfaction. Try to smooth over any problems for the time being.
Cycle 3 (and subsequent cycles, if any)	Play y rounds under the new modified rules.	Promote/demote 'big' winners/losers as before.
Organize a third meeting of the three groups. Observe the dynamics of the meetings for signs of unrest.	Players present new suggestions of rule changes. Accepted or rejected by the squares.	Observe the group interactions to decide if another session is necessary. Suggest further cycles until play breaks down.
3. Debriefing Shout *Revolution!* to stop play. Ask why play is breaking down. Ask each group to comment on the other groups' actions. Ask each group to analyse its own behaviour. Ask what similarities/differences they see to general social behaviour.	Players should: identify factors that led to breakdown; analyse the group's behaviour, contrasting it with their personal views on acceptable/just behaviour; identify analogies to social situations.	Analyse the players' insights into their own behaviour. Prompt deeper levels of introspection, if necessary. Extract the principles illustrated. Generalize and promote transfer to real-life situations.

Figure 12.12 *A detailed three-column plan for STARPOWER*
(this plan clearly specifies any modifications
that the author's plan wishes to introduce)

There are certain special skills involved in the development of these materials, and the skills differ for each game format. In the case of a game li' RUST, for example, the special skills involved are photography and photo selection, needed to create a satisfactory set of examples and non-examples. In a Monopoly-type board game, the skills involve the design of boards that are both fun to play and actually playable – we know of a Snakes and Ladd' type board on which it is practically impossible to miss all the snakes, and games can take days to complete. There is no substitute for attempting to design some games and seeing what snags occur during the field testing stage'

12.5.5 Designing simulations and simulation games

Common elements in all simulation games

Much of what we have said in previous sections is also relevant to the design simulations and simulation games. We recall the schema which we introduce at the beginning of this chapter illustrating the relationship between the various types of simulation and gaming techniques. When designing a full simulation, one generally has data to extract from reality and present to the learners. The designer starts with the planning of a case study. Most full simulations involve the participants taking on certain specific roles. Thus the simulation designer may need to plan and script the roles to be played. The difference between a pure simulation and a simulation game is the gaming element. All that we have said about game design may thus be relevant to th design of some aspects of a simulation game.

The one aspect of our discussion so far that may seem to have less genera relevance is the comment on the design of simulator devices for psychomotc skills. The design of such simulators has some unique characteristics. Howeve our analysis of the use of feedback and guidance in that context may have some general relevance for the design of simulations. The distinction betwee action feedback and learning feedback has a parallel with the immediate resu of particular actions or decisions and the long-term results.

One often hears the complaint that management development is difficult to evaluate – and hence difficult to plan systematically – because the consequences of a manager's actions are often apparent only very much late Managers are reinforced by the immediate results of their actions, not by th long-term consequences. Because of this, they may often be misled into attaching too much importance to immediate results – like staving off tomorrow's planned strike – and too little to the ultimate consequences – like impoverishing the company by too many wage settlements not accompanied by productivity increases. The simulation designer must bear t in mind, remembering that one great benefit of the use of simulation techniques is to compress time and thus bring the long-term consequences more to the fore, enhancing the real learning feedback that a management development programme should offer.

Experiential and expositive strategies in simulations

Similarly, the distinction we drew between feedback and guidance is of general value. Simulators that enhance the feedback in the task are employir a form of experiential strategy, whereas the use of guidance generally implie the adoption of an expositive strategy. Most simulation games in the social skills and attitudes area pride themselves on being experiential learning at its best. One would not therefore expect to meet much use of guidance in such simulations. In reality, however, many simulations are designed to develop specific skills, such as selling, interviewing and teaching. In these forms of simulation, we see extensive use of guidance. For example, in microteaching it is almost mandatory to present models of the skilled behaviour expected, either with live presentation or with videotape. Indeed, microteaching uses both guidance and feedback.

The parallel, from a design viewpoint, between microteaching and physic skill simulators, such as the panel beating exercises discussed earlier, is mark Once more we note the value of the distinction we drew between expositive and experiential strategies as a guide to instructional design decisions.

There is one aspect, peculiar to the design of simulations, which we have
not discussed in detail, though it was mentioned at the beginning of the
chapter. This is the incorporation in the simulation of a working model of the
real-life situation being studied. If the learners cannot manipulate the exercise
in a realistic way, and the exercise does not respond in a realistic way, we
do not have a simulation in the full sense of the word. We may have a case
study, which represents reality but does not react to the learner's decisions,
or an excellent and absorbing game such as Monopoly (which appears to
represent the property dealing world, but does not really react to the players'
courses of action in a realistic manner at all). To be a simulation, or a
simulation game, however, the life-like working model element must also be
included. As an example, Figure 12.13 (on p 212) gives a picture of the board
used in the NORTH SEA game, developed by Ellington and Addinall for Shell
UK Exploration and Production Ltd. In their description of the game,
Ellington and Addinall take great pains to explain that:

> all the three phases of the process by which actual offshore oilfields are discovered
> and developed are realistically simulated: first, the exploration phase, . . . then the
> development phase, . . . and, finally, the actual production phase . . . As in real life,
> there is a certain amount of luck involved, but players must also make strategically
> correct decisions, at all stages of the game, if they are to play effectively. (Ellington
> and Addinall, 1978.)

This model of the real world situation is perhaps the most important aspect of
the design to get right. Structural defects will show up during play, but the
learning of warped concepts and principles in relation to how reality works
may not be revealed until much later. Of course, simulations are also
simplifications of reality. They often enhance important aspects and play down
or eliminate the less important ones. This simplification process should not,
however, rob the simulation of its essential realism or its capacity to react
to the learners' manipulations in a sufficiently lifelike manner.

In order to achieve this balance it is well to follow some guidelines such as
those suggested by Livingston (1974) for planning simulation games:

1. Identify the roles of participants in the real-life situation and of the players in
   your game. In some games all players take the same role; in others they take
   different roles. But in any good simulation game, players represent only those
   persons or groups whose decisions affect the outcome.
2. Determine each player's goals and choose a measure of success for each player.
   The measure may be a concrete unit (such as dollars or votes) or an abstract unit
   (such as points or credits). Of course, two players cannot compare their scores
   unless the scores are expressed in the same unit of measurement.
3. Identify the resources available to each player, which he can use to influence the
   outcome in his favour. These also may be concrete objects (such as factories, men
   and money) or abstract qualities (such as prestige or ability). When you have
   identified each kind of resource, determine its relative importance — that is, its
   power to influence the course of events, either directly or by influencing the
   decisions of other players.
4. Determine the interactions between players in the game — that is, the way in which
   each player's actions affect the other players and their chances of success.
   Generally, interactions can be classified as cooperative or competitive, although
   two players may both cooperate and compete with each other in the same game.
5. Determine the sequence of events. This may be a series of repeating cycles or a
   single, non-repeating sequence. It may have a natural conclusion or be of
   indefinite length. If it is of indefinite length, you will have to devise a means
   of deciding when the game is over. This could be at the end of a given time (as
   in basketball or football), at the end of a given number of repetitions of the
   sequence (as in baseball), or when one player has reached a certain score (as in
   volleyball or ping-pong). If you do use an artificial means of ending the game, you
   may have to adjust the scoring to avoid encouraging special end of game strategies
   that wouldn't make sense in the real-life situation.
6. Determine the external factors — those outside the player's decisions and actions —

Top row of board squares (left to right): Collect monthly production income | Decision | Pentland refinery site | Lyness supply base | Chance factor | Ness refinery site | Decision | Decision | Lerwick supply base | Pay monthly interest

Right column of board squares (top to bottom): Decision | Sullom Voe supply base | Decision | Chance factor | Tyne refinery site | Decision | Stavanger barge base | (blank) | Collect monthly income from head office

Bottom row of board squares (left to right): Pay monthly running costs | Tees refinery site | Decision | Decision | Chance factor | Decision | Lowestoft supply base | Decision | Methil start/yard | Collect monthly income from head office

Left column of board squares (top to bottom): Collect monthly production income | Decision | Chance factor | Aberdeen supply base | Tay refinery site | Decision | Dundee supply base | Forth refinery site | Decision | Pay monthly running costs

1	2	3	4	5	6	7	8	9	10	11	12
2					LB	LB	LB	LB			
3				LB	DB	DB	DB	DB	LB		
4			LB	DB	P	DB	P	P	DB	LB	
5		LB	DB	P	DB	DB	DB	DB	P	DB	LB
6		LB	DB	P	DB	LB	LB	LB	DB	DB	LB
7	LB	DB	DB	P	DB	LB			LB	LB	LB
8	LB	DB	P	DB	LB						
9	LB	DB	P	DB	LB						
10	LB	DB	P	DB	LB						
11	LB	DB	DB	DB	LB						
12		LB	LB	LB							

Note: For reproduction in black and white, the squares on the board, which represent licence blocks with different probabilities of containing oil, have been labelled, to indicate the colours used on the original board, as follows: P: purple – probability 5 in 6; DB: dark blue – probability 4 in 6; LB: light blue – probability 3 in 6; white squares – probability zero.

Figure 12.13 *The layout of the board for the NORTH SEA*

that will affect the outcome. These would include the actions of participants in the real-life situation who are not represented by players in the game. Some of the external factors will be constant, some will depend on the other conditions of the game, and some will be affected by chance. You can allow for chance factors by using dice, cards, or spinners, but the probabilities implied should match those in the real-life situation (if it is possible to know what they are).

7. Identify the physical factors affecting the outcome of the situation and organize them on to a playing board. (Sometimes it may be convenient to have a separate board for each player instead of one large board for the whole game.) If the most important physical factors are geographic, the board will probably take the form of a map. If they are not geographic, it will probably be a systematic diagram of some kind. If the physical factors are important, there may be no board at all.

8. The final version (if indeed there is such a thing) of a simulation game is very seldom the same as the designer's first version. Several experimental playings of a game are usually needed to get all the 'bugs' out of it. In revising and refining a simulation game, there are two basic considerations: realism and playability.

9. Realism demands that the choices of strategy available to the player in the game correspond to those available to the participant in the real-life situation. It requires that the immediate results — the rewards or punishments for the player — correspond to those which he would experience as a participant in the real-life situation. And it requires that the final outcome of various combinations of player strategies and external factors reflect those of the same combinations of factors in the real-life situation.

10. The requirements of playability are somewhat harder to define, but it is generally a good idea to avoid the following characteristics:
   (a) Idle time for the players.
   (b) Complex calculations that must be made during the game — they often produce errors. (Sometimes these can be avoided by making a table that players can consult during the game.)
   (c) Complicated or confusing materials, board layouts and rules.
   (d) Rules that are easily misunderstood or likely to be unintentionally violated.

Livingston's 10 commandments nicely sum up the general approach to the planning of simulation games which, like the NORTH SEA example, explore a complex phenomenon or system under simulated game-like conditions. As he says, you may or may not need a board, and may or may not need cards or dice or counters or tokens. But you must ensure *realism* and *playability*.

This approach may also be applied to the design of social simulation games of the STARPOWER type. In this case, however, one may have to plan more carefully, to ensure that the hidden social objectives only emerge at some point well into the game. In a game that hopes to lead the players to an understanding of what it feels like to be discriminated against for holding a particular belief, it is essential that the players do not realize from the outset that the game is about discrimination, otherwise the strategies of the players may be influenced and much of the value of the exercise lost.

checklist
the design
social
ulations

This is not necessarily the case, however, in social simulations that aim to impart the feeling of being involved in a process, such as elections or race relations negotiations. In such simulations, we may follow the suggestions of Michalski (1974):

1. Select a problem or issue that has alternatives in the solution, and provide an opportunity to identify them. Students then formulate a list of their ideas and share them with the class in a brainstorming session.

2. Determine the position of simulated groups. These groups may be governmental bodies, local conservation groups, institutions, businesses, citizens' groups, etc. (The designer should be familiar with the arguments for each of the groups.) A group representing the decision-making body must also be selected. This group may represent a city or county council, an environmental protection agency, a judicial body, etc.

3. When the role or group assignments are defined, participants should have time to gather data related to their group's position. The teacher may wish to help groups to find sources of primary data. For example, the group representing the

decision-making body may actually visit a meeting of the city or county council to see how they hear a case regarding a local problem. While the groups representing various sides of the issue are gathering factual data regarding the problem, the decision-making body should be gathering information about the process of decision-making. They should consider methods of presentations, whom they represent, what their criteria are going to be, and how to structure the hearing

4. The simulated groups should be allowed to present their data to the decision-making body by a method that they have determined to be the most effective. Ea group should have teacher assistance in getting the types of materials necessary for effective presentation.

5. Establish limits for presentation time, research activities, etc. You will want to develop time-limits that simulate the actual time pressures which exist in real life.

This type of approach to social simulation is really an interactive case study, with an element of role-play. There is no attempt to build in any artificial gaming element, although the mere participation in the exercise can be very entertaining and competition may develop (as it does in real life) between the various social groups represented.

12.6 Conclusion

To summarize, we have come full circle, from a study of specific examples of games and simulations designed to develop all types of skill and knowledge in all four domains of learning, to the gradual building of a methodology for the design of simulation games. That methodology embraces the basic components of interactive case studies, role definition and role-play, effective use of guidance and feedback as learning aids, the design of simple educational and instructional games in all manner of formats and, finally, the combination of any number of these elements around a true working model of the real-life system under study.

We have tried to show that, contrary to common belief, simulations (as well as simple games) may sometimes follow an expositive strategy, although their use for experiential learning is undoubtedly one of their main attractions to the educator.

13. The Evaluation of an Instructional System

13.1 Context, input, process and product (CIPP)

This chapter considers the detailed evaluation of an instructional system. We will assess four 'moments' — perhaps better described as four functions — of evaluation at the lesson delivery, or operational, stage:

☐ *Context:* the climate in which the instruction is given;
☐ *Inputs:* the resources available for carrying out the instructional plan;
☐ *Process:* the manner in which the plan is put into action;
☐ *Products:* the results of instruction.

We will continue to apply our basic systems concepts as a general framework for our approach to evaluation. This type of approach is quite common, and many authors have developed models for 'systemic' evaluation of instructional systems. Some readers may be familiar with the CIPP (Context-Input-Process-Product) model advocated by several writers. Our approach is based on this model, though we will only deal briefly with the evaluation of the context in which our instructional system operates.

aluation
the
ntext —
icro level

Evaluation of the context is concerned with the initial decisions that the instructional designer must take when considering whether a course is really necessary. The techniques of front-end analysis, discussed in Chapters 4 and 5 and described in detail in *Designing Instructional Systems*, illustrate one aspect of context evaluation. When we analyse to what extent training can resolve a given performance problem, we are evaluating the factors in the potential trainee's job environment (or context) that may impede satisfactory performance, even when the performer has the necessary knowledge and skills. Another example of context evaluation is the technique of systems analysis applied to the identification of conflicts that exist between systems, either in terms of opposed objectives or competition for scarce resources. This forms part of the analysis of the viability of a given project. Both these examples are part of the initial stages — Level 1 — of instructional design.

It is possible to analyse the causes of failure or partial success, after a project has been executed, by means similar to those described above. Many courses do not produce the long-term returns that were expected because the context in which students live or work militates against long-term success. This is the fate of much general management development, which fails to take into consideration the reality of the organizational climate in which the trainee works. The course participants learn new techniques or approaches which, although theoretically sound, are so different from current traditions that they have no chance to put their newly gained skills into practice.

The approach to management called 'management by objectives' (MBO), which is a highly democratic yet performance-based methodology, has failed in many organizations as a result of adverse contextual factors. Many keen managers are trained in the principles and procedures involved, only to be defeated by the autocratic viewpoints of the majority of top managers who resist the introduction of MBO in their departments.

An example from the education context is the relative failure of educational systems to change attitudes to religion, race, colour or sex. However great an effort teachers make to encourage more tolerant attitudes, the context in which schools operate — society itself — only reinforces the prejudices teachers try to break down.

All these examples are at the macro level of analysis and decision-making. Some aspects, such as the availability of support and a 'favourable climate for change', may be Level 2 considerations.

Evaluation of the context — micro level

At Level 3 — the planning of specific lessons — contextual aspects are limite to the 'climate' that exists in relation to the course, the content of the course or the methods and resources used in the course. For example, a particular course may have a reputation for being boring or difficult, and this may have a negative effect on students' attitudes. Thus, if the course content is considered difficult or irrelevant by course participants, they will not give sufficient attention to lessons, however well planned and executed they may I

No questionnaires or standard recipes exist for context evaluation. It simp requires observation, analysis and critical evaluation of events that occur duri the learning process, or of comments made by learners during and after the lesson, to identify factors, other than those planned by the instructional designer, which influence the effectiveness or efficiency of instruction. These factors may vary widely according to the project. We have identified cultural factors that make it difficult to expect any 'homework' task to be performed regularly, that make rigid timekeeping a pipe-dream, that make the use of diagrams and graphs virtually useless as communication aids, that invalidate t use of any individual self-study methods, and so on. Very often, these have been identified in the middle, or at the end, of a project as the principal causes of disappointing results. Generally, there is very little that the instructional designer can do to influence these contextual factors, but he should take them into account and design systems that fit the context.

13.2 Evaluating the lesson inputs

With the other three components of the CIPP model, specific procedures and instruments can be applied at the lesson design and execution level. We shall now discuss each of these three components in turn.

Three types of input to be evaluated

There are three principal types of input to a lesson:

☐ The lesson plan itself, its structure and content, and the methods selecte
☐ The resources to be used during the lesson, especially the instructional resources — learning materials and teaching aids.
☐ The human resources employed — the teachers/instructors and perhaps other assistants/monitors — especially their level of training and preparedness to execute the plan.

It usually pays to evaluate the quality of the inputs before the lesson is given, to avoid the possibility of wasting resources and time. However, in the case of a lesson that did not quite measure up to expectations, it is worth checkin to what extent the weaknesses are due to the way in which the lesson was giv (the process aspects), and to what extent it was just badly planned, or used poor materials or poorly prepared teachers (the input aspects). The technique and sample instruments we shall be presenting can be used both *before* and *after* the lesson is given (pre- and post-evaluation).

13.2.1 Evaluating the lesson plan

The questionnaire presented in Exhibit 13.1 on pp 217-218 is a suggestion th. readers may wish to adopt when evaluating a lesson plan. It may be applied to any plan, whatever the style of lesson and whatever the format of presentation of the plan. However, readers will note that the questions adher closely to the lesson planning methodology outlined in Chapter 10. In some cases it may be advisable to include other questions, or to skip some of the ones listed, to adapt the instrument to specific styles of lesson.

	Your evaluation of the plan			
Key questions: ask only those that are relevant to the type of lesson being evaluated	*Yes*	*Partly*	*No*	*Cannot say on basis of data*
1. Does the plan specify the terminal objectives of the lesson?				
2. Does the plan indicate the general instructional strategies to be adopted during the lesson?				
3. Does the plan describe a procedure to be used to gain the learner's attention and motivate him?				
4. Does the plan describe a procedure for informing and explaining the lesson's objectives to learners?				
5. Does the plan describe a procedure for recalling/refreshing the prerequisite knowledge/skills?				
6. Does the plan describe all the steps of the instructional process to be implemented during the lesson?				
7. Is the instructional process in accordance with the principles of the general strategies (see 2)?				
8. Does the description of the process indicate what new information is to be communicated to learners?				
9. Does the description indicate the specific *tactics* to be used to explain content/facilitate learning?				
10. Does the description state the examples/analogies to be used and at what point in the lesson?				
11. Does the description state what learning materials will be used and when?				
12. Does the description state what activities should be performed by the learners at each step of the lesson?				
13. Does the description state how the instructor should evaluate progress at each step of the lesson?				
14. Alternatively, does it state how the learner may evaluate his own progress during the lesson?				
15. Does the plan indicate what the instructor should do to correct or reinforce learning at each step?				

Exhibit 13.1 *(continued)*

Key questions: ask only those that are relevant to the type of lesson being evaluated	Your evaluation of the plan			
	Yes	Partly	No	Cannot say on basis of data
16. Alternatively, does it indicate what reinforcing activities learners may undertake on their own?				
17. Does the plan include an adequate amount of practice/repetition to ensure that learners reach the proposed criteria of competence?				
18. Does the plan provide opportunities, when necessary, for the *transfer* of learning to a variety of problem-solving situations?				
19. Does the plan state how the final lesson evaluation should be carried out?				
20. Is this final evaluation valid for the objectives proposed (see 1)? Are the criteria stated and valid?				
21. Does the plan indicate how the lesson will be summarized, linked to other related topics and closed?				
22. Are some indications given on how and where interested students might find more information/get more practice?				
23. Does the plan include a timetable which apportions time to each step of the lesson/ each objective?				
24. Does this timetable seem realistic and well-planned in the light of the lesson's content and the learners' skills?				
25. As a whole, is the plan sufficiently clear? (Test: could another teacher of the subject use it without being given explanations?)				
26. In general, would you be happy about using this plan to give the lesson?				

Exhibit 13.1

Questionnaire for the technical evaluation of lesson plans

The questionnaire presented in Exhibit 13.1 is perhaps more detailed than would be fair for lesson plans written in a more sketchy manner than that suggested in Chapter 10. Accordingly, we have included the 'cannot say' column in the questionnaire. When some aspect of the 'ideal' plan — say, the general strategy — is not explicitly defined, then related questions — such as the coherence between the tactics and materials used and the underlying general strategy — cannot be evaluated.

Not all lesson plans need always be developed to the level of detail illustrated in earlier chapters. It is therefore sometimes necessary to cut out a proportion of the questions. However, as an aid to the pre-evaluation of one's own lesson plans, the complete list of questions is invaluable, as it helps to check whether the plan is sufficiently detailed to reduce the chances of surprises during the actual lesson. Running through the questions, one picks up aspects of one's plan which have not received sufficient thought. When, on the other hand, a given question triggers off the reaction 'No, the plan does not state . . ., but it is obvious to me what I would do in the lesson at this point', you just ignore the question and proceed.

When using the questionnaire to evaluate some other teacher's plans, one has to be more careful, as one does not usually know enough about the author to be able to decide whether more detail is needed or whether he can be relied on to complete the details during the lesson. When training instructors, it is a good idea to insist on fully detailed plans in the initial stages, so that one can fully evaluate the trainee's knowledge and skills. In that case, the questionnaire serves to check, in the first instance, whether the trainee has followed instructions in preparing his lesson plans. Later in his training, the trainee should take responsibility for evaluating his own plans.

The questionnaire is also useful for centralized production projects that set out to produce teacher packages with everything necessary to deliver the lessons, including detailed lesson plans. This is not very common in the educational context, but in industrial training it is sometimes a very effective way of providing large-scale, standardized training, in many different locations, which is independent of individual instructor idiosyncrasies or differences in teaching skills.

For example, this approach was adopted in one large project in Brazil, which developed over 100 technical courses in telecommunications. The recently formed national telephone holding company inherited several hundred telephone companies, operating in different cities, using different makes of equipment and following different operational procedures to different standards. In order to knit these into one national system, common programmes of training were to be adopted. It was essential to standardize the content of all training courses and necessary to repeat the same courses in many localities. Most of the courses required live demonstrations, practical exercises and other activities which make self-instruction (eg programmed texts) inadequate. In any case, a high percentage of the lower level technical staff were only semi-literate and unaccustomed to self-instruction. There were numerous local technical specialists, but they had no experience as instructors.

In this context, 100 courses were designed to produce instructor-delivered, pre-planned modules. Each module was in reality a kit containing all the necessary instructional materials — slides, transparencies, charts, models, hand tools, etc, and learning materials — self-study texts and reference materials — and a comprehensive instructor's manual.

This approach proved most effective, operating nationwide, using part-time instructors recruited from the experienced workforce and trained on a three-day course, to apply the appropriate instructional modules. In this project, a questionnaire like the one shown earlier would have been useful to control the quality of the many thousands of lesson plans produced by the 75 instructional designers involved.

13.2.2 Evaluating the lesson's instructional materials

Two viewpoints on materials evaluation

The question of the evaluation of instructional materials may be approached from several angles. We must distinguish the approach of the designer of the materials from that of the user. The first is concerned with the identification of specific weaknesses and opportunities for improvement, while the second is primarily concerned with the selection of appropriate, effective and efficient materials for inclusion in the lesson. This distinction is often blurred, for the lesson planner may indeed take it on himself to develop special materials, or may wish to adapt some existing set of materials to the specific needs of his lesson. Here, we shall discuss the evaluative questions that the lesson planner should ask in order to assess existing materials and evaluate their suitability for use in a given lesson.

Validation and evaluation

At both these points of the design process it is, however, useful to distinguish between the *technical validation* of the materials and their *pedagogical evaluation*. We use these terms in the following senses:

☐ Technical validation: the verification that the content of the materials is technically correct, up to date, stated in appropriate technical language, sufficiently complete to achieve the lesson objectives and not full of inessential information, to the detriment of clarity or efficiency.

☐ Pedagogical evaluation: the verification of the quality of the materials as an instructional resource; whether they are likely to achieve the specific objectives for which they are being selected/prepared (or whether indeed there is evidence that they do so); whether they are well-structured, easy to use, clear, and use the special effects of specific media to full pedagogical advantage, etc.

Some authors use the word 'validation' for both these aspects, distinguishing between validation and evaluation in terms of what is done before, or during, instruction (validation) and what is done after instruction, especially in terms of the long-term follow-up of performance changes and benefits (evaluation). We prefer, however, to use the term evaluation in all cases where learning or other results are measured or predicted (whether before, during or after instruction) and reserve validation for the comparison of content and its treatment with the technical expert's view of what is correct or important. This differentiates the task of the subject matter expert – validation of the material – from the task of the instructional designer – evaluation.

The interface between validation and evaluation

As we are not writing a book for technical experts, we need say little about validation, other than to define it and to stress the importance of performing this task before the implementation of the materials. We should add that the instructional designer also has a role in the validation process. When he is actually producing the materials, his role is obvious, as he will be working with subject matter experts throughout the process. When selecting materials for inclusion in a given lesson, the designer has the task of orienting the subject matter expert, who may well be inclined to include aspects of the subject that especially interest him, even when they may not be particularly relevant to the lesson's objectives. Some interesting 'padding' is not a bad thing, but the designer should not allow the subject expert to get carried away by his interests and drift dangerously away from the main objectives.

An instrument for the evaluation of materials

We shall leave the technical validation and now concentrate on the designer's principal task of evaluating the soundness of the materials from a pedagogical viewpoint. Exhibit 13.2 on pp 221-222 presents a questionnaire that may be used for the pre-evaluation of existing materials in terms of both suitability in a given lesson and general pedagogical quality.

Questions: answer only the questions that apply to a given case	Your evaluation			
	Yes	*Partly*	*No*	*Cannot say*
General aspects 1. Do all the materials specified in the lesson plan actually exist, and are they available for inspection?				
2. Have the materials passed the technical validation stage, and are they considered suitable in content?				
3. Bearing in mind the strategies and tactics specified in the plan, is the type of material appropriate?				
4. Does the material appear to be adequate to achieve the objectives set for it in the lesson plan?				
5. Are the materials really necessary? Do they contribute to the lesson in a manner that justifies the time/cost?				
6. Are the media employed appropriate for the objectives to be achieved and the content?				
Questions for written text 7. Are the style and language used appropriate for the target students?				
8. Does the material really say what it sets out to say? Are the sentences logically structured, well-organized, etc?				
9. Are sufficiently well-chosen examples included to define all new concepts clearly and adequately?				
10. Are there sufficient well-designed illustrations and graphics to support or summarize the text adequately?				
11. Is good use made of spacing, blocks, underlining, colour, typography and other aids to communication?				
12. Are worked examples, self-tests, practice exercises, introductions, summaries, glossaries, references and indexes used adequately and to good effect?				
Questions for audio recordings 13. Do the scripts obey the criteria of style, language and structure defined above for the target population?				

Exhibit 13.2 *(continued)*

Questions: answer only the questions that apply to a given case	Your evaluation			
	Yes	Partly	No	Cannot say
14. Are the recordings of a reasonable length, generally not exceeding five minutes?				
15. When appropriate, is the first person singular used to address the learner? Is informality maintained?				
16. Are special effects, such as background music, used sparingly, to ensure that they do not interfere with the main message?				
17. Are the voices of the speakers clear and pleasant in tone, varied to emphasize important points, etc?				
18. Is the quality of recording adequate for clear comprehension in normal conditions of use?				
Questions for visuals 19. Are the notation, conventions and graphic symbols used in visuals known to the learners?				
20. Is the intended message well conveyed by the visual? Does it use the visual medium to good effect?				
21. Are the size and style of lettering used appropriate to the size of projection screen/room?				
22. Is the layout of the visuals clear and uncluttered, illustrating the key points of the message?				
23. Is the quality of the artwork and the use of colour and shading of adequate quality for communication?				
Questions for audiovisuals 24. In addition to meeting the above criteria, do the audio and visual elements complement each other?				
25. Are the rate of change of visuals and the quantity of commentary well planned and varied?				
26. Are the structure of the shots, their sequence, special effects, etc designed for pedagogical, rather than artistic, effectiveness?				

Exhibit 13.2

A questionnaire for the pedagogical evaluation of the instructional materials to be included in a given lesson

Once again, it is clear the questionnaire must be used carefully, selecting the questions that are relevant to particular cases. The questions presented cover most of the aspects that may be pre-evaluated, by means of inspection, with most types of instructional materials. However, some special types of materials may require supplementary questions. One such class of materials includes programmed texts, learning modules, learning activity packs and audio-tutorial programmes. Questions may arise in relation to the applicability of the structure to the content, target population and objectives.

There is, however, a question that we should ask at this stage in relation to any form of self-instructional materials. As they set out to be self-instructional they take upon themselves the role of leading the learner to the achievement of specified objectives, without the help of supplementary explanations, drills or feedback from the teacher during the lesson. Having taken on this full instructional role, they have the concomitant responsibility to provide *evidence* that certain learning objectives can be achieved by certain groups of learners, through the individual study of the materials. What we are arguing for is the availability of *field test data.*

Anyone thinking of selecting published self-instructional materials for use in a given course is entitled to ask: *'What evidence can the authors, publishers or promoters of the materials present to show the effectiveness and efficiency of the materials when used with certain types of learners, or under certain defined conditions?'* If he gets a satisfactory reply, the designer may ask himself: *'What is the likelihood of similar results being obtained in my case? How do the learners or conditions differ?'* The problem is that, all too often, no satisfactory answer to the first question is obtained, forcing the designer to field test the materials before making a final decision.

13.2.3 Evaluating the human resources to be employed

The evaluation of instructors, teachers and lecturers, demonstrators, course coordinators and other staff involved in instruction can be approached from different perspectives. One is the evaluation of job performance for promotion or bonus payment purposes — an aspect that interests us little in the present context. Another is the evaluation of a specific teaching technique, by observation and analysis of lessons, in order to improve teaching performance. This is an aspect of the evaluation of the instructional *process* which we discuss later in this chapter. A third perspective is the pre-evaluation of the knowledge, skills or experience of the teachers we intend to select, in order to diagnose their level of preparedness for teaching the type of course we have in mind. This helps us to select potentially competent teachers or to define the content of training to be given to the teachers before the course begins. These *input* aspects are the subject of our current discussion.

Many techniques have been developed for the evaluation of teacher performance. They vary from the identification and observation of certain specific basic skills, as in some systems of microteaching, to counting and classifying the interchanges between teacher and students, as in some forms of Interaction Analysis, which is a special application of Transactional Analysis, adapted to the teacher-learner transactions that normally occur in lessons. These approaches depend, however, on fairly intensive observation of the teacher in action. They are therefore more suitable for the evaluation of the *process* of instruction than for the initial *input evaluation* of what the teacher brings with him in terms of prior experience. We generally do not have the opportunity, nor the time, to observe and analyse in depth the performance of the teachers we are thinking of employing. Some form of interview is generally all that is used. However, we have found it much more reliable to let the potential teacher evaluate his or her own state of preparedness, using self-analysis questionnaires of the type illustrated in Exhibit 13.3 on pp 224-233.

Knowledge of:

	1. Importance	2. Competence	3. Competence profile
			-4 -3 -2 -1 0 1 2 3 4
1. Theories of communication	2	3	
2. Modern communication technologies	2	2	
3. Essential aspects of clear one-way communication	5	3	
4. Essential aspects of two-way instructional communication	5	2	
5.			
6.			
7.			
8.			
9.			
10.			

Skills in:

	1. Importance	2. Competence	3. Competence profile
1. Reading rapidly and with good levels of comprehension	3	4	
2. Clear oral communication — unimpeded speech	4	5	
3. Writing clear, concise and correct text	4	4	
4. Listening to others with attention and comprehension	4	2	
5. Communicating ideas by means of creative visuals	4	2	

Exhibit 13.3 *Table 1 (continued)*

	1. Importance	2. Competence	3. Competence profile -4 -3 -2 -1 0 1 2 3 4
6. Use of non-verbal communication in the classroom	3	2	
7. Public speaking and debating	4	4	
8. Leading and animating small group discussions	5	3	
9. Participating as a member of a discussion group	4	4	
10. Using questions for diagnosis of learning difficulties	5	3	
11. Presenting and controlling expositive classroom instruction	5	4	
12. Correcting and providing feedback on students' learning activities	5	2	
13. Writing effective instructional/self-instructional materials	2	3	
14. Counselling and advising students	3	3	
15. Acting as an individual/small group tutor	3	4	
16. Interviewing and selection/classification of students	4	4	
17. Presenting audio/audiovisual programmes, voiceovers, recordings, etc	2	4	
18. Negotiating with superiors or outside agencies effectively	4	4	
19.			
20.			
21.			
22.			
23.			
24.			
25.			

Note: This table has been completed, to act as an example.

Exhibit 13.3

Table 1. Competence as a communicator

Knowledge of:	1. Importance	2. Competence	3. Competence profile
			-4 -3 -2 -1 0 1 2 3 4
1. Learning — its definition and characteristics			
2. Principles of retention, forgetting, learning curves, etc			
3. Teaching/learning as a systematic process			
4. Effects of 'nature' and 'nurture' on learning			
5. Basic aptitudes and how to recognize/classify them			
6. Effects of attitude/interest/motivation on learning effectiveness			
7. Effects of the learning environment on the learning process			
8. Special factors influencing early learning — development of the child			
9. Special factors influencing the learning of adults — andragogy			
10. The roles of the teacher/instructor in promoting learning			
11. Theories of learning based on behaviourism			
12. Theories of learning based on cognitive psychology			
13. Theories of learning based on *gestalt* psychology			
14. Theories of learning based on cybernetics			
15. Theories of learning based on neuro-linguistics, etc			
16. General instructional strategies — expositive			
17. General instructional strategies — experiential			

Exhibit 13.3 *Table 2 (continued)*

	1. Importance	2. Competence	3. Competence profile -4 -3 -2 -1 0 1 2 3 4
18.	Theories of motivation		
19.	Theories of leadership		
20.	Theories of concept formation, assimilation, accommodation, etc		
21.	Theories related to cognitive schemata, structures and strategies		
22.	Theories related to knowledge structures, content analysis, etc		
23.	General systems theory and the systems approach		
24.	Models for the classification of objectives/learning categories		
25.	Models for the planning of instructional systems/lessons/materials		

Skills in:

	1. Importance	2. Competence	3. Competence profile -4 -3 -2 -1 0 1 2 3 4
1.	The application of theoretical principles to the design of instruction		
2.	The application of theoretical principles to the delivery of instruction		
3.	The application of theoretical principles to the evaluation of learning		
4.	The application of the systems approach as a model for problem-solving		
5.	The analysis of complex systems, using systems thinking/concepts		
6.	The use of skills analysis/behavioural analysis/task analysis		
7.	The use of subject matter/topic/concept analysis		
8.	The use of knowledge/skill schemata for instructional design		
9.	The use of theoretical models for instructional design/production		
10.			

Exhibit 13.3

Table 2. Competence in theoretical aspects

Knowledge of:

	1. Importance	2. Competence	3. Competence profile
			-4 -3 -2 -1 0 1 2 3 4
1. Practical systems for the design of instruction			
2. The contributions of Skinner, Gagné, Bruner, Ausubel, Bloom			
3. The contributions of Seymour, Austwick and others to skill training			
4. The contributions of Polya, Skemp, Piaget, Landa to cognitive training			
5. The contributions of Mager, Gilbert, Glaser, etc to programming			
6. Theories and models of individualized instruction			
7. Theories and models of small and medium group learning			
8. Theories and techniques of group dynamics			
9. Theories and principles of mediated instruction and distance learning			
10. Principles and models for the design of instructional materials			
11. Principles and models for computer-assisted learning			
12. Techniques for the implementation and organization of instruction			
13. Techniques for the effective delivery of classroom instruction			
14. Techniques for the control and evaluation of instructional systems			
15. Techniques for the long-term evaluation of the effects of training			
16.			
17.			
18.			
19.			

Skills in:	1. Importance	2. Competence	3. Competence profile									
			-4	-3	-2	-1	0	1	2	3	4
1. Identification and definition of training/education needs											
2. Definition and formulation of instructional objectives											
3. Overall planning of training programmes and projects											
4. Job/task/knowledge/skills/topic/concept analyses											
5. Selection of instructional strategies and specific methods											
6. Selection of instructional media and materials											
7. Planning and production of evaluation instruments/tests/etc											
8. Planning lessons/preparing detailed lesson plans											
9. Planning materials – writing instructional text											
10. Planning materials – producing outlines for visuals/graphs/etc											
11. Planning materials – writing scripts for audiovisuals/tapes/etc											
12. Planning materials – writing individualized instruction materials											
13. Planning materials – writing outlines for CAI materials											
14. Planning materials – writing outlines for job aids/reference manuals/etc											
15. Adapting existing instructional systems to changed needs/target groups											
16. Implementing pilot projects and field tests of new instructional systems											
17. Measuring, interpreting and evaluating the results of instruction											
18. Revising and improving instruction on the basis of evaluation feedback											
19.											

Exhibit 13.3
Table 3. Competence in instructional design

Knowledge of:	1. Importance	2. Competence	3. Competence profile
			-4 -3 -2 -1 0 1 2 3 4
1. Expositive teaching methods — lecture, demonstration, etc			
2. Experiential teaching methods — group study, games and simulations, etc			
3. Case studies — their use, preparation and evaluation			
4. Brainstorming and other methods for creative problem-solving			
5. Sensitivity training — T-groups, Coverdale, grid, etc			
6. Phillips 6-6, integrated panel and other methods of small group study			
7. Group dynamics and methods for influencing them			
8. Laboratory and workshop-based practical training methods			
9. Programmed instruction and derivative methods of self-study			
10. Role playing and dramatization (sociodrama) techniques			
11. Simple and complex instructional games — uses, design, application			
12. Paper, group and computer-based simulations — uses, design, examples			
13. TWI and derivative methods of in-service training			
14. Keller Plan and other forms of modular/competence-based instruction			
15. Correspondence and distance education — methods, uses, limitations			
16.			
17.			
18.			

| Skills in: | 1. Importance | 2. Competence | 3. Competence profile |
			-4 -3 -2 -1 0 1 2 3 4
1. Lecturing and large group teaching			
2. Conducting practical demonstrations and drill and practice exercises			
3. Conducting case study, role-play and social simulation exercises			
4. Using games and simulation games in education and training			
5. Conducting and motivating group discussions and small group learning			
6. Planning and implementing individualized systems of instruction			
7. Planning and implementing/executing on-the-job training programme			
8. Organizing and implementing competence-based learning contracts, etc			
9. Organizing effective meetings, brainstorms, etc for problem solving			
10. Using objectives for planning, organizing and controlling instruction			
11. Use of behaviour modification, reinforcement, shaping, etc			
12. Use of briefing and debriefing in experiential learning			
13. Use of advance organizers, schemata, maps, networks for guidance of learning			
14. Use of questioning for diagnosis, motivation, evaluation, etc			
15. Using social forces/group dynamics/modelling for motivation/attitudes			
16.			
17.			
18.			

Exhibit 13.3
Table 4. Competence in teaching methodology

Knowledge of:

	1. Importance	2. Competence	3. Competence profile
			-4 -3 -2 -1 0 1 2 3 4
1. Advantages/uses/limitations/costs/techniques of slides and filmstrips			
2. Advantages/uses/limitations/costs/techniques of overhead projector			
3. Advantages/uses/limitations/costs/techniques of audio recordings			
4. Advantages/uses/limitations/costs/techniques of video recordings			
5. Advantages/uses/limitations/costs/techniques of chalkboards, etc			
6. Advantages/uses/limitations/costs/techniques of felt boards, etc			
7. Advantages/uses/limitations/costs/techniques of flip charts, etc			
8. Advantages/uses/limitations/costs/techniques of hand-outs, texts, etc			
9. Advantages/uses/limitations/costs/techniques of printing/repro systems			
10. Advantages/uses/limitations/costs/techniques of CAL and CML systems			
11. Principles of selection of media — pedagogical, economical, practical			
12. Principles of design of visuals, charts, posters, transparencies, etc			
13. Principles of operation of electric projection equipment, audio, etc			
14. Principles of preventive maintenance applied to audiovisual equipment			
15.			
16.			
17.			
18.			

Skills in:

	1. Importance	2. Competence	3. Competence profile -4 -3 -2 -1 0 1 2 3 4
1. The use of simple slide, filmstrip and opaque projectors			
2. The use of the overhead projector			
3. The use of chalkboards, white boards and other free-writing surfaces			
4. The use of feltboards, magnetic boards, etc			
5. The use of flip charts and other partly prepared paper visuals			
6. The use of 16mm and 8mm film projectors			
7. The use of audio recorders for playing, recording and copying/editing			
8. The use of video equipment for recording, playback, copying, editing			
9. The use of photographic equipment for slide and photo production			
10. The use of xerox and offset/litho printing equipment			
11. The use of printed materials effectively, in the classroom			
12. The use of computers (ready programmed) for teaching/administration			
13. The use of CAI systems for the generation of course material			
14. The planning and preparation of simple visuals for classroom use			
15. The planning of slide sequences and video sequences			
16. The planning and operation of a visual aid cataloguing system			
17. The planning and operation of a preventive maintenance system			
18.			

Exhibit 13.3

Table 5. Competence in the use of media and materials

Instruments for the evaluation of a teacher's competence

These questionnaires are the result of a fairly detailed occupational analysis of typical teachers and instructors. The resultant list of tasks — which some, if not all, of the teachers questioned performed fairly regularly — was then transformed into a list of necessary knowledge and skills. These were then classified into a series of areas of competence. Exhibit 13.3 shows five areas of competence which seem to summarize the tasks performed by most teachers. (We have excluded administration and curriculum planning, concentrating on those tasks which the majority of teachers and instructors perform.) The five competency areas, described in the five tables of Exhibit 13.3, are:

- the teacher as communicator;
- the teacher as expert on the theory of learning and instruction;
- the teacher as instructional designer;
- the teacher as expert in teaching methodology;
- the teacher as user of instructional media and materials.

Each table lists knowledge and skill areas identified. The columns on the right of each table may be used to identify, for each teacher, the knowledge and skills relevant to his job and the degree of importance that each area represent in relation to the real job requirements. Once the areas of importance are identified, the teacher may evaluate his current levels of competence in each area, thus comparing, area by area, what the job requires with what he has to offer. This comparison may be expressed in the form of a profile that reveals the teacher's strong and weak points, and the latter can be redressed by training.

The charts may be used very flexibly. Not all the tables need be used. For example, in the case of the part-time instructors we described earlier in the Brazilian telephone company project, the table listing competence in instructional design would not be required, as the specific job structure of those instructors precludes their performing any instructional design. In addition, many of the specific items in the other tables would also be omitted. This identification of the relevant items is performed by someone who has analysed the instructor's job as it is actually performed in the specific organization or project for which we are selecting personnel. The person being selected can then indicate his own opinion of his current preparedness, by defining his present degree of competence on a five-point scale. Alternatively, the potential instructor's current supervisor may be asked to complete the evaluation. The results may be used for selection, for task allocation in a team teaching system or for the planning of individual training and development programmes for staff. Later on, the same questionnaires may be used as a means of periodic job performance appraisal, if the training manager or head teacher wishes to install such a system.

The procedure for using the questionnaires is as follows:

1. Select the tables that are relevant to the tasks actually performed, or to be performed, by the person to be evaluated.
2. An expert in the job that is being evaluated reads the list of knowledge and skill areas on the selected tables and identifies those that are of some relevance to the particular job. He may also identify some areas that are relevant, but are not listed in the tables. These extra items are added in the spaces which have been left blank in each of the tables.
3. The job expert then evaluates the importance of each of the relevant items on a five-point scale (see Figure 13.1 on p 235), and writes the evaluation down in column 1 at the right of the table.
4. This procedure is repeated for all the relevant items on all the relevant tables.
5. Now the person to be evaluated assesses his current state of knowledge or skill in respect of each item that was deemed relevant. Although it

(5) *Essential:* It is absolutely impossible to perform some of the tasks in this job without a high degree of mastery of this item.

(4) *Very important:* It is difficult to perform some of the tasks satisfactorily without an almost perfect degree of mastery of the item.

(3) *Important:* It is desirable to have a reasonably complete degree of mastery of this item, in order to guarantee satisfactory job performance.

(2) *Fairly important:* The job can be performed satisfactorily with only an average degree of mastery of this item.

(1) *Very little importance:* A general notion about the item is desirable, but the job may be performed satisfactorily with quite low degrees of mastery.

(0) *No importance whatever:* This item is not relevant to the job that the person to be evaluated executes/will execute. We may eliminate this item from our table.

Figure 13.1 *Five-point scale for evaluating the importance of a given area of knowledge/skill for the maintenance of satisfactory job performance*

may seem unreliable to ask the teacher to assess his own competence in relation to a job he is not yet performing, we have found that teachers with some experience are surprisingly accurate in identifying their strong and weak areas of competence when using the tables. If one has access to a person who knows the teacher professionally, (who has been the teacher's supervisor, for example), reliability may be improved by asking this person to evaluate his subordinate. This evaluation is also performed using a five-point scale (see Figure 13.2 below).

6. This procedure is repeated for all the relevant items on all the relevant tables.

7. We now have two scores for each item: *importance* of the item for effective job performance and current *competence* of the teacher in relation to the item. Each is assessed on a scale from 5 to 0. By subtracting one score from the other, we obtain a measure of the *gap*

(5) *Total mastery:* The person is an expert/specialist on the topic, totally up-to-date with relevant knowledge and with considerable practical experience.

(4) *Almost total mastery:* The person is very well informed and skilled with respect to this item, although not reaching the level of a fully up-to-date expert or specialist. Has much practical experience.

(3) *Good level of mastery:* The person is reasonably well informed/skilled with respect to this item. Has a certain, perhaps slight or not comprehensive, practical experience.

(2) *Fair level of mastery:* The person has a certain amount of knowledge/skill with respect to the item, but very little or no practical experience in applying the relevant knowledge or skill to the real job situation.

(1) *Very sketchy mastery:* Has a certain amount of knowledge/skill with respect to the item, but no real practical experience and as a result does not feel secure about applying even the little he knows. Can probably apply what he knows if he can rely on assistance/explanations/evaluation and feedback from more experienced fellow workers.

(0) *No mastery:* The person may have heard/read something with respect to the item, but he has never really studied it fully and has never used the item in practice.

Figure 13.2 *Five-point scale for evaluating the current level of competence with respect to a given area/item*

between job requirements and current level of competence. By subtracting the value in column 1 from the value in column 2, we get a:

positive result when competence is greater than the job requires, and *negative* result when competence is below the job requirement.

8. The plotting of these results in column 3 produces a competence profile which illustrates the general preparedness of the teacher to perform the specific job. It also highlights his strong points — these might be exploited through intelligent delegation of tasks — and his weak points, which might be countered by appropriate training and development.

An exercise for the reader

The reader may wish to use the tables to analyse his current competence in relation to the job that he currently performs. The items in Tables 2, 3 snd 4 may be compared with the subjects covered in this book and in *Designing Instructional Systems*. Readers might thus evaluate what they have gained from reading the two books. This exercise will reveal a fairly full coverage of the items in Table 3 and a fair selection, though not all, of the items in Tables 4 and 5.

No doubt readers will agree that the two books provide a fairly good grounding in the knowledge items (how thorough a grounding is up to you to judge), but do not really develop the skill items at all. These items would need appropriate practice exercises and corrective feedback. As most of the exercises would, by the nature of the skills, have to be of an open-ended, creative nature, it would be very difficult to provide full coverage of the skill items in any book. This is left as the task of each individual reader, in his own job environment, or of an instructor who decides to build a practical workshop-type course around the models and techniques presented in the books.

13.3 Evaluating the process aspects

The evaluation of the teaching/learning process may also be approached from several different angles. For the instructor giving the lesson, the main aim of evaluating the process is to pick up weak aspects as and when they appear and take immediate corrective action. For the instructional designer, the principal aim is to identify aspects of the lesson design that can be improved *next* time the lesson is given. For the training manager or head teacher, the main purpos may be to evaluate the teacher's performance to put into action some specific teacher training, or to use the lesson session itself as an in-service training opportunity by giving the teacher advice on his performance. Finally, the learners themselves may be interested in participating in the evaluation of the teaching/learning process, in order to be able to voice their opinions on the methods used and to feel involved in the planning or development of the course they are studying. Many writers argue that it is particularly important for the adult learner to be able to influence the process and bring it more in line with personal objectives.

Techniques for the evaluation of the instructional process

The evaluation of the teaching/learning process must obey the rules for any process evaluation. We are less interested in the results than in the way in which they are being achieved. This requires direct observation and measurement of the process in action. Techniques which can be used include:

☐ Free observation and later debriefing-style evaluative discussion.
☐ Free observation, with the aid of videotape, to enable the process to be observed and analysed later. That analysis may include the performer and, indeed, the great advantage of this approach over the former technique is that the performer being evaluated is involved in self-evaluation. He can see himself and the errors that others are pointing out, and he is thus more likely to accept criticism constructively.

☐ 'Instrumented' observation, based on a prepared questionnaire completed by the evaluator. The questions are usually based on some model of the desired performance.

☐ 'Instrumented' observation, supported by a videotaped record of the performance. This method combines the rather greater objectivity of a questionnaire-based evaluation with the advantages of greater credibility and feedback to the performer already mentioned in relation to the use of videotape.

☐ Objective measurement techniques, such as activity sampling or interaction analysis. These are designed to remove the element of subjective measurement present in all the earlier examples, thus making the evaluation process more scientific. One activity sampling method involves the observation of instances in a series of lessons sampled by a randomly spaced series of visits. A count is made of the number of instances observed in which the teacher was active and the students passive, the students active and the teacher passive, both active, and so on. The frequency of the different types of activities are used to evaluate the teacher's style, by comparison with standards considered indicative of teacher-centred, learner-centred or other basic styles. Interaction analysis techniques differ in that they are based on the observation of whole lessons and directly measure the time spent by the teacher talking, by students responding, working in groups, working individually and so on. These measurements can be presented in the form of a profile of the lesson, indicating the percentage of total time spent on different categories of activity/interaction.

This last group of techniques, although more scientific and perhaps of great use for basic research into teaching styles, does not yield the detailed information needed for a formative evaluation and revision of the procedures adopted in a given lesson, or even in a given step of the lesson. For example, the sort of information that is useful to both the instructor and instructional designer is that the way of presenting example 3, of concept 4, in lesson 6, did not come over very well, indicating that certain modifications of content, sequencing or method are necessary.

The use of video

The observation techniques, both instrumented and 'free' and with or without the support of video recordings, are the ones most useful to instructors and instructional designers. Video is particularly useful when instructor development is envisaged or when the instructional designer cannot be present to observe the lesson directly. When the instructor and designer are one and the same person and the principal purpose of the evaluation is to 'debug' a newly designed lesson, video is less important, as the instructor/designer probably has the experience and skills necessary to identify weaknesses as they occur, take note of them and take corrective action, either during the lesson or later.

The use of questionnaires

The use of questionnaires is particularly useful when other people are to furnish feedback to the instructor, especially when they are not skilled teachers and evaluators of teachers, eg when the students are involved in evaluating the teaching process. Exhibit 13.4 on p 238 is an example of the type of questionnaire that may be used to instrument the collection of feedback data from students to instructor, instructional designer or course administrator.

Questionnaires can also be very useful when a skilled evaluator is furnishing feedback to a trainee instructor, as the questions may be analysed by both, before the performance, thus telling the instructor what the evaluator will be looking for. During debriefing, the questions and the evaluator's comments can then be analysed in detail, and, if necessary, challenged by the trainee instructor. Finally, the completed questionnaire may remain with the trainee as an aid to the planning and execution of further lessons, possibly being compared in the future with evaluations, using the same set of basic questions, of other lessons. This provides a means of measuring the improvement of the trainee. The

	← Yes — No →			
	4	3	2	1
1. Teaching technique				
1.1 Audible? Could I hear the teacher clearly at all times?				
1.2 Intelligible? Could I understand what the teacher was trying to say?				
1.3 Variable? Was there sufficient variation in the tone and pitch of the teacher's voice to indicate his exact meaning?				
1.4 Rhythmical? Was the speed and rhythm of the presentation such that I could grasp one topic/idea before another was introduced?				
1.5 Fluent? Was there adequate continuity of presentation to facilitate my understanding and inspire confidence in the teacher?				
2. Lesson organization				
2.1 Objectives? Could they be identified clearly from the start of the session?				
2.2 Sequence? Was the sequence of presentation logical, coherent and easy to follow?				
2.3 Content? Was the amount of new content presented reasonable for the time available?				
2.4 Examples? Were there sufficient, well chosen examples to clarify all new concepts?				
2.5 Teaching aids? Were the visuals and other aids well chosen and designed to clarify and support the verbal presentation?				
2.6 Teaching methods? Did the methods used succeed in stimulating my practice/activity/thinking adequately?				
2.7 Evaluation? At the end of the lesson, did both I and the teacher know what objectives I had achieved and where I had failed?				
3. Interpersonal relationship				
3.1 Group needs? Did the teacher show an understanding and interest in *our* objectives?				
3.2 Individual needs? Was any attempt made to cater for individual differences/needs?				
3.3 Interaction? Was the presentation two-directional? Were we involved?				
3.4 Interrelation? Did the teacher get on to our wavelength? Was there mutual understanding?				
3.5 Our reaction? At the end of the lesson were we more motivated towards the topic and to future study/participation than at the beginning?				

Exhibit 13.4 *A lesson evaluation questionnaire designed to be used by course participants (based on a similar instrument in* University Teaching in Transition *by Arthur Wise, Oliver and Boyd, Edinburgh, 1968)*

questionnaires used for this purpose should be much more detailed and technical than those intended for evaluation by course participants. They are generally based on some theoretical model of the teaching process, for examp on the analysis of basic teaching skills that forms part of most microteaching systems. Exhibit 13.5 (see p 239) is part of a questionnaire of this type. The skill in question is verbal exposition/explanation.

1. The sequence and structure of the presentation	4	3	2	1
1.1 *The argument/message presented*				
1.1.1 Are they the same in content and meaning as was intended and defined in the plan?				
1.1.2 Are they relevant to the achievement of the proposed learning/objectives?				
1.2 *The examples used*				
1.2.1 Do they illustrate clearly and accurately the ideas presented in the message?				
1.2.2 Are they well chosen for the level of knowledge and interests of the listeners?				
1.2.3 Are they interesting and motivating?				
1.3 *Continuity and sequence*				
1.3.1 Is there a clear interrelation and flow of ideas from one sequence to another?				
1.3.2 Are the objectives sequenced in a manner that facilitates comprehension?				
1.4 *Visual and other communication aids*				
1.4.1 Are visuals used where appropriate to clarify/emphasize the message?				
1.4.2 Are the visuals effective/correct representations of the idea being communicated?				
1.4.3 Are they inventive and well drawn? Do they break away from the conventional?				
1.5 *The sentences*				
1.5.1 Are they of a reasonable length?				
1.5.2 Are they of relatively simple construction?				
1.5.3 Are they grammatically correct?				
1.5.4 Are they idiomatically well structured?				
1.5.5 Do they have interesting sound/rhythm?				
1.6 *The words*				
1.6.1 Are they the simplest available for the idea that is to be communicated?				
1.6.2 Are they within the vocabulary of the audience?				
1.6.3 Are they relatively free of slang?				
1.6.4 Is non-essential jargon avoided?				

Exhibit 13.5 *Part of a questionnaire designed for the 'specialist' evaluation of verbal expositions*

Evaluation of the learning process

So far, we have been considering the evaluation of the teaching process, rather than the learning process. We have been collecting data on the classroom performance of the teacher and the impressions that he is making on the learners. Our questionnaires do not investigate the performance of the learners, whether they are understanding the messages of the lesson in the way the teacher intended, whether they are carrying out the learning activities that are necessary in order to learn and whether they are indeed learning what the lesson was planned to teach.

The evaluation of the learning process is, of course, one of the principal tasks of the teacher, which he carries out through continuous observation of the learners, through questions aimed at verifying comprehension of individual concepts or principles as they are introduced, and through the setting of learning tasks that show the learners' ability to apply the newly gained information to specific problems, or their ability to relate the new information to earlier learning in ways that lead to the formation of more powerful cognitive schemata.

The competent teacher may have a high level of skill in picking up the signs of learning success or difficulty that the students are experiencing, simply on the basis of the dialogue which takes place naturally during the lesson. Howe when dealing with medium and large groups of students, such a dialogue becomes impossible, or at least very difficult, tending to involve only one or two of the students in the group. It becomes necessary to plan and implemen activities specially designed to create the feedback on the learning process needed to assess the effectiveness of teaching.

It is therefore a good idea systematically to plan the feedback activities as part of the overall lesson plan. And it is for this reason that we have been suggesting the three-column model of lesson planning. This approach forces u to consider the desired learning activities that should occur during the lesson the signs that may be used to evaluate the progress of these activities and the feedback activities that the teacher may resort to if the learning is not progressing as well as was hoped.

Use of the lesson plan as an instrument of evaluating the learning process
The instrumentation for the evaluation of the learning process is thus contained in the lesson plan itself. Every lesson, because of its special conten and objectives, requires its own special evaluation plan. As the object of the activities that make up this plan is to *diagnose* the difficulties in comprehending or applying the new lesson content being presented, in order to take immediate corrective action, we can refer to this part of our overall lesson plan as the 'diagnosis plan'.

This specifies the behaviours, verbal or otherwise, that the learning activit should lead the learners to perform and the characteristics/criteria of these behaviours that may be used by the teacher (or some other component of th instructional system) to diagnose the causes of learning difficulties. Our three column model of lesson planning, when properly applied, would detail these behaviours and criteria in the second column, and, in the third column, woul specify the remedial actions for every significant type of learning difficulty that is known to occur in practice.

It is as well to remember that the lesson plan should be of use to the teach both *before* and *during* the lesson: before, to enable him to prepare all the necessary examples, exercises and materials; and during, as a reminder of wh to do at specific stages of the lesson. Thus the first column of the plan shoul remind the teacher what to present and how to present it. The second colum should remind the teacher what to look for in the learning activities of the students in order to be able to diagnose probable causes of any learning difficulties that may occur. The third column should remind the teacher of how to deal with specific types of learning difficulties.

When prepared in this way, the lesson plan is an excellent instrument for quality control of the lesson. Figure 13.3 (see p 241) presents part of a lesson plan which is intended to lead students to mastery of the concept of 'break-even' and its use in economic analysis of alternatives. Notice that the plan contains a detailed account of what to watch for in diagnosing learning difficulties and what to do in the case of each type of difficulty.

13.4 Evaluating the products of instruction

Whereas during the steps of the lesson the teacher is evaluating *progress* towa certain objectives, at the end of the lesson he will wish to evaluate to what extent the objectives *have actually been achieved*. This evaluation may serve summative purposes, such as informing the learners that they are 'doing well' or that they 'could do better', or even, in systems that adopt a philosophy of continuous evaluation, to grade the learners. It may also have a formative purpose, suggesting that certain aspects of the lesson should be modified in future courses or that further practice of the content should be undertaken before progressing to more advanced related work. Figure 13.3 gives an exampl in the debriefing session described, of an attempt to evaluate whether furthe exercises of a similar type to that included in the lesson should be planned.

Teaching activity	Learning activity	Feedback activity
1. *Explain objectives:* 'to use the concept of "break-even point" in decisions between alternatives.'	Respond to teacher's questions: 'what do you understand by the term "break-even point"?'	Modify and complement the explanation given, if necessary.
2. *Demonstrate* the break-even points in several cases, using transparencies of the cost/time graphs for each alternative course of action.	Show comprehension of the graphs, by identifying the break-even points or explaining the absence of such points on the graph.	Resolve any difficulties of comprehension by further explanation and analysis of extra cases, until all the learners show skill in interpretation of break-even graphs.
3. *Supply practice* in the form of a case study, for example three ways of increasing the productivity of the typing pool: (a) recruit more staff; (b) use external course; (c) use on-the-job training. Supply all necessary data to compute the annual costs over four years, including any initial investment costs. Form small groups (of three) to prepare break-even graphs and then make a decision between alternatives, in the form of a management report.	Learners work in groups, using any references or texts as aids and asking for help from instructor if necessary. They should: (a) compute the costs of each alternative; (b) draw graphs; (c) make reasonable decisions between the alternatives and justify them. Observe the work of the groups and intervene if necessary.	(a) In case of errors in computation of the costs, call attention to error, and check if it is due to incorrect interpretation of data or merely incorrect arithmetic; (b) In case of errors in drawing the graphs, refer group to the place where they will find a worked example; (c) In case of poor decision-making, let the other groups comment and argue different viewpoints during the debriefing session (see below).
4. *Evaluate* the learning that has occurred by asking each group to present its report to the others, who should point out any errors or alternative decisions. Run this as a form of debriefing session, intervening, if necessary, to ensure that all the alternatives are fully explored.	Learners should show ability in making appropriate cost/benefit decisions, and in identifying the implications of the decisions taken by other groups.	(a) As regards differences in decisions, leave the groups to correct each other, intervening only if learners fail to identify key implications or valid alternatives; (b) As regards the general level of logic/argument, decide whether or not more such exercises are needed.

Figure 13.3 *Extract from a lesson plan illustrating the use of the second and third columns for planning diagnostic and feedback actions*

In one sense, any learning that takes place during the lesson is a product, and the behaviours observed to monitor the steps of the lesson are sub-products of the final product. They are the *component behaviours* of the more complex *end-of-lesson behaviours* specified in the lesson objectives. Much of what we will say in this section is therefore relevant to the planning of end-of-lesson tests, or to the planning of questions to be asked during the lesson, in order to evaluate progress towards the end-of-lesson objectives. As the lessons in a course are interrelated, leading to the achievement of yet more complex end-of-course objectives, we can conceive of the products of a lesson as sub-products of the course. Some of what we shall say in this section will therefore also apply to the evaluation of whole courses.

A schema of levels of evaluation

It is useful to visualize these different levels of product as part of an overall schema of evaluation related to our model of levels of instructional design. In Figure 13.4 on p 243 we present a visual representation of instructional design and evaluation as two multi-level processes, linked at each of the levels by appropriate testing systems and instruments. This enables formative decisions to be taken and modifications implemented at all the system levels, as indicated by the dotted arrows in Figure 13.4.

This diagrammatic representation of the various levels of objectives specification and evaluation may, because of the terminology employed, appear to be couched very much in the context of job-specific training. However, a parallel model of levels may be drawn up for the education-in-society context. The 'wider system' is the society that sends its children to educational institutions. The 'jobs' system is the role, or roles, that these children later adopt in society, either in a vocational sense or in the general sense of 'being a good and competent member of society'. The objectives at this level are the social skills that so many modern curricula emphasize. From this point on down the levels, the distinctions between the training and education contexts is progressively blurred. It is in the upper levels that the greatest differences in philosophy and methodology of evaluation exist. Also, it is much more difficult to perform valid long-term evaluation in the educational context as the time-scale is so much greater and so much unplanned learning goes on outside the confines of the school. Nevertheless, the importance of the evaluation of total educational systems and their contributions to the society in which they are embedded is of the utmost concern to educators and politicians alike.

Products, outputs and outcomes

As an aid to the clear understanding of the long-term evaluation of education, some attempts have been made to define stages, or levels, of evaluation and the associated terminology. Our own model, presented in Figure 13.4 on p 243, indicates the structure and complexity of the evaluation process. Others, notably Roger Kaufman, have written on the need to define the terms used with more care. Kaufman argues that terms such as products, outputs and outcomes are used indiscriminately as synonyms or near-synonyms by some educators, whereas for others slightly different meanings are attached to each of the terms. He suggests that we should be more rigorous in our use, and presents a model in which 'product' means the learning that has taken place, 'output' means the job or social skills acquired and later applied successfully, and 'outcome' or 'result' means the changes that occur in the wider system — society or work — as a consequence (Kaufman and English, 1979).

Our main concern in this chapter is with the evaluation of lessons and lesson plans, so our use of the term 'product' accords with Kaufman's suggestions. We are not directly concerned here with the evaluation of outputs and outcomes, though sometimes it is not that easy totally to separate the various levels. We dealt in *Designing Instructional Systems* with some of the major aspects of long-term evaluation or follow-up (Romiszowski, 1981), and reproduce here, to provide a general framework, one of the maps used to summarize the upper levels of evaluation (see Figure 13.5 on p 244).

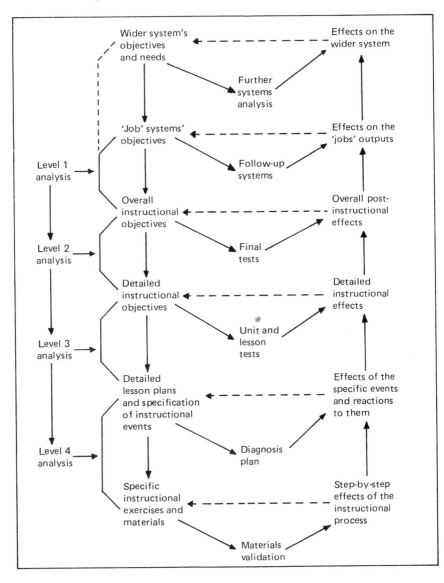

Figure 13.4 *A schema of instructional design and evaluation*
as two multi-level processes, interlinked by 'testing-evaluation-revision'
loops (Romiszowski, 1981)

levels
: which
roducts are
valuated

Our schema includes several levels at which learning is evaluated. These are:

1. Overall instructional effects evaluated at the end of a course, or at key points during the course in systems that employ continuous evaluation.
2. Detailed instructional effects, evaluated at the end of each lesson or unit of interrelated lessons.
3. Effects of specific instructional events, evaluated during the course of the lesson.
4. Step-by-step effects of the instructional process, which seems to be another way of saying the same thing as in (3).

Introduction	In follow-up, it is never possible to say for sure whether the measured improvements are due entirely (or even in part) to the learning that has occurred. There are usually other factors at play that must, if possible, be controlled or allowed for in the assessment of effects. The evaluation of follow-up data must therefore be done carefully. Usually there is need for 'before' and 'after' data in situations where all other factors that may influence job performance have been kept from changing. This is easier said than done. However, many viable techniques do exist.
Techniques for measuring long-term performance changes	One may obtain information about past and present performance levels by three main routes: ☐ Direct observation (of the performers) ☐ Indirect measures (of the effects of the performance) ☐ Secondary measures (by asking someone else). Some practical techniques that may be used, both in the educational and training contexts, are given below.

Direct measurement techniques	**Training context**	**Educational context**
	Job performance evaluation system, by regular formal reports from supervisor.	As there is no formal job, no formal system of reporting is possible.
	Observer diary, kept by an expert, over a given period, recording changes in post-training performance.	A sample of past students may be observed and a diary kept. A sophisticated example is Project 'TALENT'.
	Critical incident methods: an analysis of how the trainee deals with exceptional job situations.	Very effective in the educational context. Does schooling contribute to success/happiness?
Indirect measures of effects	Changes in productivity, error rates, speed or quality of work, rates of wastage/scrap, human relations, turnover.	Changes in standard of living, quality of life, social awareness, participation in government.
Secondary information	Interviews of performers. Questionnaires. Diaries kept by the performers. Interviews of superiors.	All the sociological techniques of interviews and questionnaires used to investigate people's life-styles.
Techniques for measuring long-term reactions	Direct observation of attitude to the job. Indirect measures of job changes, drop-out rates, etc. Secondary information through attitude questionnaires or interviews, on reasons for job change.	Direct observations of voluntary continuing education efforts. Indirect measures of demand for education. Secondary information through questionnaires and interviews.

Figure 13.5 *A map of the principal techniques of long-term evaluation or follow-up of the effects of instruction* (Romiszowski, 1981)

The last two levels of evaluation are indeed similar, but we have put them in our diagram as separate levels, to distinguish between the evaluation that occurs during instruction — carried out by the teacher as part of his teaching methodology — and the evaluation that occurs during materials development, in special conditions, with specially selected samples of the target population. This is often conducted by specialists in materials design, and is performed before the materials are released for general use by teachers.

luating overall ructional ects

As far as the overall instructional effects are concerned, our main interest is to perform a summative evaluation of what has been learned from a particular course or unit of the course. We wish to measure the final level of mastery achieved by the participants on the terminal objectives. We generally do not have the opportunity to set a very detailed test that evaluates the achievement of all the specific enabling objectives that were studied during the course. This would take too much time, and would involve the use of very unwieldy testing procedures.

The use of these 'final results' is often restricted to the grading or certification of the course graduates. In the educational context, the final test is often a small sample of what was taught during the course, serving only to give a general idea of how well a given student has learned. The results may not be used to identify exactly what has been learned and what has not. In the training or vocational education contexts it is more common to try to test all the course objectives. However, this testing is done by means of composite test items that attempt to evaluate the performance of whole tasks, which might involve several sub-skills and many specific items of knowledge.

For example, the end-of-course test for a secretarial course may include exercises in typing, letter composition, filing, answering the telephone and so on. However, the exercises will not break the tasks down into their separate components. The filing test, for example, will not ask separate questions on the principles of filing systems, the different classifications that exist in the organization's filing system, the number of copies of specific types of documents that should be filed, etc. Rather, all these component items of knowledge and sub-skills will be tested indirectly, through the evaluation of the overall performance of the trainee on filing tasks.

w to pare d tests

The importance of test design is to *match* the behaviour required by the test to the behaviour specified in the objective. The end-of-course objectives usually describe tasks that are part of a future job, or part of the student's future role in society. The end-of-course test items should therefore *simulate* these tasks as closely as possible. Failure to apply this simple rule may lead to invalid testing or worse.

case dy: the ting of gnostic lls

As an example of what we mean by invalid testing and what we mean by worse, let us examine a case that came up in a project executed by the author some years ago. It involved the analysis of teaching and examination in some institutions of medical education. The reasons for the project were dissatisfaction with the performance of doctors after training on some important tasks. One of these tasks was the diagnosis of disease. Much time was devoted on the courses to the teaching of diagnosis, both the basic diagnostic skills required and the special knowledge needed to diagnose specific diseases correctly. So why was later performance not very good? Was there something wrong with the course structure?

We discovered that there was indeed something wrong with the course, but that the root of the problem lay in the methods of evaluation used. Because of the large numbers of medical students in the institutes concerned, the organization of practical examinations presented serious problems. The tendency was to examine by means of written papers. Immediately we notice a discrepancy between the ideal way to test a diagnostic skill and the methods actually employed. Practical diagnostic skills depend on visual observation of symptoms and appropriate questioning of the patient. These aspects are difficult to reproduce in a written examination question. Worse still, however, was the tendency in the examination papers to ask questions of the type — 'What are the symptoms of disease X?' This is a nice, short question (for the examiner) which may require a quite lengthy essay on the part of the student, especially if the question continues 'and how would you treat it?'. It is easy to compose and to mark such a question. However, what the student is doing in responding bears little relationship to the stated objective. The behaviour implied by the objective 'diagnose diseases' is of the form:

> Given a set of symptoms to be observed, tested for or deduced from interviewing a patient, the learner should be able to identify the disease or diseases from which the patient is suffering, to criteria of correct identification in X per cent of cases presented that involve the Y most common diseases (list attached).

End-of-course objectives are seldom stated as precisely as the above model suggests. This is a pity, for it may help to avoid the sort of distortions that we are beginning to identify in this case study. If we analyse the behaviour being tested by the typical examination question we mentioned above, we get:

> Given the name of a disease (taken from the Y most common diseases — see list attached), the learner should be able to list the symptoms associated with this disease, to criteria of correctly listing at least Z per cent of the symptoms that might be associated with the given disease

Note that the behaviour tested is quite the inverse of the behaviour of diagnosis. Instead of identifying diseases from given symptoms, the learner is identifying symptoms for given diseases. No wonder he could do well on the test, yet not perform well on the job. The test is invalid for the objective.

Influence of testing on teaching

But why did he do badly on the job? What has the invalid final test got to do with poor on-the-job performance? Well, of course, it need not have anything to do with it. If the course itself were to teach the necessary diagnostic skills and the necessary knowledge effectively, then on-the-job performance would be satisfactory, even though the final test used on the course could not be considered as a valid predictor since it tests something quite different.

But the course was not effective, and one reason for this was that the *teaching* on the course followed the criteria that were being set by the *testing* system employed. Students and teachers were, in time, influenced by what the exam tested, to teach and learn lists of symptoms for given diseases, as rote memory learning of factual information, rather than to practise the skills of diagnosis and build special conceptual schemata that might link specific patterns of symptoms to the probability of specific diseases. Without a doubt, the inadequate testing system was one factor that led to the formation of an inadequate instructional system.

Similar cases may be identified in all the areas of education and training. Students learn lists of facts when they should be forming new concepts, of which the lists are merely examples. Problem-solving is learned as a fixed algorithmic procedure, when it should be a flexible, heuristic strategy. People learn to verbalize — to talk about what should be done — instead of mastering the skills necessary actually to do it. And very often the teacher is not even aware that what has been learned does not match the real objectives, reassured by the satisfactory results obtained by the learners on final tests which do not match the real objectives.

Tools for ensuring the validity of test items

For this reason, special attention should be paid to the validity of the test items that are used. Several tools have been developed to help one do this. One such tool is the behavioural objective. As in the example of medical diagnosis mentioned above, the specification of all course objectives in formal behavioural terms, stating in quite unambiguous language what the learner should *learn to do*, under *what test conditions* and to what *criteria* of excellence, makes it very difficult to unknowingly employ an invalid testing and evaluation procedure. The objective states, in reality, the test situation that should be used at the end of the course.

Another tool, which avoids the specification of all objectives in strictly formal behavioural terms, is the use of a classification or taxonomy, such as the taxonomies of cognitive and affective objectives prepared by Bloom (1956) and Krathwohl (1964) and their colleagues. These taxonomies use a classification schema which allows test designers to talk of categories of objectives that should be aimed for, and then proceed to design test items for the desired categories. This approach is particularly useful in the educational context, where end-of-course examinations generally test only a sample of the learning that has taken place. The taxonomical approach can ensure that the sample of behaviours tested is well chosen from a pedagogical viewpoint.

Yet another tool that can be used is our own schema of skill and knowledge categories. Figure 13.6 on p 248 presents a summary of guidelines for the selection of suitable evaluation techniques for each of the principal categories of skill. Note the differences between techniques suitable for productive and for reproductive skills. Reproductive skills, whatever their basic category, can be evaluated in a fairly mechanistic manner.

In the cognitive domain, mathematical calculation skills of a repetitive nature may be evaluated in terms of the number of problems solved correctly in a given time. An answer sheet may be prepared, so that almost anyone, including a monitor, a secretary, a computer or even the learner himself, may evaluate performance and progress towards achievement of the terminal objectives.

In the psychomotor domain, criteria of speed and accuracy for a given task may again be predetermined, so that evaluation may be carried out mechanically, as in the case of counting characters per minute and errors per page as a means of evaluating a typing course.

In the reactive domain, the counting of 'approach behaviours' — helpful comments, punctuality, voluntary participation, borrowing books from the library, etc — may be used to evaluate the formation of positive attitudes towards a given subject, and the counting of an increase in 'avoidance behaviours' — interruptions that disrupt the lesson, lateness, non-participation, etc — to indicate the formation of negative attitudes (see Robert Mager's *Developing Attitudes Toward Learning*, Mager, 1968). In the interactive domain, a similar counting of signs of good manners, pleasant interaction and cooperation may be used as measures of the simpler, reproductive, interpersonal skills.

In the case of productive skills, however, the problem of evaluation is more complex. In order to demonstrate that the skill has been mastered, the learner must perform some form of creative activity. In the cognitive domain, an unfamiliar problem must be solved by the application of general principles. There may be only one correct answer or there may be many, but there are always many ways of arriving at the answer and some are quicker, more economical, more sophisticated, more unusual or more elegant than others. The evaluation procedure must study the *process* by which the problem was solved as well as the actual *result* obtained.

The same is true in productive psychomotor tasks. The evaluation of a football game does not restrict itself to the counting of goals scored, but considers the whole process of play, the strategies adopted by the players, what paid off, what did not — and why. In the reactive domain, higher order skills, involved, for example, in planning and living according to particular philosophies or religious beliefs, may once again only be evaluated by a close analysis of the decisions taken in difficult, non-standard situations. In the interactive domain the same holds true. Evaluation of a leadership skill means more than counting the votes that a given candidate receives for his popularity and effectiveness as a leader.

Techniques for the evaluation of skilled performance	We may use our schema of skill categories to list some of the more useful techniques.	
	Reproductive skills	**Productive skills**
— cognitive skills	Problems of a *familiar* type to be solved to predetermined standards of accuracy, speed, etc (eg long division drills) (closed, objective methods)	Problems of an *unfamiliar* type to be solved, often with no unique solution. Evaluation of the process as well as the solution (open ended methods)
— psychomotor skills	Performance tests on real or simulated task. Criteria of speed, accuracy, quality applied objectively (eg typing skills, machine operation skills)	Productive tasks which require planning of a strategy. Evaluation of result and of planning process by observation and discussion
— reactive skills	Directly, by objective counts of 'approach' or 'avoidance' behaviours. Indirectly by attitude questionnaires, etc (see Mager, 1968 for approach/ avoidance)	Directly through observing people's value systems in action, outside school. Indirectly through analysis of positions taken during debates on key issues and the arguments used
— interactive skills	Directly, by counts of frequency of 'good' habits, manners, etc, being displayed under voluntary conditions	Observation of complex interactive skills under real or simulated social conditions, followed by evaluation debriefings to examine the planning element
Techniques for the evaluation of knowledge	At the post-instructional stage, the separate evaluation of knowledge is only necessary if the objectives are purely to acquire knowledge (ie we are dealing with an information problem). In the case of performance problems, the necessary knowledge is indirectly tested by the skills testing, as above. If necessary, knowledge may be tested as follows:	
— recognition	Multiple-choice questions demanding identification of the correct fact, definition, example, etc	
— recall	Direct open ended questions, phrased so as to elicit one unique answer	
— comprehension	Multiple-choice questions demanding the identification of errors, correct/ incorrect statements, conclusions or classifications. Matching lists of concepts and examples, rules and applications, steps and sequence, etc. Open ended essay questions requesting explanations, restatement in own words, examples, etc.	

Figure 13.6 *A map of the chief characteristics of valid tests for the evaluation of overall instructional effects* (Romiszowski, 1981)

All of these examples illustrate the need for a much more complex approach to the evaluation of productive skills, an approach that stresses the evaluation of the planning and decision-making process that led to specific actions. This evaluation generally requires conversation between the evaluator and the person being evaluated, a conversation that leads to the analysis of the reasons behind the selection of specific courses of action and the rejection of others. Ultimately, this conversation should lead to the analysis of the cognitive schemata that the learner has formed in respect of the subject. Thus, the knowledge required to perform a skilled task (and its structure in the mind of the learner) is evaluated indirectly, as part of the evaluative conversation, or debriefing, that should follow any exercise that aims to develop productive skills.

Figure 13.6 also illustrates the rather limited role that the testing of pure knowledge should play in end-of-course evaluation. Verbal tests of knowledge are justified at this stage only in courses where the terminal objectives are limited to the transmission of knowledge. This is quite common in the field of general education, but rarely justified in any training or vocational education context. In such cases, knowledge is generally transmitted in order to facilitate the learning of a task and can thus be tested indirectly, through the correct execution of the task.

The case is quite different, however, in testing and evaluating individual lesson objectives. In planning the detailed evaluation of learning, lesson by lesson, we focus on the *specific objectives* of each lesson. These may be certain specific skills, that will later be used in combination with others to attain the overall objectives envisaged, or they may be certain items of knowledge, necessary to enable the learner to perform some more complex task later. The principal value of testing the learning that has occurred in a given lesson is to perform a formative evaluation that leads to modifications in the lesson's structure and perhaps the incorporation of extra teaching to overcome any failure of the lesson to achieve its objectives.

The end-of-lesson evaluation should be sufficiently detailed to enable the teacher to identify exactly what has gone wrong. It is necessary to test each specific objective separately. When the lesson teaches some new knowledge and then develops skill in its application, the testing system used must be sufficiently sensitive to distinguish between failure to acquire the knowledge and failure to use it correctly. This means that the test would include items that separately measure the recall of the knowledge, its comprehension and its practical application.

If certain essential sub-skills are involved in the application of the knowledge (for example, special levels of visual perception or unusually high levels of dexterity), the testing system must be capable of identifying whether learning difficulty is due to the present lesson's content, or to inadequate mastery of specific sub-skills. A thorough test should therefore be part and parcel of each lesson. It is not practical to enter into such detail in end-of-course or end-of-unit tests, as the tests would be very unwieldy and long. Moreover, the moment when teachers most need this detailed feedback is when they still have a chance to do something about correcting their teaching performance, that is, during and immediately after the lesson.

As a general guide, we reproduce, in Figures 13.7 and 13.8 on pp 250 and 251, a summary of how our skill cycle and our schema of knowledge categories may be used as an aid to deciding what kinds of tests are appropriate for a given lesson.

By matching our lesson objectives to the categories of sub-skill and knowledge of our model, we can find in the two maps presented (Figures 13.7 and 13.8 on pp 250 and 251) guidelines to the most appropriate types of testing. Note how often something other than a written test is called for. Often, the appropriate testing method is the observation of the learners' behaviour in a given situation. On other occasions, the only method of testing

uating detailed uctional ts

ching type of to the e of skill nowledge

Introduction	Remembering that the principal function of evaluation *during* the instructional process is to *improve* the instruction, the evaluation techniques and instruments must be sufficiently sensitive to indicate exactly what parts of the instructional plan are working and what parts need to be improved. We may no longer test for prerequisite knowledge indirectly by testing its application in skilled performance. We need to have instruments which will identify what aspect of the skilled performance is poorly mastered.
Use of the skill cycle	We may employ our basic skills cycle to identify the questions we should be asking in the detailed evaluation of a skill.
Perception tests — cognitive skills	Does the learner understand the problem? Can he restate it/put it into symbolic form/identify the unknown quantity that he should seek/recognize when it has been solved/recognize degrees of difficulty in the problem?
— psychomotor skills	Can the learner perceive the external signals that guide the skilled activity? Can he discriminate between relevant and irrelevant information? Does he have the requisite level of perceptual acuity?
— reactive skills	Does the learner attend to external events and show an interest in them? Is he sensitive to events?
— interactive skills	Does the learner attend to the reactions of others and is he sensitive to their feelings?
Prerequisite tests — all skill categories	Tests of the requisite knowledge: the procedures and the principles that must be stored.
Strategy tests — productive skills	Tests of the requisite ability to analyse relevant problems, generate alternative solution strategies and pre-evaluate them by thinking through at a reflective level (open ended verbal tests).
Performance tests — cognitive skills	Can the learner put it all together in order to perform the cognitive task to required standards of accuracy, speed, long-term productivity, etc?
— psychomotor skills	Can the learner perform and continue performing at required productivity, accuracy and quality standards?
— reactive skills	Does the learner actively respond in the appropriate manner at every opportunity Does he seek opportunities to practise his values and life skills?
— interactive skills	Does the learner actually respond to others in the expected manner? Does he seek to interact effectively and frequently? Does he seek to improve his skills?
Observation	Naturally, the above suggestions are very general. Every skill requires its own set of specifications.

Figure 13.7 *A map showing the use of the 'expanded skill cycle'*
as a tool for planning a detailed evaluation
of the instructional effects of a lesson (Romiszowski, 1981)

Introduction	The comments made on 13.6 regarding the evaluation of knowledge referred only to the type of testing instruments that may be used for the testing of knowledge. After Level 3 analysis, we have a more detailed picture of the knowledge to be taught. We can classify the items of knowledge into the four basic categories of *facts, concepts, procedures* and *principles*. Furthermore, we can build up a sequence, or hierarchy, for the learning of this knowledge. Certain facts must first be learned in order to be linked together into procedures. Certain concepts must first be learned in order to enable the learning of further more complex concepts and to later be linked with other concepts in order to form rules, rule sets and finally complex problem-solving strategies. The *knowledge structure* that we uncover helps us to determine the sequence of lessons in our course and the content of each lesson.
	Thus, for each lesson, we are in a position to develop appropriate tests.
Questions for various types of knowledge	The table below suggests typical questions that should be asked at the lesson level, for each of the four main categories of knowledge.

	For *recall*, ask student to:	For *comprehension*, ask student to:
Facts — verbal – concrete	State the facts Recognize the fact	Restate in own words Explain its significance
Concepts – concrete – defined	Recognize examples State definition	Classify examples and non-examples Classify examples and non-examples
Procedures	State the steps in correct sequence	Explain the key points which govern effective performance
Principles	State the rule or set of rules	Give an example of their application. State if they apply to a given example

| Observations (1) | Only recall and comprehension are included as the aspects of knowledge that are worth testing by direct questioning. Recognition is a somewhat simpler behaviour than recall. It may be tested as a step towards the testing of unaided recall, but, at the end of a lesson or unit of instruction, essential knowledge at least should be recallable. Testing for comprehension is an attempt to ensure that the knowledge is stored in an efficient way, related to other knowledge as a meaningful schema. |
| (2) | The other categories of Bloom's taxonomy are not used, as *application* of knowledge is tested via the performance of *all skills* and the *creation* of new knowledge (through analysis, synthesis and evaluation) is tested through evaluation of *productive skills*. |

Figure 13.8 *A map of the principal considerations to take into account in planning the detailed evaluation of the knowledge content to be transmitted by a lesson* (Romiszowski, 1981)

which is valid involves prolonged observation and counting of the frequency of certain behaviours during a given period of time after the lesson, or during subsequent lessons. This is particularly true in the reactive and interactive domains. In order, for example, to test whether the learner has developed the ability to recognize other people's views on a subject and to understand the reasons that lead to different views on a subject (we might call this the sub-skill of empathy), it would probably be necessary to observe how that individual handles a number of different situations in which a clash of views is encountered. No doubt some practice in the handling of such situations may be arranged by suitable simulation games, or in role-play sessions. However, the learners know that they are in an artificial situation and this m influence their behaviour considerably. The instructor may therefore wish to evaluate this skill in situations in which the learners do not know that they are being evaluated. The instructor might, for example, arrange as part of sor other lesson a situation which involves a conflict of views on a given topic. The exercise ostensibly aims to achieve some other specified objectives, but the instructor is making observations to evaluate the empathy skills that were learned in earlier lessons. This is a 'hidden agenda' approach, similar to the on used in STARPOWER, which was described in Chapter 12.

The maps presented in Figures 13.7 and 13.8 on pp 250 and 251 are self-explanatory. The suggestions made in them are derived from research, teachin experience and common sense, organized around our basic schemata of knowledge and skills. Note the difference in detail of our treatment of the end-of-course evaluation procedures and the end-of-lesson procedures. In the former case, we tend to test whole tasks all at once. The knowledge content - when indeed it needs to be tested directly at all — may also be tested in large chunks. These may cover lists of facts, as in 'write a report on . . .'; procedure as in 'describe how to . . .'; conceptual schemata, as in 'explain the relationshi that you see in . . .'; strategies or theories, as in 'how would you attempt to solve the following problem . . .?', or 'how do you explain the following phenomenon . . .?'.

At the lesson evaluation level, however, one descends to the detailed testir of each component sub-skill and each specific item of knowledge to be mastered. We should design separate test items for the perception skills, separate tests for the knowledge necessary (taking into account the type of knowledge), separate tests for the basic intellectual skills of analysis that are necessary to plan the appropriate course of action in productive activities, an separate performance tests to check whether the learner can 'put it all togeth without inhibition, fear, lack of dexterity, lack of stamina, or any other factor that may lead to poor performance.

The adoption of such a detailed approach to the evaluation of the product of a given lesson offers all the data that may be required to identify and correct any weak aspect of the instructional plan or of its execution.

As a practical example of such a detailed approach to lesson evaluation, w might consider a hypothetical lesson (or series of two or three lessons) on the **A case study:** use of the AIDA model of salesmanship. This model is quite simple: the idea **the detailed** is that a typical selling/buying interaction takes the potential buyer through **evaluation** four progressive states or attitudes:
plan for a
lesson on   1. *A*ttention to the salesman and the product or service being offered.
salesmanship   2. *I*nterest in the product or service, to the extent of wishing to know
                      more/see a demonstration.
                   3. *D*esire to acquire the product or service being offered.
                   4. *A*cceptance — the closing of a deal.

We may analyse the skills of a salesman who is using this model by means of our expanded skill cycle:

nalysis of
e basic
ills
quired

1. *Perception. Attention* to the customer's comments and to non-verbal signs of interest is critical. *Perceptual acuity* is necessary to a reasonable degree in order to identify when a customer has reached a particular stage of the model. *Discrimination* (in a 'noisy' environment) may be an important skill in some real selling situations, where, for example, the client has hidden motives for appearing to be less interested than he really is.

2. *Knowledge. Conceptual schemata* are required in order to understand the basic concepts of the four AIDA stages. The four concepts of attention, interest, desire and acceptance must be clearly understood. *Procedures* of a standard nature are *not* involved in the application of the AIDA model. The process is heuristic. There may be some specific demonstration procedures related to a particular product or service, but this is not a direct part of the methodology. *Principles*, on the other hand, do exist and must be known and understood by the salesman. Many psychological principles are involved in the awakening of interest.

3. *Planning.* The intellectual skills of analysis, synthesis and evaluation are used by the salesperson in the planning of a specific strategy for a specific case.

4. *Performance.* Many basic skills influence successful performance by a salesperson who has the necessary knowledge and the perceptual and intellectual skills described above. These include skills of *verbal expression, persistence* and *self-evaluation*, as well as characteristics such as a lack of inhibition, pleasant voice and strong self-motivation. These are required to ensure the *initiation, continuation* and the self-regulating *control* of the selling process.

nalysis of
e sequence
d structure
f the
aluation
an

A further analysis of the interrelationships between the knowledge and the skills identified above leads us to the construction of an interdependence diagram, or hierarchy (see Figure 13.9 on p 254). This diagram is similar to an objective hierarchy, such as those already mentioned in Part 2 of this book and studied in depth in *Designing Instructional Systems*. However, in this case, we have used the four main stages of our skill cycle as a means of organizing the diagram. We have spread out these four stages along the top of the diagram and have placed the skill and knowledge elements identified as important in the appropriate columns.

The diagram suggests that the final objective of the lesson(s) is to lead the salesman to apply the AIDA model successfully in his selling, success presumably being judged by improved sales performance. The testing of this final objective may, or may not, be considered as part of the evaluation plan for the lesson. We may choose to consider the simulated selling sessions at the end of the lesson to be the lesson evaluation, and on-the-job performance to be part of the end-of-course evaluation. If, on the other hand, our diagram portrays the whole course (composed of only a few lessons dedicated to the AIDA model), the distinction between end-of-course and end-of-lesson evaluation becomes blurred.

esign of
plan for
e lesson
aluation

The diagram also indicates, however, that a full evaluation of the lesson(s), for formative evaluation purposes, should assess the level of competence gained in respect of the various sub-skills and items of special knowledge. Assuming that there is no need to test the basic abilities of paying attention to the customer and his reactions, we still have a total of 10 different tests that should be applied, at least seven of them during or immediately after the lesson. These are, in probable order:

1. Testing for the acquisition of the four basic concepts of attention, interest, desire and acceptance.

2. The identification of each of the four stages in example situations, presented to the learners as role-plays or as films or videos of master performances by crack salesmen.

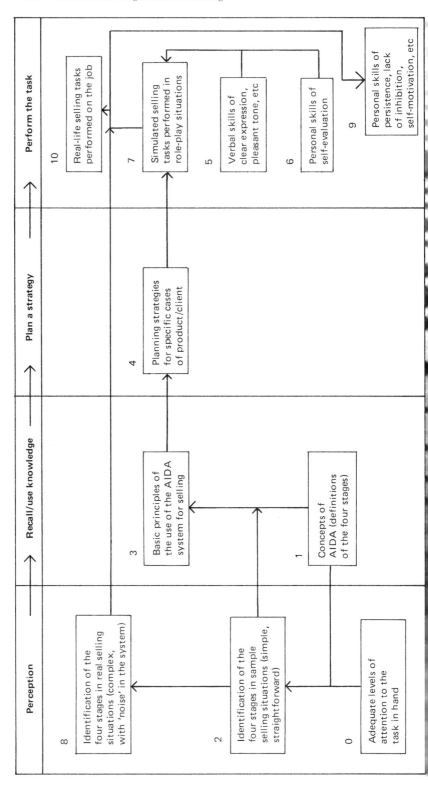

3. The definition and identification of the basic principles of psychology or salesmanship which govern how one should approach the implementation of each stage of the model.
4. The planning of sales strategies for given cases. This is an open ended testing situation, which should be evaluated by analysis of the decision-making processes — not just the decisions and strategies finally formulated.
5. The testing for the presence of necessary levels of basic communication skills and verbal expression.
6. The testing for the presence of adequate levels of self-evaluation skills, necessary for the control of the selling process.
7. The bringing together of all the previously mentioned capabilities in simulated exercises.

If one considers this to be the final objective, one might stop at this point. However, there are some very important sub-skills not yet practised or tested. These include:

8. The development and testing of the higher levels of perceptual discrimination skills that may be necessary to deal with some unusually difficult selling situations. These may best be learned and tested in the on-the-job training that follows the initial lesson.
9. The development and testing of the levels of persistence, self-motivation and free, uninhibited interaction necessary to ensure success as a salesperson.
10. The ultimate test situation: evaluation of the on-the-job performance of the salesperson, with all the pressures and difficulties that exist in reality.

Such a sequence of separate test situations, each one leading to formative revision of sub-skills or knowledge found to be below acceptable standards, will ensure:

(a) that students do not find themselves with tasks to perform that are wholly outside their present capabilities, and
(b) that instructors and instructional designers will not find themselves at a loss in trying to identify the reasons for any specific learning difficulties encountered by the students.

We do not wish to imply that, in this example, one should have ten formal examinations. Very often, the tests may be in the form of questions asked casually at key points. At other times, the tests are simply observations of the students' activities.

13.5 Conclusion: other aspects to evaluate

The topic of evaluation is so vast that in a single chapter we may only scratch the surface. We have tried to give a general view of the systems approach to evaluation and its four main components — the evaluation of context, inputs, process and products. We have shown how each of these components of a total systems evaluation may be performed at the lesson planning level of instructional design and during the delivery of the lessons. This we call Level 3 evaluation. It was made clear that similar evaluations may be made at the other levels of instructional design. Aspects of 'political' evaluation of projects as a whole (Level 1) and of the 'strategic' evaluation of long-term results, benefits and cost/benefits (Level 2) were discussed in *Designing Instructional Systems*.

At several points in our discussion, we have mentioned other aspects of the evaluation of instruction. One such aspect is the evaluation of student attitudes or reactions to the instructional system. We mentioned this as part of the evaluation of the *process* of instruction, even presenting a questionnaire that may be used to measure student opinions of the teacher and the lesson. We also mentioned the evaluation of reactions as part of the evaluation of the *products* of instruction, when we discussed the use of 'approach' and 'avoidance' behaviours as a means of measuring changes in the learner's attitude towards the learning process itself or the content of specific subjects in the course curriculum.

Much more could be said in respect of the evaluation of reactions and many more examples of typical questionnaires could be presented. However, we shall not do this for two reasons. First, the constraints of space: we have already devoted many pages to the presentation of sample instruments, most of them not very well known and not much used, whereas student opinion questionnaires are well known and many examples are to be found in other sources.

Our second motive is priority. Not only are student opinion questionnaires well known; they are also used widely and often are the only form of systematic evaluation that is made of a course. A research study performed by Lusterman (1975) in over 600 organizations in the USA showed that in the case of specific job-related training, about 75 per cent of all courses used some form of student opinion questionnaire, while only about 33 per cent of them applied a final objectives-related test and only about 50 per cent performed some form of later on-the-job performance evaluation. In the case of management and supervisory training, the figures are even more one-sided. Over 90 per cent of all courses in these categories used opinion questionnaires, whereas only about 25 per cent used end-of-course, objectives-related, tests and only about 33 per cent attempted later job performance evaluation.

We do not therefore see that it is necessary for us to devote space here to a discussion of the evaluation of reactions. We do not wish to imply that the testing of student reactions is of no value. If well planned and implemented, it may be of immense use for formative evaluation. But it is by no means the only, nor the most important, aspect of evaluation. Also, if badly planned or implemented, it may produce distorted results, which hide or exaggerate weak points, thus reducing the value of the data collected.

A second aspect that we have mentioned in passing is the evaluation of unexpected results and by-products. Some of these may be problems caused by contextual aspects not taken into account in the planning stages. Others may be opportunities for improvement of the system, by the incorporation of hidden resources or the exploitation of voluntary and enthusiastic help that appears during the course of the project and had not been counted on in the initial planning. Very often these unexpected effects, both the problems and the opportunities, are not recognized until it is too late.

We will touch on some of these aspects in the next chapter, which ties up our discussion of the evaluation of instruction by considering the question of evaluating the evaluation system we are using.

14. Evaluating the Evaluation System (or, Why Instruction Fails)

14.1 The self-correcting system

e
structional
ocess

The title of this chapter may, at first glance, appear strange, but a little reflection on the nature of the instructional process should quickly convince us that, in the long run, instruction most commonly fails due to the absence of an adequate system of evaluation. At this point it is perhaps necessary to recall the basic model of the instructional process (see Figure 14.1).

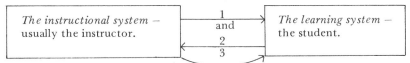

Figure 14.1 *The instructional process*

Instructional learners are linked by a *two-way communication* system that permits *three basic types of interaction.*

1. Information, and instructions on what to do with it, must flow from the instructional system to the learning system, in order to involve the learner in relevant activity.
2. Information on the results of learning must flow from the learning system to the instructional system, to enable measurement of the results as a basis for the evaluation of learning.
3. If the evaluation reveals that the learner has not learned, further information must flow from the instructional system to the learner to overcome any difficulties and to lead the learner to full mastery of the instructional objectives.

e systems
proach

These three forms of information flow, when well planned and well implemented, give our teaching-learning system the quality of self-correction. In principle, any initial defects in content, structure, strategy or tactics should be detectable and correctable during a succession of field test sessions, or indeed during normal use of the system, from one course to the next. This cyclic, or iterative, process of design, testing, evaluation, analysis and redesign is an essential characteristic of our basic systems approach to the design and development of instruction.

Human activity systems are both highly complex and highly probabilistic. It is seldom possible to 'get things right' first time. Previous experience may help us to make a reasonable first attempt, but we should always be ready to modify our approach in the light of feedback, generated by an efficient system of evaluation.

14.2 A systems view of evaluation

1at makes
evaluation
stem work?

To be efficient, an evaluation system must have two essential characteristics:

☐ It must be comprehensive/complete
☐ It must be viable

In other words, it should be set up to observe and measure *all* aspects of the instructional system that might possibly contribute to poor performance and it should be possible to make the necessary measurements, analyse the causes of failure and take appropriate action in order to eliminate these causes.

There is no hope of improvement in an instructional system that is not set up to measure key performance indicators by means of appropriate procedures. There is also not much hope if the appropriate remedial actions are not able to be taken — for political, economic or other reasons.

Finally an evaluation system, even when comprehensive and viable, may not actually work in practice due to poor management. We will not concern ourselves here with this last factor, but will concentrate on the two aspects mentioned earlier. These are, after all, an integral part of the instructional design and development process.

In this book, we have been concentrating on the micro-design or development aspects of the overall instructional design/development process. Specifically, we have analysed how an overall design for an instructional system can be transformed into a set of detailed module or lesson plans. Starting from a general map of the proposed instructional system (illustrated in Chapter 6), which details the preferred *strategies*, we have prepared lesson and exercise plans that specify a sequence of specific *tactics* to be adopted, step-by-step, during instruction. In Chapter 13 we considered the evaluation of our plans at this module and lesson level.

A multi-level model for evaluation

In order to be comprehensive, however, our system of evaluation must stretch beyond the bounds of the part of the instructional system that is our responsibility. A classroom teacher, for example, may be applying a series of tests and other evaluative methods, which lead him to be quite happy about the progress of his classes. However, the students may not be that happy later on when they find that what they have learned is out of date, or that the course objectives do not match the requirements expected by future employers.

As a general rule, our system of evaluation should stretch to at least one level above and one level below the level for which we are directly responsible. The classroom teacher should ensure that, at the very minimum, his evaluation system is in tune with the overall course objectives. He should also be able to check whether learning difficulties encountered during his teaching are caused by his planning and execution of the lesson or, perhaps, by weaknesses in textbooks adopted for the course. Unless the teacher is capable of evaluating the system on all three of these levels he will have difficulty in deciding exactly what steps to take to improve the instructional system.

We have been operating on the basis of a four-level model of the instructional design and development process. It follows logically that we should also view evaluation in terms of this model. Such a multi-level model of evaluation was developed in *Designing Instructional Systems* (Romiszowski, 1981) and reproduced in the last chapter (Chapter 13) as Figure 13.4 (see p 243). We note that this figure appears to illustrate five or more levels at which evaluation may take place. However, these can be conveniently grouped into four levels, if we consider together everything that happens during instruction.

In this case, the application of lesson and unit or module tests, at specific points in the course, and the constant monitoring and evaluation of learning progress during each lesson, may be considered as two aspects of evaluation that are the direct responsibility of the instructor. Taking these aspects as Level 3 of evaluation we have, below this, the rather specialist tasks of pre-evaluation of instructional materials, and above, the final course or project evaluation. All this is of interest and importance to the instructor, although he may only be directly involved in the execution of Level 3.

The upper levels of design and evaluation, shown lumped together as Level in Figure 13.4, are of some relevance to the instructor's task. Although the instructor may never be directly involved in evaluating the future job performance of his trainees, nevertheless he is contributing to this performance by attempting to achieve the overall instructional objectives designed for the project. If these are not directly related to real job requirements then the instructor is wasting both his and his students' time. The instructor *may* need to know how his students fare in later life. The instructional designer, however, *must* know this.

In order to establish perspective, and also to help the instructional designer, whatever his level of action, to plan a sufficiently comprehensive evaluation system, Figure 14.2 on pp 260 and 261 presents a conceptual schema of the aspects that may need to be included in its design. This schema is in the form of a matrix, based on the combination of two sets of concepts that we have already used in this book. On the vertical scale, we have the four levels of system design that we are using as an organizer for the instructional design/ development process. On the horizontal scale, we have the CIPP model for project evaluation, which was used as an organizer for the various techniques of evaluation discussed in the last chapter. Together, these dimensions form a matrix, or table, on which we can conveniently organize and classify the aspects of any project that we think may require measurement and evaluation.

Figure 14.2 presents a fairly comprehensive, but not necessarily complete, list of items for evaluation. It is probable that not all of these items would need to be formally evaluated in any one project. It is equally possible, however, that yet other important items may be identified.

Some observations and comments may help the reader to better understand and use this schema. Firstly, we may localize ourselves within the schema by comparing the items listed at Level 3 with the contents of Chapter 13. Almost all of the items listed in the schema were discussed and exemplified with sample methods. In relation to the *product*, we discussed types of tests applicable for different categories of skill and knowledge, the validity of tests, etc. In relation to the *process*, we studied examples of methods for the evaluation of a teacher's classroom performance and the use of a lesson plan as a technique for organizing the progress of the learners towards mastery of all the lesson's objectives. In relation to the *input*, we saw how a teacher may self-evaluate his/her existing level of knowledge and skill, how a lesson plan may be technically and pedagogically validated and how to select appropriate instructional materials and media. In relation to the *context*, no methods were presented, as much of this part of the evaluation process depends on the maintenance of a 'systems view' of the project in its context, in order to notice the signs of unexpected negative effects before they cause the project to get out of control. We show this need for systems analysis in our schema as a vertical balloon.

At Level 2, we note that many of the items listed have also been discussed elsewhere. The evaluation of terminal objectives at the end of a course was discussed in the last chapter, together with the evaluation of reactions. In Chapter 6, we used a method for the evaluation (or, rather, validation) of the overall course plan. We have not discussed other items at Level 2, as they are more often the responsibility of the project manager than the instructional developer.

We have not studied the Level 1 items in depth as they fall outside the scope of this book. They are, of course, relevant in the planning of a truly comprehensive evaluation system. Readers interested in the subject will find a thorough analysis of all the Level 1, and many of the Level 2, items in the earlier book *Designing Instructional Systems*.

Finally, Level 4 and its evaluation has been mentioned at several points, particularly in relation to selecting appropriate ready-made media for inclusion in a course or lesson plan. Other aspects of the pre-evaluation of materials and media, and of their technical and pedagogical validation, will be covered in the second volume in this series, *Developing Auto-instructional Materials*.

	Context	Input
Level 1 *The job or society* — long-term effects — benefits	Analysis/evaluation of long-term organizational/societal needs and resources used to evaluate future policy/plans Front-end analysis of performance problems used to identify the causes of performance deficiencies and thus to evaluate the applicability of alternative forms of solution	
Level 2 *The project as a whole* — terminal instructional objectives	Evaluation of institutional climate and its effects on the students' attitudes and study habits	Evaluation of student selection policy/practice Evaluation of student expectancies/personal objectives Validation of curriculum relevance/content/planning Evaluation of project's resource requirements (including finance)
Level 3 *Specific units/ modules/lessons* — intermediate instructional objectives	Evaluation of the physical environment of instruction — space — illumination — noise — distractions	Evaluation of teachers' knowledge/skills Evaluation of students' prerequisites in relation to the lesson(s) to be given Validation of lesson and exercise plans Evaluation of the condition and quality of media and materials to be used
Level 4 *Specific exercises and materials* — component behaviours	Evaluation of the physical environment of study, all factors listed at Level 3, plus — signal reception — electricity supply — maintenance of equipment, etc	Evaluation of students' and teachers' skills and attitudes with reference to the proposed media Technical validation of the proposed content by subject-matter experts Evaluation of resources necessary to prepare the media/materials (including time)

Vertical label spanning Levels 1–4 between Context and the Level column: Systems analysis used to evaluate possible conflict between the system being designed and other related systems/sub-systems

Figure 14.2 *A conceptual schema for the planning or evaluating of an evaluation system*

Process	Product
Organization and methods, work study, etc applied to evaluate jobs/occupations	Organizational performance evaluation
	Job-performance evaluation used as feedback to the performer
	Job-performance evaluation used as feedback to the trainer
Evaluation of administrative structure and procedures	Evaluation of learning in terms of final objectives — use performance criteria — emphasis on skills — simulation of job situation
Evaluation of project implementation procedures	
Evaluation of project execution and coordination	Evaluation of students' reactions in relation to — expectancies satisfied — instructional process — content relevance
Control of resources and their utilization	
Evaluation of teachers' classroom performance	Evaluation of learning in terms of intermediate objectives — use behaviour criteria — emphasis on knowledge — practice of sub-skills
Control of the execution of lessons according to plan	
Evaluation and control of the learner's progress	Evaluation of attitude changes in relation to course — approach behaviours — avoidance behaviours
Developmental-testing of all materials during the production process on a one-to-one basis	Field testing of all finished materials on groups representative of the target audience — simulating the future study conditions — measuring achievement of specific objectives — measuring reactions to the materials/media used
Pedagogical validation of the structure/tactics adopted by other instructional experts	
Quality evaluation/control of artwork, photography, etc	

14.3 Checking out an evaluation system

The schema presented in Figure 14.2 serves to give a comprehensive view of aspects that *may* need to be included in a given evaluation system. What actually *should* be included must be decided by the instructional developer in the light of his analysis of the given project and of the practical, economic and political constraints that may exist. It is not always possible to measure all the factors relating to the project. Sometimes, the problem is lack of resources; other times, it is lack of access to the data required; in yet other cases, it may be that the attempt to collect and use the required evaluation data will cost more, in terms of time, money or interpersonal difficulties, than the value of any possible improvement in instruction.

The use of a planning sheet
The planning of a comprehensive, yet viable evaluation system is, therefore, a heuristic process. No algorithm is available. The instructional developer must take into account all the relevant factors of the project in hand in a creative and balanced manner. It is useful, however, to have some planning tools to help in this task. One such tool is the conceptual schema in Figure 14.1 on p 257. Another is the planning sheet, which we present in Figure 14.3 on pp 264 and 265.

This sheet is largely self-explanatory. It is based, vertically, on our four-level model. The horizontal dimension is divided into columns that serve for the listing of the decisions taken by the instructional developer, in relation to what should be measured, with what methods, who should prepare the methods, who should apply them to collect the necessary data, who should receive the data and what actions they should be prepared to take.

The planning sheet presents a picture of the decisions taken by the instructional developer, which can be analysed and evaluated for *coherence*, *comprehensiveness* and *viability*. It also shows how the instructors, course coordinators, instructional developers, managers and other staff, should cooperate in the preparation or use of certain procedures. It shows where there is need for inter-departmental cooperation, which may need to be carefully planned and orchestrated. It identifies methods or data which are not at present available, thus defining the work that has to be done to turn the plan into an actual situation. It may expose the need for training certain staff members in certain evaluation skills. There are yet other possible uses.

An example of an evaluation plan
The example shown in Figure 14.3 on pp 264 and 265 was prepared for a training course for production line, and other similar, supervisors in a large factory. The earlier stages of instructional design had defined the overall instructional plan as described below. The training was to be divided into five modules:

☐ Human relations training
☐ Work study and measurement
☐ Workflow planning and control
☐ Administrative duties and procedures
☐ Evaluating and improving workers' performance.

Each module was composed of several texts and self-evaluation exercises, designed to impart the knowledge content and to be studied during slack periods or at home, in preparation for regular, one-day-a-week, group sessions. The group sessions were to be used in order to clear up doubts and to give more examples of the knowledge content as well as to develop practical application exercises for skills building (technical and interpersonal skills).

This short description should suffice to allow the reader to appraise the example shown, which plans the system of evaluation at all four levels. The analysis of this example should explain how such a planning sheet may be used to assess an existing system of evaluation, as well as how to plan for a totally new system.

14.4 Why instruction fails?

We now have a plan of a comprehensive and, theoretically, viable evaluation system for our instructional system. All that remains for us to do is to put it into practice. This is not always done as well as it should be and, probably, is one of the chief reasons why instructional systems fail in the long term. Human activity systems do not stay static from one period to the next, but, on the contrary, are in a permanent state of dynamic change. The instructional system may appear to be in a state of dynamic equilibrium, producing the same number of graduates per year, while consuming the same quantities of time and other resources. However, at a detailed level of analysis, things are not static at all. The teacher meets new and different students each year, who have their own, unique, learning problems. No well delivered lesson turns out exactly the same on any two occasions. The teacher needs to pay constant attention to the changes and take appropriate actions to modify his delivery. In other words, there is always a need for formative evaluation.

Evaluation — a continuous process

Promising new instructional systems have been known to fail because no account has been taken of this simple principle. Once the initial field testing stage has come to a close, yielding excellent results, the project enters its final phase of regular, large-scale use and, slowly, a form of 'drift' takes place, carrying it further and further away from the changing reality in which it was implanted. Thus, as in the case of an alien organ implanted without due care in a living organism, a rejection phase is reached — the new instructional system is eliminated, killed off by the 'antibodies' in its environment. The way to avoid the rejection of an implanted sub-system is to maintain a high level of compatibility between the new system and older, more established, systems in its environment. As these are in constant change, the new system must also constantly adapt itself.

The methodology that we have adopted for instructional design — the *systems approach* — is exceptionally well suited to the task of dealing with changing, probabilistic systems. As such, we may use it to detect signs of incompatibility and control the 'drift' before the rejection phase is reached. Figure 14.4 on p 266 illustrates each stage of the systems approach and what it produces in the context of instructional development.

In the right hand column of Figure 14.4 is a list of possible causes of ultimate failure of the system. It should be noted that all stages of the system depend for their efficiency on the evaluation stage. As instructional systems involve human beings and are, therefore, probabilistic in nature, we can never guarantee to get things right first time round. We are forced to use an iterative process of successive approximations to what we hope to achieve. Evaluation plays a key role in this process.

Assess the system of evaluation

For this reason, we should be particularly careful to assess the evaluation system we are using:

☐ Are we measuring and evaluating all the aspects of the system that might possibly lead to failure? *Is the evaluation system adequately comprehensive?*

☐ Are we using appropriate measures and reliable measuring procedures? *Is the evaluation system valid?*

☐ Are we capable of obtaining what we require? Is the cost of evaluation reasonable in relation to the possible benefits? *Is the evaluation system viable?*

☐ Do we have the necessary skills to interpret and analyse the data collected? Do we have all the methods ready? Do we have the necessary resources and political support to implement the changes that our evaluation data might suggest to be necessary? *Is the evaluation system operational?*

☐ Are we actually putting into practice what we originally planned? Are the measures being made? Are the methods completed regularly? Are we

	What should be measured?	What methods should be used?	Who should prepare the methods?
Level 1 *The production and other 'line' departments*	Productivity of department and costs of errors or waste	Normal production control statistics	Already exist in the organization
	Job performance of the section supervisors	Criterion-referenced 'MBO' system of job evaluation	Performance technologist and job experts
	Causes of poor supervision	'Front-end' analysis schema	Already exists (Romiszowski, 1981)
Level 2 *Supervisor training project (course)*	Overall results — the supervisory skills mastered	Simulations of typical supervision tasks and problems	Performance/ instruction technologist and job experts
	Trainees' and instructors' reactions	Attitude questionnaires and interviews	Instructional technologist and psychologist
	Predicted and actual costs	Internal cost-control system	Training department management
Level 3 *Specific modules and lessons*	For each of the five modules separately: — skills acquired — knowledge acquired	Practical exercises (individual/group) Written post-tests	Instructional technologist
	For each lesson: — specific objectives — attitude changes	Prepared questions and tasks, listed in each lesson plan	Each instructor, with assistance from instructional technologist
Level 4 *Specially prepared exercises and materials*	For each text and practice exercise, separately: — specific objectives — clarity of communication — acceptability	— Pre- and post-tests — Quality control checklists — Expert validation guides — Reaction questionnaires	Instructional technologist and media production specialists

Figure 14.3 *A planning sheet used to design a comprehensive evaluation system*

Who should apply the methods?	Who needs the results — and why?	What type of action should be taken?
Department managers<hr>Department managers and section chiefs<hr>Section chiefs and performance technologist	Department managers — for 'MBO' Section chiefs — for job control Supervisors — for self-development Training department for needs analysis	Review of department targets and methods OD interventions to improve climate Corrective feedback to job performers Training needs identification
Course instructors and coordinator<hr>Course coordinator<hr>Training department management	Trainees and their department managers<hr>Training staff in general — for formative actions Instructors and coordinators — for self-development	Summative — pass or fail<hr>Revision of course — objectives — content — structure, etc<hr>Cost-effectiveness and cost-benefit analysis
Instructors and course coordinator<hr>Each instructor in group sessions<hr>Trainee in self-study sessions	Training staff in general — for formative actions Coordinators — for course control Instructors — for self-development and feedback to trainees	Revision of modules and lessons — sequence — structure — content, etc<hr>Individualization of the instructional process
Instructional technologist and media production specialists	Instructional technologist — for revision of scripts, content, etc Media staff — for control of the production process	Materials revision and repeated field testing, as necessary

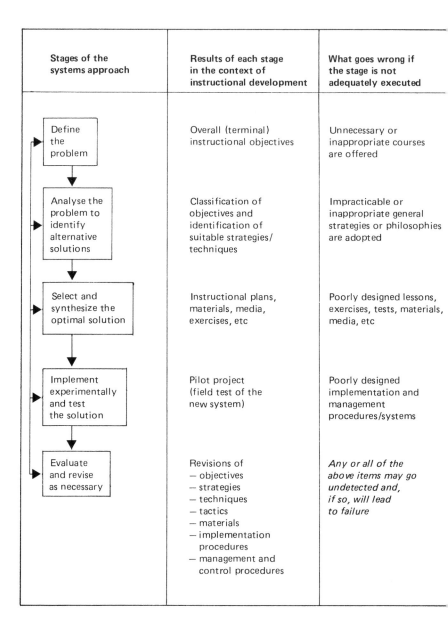

Stages of the systems approach	Results of each stage in the context of instructional development	What goes wrong if the stage is not adequately executed
Define the problem	Overall (terminal) instructional objectives	Unnecessary or inappropriate courses are offered
Analyse the problem to identify alternative solutions	Classification of objectives and identification of suitable strategies/ techniques	Impracticable or inappropriate general strategies or philosophies are adopted
Select and synthesize the optimal solution	Instructional plans, materials, media, exercises, etc	Poorly designed lessons, exercises, tests, materials, media, etc
Implement experimentally and test the solution	Pilot project (field test of the new system)	Poorly designed implementation and management procedures/systems
Evaluate and revise as necessary	Revisions of — objectives — strategies — techniques — tactics — materials — implementation procedures — management and control procedures	*Any or all of the above items may go undetected and, if so, will lead to failure*

Figure 14.4 *The systems approach as a means of avoiding failure of instructional systems*

interpreting the data as soon as it is available? Are we actually implementing the changes that appear to be necessary? Are we revising the evaluation system to take into account the implemented revisions in the instructional system? *Is the evaluation system actually operating?*

The first three of these questions are part of the instructional development process and have been dealt with in this book. The last two are more in the area of project management and may be discussed by the author in another book to be published in the future.

15. Establishing Perspective (Where Are We? Where Are We Going?)

15.1 The 3-D model

In the last chapter of *Designing Instructional Systems* a series of structured 'information maps' were presented to illustrate the overall structure of instructional design and development projects and to analyse the common causes of failure that occur in practice. Three of these maps are reproduced here (Figures 15.1, 15.2 and 15.3) to act as a structure for the closing chapter of this book.

Figure 15.1 on p 270 presents what may be called the 3-D model of how a new education or training project comes into being. Not all projects follow this model to the letter. In small, one-institution or one-teacher, projects, it is difficult to distinguish between the second, development, stage and the third, dissemination, stage. The teachers concerned design and develop a set of new materials by applying them to the groups of students at their disposal. Revisions occur from one course to the next, but it is the same group of teachers, who originally designed and developed the system, who continue to apply and perfect it from one year to the next. There is no real distinction between a 'pilot project' and a 'full-scale' project, so the only sign that the development stage is over is when the results achieved in the normal teaching situation are such that no further major changes in the system are considered necessary.

With regard to larger projects, however, especially those that employ some form of centralized design and development team, the three stages are quite clearly identifiable. It may be that the comment made at the foot of Figure 15.1 is not always observed. Projects may 'drift' from the design stage into the development stage and then on to large-scale dissemination without acquiring systematic evaluation and approval (or revision) between each of the stages. Nevertheless, the flow-chart in Figure 15.1 represents the ideal process, which, if deviated from, may lead to problems later on.

In terms of our 4-level model of instructional design/development, we may consider the first, initial design stage to include Levels 1 and 2 of our decision-making model and the second, development stage to include Levels 3 and 4. The third 'D' — dissemination — is then largely a management and logistics problem area.

15.2 The development stage

Figure 15.2 on p 271 presents an analysis of the development stage, identifying four principal sub-systems, or areas of activity. There is an introduction contained within this figure which states that if any one of these essential sub-systems functions badly the system as a whole is likely to fail. In the last two chapters we have seen the importance and complexity of the last two of these sub-systems — the controlled implementation of the proposed instructional system and its thorough evaluation and revision. We concluded that the most important factor which might prevent the failure of our instructional system in the long term is a system of evaluation which is comprehensive, workable in theory and actually works in practice.

Throughout this book we have also seen stress placed on heuristic

Introduction	Any project that is worth carrying through should produce results, that is, it should solve a problem, to convert 'what is' into 'what should be'.
The three main stages of a project	To achieve this the project passes through three principal stages: 1. *Design stage:* proposals, objectives, methods, content, etc leading to a *plan*. 2. *Development stage:* detailed design, production and validation of materials, development of implementation and management systems, etc leading to a *pilot project*. 3. *Dissemination stage:* application of the tested system on a large scale in many institutions, building up to the *full-scale project*. 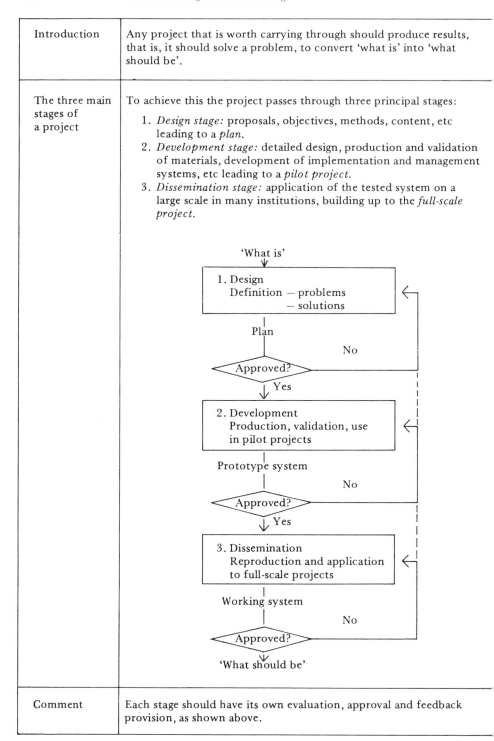
Comment	Each stage should have its own evaluation, approval and feedback provision, as shown above.

Figure 15.1 *The principal stages of
an instructional design and development project*

Introduction	Each of the principal stages may be regarded as a system made up of a series of *essential* sub-systems. If any one of these essential sub-systems functions badly, the system as a whole is likely to fail.
The instructional development stage	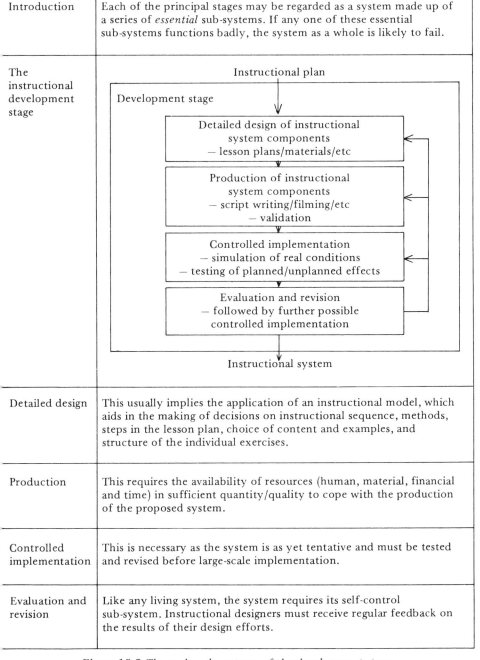
Detailed design	This usually implies the application of an instructional model, which aids in the making of decisions on instructional sequence, methods, steps in the lesson plan, choice of content and examples, and structure of the individual exercises.
Production	This requires the availability of resources (human, material, financial and time) in sufficient quantity/quality to cope with the production of the proposed system.
Controlled implementation	This is necessary as the system is as yet tentative and must be tested and revised before large-scale implementation.
Evaluation and revision	Like any living system, the system requires its self-control sub-system. Instructional designers must receive regular feedback on the results of their design efforts.

Figure 15.2 *The main sub-systems of the development stage*

decision-making with respect to all aspects of the system's design — objectives, content, strategies, tactics and media — on the basis of a conceptual model of the instructional process. The only sub-system that we have not yet studied is the production of instructional system components — script writing, programmed text preparation, audio and video programming, computer-based materials, etc.

15.3 Where are we?

A more detailed study of the two maps discussed so far will indicate quite clearly just where we are in the overall design/development process.

Initial design

The initial design stage was reviewed in Part 2 of this book and some examples of the resultant overall instructional plans were presented in Chapter 6. The account of this stage, given in Chapters 4 and 5, is necessarily very condensed and does not present the detailed arguments for the approach and models used. These may be found in *Designing Instructional Systems* (Romiszowski, 1981), which discusses in great detail Levels 1 and 2 of instructional design.

Individual- ization

In Part 1 of this book we analysed the concept and some well-known methodologies of individualization of the instructional process. This analysis was useful for two reasons. It led to the conclusion, voiced at the end of the last chapter and exemplified by all the chapters of Part 3 of the book, that individualization is an essential factor in any instructional system, whether based on self-study materials, small group study, simulations and games, or even conventional expositive classroom teaching.

Part 1 is also important in relation to the portion of the development stage which we have not yet studied, namely the development of specific types of media and materials. This will be the subject of the second book in the Instructional Development series, namely *Developing Auto-Instructional Materials*, to be published later in 1984.

Tactical planning

In Part 3 we analysed the nature of knowledge and skill acquisition in great depth and developed heuristics for the selection of instructional tactics in relation to the nature of the objectives and content of the lesson being planned. Then we developed a method for lesson planning which takes into account the individual or common learning difficulties that may occur at each step and prepares to cater for them by incorporating into the lesson plan a series of review, revision or recycling activities. The method attempts to make every lesson a self-correcting system, attuned to the specific learning difficulties of individual students. If, actually, this is not always attainable, due to practical difficulties, there are, nevertheless, many instances when the method has led to a much greater level of individualization, even within the conventional medium or large group situation.

Use of a model

Part 3 is also important for establishing a theoretical model for the detailed design steps. As Figure 15.3 on p 273 illustrates, the principal causes of failure in this sub-system are due to the lack of a theoretical model, the use of an inadequate model, or the inappropriate use of a basically adequate model. No doubt the reader could add to the list of examples from his own experience. The author could, if space permitted, document several dozen real-life case studies of instructional systems that failed in the development stage because of inadequate theoretical bases and practical experience on the part of the instructional developers. Very often, the root of the problem is that a basically algorithmic, step-by-step, rigidly controlled design procedure is adopted in a problem-area that requires heuristic, highly flexible and messy creative problem-solving strategies to be used. In both *Designing* and *Producing* we have repeatedly stressed the heuristic nature of the instructional design process and have tried to develop conceptual tools, in the form of schemata, that may promote the kind of multi-faceted, non-linear, almost lateral-thinking, approach to instructional design that, we believe, is essential for success.

The need for an instructional design model	The detailed design sub-system develops, and indeed often originates, the lesson plans, reading assignments, tests, media, materials and exercises, etc that do much of the instructing.
	If the design of these system components is not based on a clear instructional design model, it is difficult for instructional designers to check their work, learn from their successes and failures, communicate to other designers and learn from others.
Sources of failure 1. Lack of a defined model	The designers follow traditions, including objectives, content and methods, which are commonly applied in similar courses, without checking the real needs of the specific problem they are trying to solve. If they do not succeed, they just prescribe more of the same instructional medicine applying the same techniques for any situation.
— examples (a) (b) (c)	The traditional belief that any performance problem can be solved through training, or any behavioural deficiency needs a course. The traditional belief that there is no substitute for the 'personal contact' between teacher and pupil. The vogue for programmed instruction, ETV, Keller Plan, etc.
2. Use of the wrong model	Not all learning problems can be solved by applying the same instructional model. Some models apply to only certain categories of learning problems, or to only certain steps in the total instructional process.
— examples (a) (b) (c)	The behaviourist model of Skinner is excellent for teaching some reflexive or reproductive skills, but is inadequate for higher level productive skills and for knowledge. Bloom's taxonomy was developed solely to assist in the preparation of tests for subject-based curricula, but has been applied as an instructional model, even in the (inappropriate) training context. The use of a model imported without adaptation to allow for cultural differences, different levels of sophistication, or different data.
3. Lack of experience in using the model	The model may be adequate, but the designers lack skill and experience in its application. They go through the motions, but without understanding or creativity.
— examples (a) (b)	Task analysis forms, duly filled in with useless information. Long lists of objectives that bear no relation to subsequent lesson exercises.

Figure 15.3 *Sources of failure in the 'detailed design' sub-system*

15.4 Where are we going?

Individual-
ization —
limitations
imposed by
student/
teacher
ratios

The full individualization of instruction usually implies that at least part of the instructional load is taken on by media other than the teacher. As long as the teacher uses merely informational materials, such as slides, transparencies or even very conventional text books, he remains firmly in the centre stage as the only element in the system that evaluates progress, takes decisions in respect of the feedback and remedial activities necessary to overcome learning difficulties, adapts the content to the needs or preferences of individual students, etc. The student-teacher ratio, usually operative in education and training, imposes severe limits on how far individualization can really progress under these circumstances.

The solution is to delegate some of the tasks of instruction to other media. The obvious and traditional choice is to delegate the dissemination of information — and Gutenberg takes much of the credit (some say blame) for facilitating this process by the invention of the printing press. All later informational media have merely extended and sophisticated the Gutenberg revolution. The current video boom is no exception.

Delegation
of the
evaluation
function

However, individualization is still hampered by the teacher's limited capacity to attend to all the needs of a large and varied group of students. Thus, new and very efficient information dissemination media might communicate more, better and faster, but cannot really lead to significantly greater levels of individualization than exist in some of today's quite traditional classrooms. The key is for the teacher to delegate some of his evaluation and formative decision-making tasks. Then the practice of individualization can really be extended. As we saw in Part 1, early attempts were mainly based on administrative reorganization of the conventional classroom situation, in which the students themselves took on some of the tasks of evaluation — self-evaluation as in linear programmed instruction, and many earlier self-study schemes, or peer-evaluation as in the Keller Plan and earlier monitorial systems, or as in microteaching or many other small group, highly interactive, games and simulations.

However, this is the tip of the iceberg. We have come quite a way along the road of self-instruction in the 30 or so years since the first linear teaching machines appeared. We have come a long way since Lewin invented the T-Group. And we are now going to move much faster.

The promise
of the
computer

The reason for this is, of course, the application of the computer to the evaluation and control tasks that until now have been the teacher's sole province. The potential of the computer as a tool for the individualization of instruction has yet to be fully assessed, but already it is seen to be immense.

This is the area that we will be exploring in the second volume of this series, *Developing Auto-Instructional Materials*. As the title suggests, we will analyse self-instructional materials development as exercised by the best of the early practitioners and, from there, we will trace developments in the domains of expositive, print-based materials, print-based experiential materials, audiovisual instruction and, finally, applications of the computer to the instructional process. In all this, we shall be emphasizing the essentially individualizing nature of the current trends and analysing some of the tantalizing prospects that current developments are opening up for the educational and training systems of the future. No instructional developer can afford to ignore these new forms of auto-instructional systems.

Bibliography

Annett, J and Kay, H (1957) Knowledge of results and skilled performance. *Occupational Psychology*, 31.

Ausubel, D P (1968) *Educational Psychology: A Cognitive View*. Holt, Rinehart and Winston, New York.

Azzi, R (1965) A personal course – Second Report. University of Brasilia, Brazil.

Azzi, R and Keller, F S (1964) A personal course. First Report. University of Brasilia, Brazil.

Banks, B (1969) Report on an auto-instructional course in mathematics. *Programmed Learning and Educational Technology*, 6, 1, January.

Banks, B (1970) An experimental auto-instructional course in mathematics. In Bajpai, A C and Leedham, J F (eds) *Aspects of Educational Technology* IV. Pitman, London.

Biran, L (1974) The limitations of programmed instruction. In Romiszowski, A J *The Selection and Use of Instructional Media: A Systems Approach*. Kogan Page, London.

Bloom, B S *et al* (1956) *Taxonomy of Educational Objectives, Handbook I: The Cognitive Domain*. McKay, New York.

Briggs, L J (1970) *Handbook of Procedures for the Design of Instruction*. American Institutes for Research, Pittsburgh.

Bruner, J S (1966) *Towards a Theory of Instruction*. Harvard University Press, Boston.

Covington, M V and Crutchfield, R S (1965) Facilitation of creative problem solving. *Programmed Instruction*, 4, 4. NSPI, USA.

Crowder, N A (1963) Intrinsic programming: facts, fallacies and future. In Filep, R T (ed) *Prospectives in Programming*. Macmillan, New York.

Croxton, P C L and Martin, L M (1970) The application of programmed learning in higher education. In Bajpai, A C and Leedham, J F (eds) *Aspects of Educational Technology* IV. Pitman, London.

Davis, R E (1972) Many roads lead to individualization. *Educational Technology*, 12, 3, March.

De Haan, R F and Doll, R C (1964) Individualization and human potential. In Doll, R C (ed) *Individualizing Instruction*. Association for Supervision and Curriculum Development, Washington, DC.

Dienes, Z P (1960) *Building Up Mathematics*. Hutchinson, London.

Edling, J V (1970) *Individualized Instruction: A Manual for Administrators*. DCE Publications, Oregon State University, Oregon.

Ellington, H and Addinall, E (1978) NORTH SEA: a board game on the offshore oil industry. In Megarry, J (ed) *Perspectives on Educational Gaming and Simulation: 1 and 2*. Kogan Page, London.

Ellington, H, Addinall, E and Percival, F (1981) *Games and Simulations in Science Education*. Kogan Page, London.

Ellington, H, Addinall, E and Percival, F (1982) *A Handbook of Game Design*. Kogan Page, London.

Featherstone, J (1967) *Schools for Children: What is Happening in the British Classroom?* The New Republic, August.

Fitzgerald, W M (ed) (1974) Mathematics laboratories: implementation, research and evaluation. ERIC Information Analysis Center for Science, Mathematics and Environmental Education. Columbus, Ohio.

Flanagan, J C (1968) Project plan. In *Technology and Innovation in Education*. Praeger, New York.

Gagné, R M (1965) *The Conditions for Learning*. Holt, Rinehart and Winston, New York.

Gagné, R M (1975) *Essentials of Learning for Instruction*. Dryden Press, Illinois.

Gagné, R M and Briggs, L J (1974) *Principles of Instructional Design*. Holt, Rinehart and Winston, New York.

Gibbons, M (1971) *Individualized Instruction: A Descriptive Analysis.* Teachers College Press, Columbia University, Washington, DC.

Gilbert, T F (1961) Mathetics: the technology of education. *Journal of Mathetics,* 1 and 2. Reprinted (1969) as Supplement 1 of the Review of Educational Cybernetics and Applied Linguistics. Longmac, London.

Gilbert, T F (1969a) The sensible teaching of social science, or mathetics revisited. *NSPI Journal,* 8, 1. National Society for Performance and Instruction, USA.

Goldstein, M and Rittenhouse, C H (1954) Knowledge of results in the acquisition and transfer of a gunnery skill. *Journal of Experimental Psychology,* 48.

Green, B A (1976) The personalized system of instruction, or should university teaching be improved? *Programmed Learning and Educational Technology,* 13, 1, February.

Guilford, J P (1967) *The Nature of Human Intelligence.* McGraw Hill, New York.

Hamer, J W and Romiszowski, A J (1969) A computer managed individualized remedial mathematics course at undergradute level. In Mann, A P and Brunstrom, C K (eds) *Aspects of Educational Technology* III. Pitman, London.

Harris, C W (ed) (1960) *Encyclopaedia of Educational Research.* Macmillan, New York.

Hodgson, A M (1968) A communication technique for the future. In *Ideas No 7.* Curriculum Laboratory, Goldsmith College, University of London.

Hodgson, A M (1971) An experiment in computer guided correspondence seminars for management. In Peckham, D *et al* (eds) *Aspects of Educational Technology* VI. Pitman, London.

Horn, R E *et al* (1969) *Information Mapping for Learning and Reference.* Information Resources Inc, Lexington, Massachusetts.

Horn, R E *et al* (1971) *Introduction to Probability.* Information Resources Inc, Lexington, Massachusetts.

Jackson, P W (1968) *The Teacher and the Machine.* University of Pittsburgh Press, Pittsburgh.

Keen, T R (1980) Playing MISUNDERSTOOD. In Race, P and Brook, D (eds) *Perspectives on Academic Gaming and Simulation: 5.* Kogan Page, London.

Kaufman, R and English, F W (1979) *Needs Assessment: Concepts and Applications.* Educational Technology Publications. Englewood Cliffs, New Jersey.

Keller, F S (1967) Neglected rewards in the educational process. *Proceedings of the 23rd American Conference of Academic Deans,* Los Angeles, California.

Keller, F S (1968) Goodbye teacher. *Journal of Applied Behavioural Analysis,* 1.

Keller, F S and Sherman, J G (1974) *The Keller Plan Handbook.* Benjamin, New York.

Kessler, B M (1972) Individualizing mathematics learning through the maths lab. *Educational Technology,* 12, 3, March.

Krathwohl, D R, *et al* (1964) *Taxonomy of Educational Objectives, Handbook II: The Affective Domain.* McKay, New York.

Landa, L N (1976) *Instructional Regulation and Control: Cybernetics, Algorithmization and Heuristics in Education.* Educational Technology Publications, Englewood Cliffs, New Jersey.

Larsson, I (1973) Individualized mathematics teaching: results from the IMU project in Sweden. Lund/CWK, Gleerup, Sweden.

Lippey, G (1972) *Computer Assisted Test Construction.* Educational Technology Publications, Englewood Cliffs, New Jersey.

Livingston, S A (1974) How to design and how not to design a simulation game. In Stadsklev, R (ed) *Handbook of Simulation Gaming in Social Education.* Institute of Higher Education Research and Services, The University of Alabama.

Lusterman, S (1975) *Education in Industry.* Conference Board, New York.

MacPherson, E D (1972) How much individualization? *The Mathematics Teacher,* May.

Mager, R F (1968) *Developing Attitudes Toward Learning.* Fearon, Belmont, California.

Mager, R F and McCann, J (1961) *Learner Controlled Instruction.* Varian, Palo Alto.

Markle, S M (1970) Programming and programmed instruction. One of the support papers for a Report to the President and the Congress of the USA, by the Commission on Instructional Technology — To Improve Learning. Academy for Educational Development, Washington, DC.

McAleese, R (ed) (1978) *Perspectives on Academic Gaming and Simulation: 3.* Kogan Page, London.

McCord, B (1976) Job instruction. In Craig, R L (ed) *Training and Development Handbook* (2nd edition). McGraw Hill, New York.

McPhail, P (1974) Building a role playing exercise: the after-the-party scene. In Stadsklev, R (ed) *Handbook of Simulation Gaming in Social Education.* Institute of Higher Education Research and Services, The University of Alabama.

Mechner, F (1965) Science education and behavioral technology. In Glaser, R (ed) *Teaching Machines and Programmed Learning II: Data and Directions.* Department of Audiovisual Instruction, NEA, Washington, DC.

Megarry, J (ed) (1978) *Perspectives on Academic Gaming and Simulation: 1 & 2.* Kogan Page, London.

Megarry, J (ed) (1979) *Perspectives on Academic Gaming and Simulation: 4.* Kogan Page, London.

Michalski, J (1974) Developing a social simulation: the land use simulation. In Stadsklev, R (ed) *Handbook of Simulation Gaming in Social Education.* Institute of Higher Education Research and Services, The University of Alabama.

Moore, O K (1962) *The Automated Responsive Environment.* Yale University Press, New York.

Neill, A S (1960) *Summerhill.* Hart, New York.

Nichols, E D (1972) Is individualization the answer? *Educational Technology,* 12, 3, March.

O'Daffer, P G (1976) Individualized instruction: a search for a humanist approach. *Arithmetic Teacher,* January.

Parkhurst, H (1922) *Education on the Dalton Plan.* Dutton, New York.

Pask, G (1960) The teaching machine as a control mechanism. Transactions of the Society of Instrument Technology, London, June.

Pask, G (1972) Anti-hodmanship: a report on the state and prospects of CAI. *Programmed Learning and Educational Technology,* 9, 5, September.

Pask, G (1976) Conversational techniques in the study and practice of education. *British Journal of Educational Psychology,* 46. Reprinted in Hartley, J and Davies, I K (eds) (1978) *Contributions to an Educational Technology,* 2, Kogan Page, London.

Pask, G and Scott, B C E (1972) Learning strategies and individual competence. *International Journal of Man-Machine Studies,* 4, 3.

Percival, F and Ellington, H I (1980) The place of case studies in the simulation/gaming field. In Race, P and Brook, D (eds) *Perspectives on Academic Gaming and Simulation: 5.* Kogan Page, London.

Piaget, J (1965) *The Child's Conception of Number.* Norton, New York.

Polya, G (1945) *How To Solve It: A New Aspect of Mathematical Method.* Princeton University Press, Princeton, New Jersey.

Postlethwait, S N et al (1972) *The Audio-Tutorial Approach to Learning.* Burgess Publishing Company, New York.

Race, P and Brook, D (eds) (1980) *Perspectives on Academic Gaming and Simulation: 5.* Kogan Page, London.

Romiszowski, A J (ed) A systems approach to education and training. APLET occasional publication, 1. Kogan Page, London.

Romiszowski, A J (1974) *The Selection and Use of Instructional Media: A Systems Approach.* Kogan Page, London.

Romiszowski, A J (ed) (1976a) Individualization in higher education. *Programmed Learning and Educational Technology,* 13, 1, London.

Romiszowski, A J (1976b) Computer-generated examinations and tests. In Howe, A and Romiszowski, A J (eds) *International Yearbook of Educational and Instructional Technology: 1976/77.* Kogan Page, London.

Romiszowski, A J (1976c) A study of individualized systems for mathematics instruction at the post-secondary levels. Unpublished PhD Thesis available in the library, The University of Technology, Loughborough, England.

Romiszowski, A J (1979a) What's happening to individualized mathematics? *Programmed Learning and Educational Technology,* 16, 2, May.

Romiszowski, A J (1979b) De instrucao programada a tecnologia de desempenho nas empresas. Parte 2: o enfoque sistemico em micro e macro escala (From programmed instruction to performance technology in industry. Part 2: a systems approach in micro and macro scale of application). *Tecnologia Educacional,* 26 (*Journal of the Brazilian Association for Educational Technology − ABT*), Rio de Janeiro.

Romiszowski, A J (1980a) Problem solving in instructional design: a heuristic approach. In Howe, A (ed) *International Yearbook of Educational/Instructional Technology: 1980/81.* Kogan Page, London.

Romiszowski, A J (1980b) A new approach to the analysis of knowledge and skills. In Winterburn, R and Evans, L (eds) *Aspects of Educational Technology* XIV. Kogan Page, London.

Romiszowski, A J (1981a) *Designing Instructional Systems.* Kogan Page, London.

Romiszowski, A J (1981b) A new look at instructional design. Part 1 − learning: restructuring one's concepts. *British Journal of Educational Technology,* 12, 2.

Romiszowski, A J (1982) A new look at instructional design. Part 2 – instruction: integrating one's approach. *British Journal of Educational Technology*, **13**, 1.

Romiszowski, A J and Atherton, B (1979) Creativity and control: neglected factors within self-instructional programme design. In Page, G T and Whitlock, Q (eds) *Aspects of Educational Technology* **XIII**. *Educational Technology Twenty Years On*. Kogan Page, London.

Romiszowski, A J, Bajpai, A C and Lewis, P E (1976) The tutor's role in the individualization of service courses in mathematics. *Programmed Learning and Educational Technology*, **13**, 1, February.

Romiszowski, A J and Biran, L (1970) Programmed instruction: an analytical survey of European research activity and an inventory of research centres in Western Europe. Report, in two volumes, on an international study commissioned by the Council of Europe, Council of Europe, Strasbourg.

Ruskin, R S and Hess, J M (1974) *The Personalized System of Instruction in Higher Education: An Annotated Review of the Literature*. Centre for Personalized Instruction, Georgetown University, Washington, DC.

Rushby, N J (1979) *An Introduction to Eduational Computing*. Croom Helm, London.

Scanlon, R G (1970) Individually prescribed instruction. *Educational Technology*, **10**, 12, December.

Schramm, W (1967) *Big Media – Little Media*. Sage Publications, Beverly Hills, California.

Search, P (1894) The Pueblo Plan of Individual Teaching. *Educational Review*, **8**, June.

Seymour, W D (1954) *Industrial Training for Manual Operations*. Pitman, London.

Seymour, W D (1966) *Industrial Skills*. Pitman, London.

Seymour, W D (1968) *Skills Analysis Training*. Pitman, London.

Shane, H G (1962) The school and individual differences. In Henry, N B (ed) *Individualizing Instruction*. (61st Yearbook of the National Society for the Study of Education). University of Chicago, Press, Chicago.

Sherman, J G (1974) *Personalized System of Instruction: 41 Germinal Papers*. Benjamin, New York.

Skinner, B F (1954) The science of learning and the art of teaching. *Harvard Educational Review*, 24. University of Harvard.

Skinner, B F (1961) Teaching machines. *Scientific American* 205, November.

Suppes, P et al (1968) *Computer Assisted Instruction: Stanford's 1965-66 Arithmetic Program*. Stanford University Institute for Mathematical Studies in Social Science, Stanford, California.

Tansey, P J (1971) *Educational Aspects of Simulation*. McGraw Hill, London.

Taylor, L C (1971) *Resources for Learning*. Penguin Books, London.

Thomas, R M and Thomas, S M (1965) *Individual Differences in the Classroom*. McKay, New York.

Toggenburger, F (1973) Classroom teacher support system. *Educational Technology*, Marc

Vaughan, B W (1972) The application of the operations research technique of network analysis to primary mathematics. In Austwick, K and Harris, N D C (eds) *Aspects of Educational Technology* **VI**. Pitman, London.

Walford, R (1971) The role of simulations and games in the development of geography teaching. In Tansey, P J (ed) *Educational Aspects of Simulation*. McGraw Hill, London.

Wallach, M A and Kogan, N (1965) *Modes of Thinking in Young Children*. Holt, New York.

Washburne, C and Maryland, S P (1963) *Winnetka: The History and Significance of an Educational Experiment*. Prentice Hall, New York.

Wellens, J (1974) *Training in Physical Skills*. Business Books, London.

Williams, R G (1977) A behavioral typology of educational objectives for the cognitive domain. *Educational Technology*, **17**, 6.

Willoughby, S S (1976) Individualization. *The Mathematics Teacher*, May.

Wise, A (1968) *University Teaching in Transition*. Oliver and Boyd, Edinburgh.

Wyant, T G (1973) Syllabus analysis. In Budgett, R and Leedham, J (eds) *Aspects of Educational Technology* **VII**. Pitman, London.

ubject Index

Author Index